BROOKLANDS COLLEGE LIBRARY
HEATH ROAD, WEYBRIDGE, SURREY KT13 8TT
Tel: (01932) 797906

This item must be returned on or before the last date entered below. Subject to certain conditions, the loan period may be extended upon application to the Librarian

27 NOV 2007

-5 OCT 2009

AUTHOR ..... JONES

TITLE ..... Flight Catering

CLASSIFICATION NO. 641.575

ACCESSION NO. 094241

JA

...tering

...d edition

Edited by

...ter Jones

BROOKLANDS COLLEGE LIBRARY

094241

BROOKLANDS COLLEGE LIBRARY
WEYBRIDGE, SURREY KT13 8TT

ELSEVIER
BUTTERWORTH
HEINEMANN

AMSTERDAM BOSTON HEIDELBERG LONDON NEW YORK OXFORD
PARIS SAN DIEGO SAN FRANCISCO SINGAPORE SYDNEY TOKYO

Elsevier Butterworth-Heinemann
Linacre House, Jordan Hill, Oxford OX2 8DP
200 Wheeler Road, Burlington, MA 01803

First published by Longman Group Ltd 1995
Second edition 2004

Copyright © 2004, Elsevier Ltd. All rights reserved

No part of this publication may be reproduced in any material form
(including photocopying or storing in any medium by electronic
means and whether or not transiently or incidentally to some other
use of this publication) without the written permission of the
copyright holder except in accordance with the provisions of the
Copyright, Designs and Patents Act 1988 or under the terms
of a licence issued by the Copyright Licensing Agency Ltd,
90 Tottenham Court Road, London, England W1T 4LP.
Applications for the copyright holder's written permission to
reproduce any part of this publication should be addressed
to the publisher

Permissions may be sought directly from Elsevier's Science and
Technology Rights Department in Oxford, UK: phone: (+44) (0) 1865
843830; Fax: (+44) (0) 1865 853333; e-mail: permissions@elsevier.co.uk.
You may also complete your request on-line via the Elsevier
homepage (http://www.elsevier.com), by selecting 'Customer
Support' and then 'Obtaining Permissions'.

British Library Cataloguing in Publication Data
Flight catering – 2nd ed.
  1. Airlines – food service
  I. Jones, Peter
  387.7′42

Library of Congress Cataloguing in Publication Data
A catalogue record for this book is available from the Library of Congress

ISBN 0 7506 6216 6

For information on all Butterworth-Heinemann publications
visit our website at http://books.elsevier.com

Typeset by Replika Press Pvt Ltd, India
Printed and bound in Italy

Contents

Foreword

It is now eight years since the first flight catering publication appeared. Since then, and particularly in the last two to three years, some fundamental changes have taken place within the industry, which will continue for many years to come. A basic innovation has been the arrival on the scene of 'no frills, low cost' carriers in Europe, the USA, and Australia. This trend will undoubtedly grow in the foreseeable future.

Since passengers on medium or long-haul journeys will want to eat, different arrangements will have to be made to satisfy their needs. At the same time, it may be that refreshments and/or meals become a source of revenue for the carrier rather than an expense should a third party be commissioned to take the full responsibility for catering and sales.

This book addresses many of these changes. Our IFCA Professor at the University of Surrey, who is the person mainly responsible for this book, has expressed his views on the subject in a very lucid manner.

We at IFCA are, as always, indebted to Professor Peter Jones for his untiring work and research related to identifying and reporting on our industry as the story unfolds.

William M. Seeman
HonMUniS Hon.F.Inst.M., M.Inst. T.
Founder President
International Flight Catering Association
M. Univ. (Surrey)

Acknowledgements

I would like to thank a great many people for their contribution to this new edition of *Flight Catering*.

The academic contributors to the first edition were Professor Michael Kipps, David Briggs, John Edwards, Professor David Foskett, Professor David Gilbert, Cliff Goodwin, Professor Nick Johns, Professor David Kirk, Maurice Palin, Professor Ray Pine, and Professor Bill Nevett.

Academic contributors to this new edition include Dr. Anita Eves, Dr. Jessica Hwang, Dr. Margaret Lumbers and Chris Smith from the University of Surrey, and Panagiota Dervisi. I was also assisted by Rebecca Simms, the IFCA Research Officer in the University of Surrey's Travel Catering Research Centre.

Industry advisors to the first edition were Jenny Sharp, Meinrad Dormann, Bruce Murray, Willi Seeman, Tony Todd and Gilbert Valterio (all on IFCA's Education Committee), along with Fons Aaldering, Andy Blake, Ernie Carter, David Coleman, Anthony Edwards, Kurt Hafner, Jane Hoare, Alec Kirby, David Letherman, Roy Moed, Bill Moon, Erland Olsen, Adrian Ort, Thomas Plakke, Sara Pilborough, Samuel Ritzmann, and Peter Stabler.

Industry contributors and advisors to this new edition include Alfred Rigler, Colin Banks, Camille Ducherme, Jan Hovora, Stephanie Weisenberger, Stephen White (IFCA's 2003 Education Committee), along with Stan Bruce, Peter Dubovy, Alfred Gafner, Malcolm Hague, Johanne Hague, Duncan Hepburn, Tim Williams, Sterling Bridge Ltd, Peter Hough, Adrian Lee, Jens Tangeberg, Danielle Medina, and Andrew Smith.

I would also like to thank industry colleagues who have allowed me to visit their facilities including Paul Breen, Joseph Chew, Guy Curtis, Stuart Guinea, Petki Salminen, Micael Zetterquist and Lionel Wilton, as well as those that have offered support in other ways—Peter Viinapuu, and Lee Walton. Thanks too to the companies that have given permission to reproduce photographs, documentation, and other materials to illustrate this text.

Finally, I would like to thank the students of the University of Surrey, some of whose assignment work or research has been incorporated into this book. I am sure that there are many others that I should thank and apologise now for any omissions.

This list of names is without doubt impressive. But what is really impressive is the time, energy, and enthusiasm displayed by my colleagues in helping to make this book as good as it can be. Since 2001, the flight catering industry has been through a difficult period. Despite this, industry friends and colleagues did not hesitate to commit themselves to this project. It has been one of the highlights of my career to work with them all on this book.

This book is therefore dedicated to everyone who has contributed in any way to its publication. All that is good in this book is theirs; any errors or omissions are mine.

Professor Peter Jones

Preface

This is the second edition of *Flight Catering*. It is considerably changed from the first edition in a number of ways. First, all of the original chapters have been revised and updated. In some instances, chapters have been expanded, reduced, or merged. Second, four new chapters have been added to cover in more detail specific aspects of flight catering. Third, every chapter now includes at least one, sometimes two, detailed case studies that illustrates the content of that chapter. Fourth, each chapter has discussion questions and further readings that enable the reader to extend their understanding of the material. Finally, the book is illustrated with new photographs and documentary materials provided by firms in the flight catering industry.

In 1995, I was a head of school at the University of Brighton, when Professor Michael Kipps from asked me to join him as co-editor of a book focused on this industry. He, along with colleagues at the University of Surrey, had been working for some time in collaboration with the International Flight Caterers Association (IFCA). The book was one of the projects being sponsored by IFCA's Education Committee (see Acknowledgements). Michael and I assembled a distinguished team of academics, each an expert in their field, to write each of the chapters (also see Acknowledgements), while the Education Committee set up a series of meetings, visits, and contacts to assist the authors with their research and writing. Little did I realise that shortly afterwards I would leave Brighton to come to Surrey. And even more surprising, I would become IFCA's first ever professor of flight catering in 2001.

From the 1940s, flight catering has been a global industry—long before hotel companies and fast food chains, and before most manufacturers developed global brands. However, until the 1990s many of the catering firms in the industry and suppliers to the industry were regionally based, while airlines also had strong national or regional identities. The relatively small scale of many firms tended to hide the fact that flight catering was a £15 billion a year industry, serving many millions of passengers with food and beverages on every continent. Someone once described it to me as a 'Cinderella industry'.

So, one of the reasons for this book is to raise the profile of this significant industry and encourage students to learn about it and academics to include it in their curriculum. It could be used in many different ways, but some examples would include:

- To understand production and operations management by looking in some detail at one specific industry (for instance, on Business Studies or MBA courses)
- To understand logistics and supply chain management in one specific industry
- To support a specialist module on travel catering on hospitality management courses at diploma, undergraduate or postgraduate level
- To support the teaching of topics on hospitality management courses such as food production technology (cook-chill, cook-freeze), mass catering, food safety, menu planning, kitchen design, food service, environmental management and so on.

But this book is also for all those dedicated people that work in this industry and who would like to know more about how it operates. Flight catering is incredibly complex. It requires a higher degree of expertise in difficult subjects—operational research, production management, supply chain and logistics, information systems, food safety, organisational behaviour, marketing, and so on. I have met many colleagues working in the industry who are enthusiastic to learn and understand more about this complex challenge.

Professor Peter Jones

Introduction to flight catering

- Provide a brief overview of flight catering
- Identify the periods of crucial development concerning the industry
- Understand the implications of the historical development of on-board food service
- Identify the key trends in the airline industry

Introduction

It is possible to dine in five-star luxury while travelling at 600 miles per hour, six miles above the surface of the earth. To the average person, now used to air travel, this may not seem remarkable. But the average person is unaware that there may be over 40,000 separate items loaded onto a Boeing 747 (popularly known as the jumbo jet). This load occupies 60 m^2 and weighs six tonnes and the loading time may be less than 50 minutes. In view of this, some might say that it is not just remarkable that air travellers may dine so well; it is remarkable that they can do so at all.

This chapter provides an overview of how in-flight meal service has developed worldwide to make on-board dining as it is today. There have been four stages of development which have had a significant impact on how in-flight catering functions and operates.

Pioneer years of in-flight foodservice

On 17 December 1903, Orville Wright made the world's first powered flight in a heavier-than-air machine, near Kitty Hawk, North Carolina (Franklin, 1980). The flight lasted 47 seconds and covered 2000 feet. As far as we know, there was no food or drink on board this historic flight. However, it was not long before food and beverage service became a feature of air travel. As early as 1914, Zeppelin airships served passengers champagne with their in-flight meal, and in the 1920s they introduced flying dining rooms with chefs preparing hot meals (Dana, 1999).

The first regular passenger service by aeroplane began in August 1919 in Europe, between England and France, and flight catering was there from the very start (Wright, 1985). Game and cream teas were served during the two-hour flight. These were enjoyed by passengers on the outward journey from England, but refused on the return trip because of the extremely bumpy flight conditions. This was at a time when few aircraft carried no more than four passengers and closed cabins were not enclosed (Franklin, 1980).

Some claim that KLM, founded in the Netherlands on 7 October 1919, was the world's first commercial airline (KLM, 2001 [online]), and that it was four days later, on 11 October, that pre-packed airline meals first appeared on the flights between London and Paris (O'Hara and Strugnell, 1997). Other European airlines were also established during this period, such as Sabena of Belgium founded in 1923.

During the 1920s Imperial Airways (one of the forerunners of British Overseas Airways Corporation, which was formed in 1939) were developing. Initially, their catering service consisted of only sandwiches with tea or coffee (O'Hara and Strugnell, 1997). The service was provided by fourteen-year-old cabin boys in monkey jackets and tight trousers who travelled the route, and who were fined if they became over 100 lbs. (40 kg.) in weight (Wright, 1985). At this time, flight safety was not strongly considered inside the plane—aircraft seats were often wicker chairs, so selected because they were lightweight.

In 1920, KLM carried a total of 345 passengers, 22 tonnes of cargo, and 3 tonnes of mail. One year later they were possibly the first airline to install a galley on their F2 aircraft. It consisted of a wooden cupboard containing liquor and glasses. It was only short lived as the screws holding it to the bulkhead shook themselves loose after being airborne for approximate 15 minutes and the cupboard fell onto the lap of a surprised passenger (Franklin, 1980). As the journey was rough, a new heated cabin was soon added to make the passengers more comfortable (KLM, 2001 [online]).

The first recorded full in-flight meal service is attributed to Air Union, instituted on 30 July 1927. They employed stewards on board to serve *hors d'oeuvres*, lobster salad, cold chicken and ham, nicoise salad, ice cream, and cheese and fruit. Drinks were also offered with the meal and consisted of champagne, wine, whisky, mineral water, and coffee. However, the service was discontinued in June 1929 because the aircraft (an F-60 Goliath) was poorly adapted for this type of service (Franklin, 1980).

Imperial Airways in 1927 offered first-class travel to Paris for £9 and second-class travel for £7.10s (Wright, 1985). In these very early days, there was no need for a curtain to separate passengers paying different fares, because the first- and second-class passengers were put on separate planes, with the second taking 20 minutes longer. This is not so dissimilar today in terms of charter and scheduled flights.

Imperial in 1927 introduced a steward on board their DH 66 Hercules aircraft who served sandwiches, fruit, and coffee from a vacuum flask (Franklin, 1980). The next year in America, Pan Am (a US airline) employed uniformed stewards and restaurant-style tables adorned with vases of flowers and silver cutlery. Western Airline (eventually absorbed within Delta Airlines) served meals brought from a restaurant to their aeroplanes. In 1929, Pan Am introduced movies on its flight between Miami and Havana (Dana, 1999).

The first full-hot food service was on Sunday, 29 April 1928, when Lufthansa introduced their 'Flying Dining Car' on the Berlin–Paris route. The B-31, which accommodated 15 passengers, had a fully equipped galley, where the steward was able to prepare and serve hot food (Franklin, 1980).

In 1929, the KLM flight to Indonesia took 12 days (KLM, 2001 [online]). The flight engineer would double up as a steward, and ensure that the passengers were comfortable during the flight. Since the flying boats had long route patterns, frequent landings, and overnight stops, most meals were eaten on the ground. Snacks, afternoon tea, and light lunches were picked up and served in-flight at tables set with white cloths, flower vases, cutlery, and glasses as in a restaurant. Some meals such as roast beef and Yorkshire pudding were served from insulated containers. Strawberries and cream, when in season, were a great passenger favourite (Franklin, 1980; Wright, 1985).

In 1930, American Boeing Air Transport (a forerunner of United Airlines) recruited eight nurses to be employed as flight attendants, and therefore, became the first airline to employ stewardesses (Franklin, 1980). Nurses were employed because aeroplanes at this time had unpressurised cabins and flew at relatively low altitudes. This meant that the flights were frequently bumpy, and along with the lower levels of oxygen at altitude, resulted in many passengers feeling unwell and vomiting. One estimate suggests that at least one in four passengers were physically sick. This is the reason why sick bags were placed in a seat pocket in front of each passenger, a practice which continues even today. In Europe, stewards appeared in 1932 for the first time on KLM and later in 1935 the first stewardesses came on board (KLM, 2001 [online]; Franklin, 1980).

In 1933, the Marriott group contract caterers saw a gap in the market and decided to serve food from one of their 'Hot Shoppes' to passengers queued up for flights out of an adjacent airport (Romano, 1993). Later, in 1934, Dobbs International Service Inc., one of America's largest in-flight caterers, was founded in Memphis, USA (Anon, 1998).

Routes began to extend during the 1930s, and by 1934 Qantas and Imperial Airways had combined their operations to fly passengers across continents in 'hops' from Croydon near London to Brisbane (some 12,7000 miles) in about twelve and a half days, costing £195 single (Wright, 1985). They served hot meals from insulated containers (hayboxes) to keep food hot (Bruce, 2001; Wright, 1985). In the same year, Pan Am introduced the S-42 on its route from Miami to Buenos Aires. The airline set a precedent by installing facilities for heating food in-flight on long over-water journeys. Stewards would take orders from passengers and radio ahead for meals, which were served to passengers in a special dining area of the aeroplane (Dana, 1999).

Intercontinental travel

As aircraft design improved, so did the meals served. From 1936, the DC3 was designed with a galley to enable hot meals to be served to passengers, thus replacing sandwiches and tea or coffee (O'Hara and Strugnell, 1997). Imperial Airways with its 'C' or 'Empire' class flying boats built up a good reputation for its in-flight service for 24 passengers. Although no food heating or refrigeration facilities were available, the aircraft had a fully fitted galley that enabled the flight attendants to serve meals comparable to first-class restaurants or hotels. The passengers ordered meals the evening before and the food was usually supplied by the hotel or guest house where the passengers had spent the night. The food was packed in bags and boxes, vacuum and thermos flasks, delivered on hand-pushed carts and loaded by hand into the aeroplane. The steward prepared drinks in a small galley and bar.

In 1938, Imperial Airways were the first to set up what today might be called a 'catering centre' (Wright, 1985), food having become an essential part of the total service that an airline passenger was now coming to expect. In the following year Boeing 307 Stratoliner became the first aircraft with a pressurised cabin that permitted commercial flights to fly above the weather. However, it was developed with a galley no more advanced that of the DC-3 (McCool, 1995). In 1946, Dobbs constructed the first independent airline kitchen which was built to serve Delta in Atlanta (Anon, 1998).

The interior design of aeroplanes began to incorporate catering functions in order to enrich the dining experience in the air. During the 1940s, Boeing 377 served passengers in staterooms with private washstands, berths, divans, clothes closets, and reclining lounge chairs. Dinner served downstairs was the highlight of the flight (Dana, 1999). In 1946, the first aircraft ovens were installed in galleys to heat the meals, instead of the food loaded hot onto the aeroplane and kept warm in either charcoal-heated or similarly insulated containers (Franklin, 1980).

By 1949 British European Airlines (BEA) was selecting an equal number of stewards and stewardesses. Once working, the stewardess on the British airline seemed more like a housekeeper in the air. For the British Overseas Airways

Corporation (BOAC), the recruits had to have good education, poise, and tact. Glamour girls were definitely not required, but patience and a pleasant, charming manner were considered great assets. Training in simple cookery and the service of meals was given to all accepted candidates. During the flight the stewardess changed from a blue uniform to a white mess jacket, and then prepared and served a light meal. In her spare time she washed up and packed away crockery because "everything had to be spic and span when the aircraft arrived" (Wright, 1985).

BOAC followed the traditions of British airlines in that full-course hot meals were served on board, even though on their Lancastrian aircraft no cooking or re-heating facilities were provided. All the food was carried in RAF-issued thermos flasks of two-gallon capacity. The desserts, such as ice cream or fruit salad, were carried in similar but much smaller one-quart flasks (Sullivan, 1995).

The 1950s became a prime period for the airlines as the aircraft became larger and the journey times became shorter. Thus, the development of improved facilities became a priority. The introduction of deep-frozen foods on board provided the answer for some of the caterer's difficulties. On board the aircraft, complete meals, which had been frozen and kept in cold storage before being transported to the aircraft, were placed in electric ovens, defrosted, and then reheated to the required temperature (O'Hara and Strugnell, 1997). Although these meals were readily accepted in the USA, European airlines were slow to adopt them (Franklin, 1980).

The airlines were faced with meeting a wide range of ethnic tastes and special diets (Franklin, 1980). Meal service was lavish on the 14-hour flight from Europe to New York. Passengers of BOAC had the choice of ordering their meat rare, medium, or well done. Breakfast eggs took time to boil, depending on the altitude, for example, 20 minutes at 9,000 feet.

As late as 1954, it was estimated that only 60 per cent of meals served to long-haul passengers were actually served in flight. In those days, refreshments and sandwiches were always served to passengers during transit stops, if a meal on board was not scheduled. Airlines were becoming more aware of the importance of in-flight service, and introduced custom-built galleys, complete with water boilers, hot cups, and flasks. Developments also took place to insure that tray equipment, such as cups, plates, cutlery and glassware, were of such a design that weight was saved and also that they could be stowed in the confines of available space.

The first folding-type first-class trolley was introduced on the Stratocruiser. These trolleys had the facilities for carrying wine and liquor during a meal service. BOAC used an economy trolley developed by Stan Bruce, which initially consisted of two tray boxes bolted together, one on top of the other, affixed with four wheels on the side. Since then 99 per cent of the airlines have introduced this type of trolley for their economy meal service, as can be seen in today's present aircraft (Franklin, 1980).

Several of the newer and larger craft were equipped with small cocktail bars, which by 1956 were proving most popular. The double-decker 'clipper' flying boats, which had cabins above and lounges below, were highly suitable to perform a complete catering service. In all but a few instances, meals, and often drinks, were complimentary. BOAC's Trans-Atlantic 'Monarch' service was an example of luxury air travel at a high standard.

Besides the choice of flying by luxury 'Monarch' service, BOAC also introduced the 'Coronet' service in the double-decked Stratocrusiers at low tourist fares. With increased tourist demand, this period also developed factors peculiar to air travel: frozen food with specially designed ovens, catering contractors, new cooking methods, new galley equipment (consisting of a quick oven, hot closet, water boiler, beverage heater, and a small refrigerator), and menu planning (such as a buffet-style service) (Morel, 1956). With the increasing travelling trend, the International Air Transport Association (IATA) developed standards stating that airline meals should include a sandwich and outlined exactly what could be served and permitted quantities (Dana, 1999).

Mass passenger travel

The early trend was for airlines to develop their own catering systems with their own catering facilities at all major stations, especially their hub airports. The introduction of the Boeing 707 jet aircraft in 1957 saw significant developments in flight kitchens and services on board. BOAC and British European Airways (BEA) between them prepared and served more than 10,000 meals each day in the air—some of them consisting of six or seven courses. Meal trolleys were modular and loaded directly into designated galley positions, including refrigeration unit positions. With the development of the new jet engine in 1959, BOAC introduced four different types of services: De Luxe, First Class, Tourist, and Economy Class.

Until the introduction of Boeing 707, the majority of catering uplifts were being made from airport restaurants, airport hotels, or units with very limited facilities. In the USA, the development of custom-built facilities was started much earlier and they were ahead in design and equipment. Also, prior to this period, the form of ground transportation was usually an assortment of vans, pick-up trucks, and at times, bicycles with a basket in front. It became necessary for development to be carried out in this area, which resulted in the introduction and development of various types of high-lift trucks (Franklin, 1980). Dobbs replaced the forklift with its first high-lift catering truck to load meals on an aircraft in Memphis (McCool, 1995).

In 1967, BEA set up its own catering centre at Heathrow and brought in throw-away tray items. They estimated that a hot meal cost them 5s 1d(25.5p), a cold meal 3s 9d(19p), and a snack 2s 2d (11p) (Wright, 1985). Around this time, airline food began to be promoted as a feature, with Miami-based Eastern Airlines introducing 'Famous Restaurant Flights', which served meals on Rosenthal china. Northeast Airlines—its principal competitor on the US east coast—responded with steak and champagne (Dana, 1999).

BOAC in 1966 began to consider the problems of catering on the new, much larger Boeing 747, an aircraft with double aisles and capable of carrying over 400 passengers. Cabin services and aircraft catering sections of BOAC together with the interior engineers, realised a whole new concept of galley design, loading and passenger service would be essential (Bruce, 2001). Due to the large quantity of meals that needed to be produced, the food became simpler. When Boeing 747 re-introduced its double-decker airline service in 1969, a new concept in galley design was developed that resulted in galleys being installed in the belly of the aircraft adjacent to the baggage and freight holds (known as 'lower lobe' galleys).

Along with the design of galleys, a great deal of improvement was also made in the design of the ancillary equipment, such as bars, trolleys, water boilers, and so on. Air Canada used the upper cabin as a bar for first-class passengers, whilst Pan Am used the upper deck as a restaurant with individual place names. BOAC designed a microwave oven in a service table in the centre of the first-class cabin. These gueridons had a spring-loaded hot-plate container (topped with flowers when not in use) and hot shelving on either side of the central microwave oven. The quick defrosting and cooking of the microwave gave a remarkable choice of six main courses (Wright, 1985). During this period one airline even installed a popcorn machine in their galley. New procedures also had to be developed for the in-flight service, ground handling and catering units.

For a quick turn around of aircraft it was essential that all uplifts were in a 'ready-to-go' situation, with little or no preparation required by the cabin crew. Flight kitchens had to be extended or redesigned in order to be able to handle the wide-body aircraft, and areas of refrigeration had to be greatly increased, especially the holding rooms (Bruce, 2001; Franklin, 1980). Chefs were kept busy assembling the meals on large tables and kitchens adopted a variety of labour-saving equipment. KLM in Amsterdam developed a fully automatic system for pre-setting trays of only KLM size. By using this system, only one person was required, whose sole responsibility was to maintain a constant supply of required items for deployment on each belt (Franklin, 1980).

In 1976, BA with Air France launched the world's first supersonic passenger services with Concorde (BA, 2003 [online]). Cabin crews had to be careful to keep the trolley brakes on at the front galley area, or it rolled away to the rear of the plane. Extra light weight crockery and slimmed-down cutlery (much prized as a souvenir) were used, since every extra pound in weight carried meant an extra £225 in fuel a year, compared with £17 on a 747. With the supersonic speed, there was no time to sell duty-free items or show a movie (Wright, 1985).

Deregulation and consolidation

Deregulation of US airlines in 1978 changed nearly every aspect of airline operation, including catering services. In the drive to reduce costs, food service was cut back or even removed completely. The fewer flight attendants and greater number of feeder flights made it difficult or impossible to offer food service (Tabacchi and Marshall, 1988). In the mid-1980s, the business of flight catering changed further as airlines began selling of their flight kitchens and outsourcing food production (Pilling, 2001).

Flight-service decisions became crucial to meet the needs and expectations of passengers and to differentiate the product. The trade-off between premium services and the costs of providing it demanded much of the airline product planner (Shaw, 1985). Lighter meals have become the trend with SAS introducing a self-service sandwich selection, Swissair introducing cuisine modern, and Air One introducing first-class meals prepared by stewards at a buffet (Dana, 1999). TWA introduced *à la carte* meals for members of the TWA frequent flight bonus programme in which passengers order flight meals up to 24 hours prior to flight time from seven special meals. Air Canada had 12 different types of special meals. Airlines in Canada discontinued the use of 48-ounce cans of juice, replacing them by Tetra-Brik packages to reduce the weight and volume (Dana, 1999). BA introduced a food tray half the usual size with the same amount of food in short-haul flights from ALPHA Flight Services, and a return catering system with chilled galley storage for trolleys at below 8°C. KLM and Lufthansa followed this method later (Mullen, 1997).

As many airlines offer no meal service on up to 1,500 daily flights, some companies are trying an arrangement whereby airlines give passengers a discount coupon instead of a flight meal. For example, Sky Chef began offering Uno pies and pizza, Northwest Airlines worked with Pepsi Company to offer Taco Bell, Pizza Hut, and KFC on the plane, and United Airlines used Macdonald's children's meals solely on flights in and out of Orlando (Romano, 1993).

However, some airlines have diversified their feeding strategies to fulfil the passengers' expectations of value for money in other ways. Japan Airlines have introduced an in-flight sushi bar. Air Canada has promoted NutriCuisine, its brand name for low-fat, low-salt, low-sugar meals and the Flex-Meal, as a cold plate available anytime during a flight (Dana, 1999). SAS adopted a gate buffet programme in 1996 on select routes within Scandinavia, with passengers able to select food taken aboard while tea and coffee are served as usual in flight (Anon, 1999 and IFCA, 2001 [online]). In addition, Air-India reports that almost 50 per cent of all its flyers pre-order vegetarian meals and Swissair have introduced organically grown foods in all classes of its in-flight catering. Continental Airlines also offer new menus for business-class and coach-class customers on South American flights by the airline's chefs which include celebrity chefs (Murray, 1994). The Singapore Airport Terminal Services (SATS) catering service has been the first flight kitchen to be awarded the ISO 9002 certificate for production of in-flight meals (Chang, et al., 1997).

Internet technology has permitted advances in the interfacing of airlines, caterers, and suppliers with a comprehensive e-commerce based system. The launch of eLSG.SKYCHEFS and e-gatematrix in 2001, has enabled the world's two largest flight caterers assist in areas of equipment management, procurement, and basic information dissemination. Airlines can then work with caterers and suppliers on food service, scheduling, menu specifications, meal ordering, and other functions (Lundstrom, 2001a). Ordering a meal is not a problem. Cathy Pacific Airways and Virgin Atlantic offer passengers in-flight e-mail and intranet services across their entire fleet (Lundstrom, 2001b).

Airlines are also responding to the global market by the larger carriers forming partnerships and alliances to rationalise services and peripheral activities. The sharing of such things as engine overhaul services, handling and catering operations at airports served by the partnership or alliance, together with the use of common reservation systems, are becoming common. For example, three inter-related private Scandinavian airlines formed the Trans Nordic Group (TNG) to gain operational and marketing benefits and exploit the liberalisation of the European air transport market after 1992. TNG also share a flight training centre and flight kitchens (Aero Chef kitchens), providing crew training and flight catering for all three airlines. Clearly though, in response to economic and market pressures, flight catering has had to become more process driven as this book will emphasise.

While growth is to be welcomed by the industry—in 1990 there were 457.3 million international tourist arrivals compared with 692.7 million in 2001 (WTO, 2002 [online])—problems emerge because of this expansion. It is generally accepted that much of the industry's essential infrastructure has almost reached its full capacity, with the maximum capacity of some traditional international hub airports already reached. Similarly, air traffic control systems in some parts of the world, especially over Europe, can handle little extra traffic.

The flight catering system

Flight catering is probably one of the most complex operational systems in the world. Some of the facts referred to later in this text provide an insight into this operational complexity. For instance, a large-scale flight catering production unit may employ over 800 staff to produce as many as 25,000 meals per day during peak periods. A large international airline company may have hundreds of takeoffs and landings every day from just their main hub. These facts and others like them make flight catering unlike any other sector of the catering industry. While the way food is served on trays to airline passengers bears some resemblance to service styles in restaurants or cafeterias, the way food is prepared and cooked increasingly resembles a food manufacturing plant rather than a catering kitchen. The way food and equipment is stored resembles a freight warehouse, and the way meals and equipment are transported and supplied has a close affinity to military-style logistics and distribution systems.

Figure 1.1 represents only an outline of the process flow in flight catering, since such operations are highly complex and have a number of alternative configurations. It is this model that provides the structure for this text.

Flight catering starts with an understanding of the number of passengers and their needs (see Chapter 3); such information is available from both market research and actual passenger behaviour. On the basis of this, airlines, sometimes in consultation with caterers and suppliers, develop their product and service specifications (discussed in Chapter 5). Such specifications determine exactly what food, drink and equipment items are to be carried on each route for each class of passenger. At the heart of the flight catering system is the flight production unit, which is part warehouse, part food manufacturing plant, part kitchen, and part assembly belt (the layout and design of which is explained in Chapter 7). In response to forecasts of passenger numbers on any given flight, the production unit follows a series of complex steps to produce trayed meals and non-food items ready for transportation to the aircraft (see Chapter 8). Transportation is usually carried out by using specialist high-loader trucks that enable trolleys to be rolled on and off aircraft (see Chapter 10). Once loaded, trolleys and other items need to be stowed on board to ensure the microbial safety of edible items and the security and safety of the crew, passengers, and aircraft (see Chapter 13). At the designated time during the flight, the cabin crew then carry out the service of meals, snacks, and other items (described in Chapter 14). On arrival at its destination, each aircraft is then stripped of all the equipment and trolleys, which are returned to the production units for cleaning and re-use (Chapter 15). In achieving this, it is

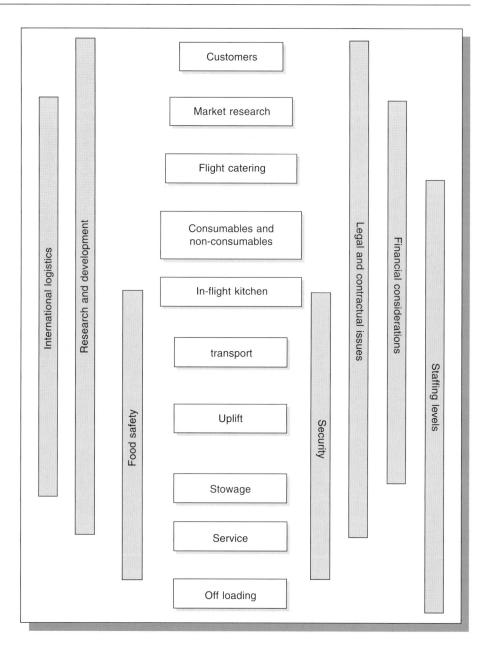

Figure 1.1
The flight catering system

necessary to understand the impact of flying on the physiology of the passenger (Chapter 4), to manage a complex supply chain (Chapter 6), assure the safety of the food and drink (Chapter 9), apply the principles of international logistics (Chapter 11), utilise increasingly sophisticated information and communication technologies (Chapter 12), and engage in on-going research and development (Chapter 16).

International operations

One aspect of the flight catering industry is that airports and flight production units are found in every corner of the globe. This means that they operate in every type of climate under a variety of conditions, from very cold to very hot, from arid to very wet. This has implications for how the operations are managed.

Very cold conditions, such as in Scandanavia, Canada and Siberia, mainly affect issues related to transportation from the production unit to the aircraft. When hi-lift trucks used in Germany were moved to an operation in Sweden, it was found they were inoperable during the winter, as they were not equipped to cope with very low temperatures. Likewise, trollies are washed and then dried centrifugally in order to remove all trace of water. This is because any water left on the trolley wheels can freeze in the short period they are moved onto planes. As a result the cabin crew reject them as 'defective' and ask for a replacement trolley, even though once the ice has melted the wheels move normally.

Climate also affects the design and layout of loading bays. In wet climates these need to be designed so that trollies can be loaded onto trucks under cover so they do not get wet, and to prevent water or snow from blowing into the trolley assembly area. In hot, arid countries the same requirement is called for, but in this instance it is to prevent the ingress of sand and dust. Particular attention may also need to be paid to the provision and use of door closures and insect screens in order to prevent foreign bodies from entering the premises and potentially contaminating the food chain.

Issues and trends

All commercial activity is subject to external forces. These forces inevitably cause an industry to change and adapt over time. Typically, companies scan the environment in order to identify factors that may affect them in the future in order to develop new policies and new products and services. Such scanning is usually organised under five main headings:

- Political forces
- Economic factors
- Social trends
- Technological change
- Environmental concerns

In reality, many external events span more than one of these categories. For instance, the creation of a single currency (the 'euro') in Europe is predominantly an economic issue, but it also has political and possibly social effects too. The flight catering industry is no exception to this. There are probably five main issues that will significantly affect the whole industry up to the year 2010.

The first key issue is **industry structure**. Until the 1990s, the industry was highly fragmented with many small companies, often with only a national or regional presence. During the last fifteen years, the industry has seen significant concentration and the emergence of two very large global companies. Linked to this has been an increase in airlines contracting out their catering provision rather than operating their own facilities.

The second key issue is **competition**. The growth of large firms in the industry has significantly increased competition in the industry. This has occurred at a time when airlines are increasingly competitive, especially with the major growth of low cost carriers. This has led to a significant pressure on costs and has implications for the profit margins of flight catering companies. This challenge has only increased due to other pressures.

The third issue is **security**. Throughout most of the second half of the twentieth century, the world order was based around the so-called 'cold war' between the western world and the Soviet bloc. With the break up of the Soviet bloc, the world order has changed significantly with a major shift towards terrorism based on religeous fundamentalism. The use of aircraft in the attack on the New York World Trade Center on 11 September 2001 has led to security becoming a major issue.

The fourth issue is **outsourcing**. Pressure on costs and increased competition has led flight catering companies to re-think their business model. They are thinking of themselves less as caterers and more as experts in logistics. Much of the production activity in kitchens is being outsourced to food manufacturers and suppliers.

The final issue is **information technology** and, in particular, the Internet. The development of this has enabled firms to redesign their processes and to manage through outsourcing. It also provides better management information, thereby helping to monitor costs more effectively.

These issues have been introduced briefly here. Their effect on specific aspects of the industry will be developed later in each chapter, where relevant. In addition, later chapters will identify other issues outside of these main ones.

Conclusion

For each of the stages in the flight catering operation, there are some features that are unique to flight catering. These derive from one simple fact: while the food is prepared on the ground it will be consumed in the air. This impacts on:

- customers and their needs—the prime motivation for travel is not eating
- menus—some food and drink items are not suitable for consumption in pressurised cabins 10 km above the ground
- production methods—the volume of business necessitates large-scale meal production
- service style—since passengers are seated in rows of aircraft seats, tray service predominates
- shelf-life—the time difference between production on the ground and consumption in the air which determines the adoption of cook–chill methodologies
- transportation—moving trayed meals from production unit to aircraft and then storing on board is based around modular trolleys

These challenges have always existed since the earliest days of commercial passenger air travel. Indeed, the industry invented or adopted a large number of ideas very early in its development which are still in use today—the aircraft galley (1920), the in-flight movie (1929), male and female cabin crew (1930), the flight production unit (1938), on-board ovens (1946), and so on. Having looked at the history and development of flight catering, this book will now examine in detail every aspect of the industry. Appropriately, it will end with a chapter that looks at innovation in the industry—what might happen in the industry in the future.

Key terms

Deregulation	Flight caterer	Flight production unit
Galley	Inflight services	Mass travel
Steward/(ess)	Uplift	
Flight attendants		

Discussion questions

1. Identify the key aspects of air travel experience. How long ago were each of these aspects introduced into passenger air services?
2. Discuss the impact of the DC-3 on service on board.
3. What was the impact of the development of jet aircraft on the in-flight catering industry?
4. How has the transportation of meals developed?
5. What has been the impact of deregulation on in-flight services?

References

Anon. (1998) "Caterer Profile: Dobbs International Services," *IFCA/IFSA Review*, 1 (1) January, 18–23.

Anon. (1999) "SAS Report Shows More Than 80 New Cabin Service Environmental Projects," *PAX International*. Mar./Apr. 42–44.

British Airways. (2003) *History of British Airways* [online], Available from: http://www.britishairways.com/press/ [Accessed 17/03/03].

Bruce, S. (2001) *In-flight Catering*. Unpublished work.

Chang, Z.Y., Yeong, W.Y., and Loh, L. (1997) "Case Studies: Critical Success Factors For In-flight Catering Services—Singapore airport terminal services' practices as management benchmarks," *The TQM Magazine*, vol. 9, no. 4, 255–259.

Dana, L.P. (1999) "Korean Air Lines," *British Food Journal*, vol. 101, no. 5/6, 365–383.

Franklin, F.G. (1980) "History of Inflight Catering: It All Began in 1903 with Orville Wright," *Airline and Travel Food Service*, September/October, 16, 21.

IFCA. (2001) *Food on the Ground* [online], Available from: http://wwwifcanet.com/environmental/useful-case-examples/useful-case-examples.html [Accessed 23/04/01].

KLM. (nd) *KLM Royal Dutch Airlines Celebrates 80 Years of History* [online], Avaiable from: http://aboutklm.com/CorporateInformation/History/frame/default.asp [Accessed 24/05/01].

Lundstrom, R. (2001a) "Global Caterers at the On-line Crossroads," *PAX International*, Jan./Feb., 14–15.

Lundstrom, R. (2001b) "Airlines Logging On to Tensing Internet System," *PAX International*, May/June, 50.

McCool, A.C. (1995) *In-flight Catering Management*, John Wiley and Sons, Inc.: New York.

Morel, J.J. FHCI. (1956) *Progressive Catering: A comprehensive treatment of food, cookery, drink, catering services and management*, Capper, W.B. (eds), The Caxton Publishing Company Limited: London.

Mullen. (1997) "Two-Way Bet," *Caterer and Hotelkeeper*, 30 October, 70–71.

Murray, M. (1994) "High Tea and Other Meals in the Air," *Hospitality*, 142, February, 30–31.

O'Hara, L. and Strugnell, C. (1997) "Developments in In-flight Catering," *Nutrition and Food Science*, vol. 3, 105–106.

Pilling, M. (2001) "Food For Thought," *Airline Business*, Jan., 48–50.

Romano, M. (1993) "Airline Food: Sky High," *Restaurant Business*, vol. 92, no. 15, 10 October, 66, 68.

Shaw, S. (1985) *Airline Marketing and Management*, 2nd edn, Longman Group Company: London.

Sullivan, B. (1995) "Speedbird Service II," *Aeroplane Monthly*, June, 20–24.

Tabacchi, M. and Marshall, R.C. (1988) "Consumer Perceptions of In-flight Food Service," *The Cornell Hotel and Restaurant Administration Quarterly*, vol. 28, no. 4, 20–23.

Wheatcroft, S. (1994) *Aviation and Tourism Policies*, World Tourism Organisation Publication, Routledge: London.

Wright, C. (1985) *Table in the Sky: Recipes from British Airways and the Great Chefs*, W.H. Allen & Co.: London.

WTO. (2002) *International Tourist Arrivals by (Sub) Region*, Available from: http://www.world-tourism.org/market_research/facts&figures/latest-data/tita01.07.02.pdf.

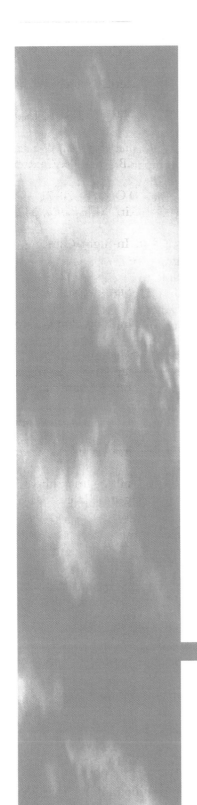

The flight catering industry

- Provide a brief overview of the relationships between the four different stakeholders concerned with flight catering
- Identify the role of the four stakeholders within in-flight service
- Explain the nature of contracts and the tendering process between airlines and caterers
- Understand the implications of alternative approaches to on-board food service

Introduction

Travelling by aeroplane can be quite hectic. Getting to the airport, check-in, immigration and security procedures are only the start. After boarding, the cabin crew undertake a carefully coordinated series of tasks, ranging from delivering blankets and headphones to drinks and meal service, all within a confined space in a finite period of time. Yet, passengers are largely unaware of the work and logistics that have gone into their flight service in order to deliver the tremendous number of meals in very restrictive conditions.

In the last chapter we saw that as flight catering developed, four separate groups—or stakeholders—emerged in the industry. Along with the passengers and airlines, suppliers to the industry were needed from the very earliest days and dedicated flight catering companies were founded in the 1940s and 1950s. In some cases, airlines formed their own flight catering divisions, in other cases these were independent of any airline.

Four stakeholders of flight services

The relationship between these four stakeholders is shown in Figure 2.1. As a result of the fragmentary and international nature of the business, tight interfaces are required between flying passengers and the airlines and between the airline and the providers and suppliers.

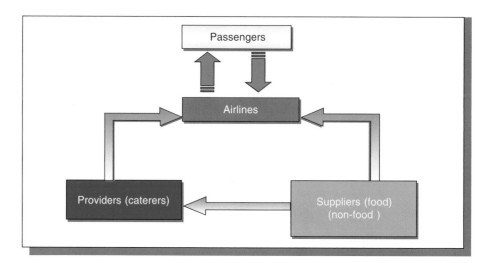

Figure 2.1
The interface between the 'players' involved in flight catering

Role of the customer

Within the flight experience, passengers largely expect the service to match the money they have paid. One research study into passenger behaviour found that some passengers may be served with an *à la carte* or seven-course dinner with a choice of five main entrees, mid-flight snack service, and hot or breakfast meal available anytime during the flight. The research also found that most customers want to have their meal service delivered at their own pace, to have more time to rest or work, and to have highly individual service delivered with "grace and elegance" (Martin, 2001). Some passengers may raise nutritional concerns. In one study women were more inclined to want lighter, more nutritious food (Tabacchi and Marshall, 1988). Chapter 3 will explain more about passenger needs and expectations and how these can be satisfied with on-board service.

As passengers are only served on the areoplane, most are completely unaware of the back-of-house activities that underpin their onboard experience: menu planning and preparing dishes and meals through a complicated supply chain, loading the very large quantity of products on an aircraft, or the cost structure. Nor are they aware of the constraints placed on caterers. Some of the constraints include:

- the time of flight
- the length of flight
- the point of embarkation and disembarkation
- the nationality or ethnicity, economy, business or first class
- the budget allowed by the airline
- the price of food
- the seasonality of food
- the cost of labour to make a food item
- the time required to serve the food
- the number of the flight attendants available to serve food
- the time needed to consume food
- the ability of meal to be consumed in a small place on a plane
- the time and effort needed to clear an item
- the odours that may penetrate the cabin
- the ability of the meal to be rethermalised
- the ability of the meal to withstand low humidity and pressures

Role of caterers

In providing all meals, beverages, and perhaps other products such as paper goods, blankets, magazines, headsets, amenity kits, and so on, caterers have two main roles: to prepare items not bought in directly from suppliers in a state ready for loading on board and to assemble trays and trolleys. To do this flight production units are located on or near major airports. They also 'manufacture' some consumable food items and assemble others. There are two main reasons why menu items are made outside of airport-based flight kitchens: the cost of space and the cost of labour. Airport space is so often at a premium that it is not feasible for a flight production unit to produce all the meals needed for every class. Some caterers make first-class, or in some cases, business-class meals and outsource all other meal production.

While the flying or fare-paying passenger might be considered as the final customer for whom the caterer ultimately works, the airline caterer, unlike a restaurant, has little, if any, immediate contact with him or her. Whether employed directly by the airline or contracted out, the flight provider works directly to and for the airline and in this respect complies with and responds to the airline's wishes. It follows, therefore, that in this case, the customer is not the fare-paying, flying passenger, but the airline.

Caterers may also have a distinctive relationship with suppliers. Although a customer of the supplier, the products used by the caterer may not be of his/her choosing but may have been determined by the airline. When products used are those purchased directly by the airline, caterers only charge for a handling and storage fee of the product but not the cost of the product. For instance, all liquor products are kept 'in bond' and are subject to customs control at any time. The bond licence is issued to the individual airline and not to the caterers. This allows the airline to 'temporarily import' free of duties not only liquor, but all the food, beverage, and equipment items needed for their operation. However, the caterer is responsible for keeping and accounting for any such products delivered directly to the caterer's production facilities. The challenge for caterers is that the products are the property of the individual airlines served by the caterer, and products belonging to one airline cannot be used for another, even if the two airlines use identical products (such as the same brand of gin).

Many airline companies operate, or have operated, their own catering companies. Depending upon the airline's finances and the vision of its executive officers, an airline may decide to sell or expand the catering component of the airline. For example, until several years ago, Sky Chefs was a division of American Airlines; likewise United Airlines sold most of its flight kitchens to Dobbs International, which was subsequently bought out by Gate Gourmet. Some caterers in the world market are Cara Operations Limited, Abela Airline Catering, ALPHA Flight Services, Eurest, Gate Gourmet, LSG/Skychefs, Nikko Inflight Catering Co., SATS, and Servair.

Role of airlines

As has been suggested, the flight caterer's customer is not the fare-paying passenger but actually the airline. The caterer must respond to the demands and wishes of the airline and any wider motives that the airline may be seeking to develop. The airline though, theoretically at least, seeks to establish what the 'flying customer' might require, and attempts, through the caterer, to interpret and respond to those wishes.

Within the airline, individual groups of people will, in turn, be customers. The cabin staff who serve the meals face a dichotomy. They often had had no input into the planning or preparation of the meals concerned, but are yet customers of the catering providers. They offer and serve a product of which they have limited knowledge to a further customer. In one study, many cabin crew believed that decisions on the number of meals and the content of menus are made by the caterers, whereas in practice these decisions were made by the airline management (Pedrick et al., 1993).

The last decade has witnessed the world's airlines creating demand and growing market share on the basis of discounted fares for both the business and leisure travel sectors. This has led to a number of weaknesses linked to revenue generation and profitability. The number of competitors is a serious problem and it is thought that the European airline industry is oversubscribed by airline operators, and while this is the case, profitability will remain a major problem. The situation was summarised for Europe when Air France's Chairman, Bernard Attali, stated, "There are about 60 airlines that matter and that's 40 too many" (*Financial Times*, 5 July 1992). More recently, in 2001, Europe had 65 carriers with revenue passenger kilometres (RPK) of 754,818 million, whereas North America had 38 carriers but with RPK of 1,116,211 million (Airline Business, 2002). The current situation is that the leading four airlines in the USA account for over 80 per cent of the entire US market (American, United, Delta, and Northwest Airlines) and their dominance is held secure due to the control they exercise of the key hubs.

Airlines concentrate on determining their customers' needs and defining the specifications of the flight service, as discussed in Chapter 5. Later in this chapter we discuss alliances between the airlines and identify the wide range of different carriers around the world.

Role of suppliers

Suppliers may supply either caterers or airlines, increasingly the latter. If, the supplier receives direct orders from the airlines, they deliver their goods to flight production units, which may be operated by contracted caterers. Airlines buy direct from suppliers for a number of reasons:

- continuity of supply in all their stations
- to negotiate a discount
- to link to the brand image of the product
- readiness of the supplier to provide products that meet the contract specification

Likewise, suppliers have two approaches to manufacturing their products. Some supply airlines or caterers with their standard products, whereas others make and supply specialist products specifically designed for the flight industry. In the first instance, the manufacture of these products is likely to take place in a factory or plant producing many other products. These products for flight service may be slightly modified for that market. For instance, spirit manufacturers need to bottle their spirits in miniatures rather than 40 ounce bottles. In the second case, the manufacturer concentrates on simply producing a cycle of food items, which often is their sole business, and hence they can produce large amounts of these items to be sold to the flight catering sector as a method of outsourcing. These food manufacturers can make these items in volume at a lower unit cost than the flight production facility can. The cost of labour to mass-produce meals is obviously cheaper at a good distance away from large cities where airports must exist. Historically, it was mainly frozen meals, or 'pop-outs' as they are called in the USA, which were outsourced in this way. Today, all kinds of specialist food items may be outsourced, such as canapés, ethnic meals, vegetarian items, patisserie, and so on.

Airline–Caterer contracts

One expert (McCool, 1996) has described the relationship between airlines and caterers: "[It] is somewhat like soliciting guests to [stay at] a [hotel] property and then, once solicited, having the guests specify the type and brand of amenities, linens and furnishings that will be in their rooms when they arrive; having the guests sometimes bring their own supply of amenities, food and beverages with them and having property secure them in safe storage and issue them on guests' request; having the guests regularly conduct quality control surveys of the property; and finally having the guest have a say in determining what rates they are going to pay for their stay." In view of this complex relationship there needs to be clarity about the nature of the contract between the two parties, and in a form that is legally binding.

The relationship between an airline and a caterer is based on service delivery. The airline requires its catering supplier to deliver on certain key variables, such as:

- consistency of food product
- accuracy of uplift
- on time delivery
- value for money
- service relationships
- health, hygiene and safety
- innovation
- overall operational performance

However, in the complex business world of today, all of these things cannot be simply agreed on the basis of a handshake. So, in the majority of cases, airlines and caterers enter into a legal relationship based on a contract between them.

Contracts between airlines and caterers may be very long and detailed documents, but they will conform to a fairly standard structure, comprising the following elements.

Terms of agreement—this specifies the length of time the contract will be in force. Typically, in this industry contracts are for one to three years. The trend is for them to be longer rather than shorter.

Definition of services—each and every element of service being provided will be defined in precise terms. For instance, terms such as 'uplift', 'menu specification', and so on will have definitions if referred to in the contract.

Charges and payments—the price to be paid for services rendered will be identified along with any relevant terms and conditions applying to such payments in relation to the timing of payment, form of payment, and so on. Currency and rate of exchange are also included, although nowadays many quotes are issued in euros or US dollars, especially in financially unstable countries.

Discounts—may form either part of the general agreement or are dealt with in a separate discount agreement. Typical are **volume** (turnover per year), **early payment** (usually 30 days, but less in countries with high interest rates, or for caterers with financial constraints). **Global**, if more than one location is involved, or where the airline serves another destination where the same caterer is present.

Title and risk—as in most cases, the caterer will be handling equipment belonging to the airline, it is necessary to identify who owns what (title) and who has the liability for any loss (risk). Typically, the airline has the title, but the caterer bears the risk.

Indemnity and liability—these clauses of the contract limit the ability of either party to the contract to sue the other party. Insurance, including the total sum insured, is also incorporated here. Since 9/11 this has become an important issue for the airline and for caterers, especially the smaller ones, insurance rates have become a burden. This has resulted in unavoidable increases in handling costs.

Warranties—in some cases one of the parties to the contract, usually the caterer, will provide a guarantee, in the form of a warranty, to the other party.

Confidentiality—most contracts contain a clause that ensures that both parties keep the terms and conditions of their contract confidential.

Termination—the contract will specify under what conditions either party can end the contract and how much notice must be given for doing so.

Force majeure—this legal term applies to allowing a suspension of the terms of the contract due to the so-called 'acts of God', that is, if events outside the control of one of the parties prevents the contract from being honoured.

Business continuity – this clause will identify what happens to the contract if one of the parties is taken over by a third party or goes out of business due to insolvency or bankruptcy.

Law and jurisdiction—this clause will specify in which country the two parties agree the contract is signed, so that the laws of contract of this country apply to any legal dispute between the two sides.

Waiver—this clause ensures that neither party is able to change any part of the contract without the agreement of the other party.

Invalidity—this clause ensures that in the event that one clause of the contract is shown to be invalid (i.e. not of legal status), this does not make the whole contract invalid.

In addition to this legal contract, attached to it or as part of the overall agreement between the airline and the caterer, there may be documentation such as a service level agreement, price list, and standards of performance criteria. A typical service level agreement would have detailed specifications of how things are to be done, relating to such elements as hygiene, punctuality, product specifications, security, equipment control, and waste management. It may refer not simply to delivering trolleys to aircraft, but to other operational aspects. For instance, some airlines require their caterers to make quarterly presentations on new menu ideas as part of their agreement. Likewise, there will be specific performance targets that caterers will be expected to meet. Such targets might include:

- number of aircraft delays allowed per month—usually the first delay is free, but time is also an important factor, e.g. more than 5 minutes or less than 15 minutes, particularly when slots are missed; delays may result in lost connections and high extra costs for the airline
- number of adverse cabin crew reports permitted
- number of catering related passenger letters
- allowable percentage of incorrect weights of product
- hygiene audit scores

If performance falls outside the allowed tolerances, the penalties to pay will be specified. Likewise, if performance is particularly good, incentives may be paid.

In most cases, caterers are invited to tender for an airline contract. Such a contract may apply to just one station, such as Schipol, or apply to all the destinations an airline flies to in a region of the world, such as the Middle East. Rarely does it apply to all the destinations an airline flies to, unless this airline is relatively small. The typical tendering process is illustrated in Figure 2.2. In some cases, caterers do not wait to be invited to tender; they make what is termed a 'pre-emptive bid'. They do this when they know a contract is likely to be coming to an end and they believe that this airline's business would be a good 'fit' with the other contracts they have. In this case the first three steps of the tendering process shown in Figure 2.2 do not happen.

Pricing of flight meals

The range of pricing methods is very wide, from a simple, 'multiply by a factor' to a sophisticated multi-disciplined approach. Some methods are straightforward in that they require the minimum of data collection and manipulation and are therefore attractive for that reason. There is little evidence to suggest that more sophisticated methods are more successful than simple straightforward ones, but they must be based on standard recipes.

Price is a determinant of demand. Pricing is never a simple matter of 'mark up over cost'. When and how to raise prices is just as critical as the amount of the increase itself. The market for the flight product appears to be becoming ever-more price sensitive and more value conscious, indicating that those flight caterers who wish to survive and increase their profitability in a much more competitive environment will need to concentrate even more on costing and pricing. Successful pricing methods are able to contribute to establishing a 'competitive edge' over very aggressive and increasingly margin-conscious rivals.

In many ground-based catering operations, price is based on raw material cost, with sufficient margin to cover labour and overhead costs. In flight catering, price is often established on the basis of separately calculating each of these elements of cost. This is because the labour cost for a meal item can vary widely depending on whether a product is simply handled or significantly processed within the flight production unit. For instance, hot entrées such as casseroles or stews may be outsourced to a food manufacturer (handling costs only) or be prepared from entirely fresh foodstuffs in the flight kitchen (production, processing and handling costs). It is therefore common for separate prices to be established for different aspects of provision, such as stock-handling and warehousing, food production, tray lay-up, transportation, and ware washing.

North American vs European and Asian school of thought

There are two distinct schools of thought in the airline catering industry, most clearly illustrated by the differences between the Asian and North American approaches. These two different strategies arose out of the origins of flight catering and the way business was conducted in the USA compared with the rest of the world.

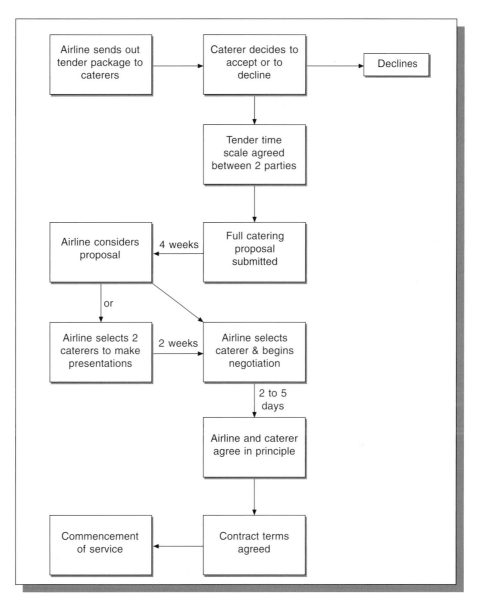

Figure 2.2
The contract tendering process between an airline and a caterer

A model of contracted-out catering was adopted widely throughout the USA, not just by the airlines but also for feeding employees in factories or offices, or students in schools and universities, or patients in hospitals. As well as the airlines contracting out, passenger use of air travel and their expectations of on-board service are quite different in the USA. Americans use aeroplanes in the same way that Europeans might get on a bus or train. Several carriers (such as Continental Airlines and US Air), therefore, withdrew catering on flights of two hours or less duration with an added reduction in cabin staffing. Even on longer flights in coach class, however, some passengers can expect only cold meals or sandwiches. The Dallas-based Southwest Airlines does not offer any meal service on any of its 1,500 daily flights (Romano, 1994). The policy of American Airlines is to cater at meal times on 90-minute sectors or more, and the carrier is pursuing a policy of using branded products such as pizzas. Benefiting from this branded bulk purchasing and product consistency, the passenger knows what to expect without guessing (Noble, 1995). Some airport restaurants have arranged either a refrigerated, quick-connection trolley to sell fresh-fruit trays, sandwiches, and chilled beverages right at the gate for on-flight consumption, or a discount meal coupon with airlines (Romano, 1994). Hotels in the USA are picking up the slack and provide take-away meals for the planes at a price, for example, the 'Food on the Fly' programmes from Hilton Hotels and In-flight menu from New York's Four Seasons hotel and Chicago's Ritz-Carlton (Blank, 1999).

In Europe and Asia the major national airlines tended not to contract out but to operate their own flight catering facilities, especially out of hub airports. During the 1990s, due to cost pressures, many airlines have divested themselves of these facilities and adopted the contracting-out model.

However, in Asia, many airlines have retained the production of their own flight meals as part of their cultural identity in order to sustain their competitive advantage. For example, since 1980, Singapore Airline's catering operation (SATS) has continued to expand and renew their flight kitchens to meet the demand for finer meal service for their thousands of passengers (Anon, 1980). SATS is equipped with an automated storage and retrieval system to store all incoming dry goods, bonded goods, and airline amenities with a bar-coded Demag conveyer system (Tansey, 1996). Korean Air has boasted that they grow the farm-fresh food served on their flights, and Japan Airlines has introduced a flight sushi bar (Dana, 1999).

Alliances and partnerships

Airline alliances

Global airline groupings dominate more than half the world transport market. There are four groupings—*Star Alliance*, *Oneworld*, *SkyTeam*, and *KLM/Northwest*. In terms of passenger traffic (RPK), they already hold close to 60 per cent of the world share and this figure excludes regional affiliates (Fig. 2.3). All the major alliances have two main partners, one European carrier and one north American carrier. This is largely due to the importance of the North Atlantic route and because it is the most profitable one. The other partners provide a global network. The main reason for the emergence of alliances is the lack of liberalisation in the industry.

While each alliance have been promising the long-term goal of seamless global services, there are wide variations in the extent of their togetherness (Gallacher 1999). An alliance may aim to cooperate on Code-sharing, Frequent Flyer Programme (FFP) integration, lounge access, seamless connections, schedule coordination and route planning, pricing and inventory management, joint marketing and sales, integration of IT systems, shared airport facilities, and joint purchasing (O'Toole, 1999). Such alliances allow firms to focus on their respective core competencies, while drawing on the benefits of scale

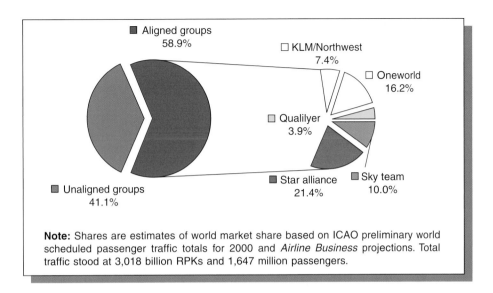

Note: Shares are estimates of world market share based on ICAO preliminary world scheduled passenger traffic totals for 2000 and *Airline Business* projections. Total traffic stood at 3,018 billion RPKs and 1,647 million passengers.

Figure 2.3
The global alliance airline groupings
SOURCE: Baker, 2001a

economies in production and marketing, and overcoming regulatory barriers and facilitating access into new markets (Dana and Vignali, 1999). These strategic alliances are generally characterised in one of two ways: vertical relationships (firms cooperating in complementary activities), or horizontal relationships (cooperation within the same activity).

Stuart (2001) has foreseen that alliance managers need to address five core business areas:

- understanding the role branding plays in market positioning and the merits of subverting to the alliance brand
- maintaining the promise of delivering value to its constituents at the operation level
- accessing information technology (for example, reservation platforms)
- the implications of alliance-based labour negotiations and actions
- understanding the regulatory bodies (for example, the antitrust immunity between British Airways-American).

Star Alliance—founded in May 1997, in 2002 it had 12 airline group members. With its joint ventures in Europe and across the Atlantic, the alliance is evolving around three geographical groups, the Americas (led by United Airlines), Europe (led by Lufthansa), and Asia (where the importance of Singapore Airlines is increasing). Table 2.1 lists its core members and associated carriers. In September 2000, StarNet, a stand-alone multi-user communication platform, was launched to enable members to keep their own legacy systems and cut down on the costs associated with a complete systems overhaul.

Core members	Pending
Air Canada	Asiana
Air New Zealand	LOT Polish Airlines
All Nippon Airways	Spanair
Austrian A/I Group	
bmi	
Lufthansa Group	
Mexicana	
SAS	
Singapore Airlines	
Thai Airways	
United Airlines	
Varig	

SOURCE: *Airline Business*, 2002

Table 2.1
Star Alliance members

Oneworld—founded in September 1998, has been held back by the inability of its core members—BA and American Airlines—to gain anti-trust immunity across the Atlantic (core members and associated carriers are listed in Table 2.2). At the IT level, Oneworld has not yet followed its major competitors in establishing a central communication platform, relying instead on different global distribution systems—Amadeus and Sabre.

Core members	Associated Carriers
Aer Lingus	TWA
American Airlines	Affiliates
British Airways	23 regional airlines affiliated to the
Cathay Pacific	Alliance
Finnair	
Iberia	
LanChile	
Qantas	

SOURCE: *Airline Business*, 2002 and Baker, 2001a

Table 2.2
Oneworld members

SkyTeam—founded in June 1999, has three founder members (Delta Air Lines, Air France, and AeroMexico) (as seen in Table 2.3). The alliance initially struggled to find new members, losing out in bids to attract bmi and Australian Airlines, but new entrants appear to be promised. SkyTeam has followed Star in introducing a stand-alone common-user IT platform, named SkyTeamNet.

Core members	Associated Carriers
AeroMexico	Air France stakes in African carriers
Air France	Aeroflot
Alitalia	
CSA Czech Airlines	
Delta Airlines	
Korean Airlines	

SOURCE: *Airline Business*, 2002 and Baker, 2001a

Table 2.3
SkyTeam members

KLM/Northwest—founded in 1989, with common purchasing and a frequent flyer programme. 'Wings' was the unofficial name for the KLM and Northwest Airlines grouping. The agreement of the group with Continental Airlines has fallen through and it has also broken up with Alitalia, but the recent agreement with Malaysia Airline Systems (MAS) could expand its relationship on an exclusive basis with the Malaysian carrier (Table 2.4). IT integration has mainly been bilateral, but a single integrated IT platform is predicted to extend the compatibility of the loyalty programmes.

Core members	Associated Carriers
Northwest Airlines	Transavia
KLM	Kenya Airways
	Malaysia Airlines

SOURCE: *Airline Business*, 2002 and Baker, 2001a

Table 2.4
KLM/Northwest 'Wings' members

Although the global alliances have swallowed up most of the world's top 50 passenger carriers, a number of major airlines are either still in the fray or have simply preferred to stay away (Table 2.5). In Asia Pacific, only Nippon Airways is currently attached and the market leader Japan Air Systems is independent. Taiwan's two main carriers are also unattached. Emerging markets such as China, Russia, and India have been identified as areas for long-term expansion by the leading alliances (Baker, 2001b).

For the time being, alliances remain more revenue-driven, focused on the gains to be made from joint marketing to customers and opportunities for world-wide outsourcing deals, but are not keen on the issues of joint branding (O'Toole and Gill, 2000).

Caterer alliances

The business of flight catering has totally changed since some airlines began selling off their flight kitchens and outsourcing food production in the mid-

Continental Airlines
Japan Airlines
US Airways Group
Southwest Airlines
America West
China Airlines
China Southern
Emirates
Saudi Arabian Airline
Alaska Airlines
Japan Air System

Note: The order is ascending by passenger traffic share (RPKs)
(SOURCE: Baker, 2001a)

Table 2.5
Major unaligned groups

1980s. The consolidation of the airline alliances and the flight catering industry are almost complete in North America and Europe. The rapid push by Lufthansa's LSG SkyChefs and GateGourmet to develop market share has intensified competition for catering contracts, and over a five-year period prices have been pushed down by some 15–20 per cent (Pilling, 2001). The relationship between the airlines and the caterers has been characterised as a 'dog fight' by Lundstrom (1998). The Airlines have asked for lower costs, faster services, high quality of products, and kitchens cleaned to standards of the Hazard Analysis at Critical Control Points (HACCP). Working with one global caterer at all of their destinations, the airlines consider cost savings and quality benefits. Most airlines have been contracting out in-flight catering and are increasingly looking for suppliers with a global presence. Through outsourcing, the industry has pushed down the costs of flight catering to about 4 per cent of the overall airline operating costs in the USA, and around 6 per cent in Europe (Gill, 1999).

Since the cost to start up a new operation is much too high in most cases, alliance and partnerships have formed between caterers. More mergers in airline catering, as predicted by Herdman (1997), have formed several global catering giants. The acquisition of Ogden Aviation Services with 11 facilities across the USA, has enhanced LSG Lufthansa Service Holding to be one of two big players; the other is Gate Gourmet, which bought Dobbs International to become the second largest caterer in the world. These two firms alone hold 85 per cent of the US market and over half of the global market (Fig. 2.4).

Consolidation is not over in this business, because although 50–60 per cent of the market is in the hands of the big players, the rest is very fragmented. The smaller caterers are competing against two large companies with significant research capability and resources that can undercut them in procuring suppliers, negotiating deals, and signing airline customers to contracts that guarantee service virtually anywhere in the word. In response, a maze of complex agreements, partnerships, and joint ownership have resulted in the new caterer alliances. They involve Servair, ALPHA flight service, Abela Catering, Flying Food Group, Eurest Inflight Services, Singapore Air Terminal Service (SATS),

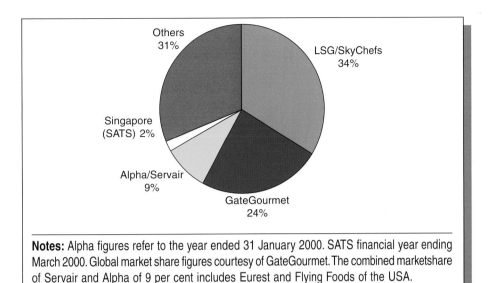

Notes: Alpha figures refer to the year ended 31 January 2000. SATS financial year ending March 2000. Global market share figures courtesy of GateGourmet. The combined marketshare of Servair and Alpha of 9 per cent includes Eurest and Flying Foods of the USA.

Figure 2.4
Major flight catering suppliers 2001
SOURCE: *Pilling*, 2001:50

and two long-time airline caterers in Italy. With the available capital for construction and acquisition, partnerships with local companies give the caterers the ability to share the best practices and offer services to more cities. In addition to equity, Servair and Flying Food have shared their personnel and marketing information on a regular basis (Lundstrom, 2001).

Since 1997 when Hong Kong returned to China, airline caterers in the Asia Pacific area have started to locate units, both large and small, around some of China's sprawling and fast-growing population centres. Beijing and Shanghai have been assigned to join Hong Kong as aviation centres in Asia (Lundstrom, 1997). LSG/Sky Chefs, Cathay Pacific Catering, and Gate Gourmet are the designated catering units for Chek Lap Kok airport (CLK) with 15-year agreements to supply flight meals for the airlines serving CLK. It is only in Asia where airlines maintain catering subsidiaries, and the combined LSG/ GateGourmet market is no more than 15 per cent (Pilling, 2001). Some have predicted that most of Asia's loss-making airlines will eventually outsource their own inefficient catering business (Anon., 1999).

In addition to the caterers' alliances, the tableware and amenity supplier DUNI (formerly DeSter ACS) started a partnership with Bernorf for supplying cutlery and other metal products and Wedgewood for branded ceramics (Anon., 2001). The two companies call the partnership an 'industry first' which offers flight services and product development. The two companies will operate separately, and no equity was involved in the new partnership. With this acquisition, DUNI emerges as a strong player by increasing the performance of flight products, which have been getting shorter and shorter product life cycles.

Case study 2.1

LSG Sky Chefs

Founded in 1966 as a subsidiary of Lufthansa, the Lufthansa Service Company (LSG) was one of the large European airline catering service companies which offered its services exclusively to other airline companies in the Frankfurt airport. The history of LSG has expanded with their acquisition of Sky Chefs (Table 2.6). Aiming for the concept of 'One Stop Shopping', they serve more than 260 airline customers from over 200 catering locations in 44 countries world-wide. With an output of 427 million meals in 2001, they employed 41,700 staff in 210 kitchen units. The timing and storing of company-owned materials and their ordering depends exclusively on demand, frequently ordered on a short-term basis. Flexibility is achieved through an automated comprehensive logistic system for both warehousing and ordering.

The new e-business subsidiary eLSG.SkyChefs, Inc. uses web-based technologies to support the electronic business-to-business (B2B) portal and aims to improve the efficiency of cooperation between the airlines, caterers, and suppliers. Partnerships with Sabre, Accenture and i2 allow eLSG.SkyChefs to offer a range of solutions covering the entire flight services, equipment management, and procurement processes.

History of LSG Sky Chefs

1942	American Airlines invests $500,000 to create Sky Chefs, a wholly owned subsidiary airline catering service based in the USA.
1966	LSG Lufthansa Service GmbH (LSG) is founded as a wholly owned subsidiary of Deutsche Lufthansa AG.
1986	Sky Chefs becomes an independent company and a subsidiary of Onex Food Services, Inc. when American Airlines' parent company, AMP Corp., sells Sky Chefs to its senior management and Onex Corp. of Toronto, Canada.
1987	Sky Chefs sells its Restaurants and Concessions Division to Delaware North Companies, Inc. of New York.
1989	With 10 Locations in Germany and an additional unit in Cairo, LSG launches a global expansion strategy under the motto 'Marketing European Quality Worldwide'.
1989	LSG enters the Asian market with the founding of LSG Lufthansa Service Asia Ltd. and investment in Sky Bird Services Ltd. New locations in Europe are also gained through a joint venture with Airest in Austria, and LSG begins operations in the USA through the formation of LSG Lufthansa Service USA Corp. and a joint venture with Marriott/Caterair.
1990	LSG forms a joint venture with Interflug in the former German Democratic Republic. LSG also enters Italy and expands operations in Asia.
1991	LSG's expansion in Asia continues when Dragon Air invests in LSG Lufthansa Service Hong Kong Ltd.
1992	Sky Chefs signs a 10-year contract with American Airlines, the largest catering contract in the history of aviation.
1993	LSG acquires a minority interest in Sky Chefs, which operates in 33 US locations. The partnership launches a joint marketing effort and the LSG Sky Chefs brand. LSG Sky Chefs becomes the largest airline caterer in the world with operations in North American, Europe, Africa, and Asia.
1994	Sky Chefs enters a partnership with Delta Daily Food of the Netherlands to establish a

new food-processing facility in Dallas, Texas. Sky Chefs also enters a joint venture as a minority partner with TAP Portuguese Airlines and forms Catering Por, SA. In addition, Sky Chefs acquires an 80 per cent interest in Servcater, an airline caterer in Sao Paulo, Brazil.

1994	LSG gains additional flight catering facilities through a 40 per cent equity investment in Canada.
1995	Sky Chef's parent, Onex Food Services, completes the acquisition of the international operations of Caterair International Corp., formerly Marriott In-Flight Services and the world's dominant independent airline caterer. Most of the acquired operations begin doing business under the name of LSG Sky Chefs.
1995	LSG Lufthansa Service Holding AG is founded as a wholly owned subsidiary of Deutsche Lufthansa AG.
1996	LSG enters South Africa with a joint venture in Johannesburg. Another joint venture with TOP Flight Catering AB opens the door to the Scandinavian market.
1997	LSG achieves further growth in Eastern Europe with units in Moscow, Kiev, Riga and Tallinn. LSG also obtains production facilities in Turkey through a joint venture with Sancak Havacilik Hizmetleri A.S.
1998	Onex Food Services acquires the airline catering division of Ogden Corp. and merges the operations with Sky Chefs, further enhancing the LSG Sky Chefs partnership.
1998	The LSG Sky Chefs 'Customer Care' programme—designed to create a global team that serves customers with the same high quality standards around the world—is launched with pilot programmes in Munich and New York.
1998	LSG signs and exclusive catering agreement with SAS Scandinavian Airlines to provide catering service in Sweden, Denmark, and Norway.
1999	LSG increases ownership in Sky Chefs to approximately 48 per cent. Coupled with that is a rights option to acquire the remaining shares.
2000	eLSG.SkyChefs, an innovative new company that provides web-based solutions for the management of in-flight services, is launched.
2001	After exercising its call option, LSG acquires the remaining shares of Sky Chefs. The two organisations officially become one global company and a world leader in airline catering.

SOURCE: LSG Sky Chefs, 2001 [online]

Table 2.6
The history of LSG Sky Chefs

Case study 2.2

Gate Gourmet International AG

Through a merger of the Swissair company ICS (International Catering Services) and the catering operations of Swissair, Gate Gourmet was founded in 1992. Several strategic acquisitions have assembled 156 flight kitchens in 34 countries on six continents with 32,000 employees. Table 2.8 summarises their history. It bought KLM's kitchen in Bangkok and has taken control of South African catering interests in Johannesburg, Durban, and Cape Town. As a result of Swissair's interest in Sabena, it has also established a relationship with Sabena Catering in Brussels. In South America, it has taken over the Lima flight kitchen of Aeroservicios Peruanos and has a presence in Argentina and Brazil with the LaMarmite kitchen in Santiago and a five-year contract with LanChile. As a result of Swissair's bankruptcy in 2001, Gate Gourmet is now a separate company owned by an American investment firm.

History of Gate Gourmet International

1992	GateGourmet is founded through a merger of the Swissair company ICS International Catering Services. The catering operations of Swissair Papadacos Catering Athens joins the Gate Gourmet Group.
1993	GG acquires AERO-CHEF, thereby increasing its number of catering units to 44 with an annual turnover of CHF 800 million (GG ranks now fifth among the world's top catering companies). Abela-Gate Gourmet joint-venture operation opens at London Heathrow.
1994	Acquisition of SSP SAS Service partner; doubling GG's Size and thus turning it into the world's third largest catering company. GG now operates 64 units in 21 countries with more than 13,000 employees.
1995	Restructuring of GG's London operations: disposal of minority shareholding in Abela, incorporation of Heathrow and Gatwick kitchen into a new Gate Gourmet London company. Acquisition of Varig kitchen Sao Paulo, Brazil. Acquisition of two ALPHA kitchens in Lisbon and Faro, Portugal.
1996	Gate Gourmet adds two new destinations to its network in South Africa: Cape Town and Durban. The Swissair Group Changes its name to SAir Group. Gate Gourmet—together with Rail Gourmet, Swissotel, Nuance, Restorama and Restosana—form SAirRelations division (former Swissair Associated Companies).
1996	Acquisition of KLM kitchen Bangkok, Thailand; acquisition of Varig kitchen Recife, Brazil.
1996	Gate Gourmet receives one of three franchise licenses for the new Hong Kong airport Chek Lap Kok.
1997	Start of Gate Gourmet's new advertising campaign: *It always pays to take a second look*.
1997	Gate Gourmet and Sabena Catering sign a cooperation agreement, making Gate Gourmet Sabena's preferred caterer.
1997	Acquisition of Aerosevivios Peruanos flight kitchen in Lima, Peru.
1997	Acquisition of LaMarmite flight kitchen in Santiage de Chile.
1997	Acquisition of British Airways' QCS and QCW kitchens at London Heathrow, joint venture with Manila Integrated Airport Services (MIASCOR) and Malaysian Airline System (MAS) for a new in-flight catering facility at Ninoy Aquino International Airport in Manila, Philippines.
1998	Opening of new GG catering operation at Hong Kong's new airport Chek Lap Kok.
1998	Opening of new GG catering operation in Manila.
1999	Inauguration of Iber Swiss Catering at Barcelona Airport in Spain.
1999	Gate Gourmet acquires Dobbs International Services, Inc. Gate Gourmet now operates 142 flight kitchens in 27 countries with approx. 26,000 staff.
1999	Acquisition of three catering operations in Mexico City, Cancun, and Monterey.
1999	Entry into the Chinese market in co-operation with China's Shanghai Pudong International Airport Authority.
1999	Commencement of operations at the new Gate Gourmet unit at Charles deGaulle Airport, Paris.
1999	Further expansion in Australia with the acquisition of seven catering units from Ansett Australia
1999	Acquisition of Ligabue Catering S.P.A. with units in Rome, Milan and Venice.
2000	Inauguration of the new Gate Gourmet flight kitchen in Zurich, which features the latest in catering and logistics technology.
2001	Opening of new flight kitchens at Port Columbus International Airport, Ohio, and San Diego, California, USA.
2001	Gate Gourmet's parent company Swissair Group goes into receivership.
2002	Swissair signs the definitive purchase agreement with Texas Pacific Group, on the sale of Gate Gourmet.

SOURCE: Gate Gourmet, 2002 [online]

Table 2.7

The history of Gate Gourmet International AG

Current issues and future developments

As the case studies in this chapter have shown, over the last decade two major global companies have emerged in the flight catering industry. This is not surprising. Industry concentration (the move towards greater market share in the hands of fewer larger companies) and globalisation are trends that are evident in many industrial sectors, from soft drink to sportswear, fast food to aircraft manufacture. Indeed, this trend is evident in the airline and supplier sectors of the industry too.

Industry concentration occurs mainly to take advantage of economies of scale. Larger firms incur lower unit costs because they can spread fixed costs (such as head office expenses and marketing) more thinly, better manage their supply chain, and engage in organisational learning. This enables them to lower their prices, which in turn increases concentration by making the large firms more competitive. To a certain extent this is what has happened in flight catering. However, there is some evidence to suggest that while prices have come down, this has been due to the highly competitive nature of the industry, rather than through actually achieving scale economies. This means that the very large firms have cut their profit margins to gain market share, and still need to exploit the opportunities that being big can offer.

Globalisation, on the other hand, is largely driven by two factors. The first is that the firm cannot grow any larger in its own home market, and the second is that its customer base is international. Since the airline industry has always been international, it could be argued that caterers have been very slow to 'go global'. In Europe a major barrier to this had been the philosophy of state-owned airlines to operate their own facilities. With privatisation and deregulation, the market for catering, as also airlines, has been opened up. In this industry, globalisation has been facilitated by two other trends—the trend towards outsourcing product (see also Chapter 9) and the development of IT-enabling technologies, notably the internet (see Chapter 11).

In terms of what may happen in the future, it seems likely that these two trends will continue. But precisely how the structure of the industry will change is more difficult to predict. One scenario is that in addition to Gate Gourmet and LSG Sky Chef, a third large firm will emerge through the merger of existing regional companies. Already, some such companies have responded to the threat posed by the larger firms by forming consortia to share expertise, increase their purchasing power, and so on. For instance, Eurest Inflight services and Catair merged into one company in 2002 (Momberger and Momberger, 2003). This would result in three global firms and many small, local companies serving niche markets. An alternative scenario is that in the short term, one or both of the big two, will be unable to exploit the opportunities offered by scale economies and globalisation, forcing them to 'downsize'. In other words, financial pressures would force them to sell off parts of their business. Given the very difficult trading condition between 2001 and 2003, this is a possibility.

Amongst **suppliers**, there already exist a large number of global food and drink manufacturers that are household names—Kraft, Nestle, and Heinz for instance. When the flight catering industry was relatively fragmented into regional and national companies, these very large suppliers, although aware of the airline market, found it relatively difficult to handle many separate accounts. With the emergence of the big two, they have seen the opportunity to sell their products globally in very large quantities through a small number of key accounts, greatly helping their sales and distribution effort. This greater engagement in the industry, along with their ongoing product development for other markets (restaurants, supermarkets, and so on), has led them to also identify an opportunity to persuade caterers to outsource the production of many items that previously would have been produced in the flight production unit (see also Chapters 6 and 8).

Strategic airline alliances have essentially emerged as a result of the semi-liberalised nature of the industry. This has to be done under strict regulation as too close cooperation is prohibited by competition laws, while full liberalisation would facilitate a wave of mergers and acquisitions at a global level. Strategic alliances can offer valuable unit cost reduction during recession periods by taking advantage of scale and scope economies. Moreover, the gradual promotion of a common brand name and a frequent flyer programme creates marketing advantages and enhances customer loyalty. All three major alliances (Star Alliance, Oneworld, and SkyTeam) focus primarily on the North Atlantic route (one of the most lucrative markets until recently) and are led by two major partners followed by a number of smaller carriers. Moreover, the current gaps in the global seamless alliance networks (mostly in the Middle and the Far East) will be probably filled by new members from these areas. In fact, the collapse of Swissair's Qualiflyer alliance and the efforts of KLM to join one of three existing groupings (in exchange or in addition to its current agreement with Northwest) show an ongoing process of fortification but also consolidation in airline partnerships. If American Airlines or United Airlines are forced into bankruptcy, due to their current high levels of debt, further dramatic concentration may occur.

So far, only traditional scheduled carriers have participated in strategic alliances. It will be interesting to see in the future whether low cost airlines will seek membership too. Although the latter claim to operate on a point-to-point rather than network basis, increased competition and subsequent product differentiation could induce them to reassess their strategy. As we move towards complete liberalisation of the airline industry at a global level, the very character of strategic alliances may also change. Instead of facilitating airline coordination, they will become a stepping stone for horizontal market integration (mergers of airlines) both at an intra- (for example, within Europe) and inter-continental (for example, between Europe and the Americas) level. Even though they may end up being a transitory phenomenon, strategic alliances will have left a permanent footprint on the evolution of the airline industry.

Conclusion

In summary, there are four major types of players in the flight catering business. These are the carriers (airlines), the providers (caterers), the suppliers (vendors and distributors), and the passengers. Each airline carrier decides what kind and how much food service and which flights need which type of service. Obviously, food service is a marketing tool and some airlines do not give as much service if there is no competition or if the flight is exceptionally short (such as under one hour). Some passengers may be willing to forgo food on 'no frills' or 'peanuts' flights if the fare prices are slashed. All of this is for the airline to decide.

The carrier must also decide whether to operate its own catering operation or to contract with an external caterer. This decision is based upon location, availability, reliability, long-term relationships, cost, and convenience. Both the caterer and the carrier must carefully negotiate costs. The carrier cannot afford to pay too much as each fraction of a penny may add up to thousands of pounds or euros per annum, while the caterer cannot afford to accept too little as food prices may fluctuate or labour costs may increase, and the caterer must deliver a quality product to preserve not only its own image but that of the airline.

Manufacturers/suppliers who prepare food for the airlines also take advantage of economies of scale to purchase raw goods for the manufacture of airline meals, desserts, beverages, and snacks. Increasingly, these suppliers can produce meals for economy class much more cheaply and efficiently than can most flight kitchens; hence catering companies tend to buy these meals from vendor/suppliers.

Distributors play dual roles for airlines and caterers. They obviously distribute materials and meals from vendor/suppliers and they can track numbers, volumes, brands, and hence the quality of food for the airlines. The airlines want value for money and one of the ways in which they ascertain value is through establishing with the caterer and the vendor certain brand and manufacturing specifications. Because caterers and airlines purchase such volumes, it is essential that someone can track purchasing, receiving, and the utilisation of products for the production of airline meals.

The interaction of the players, the airlines, the caterers, the manufacturers/suppliers, and the distributors is the key to providing quality food service to passengers on airline carriers. These four stakeholders in the industry must communicate and work in agreement to achieve excellence in their endeavours. More than any other industry, these constituents are interlinked. It is difficult to separate clearly the functions of these players as roles and responsibilities overlap. The overlap and the co-operation found in this industry are some of what makes it so unusual.

Key terms

Alliances/partnerships	Contracts	Deregulation
Fare paying passenger	Outsourcing	
Service level agreement	Suppliers	

Discussion questions

1. Discuss the roles of the four stakeholders. What might be the problem areas?
2. What are the pros and cons of airline alliances?
3. What are the implications of airline alliances for flight caterers?
4. How might the two schools of thought influence the future of flight caterers?
5. Discuss how the emergence of two flight caterer giants might impact on the global market.

References

Airline Business. (2002) "The Airline Industry Guide," *Airline Business*, Sep. 2002, 31.

Anon. (1980) "Singapore Airlines Is Building World's Largest Inflight Kitchen," *Airline & Travel Food Service*, Sep./Oct., 14.

Baker, C. (2001a) "Playing for Position," *Airline Business*, vol. 17, no. 7, 40–41.

———— C. (2001b) "The Global Groupings," *Airline Business*, vol. 17, no. 7, 42–45.

Blank, D. (1999) "Pie in the Sky," *Caterer & Hotelkeeper*, vol. 188, no. 4079, 32.

Dana, L.P. and Vignali, D. (1999) "British Airways plc," *International Marketing Review*, vol. 16, no. 4/5, 278–290.

Dana, L.P. (1999) "Korean Airline," *British Food Journal*, vol. 101 (5/6), 365–383.

Gate Gourmet International. (2002), *Corporate History*. [online], Available from: http://www.gategourmet.com/797/798/920/921/955/960.asp [Accessed 17 March 2003].

Gill, T. (1999) "Food For Thought," *Airline Business*, 75–76.

Herdman, A. (1997) "More Mergers Predicted in Airline Catering," *Hospitality Industry International*, no. 16, 13.

LSG-Sky Chefs. (2001) *History of LSG Sky Chefs*, [online], Available from: [Accessed 17 March 2003] http://lsg-skychefs.com/en/companies/lsg-holding/history/history_body.html.

Lundstrom, R. (1998) "A Caterer's Role: Implementing Programs that Please All those Passengers," *PAX International*, Aug./Sep., 21–22.

———— (2001) "Latest Round Solidifies co-operation among smaller caterers," *PAX International* May/June, 28–30.

———— (1997) "Roaring to Life: Hong Kong's Return to China Finda Cautious Optimism in Flight Catering Business," *PAX International*, June/July, 22–24.

Martin, J. (2001) "US Airways' On board Cuisine Kepps International Customers In Mind," *On-Board Services*, Feb. 21.

McCool, A. (1996) "Pricing and Cost Management for the In-Flight Food Service Industry," *The Bottomline*, Oct./Nov. 14–19.

Momberger, K. and Momberger, M. (2003) "Aviation Catering News," *Momberger Airport Information*, 10 May, 1.

Noble, M. (1995) "Catering for Profit," *Interavia Business and Technology*, vol. 52, no. 2, 32–35.

O'Toole, K. and Gill, T. (2000) "Buying Power: The Global Alliances are only Just Starting to Use Their Combined Buying Power," *Airline Business*, vol. 16, no. 1, 44–45.

O'Toole, K. (1999) "The Major Airline Alliance Groupings," *Airline Business*, vol. 15, no. 7, 36–37.

Pedrick, D. Babakus, E. and Richardson, A. (1993) "The Value of Qualitative Data in Quality Improvement Efforts," *Journal of Services Marketing*, vol. 7, 26–35.

Pilling, M. (2001) "Food For Thought," *Airline Business*, Jan., 48–50.

Romano, M. (1994) "Who's Feeding Them Now?" *Restaurant Business*, vol. 93, no. 12, 62, 64, 69.

Stuart, S. (2001) "The Global Challenge," *Airline Business*, vol. 17, no. 8, 80–84.

Tabachi, M.H. and Marshall, R.C. (1988) "Consumer Perceptions of In-flight Food Service," *The Cornell Hotel and Restaurant Administration Quarterly*, vol. 28, no. 4, 20–23.

Tansey, G. (1996) "Catering on a High," *Caterer and Hotelkeeper*, 7 Nov., 64–66.

The air travel market-place and the customer

Learning objectives

- Examine the growth in the air travel market and its relationship to in-flight catering
- Identify the future trends and success factors of leading airlines
- Explore the motivation of the travel market and understand travellers' needs and wants
- Discuss the complexity of the service encounter during flight experiences
- Recognise service priorities toward travellers, particular by in meal services

Introduction

The history of the aviation industry has been one of continuing adjustment to intense competition, pressure to achieve higher passenger numbers, and the need to monitor and control costs. Turbulence created by government regulations and constraints, and the failing health of the economies of different countries led to one of the most difficult trading periods ever experienced by the airline industry in the late 1990s. In the 2000s conditions became very much worse due to 9/11, the war in the Middle East, and the SARS outbreak in Canada and the Far East.

This is not to say that the industry has become complacent. On the contrary, a number of airlines have invested heavily in new technology and have continued to develop the quality of the product. In fact it could be argued that the airline industry has shown greater initiative and enthusiasm for improvement than any other sector of the transport industry. As the primary means of long haul and overseas travel is by air, the improvement in the provision of lower prices for air travel has caused a direct impact on the patterns of international tourism. These lower prices are being generated through major cost-cutting exercises which can mean the airline divesting itself of peripheral businesses, such as in-house catering, so as to be able to reduce prices and concentrate on the core business. This enables the airline to gain a stronger competitive advantage as prices are reduced through the use of non-unionised, lower-cost labour, and the ability to choose innovative partners who deliver quality and service. While the control of price is important, non-price factors are also used in the competitive struggle between airlines. They recognise the importance of managing and achieving high levels of customer satisfaction through customer care and service programmes.

How important are food and on-board service to the airlines? Some airlines use food as a marketing tool. A number of airlines advertise their product by making food the focal point. But food as a marketing tool has only a limited impact. The public's first concern seems to be travelling from their point of departure to their destination, in the most direct and safe fashion, and this concern seems to reflect how many airlines view their role. Indeed, there has been much discussion regarding whether air travel should be regarded as a service or as a form of transportation. Passengers appear most concerned about on-time performance, scheduling/ticketing issues, the aircraft's physical surroundings such as seat and leg comfort, and gate check-in and boarding. Passengers and passengers' companies are also concerned about prices and the more affluent passengers are concerned about price in relation to value. This means that while food is important, it is not likely to be the deciding factor in a passenger's choice. This is most clearly seen in the USA where deregulation has had a great effect upon competition and where fare wars are common. Most US airlines have implemented a no-frills policy where no meals are served on board flights within the USA. The same trend is evident in Europe, with some carriers, such as Ryan Air and Easy Jet, offering low-cost, no-frills flights between European destinations.

The global market of air travel

It is important to locate the trends in airline catering in the context of changes which are affecting the market-place, as it is these trends which will dictate the way the industry has to adapt. The World Tourism Organisation (WTO) suggested that in the period of 1990–2000 international travel trends would reflect those of the 1980s but that long-haul travel would shift the importance of specific geographic areas in terms of travel generation and expenditure. Three high-growth flows were forecast:

1. Intra-European travel (including west/east travel)
2. Asia Pacific
3. North Atlantic (originating from Europe)

This indicates that while Europe continued to attract more arrivals it was consistently losing overall market share to other tourism regions (Table 3.1).

	Europe	Americas	Africa	Middle East	Asia	Oceanic	Total	Per cent change
1994	8119	28051	173	403	5551	556	42853	
1995	8793	26680	186	454	6616	588	43317	−3.2
1996	9727	27948	205	480	7500	629	46489	7.3
1997	10390	28155	234	552	7756	680	47766	2.7
1998	10675	27513	258	587	6724	639	46396	−2.9
1999	11243	28747	274	625	6935	667	48491	4.5
2000	11597	30010	295	702	7554	731	50891	4.9

Source: *ITA Tourism Industries*: 7

Table 3.1
The trend for USA International Tourism Arrivals (000)

Globally, the growth appeared to be distributed evenly around the world (Table 3.2). The result of the 2000 *Airline Business* ranking of passenger airlines showed a strong set of operating figures. The Middle East carriers lead with double-digit growth. Even the mature European market managed 7.7 percent growth (O'Toole, 2001). Clearly such growth is affected by global events, such as war, but evidence from previous years suggests that trends overall remain fairly constant, with demand 'bouncing back' from the sharp decline experienced prior to and during these periods.

While this growth will mean there is increased market potential for airlines, there is not a corresponding benefit for the accommodation sector. It is forecast that the growth in air and surface transport will allow the business traveller more flexibility and therefore lead to a reduction in the duration of stay for European business trips. Furthermore, the increase in feeder and regional air services will reduce the need for more costly overnight stays. Such changes mean that time could be more limited at the destination which makes it more

Region	Passenger traffic (RPK) million	Change	Number of airlines
Middle East	96,420	11.4%	13
North America	1,235,996	9.2%	39
Asia-Pacific	766,994	8.6%	48
Central/South America	132,548	8.4%	22
Europe	785,420	7.7%	65
Africa	63,901	6.7%	13
Total	3,081,170	7.5%	200

Note: Based on the top 200 airlines operating in the Airline Business/Air Transport Intelligence database. Central/South America includes Mexico and Caribbean.
SOURCE: O'Toole, 2001: 79

Table 3.2
Top 200 passenger airline statistics by region 2000

difficult to organise meals. This may place more emphasis on the quality of the flight meal and lead to a higher use of business-class travel.

In the UK, the Department of the Environment, Transport and the Regions (DETR) (2000) has revealed that the key variables determining air traffic are

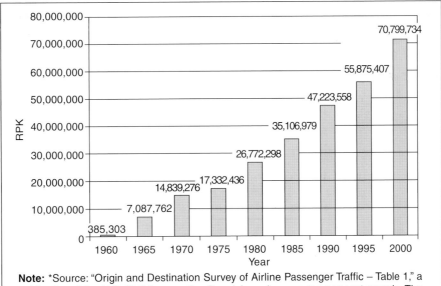

Note: *Source: "Origin and Destination Survey of Airline Passenger Traffic – Table 1," a publication of the U.S. Civil Aeronautics Board, based upon a ten per cent sample. The ten per cent sample has been expanded to 100 per cent and rounded to thousands (000) for ease of comparison with the 'Revenue Passenger Enplanements' data.
SOURCE: Bureau of Transport Statistics, 2001

Figure 3.1
The world air travel market 1970–2000

domestic and foreign economic growth (principally GDP), air fares, trade and exchange rates, and market maturity. The relationship derived from previous years' data is applied to projections of future year values of the explanatory variables to calculate forecasts of air traffic. Without the constraints of existing airport and airspace capacity, Figure 3.2 forecasts a significant pattern of growth in passenger arrivals from 2000 to 2020. International traffic is forecast to grow faster than total traffic at 4.6 per cent per annum in the period to 2020 under the central forecasts from both long haul and short haul. Similar higher growth rates are forecast for countries in Western Europe.

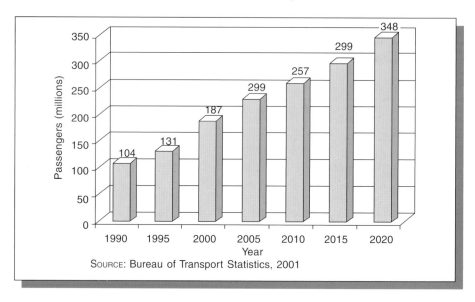

Figure 3.2
UK airport passenger numbers, forecast to 2020

Although the forecast painted a rosy picture of growth, the tragic and unforeseen terrorist attack on the World Trade Centre in New York on 11 September 2001 (now come to be called 9/11) has caused all the projections discussed here to be re-evaluated. According to IATA, passenger traffic showed a world-wide fall of 23 per cent during October 2001, bringing the cumulative change for the first ten months of 2001 to 2 per cent. North American IATA carriers experienced an average 33 per cent fall in passenger traffic in October 2001. European, Far Eastern, Central and South American carriers saw average declines of between 20 to 25 per cent (Jones, 2001). European airlines also face falling passenger numbers, added security costs, falls in their share prices and increased insurance premiums, and thousands of job cuts in adjusting their losses. For instance, Swissair subsidiary Crossair, including catering and ground services, filed for bankruptcy (BBC News, 2001 [online]) as a result of September 11. September 11 has also had a pronounced effect on the American economy, accelerating its slide into recession. Weak corporate results have led to reductions in business travel, placing further pressure on the traditional full service carriers. There may be similar outcomes from the downturn in early 2003 caused by the war in Iraq and SARS.

However, as major international airlines suffered a decline in demand, the low-cost carriers have continued to enjoy strong passenger growth, underpinned by fare reductions. New entrants to the US market place have chosen to position their product as one of low cost on high-frequency routes. This position may mean the stripping out of catering galleys in order to include more seats on the aircraft. Southwest Airlines had rapid growth due to its single class, no frills, non-seat selection, rapid turnaround and sector-specific product. Keeping a minimum of 20–25 minutes turnaround, Southwest refused to allow peanuts on their aircraft because a spilled bag could slow the turnaround (Harper and Milner, 2001). Costs are also kept down by paperless ticketing, and sales over the internet and the phone rather than through a travel agent that charges commission. Selling food and drink rather than giving them away provides additional revenue streams, so long as loading does not slow down turnaround times. Europe's EasyJet, Ryannair, bmibaby and Go all utilise this market strategy alongside Canada's WestJet and the USA's Jet Blue, which is competing with other American carriers after only its first full year in operation (O'Toole, 2001). Ryan Air has become one of Europe's airline majors as they announced a 39 per cent rise in profits and a 37 per cent load increase for the six months ending 30 September, 2001 (Labi 2001). EasyJet profits rose by 82 per cent to £40.1m in the year to the end of September 2001 and maintains its fleet expansion to more than 100 aircraft by the end of 2007, to support a growth in capacity of about 25 per cent a year.

Nevertheless the problem for most European airline companies is that intra-European services are unprofitable. For example, it was only in 1991 that British Airways (BA) was able to record a modest profit of £20m from its European service network. According to O'Brien (1993) the profitability of airlines has been linked to long-haul routes where there has been a tradition of protection based upon bilateral agreements. However, the dominance of this advantage is under pressure. The strength of European carriers may decline if the airline operators in Japan, Singapore, and other Asian countries continue to expand their operations. Transatlantic routes have already become very competitive.

Scheduled carriers operating in Europe face a great deal of competition as Europe has charter carriers as well as national airlines. Charter traffic in Europe accounts for 30 per cent of passenger kilometres flown which is higher than any other area in the world (CAA, 1993). The majority of this market is based upon catering for the leisure traveller. While the UK, Spain and Germany provide around 80 per cent of all charter air traffic in Europe, the UK dominates with half of this total. We witnessed further European rivalry because of the 1997 legislation changes which were based upon a single operating licence allowing access throughout Europe for different airline operations. A number of charter airlines, such as Britannia owned by TUI, the second largest tour operator in Europe, are routinely scheduling route operations.

Currently the airline market-place in Europe is protected from full market forces due to the subsidies given to national airlines by their governments. Most European governments have a financial link to national airlines. Many are either owned or partly owned by the government. Often, money is allowed for the national airline as part of a restructuring programme but the current community policy stresses that for the common interest of the community the objectives of the liberalisation process would be at stake if a subsidy race took place. Some European governments are signalling their intention to privatise in part or whole their national airline, notably Germany, Italy, Portugal, and France. British Airways was privatised in 1987. This will lead to a situation of freer competition and less distortion of the market-place.

To be successful airline operators are required to push down the level of costs. The growing trend is for airlines to seek as much cost efficiency as possible for their operation. This is brought about in three main ways:

Association Links between airlines through equity or cooperation arrangements, for example, KLM and Air UK, BA and TAT, Air France and Sabena. Sometimes the links are forged as part of a longer-term strategic alliance (as discussed in Chapter 2) to provide the basis for a global service. This limits rivalry and therefore price competition. It may also lead to the sharing of computer reservation systems (CRS) and shared costs for CRS development programmes.

Efficiencies through scope and scale Airlines have introduced less costly operations, for example, Lufthansa Condor owned by Lufthansa, or Iberia and Viva Air. The totality of the volumes of passengers carried by all the brands, in terms of scale, can lead to larger budgets being made available for travel agent incentives or frequent flyer programmes. This provides for specific competitive advantage.

Overhead efficiencies Cost saving through the reduction of staff, selling off peripheral services, such as catering, to increase procurement power and allowing flexibility of purchasing for the non-core functions.

According to Carter (1994) the options open to full-service airline operators in order to remain competitive were:

- withdrawal from local short-sector flights and replacement with low-cost commuter partners or subsidiaries operating on a share or franchise basis
- elimination of expensive hub operations at centres where local point-to-point traffic levels are low
- increase in international service, where viable, to raise revenue yields
- renegotiation of labour contracts with more emphasis on company share ownership but lower wages
- contract out non-airline specialist activity to external suppliers
- enter into investment and/or share partnerships with foreign airlines
- set up low-fare divisions/subsidiaries to compete with no-frills rivals
- maximise earnings from third parties for use of CRS and other specialist systems
- upgrade product standards for specific premium markets (e.g. long haul)
- freeze capacity increases and suspend unprofitable routes
- reduce staff levels and eliminate or downgrade those products or services for which the customer is not prepared to pay extra

Current airline market

Short-term declines in demand and increasing competition impacts on profitability, as shown by *Airline Business'* financial ranking of the world's top

150 airline groups in 2000 (Table 3.3). O'Toole and Ombelet (2001) commented that the airlines had the worst collective net margin (1.1 per cent) since the industry began to recover from the last recession six years ago and that growth has already shown signs of stalling as the world prepares for downturn. The emphasis is on trimming seat supply. British Airways was one of the few to cut back on seats in 2000 and KLM kept growth below 2 per cent. Lufthansa also has put its aggressive expansion on standby.

By Revenue ($m)	By Net Losses ($m)	By Net Profits ($m)
1. AMR Corp/America Airlines	1. Swissair Group	1. Delta Air Lines
2. UAL/United Airlines	2. Korean Air	2. AMR Corp/American
3. Delta Air Lines	3. Malaysia Airlines	3. Singapore Airlines
4. FedEx Express	4. AOM French Airlines	4. Cathay Pacific
5. Japan Airlines	5. Aeroneas Argentinas	5. Lufthansa Group
6. Lufthansa Group	6. Sabena Group	6. Southwest Airlines
7. British Airways	7. TWA Airlines	7. Japan Airlines
8. ANA Group/All Nippon	8. US Airways	8. ANA Group/All Nippon
9. Northernwest Airlines	9. Alitalia Group	9. Continental Airlines
10. Air France	10. LTU Group	10. Qantas Airways
11. Continental Airlines	11. Tansbrasil	11. UAL/United
12. Swissair Group	12. TAP Air Portugal	12. Northwest Airlines
13. US Airways	13. El Al	13. Air France
14. KLM Royal Dutch Airlines	14. THY Turkish Airlines	14. British Airways
15. Air Canada Corp	15. Gulf Air	15. SAS Group
16. Singapore Airlines	16. Varig	16. Emirates Group
17. Qantas Airways	17. Avianca	17. Thai Airways International
18. Southwest Airlines	18. Asiana Airlines	18. Finnair
19. SAS Groups	19. LAPA	19. Ryanair
20. Alitalia Group	20. Alaska Air Group	20. China Airlines

Source: O'Toole and Ombelet, 2001

Table 3.3
The leading airline companies of the world

The Swissair Group's $1.7 billion net deficit led it into bankruptcy. Sabena, LTU, and AOM joined the Swiss group as heavy loss-makers. However, it has been the low-cost independents, lead by Southwest Airlines, where profitability has been maintained. History suggests that they should benefit as business budgets get tighter. Notably, the top four operating margins in the latest Top 150 ranking are all taken by such carriers, led by Europe's Ryanair and veteran Southwest (O'Toole and Ombelet, 2001).

Many Asian carriers have suffered sharp traffic declines since the first half of 2000, primarily on the cargo side which saw volume drops some had never seen before on the back of a collapse in the US IT market (O'Toole, 2001). After September 11, long haul fights to Asia have seriously declined, particularly affecting flight catering. University of Surrey research showed an average 25 per cent slow down in global production of airline meals. One significant outcome of the research was the finding that catering production units in Asia were heavily reliant on full-service, long haul flights to North America.

Overall, this downturn is global, especially in companies related to the airline business. Airline revenue passenger miles were down 32 per cent domestically and 29 per cent for international flights in September 2002 compared to September 2000 (Bureau of Transportation Statistics, 2002). LSG Sky Chefs has seen a drop of 35 per cent in revenues from the United States since 11 September, as well as a 30 per cent dropped at the American division of Gate Gourmet (Lundstrom, 2001). IATA commented the monthly drop in the number of passengers travelling on international scheduled flights was the biggest since immediately after the Gulf War in 1991. Carriers registered in North America were most seriously affected, with passenger and freight traffic falling by more than 30 per cent after September 11.

Irrespective of the drop in travel since 11 September, the Travel Industry Association of the America's (TIA) announced their latest overall *Traveller Sentiment Index (TSI)* which had improved slightly in the fourth quarter of 2001 to 101.1, up from 97.1 in the third quarter (Fig. 3.3). It was driven mainly by an extremely large gain in consumer perceptions of the affordability of travel and the service quality of travel services (Keefe, 2001).

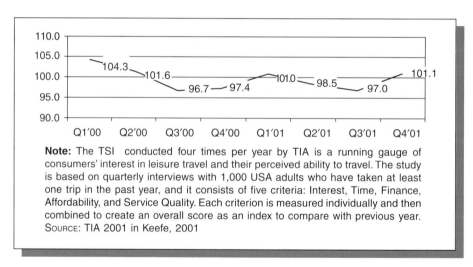

Note: The TSI conducted four times per year by TIA is a running gauge of consumers' interest in leisure travel and their perceived ability to travel. The study is based on quarterly interviews with 1,000 USA adults who have taken at least one trip in the past year, and it consists of five criteria: Interest, Time, Finance, Affordability, and Service Quality. Each criterion is measured individually and then combined to create an overall score as an index to compare with previous year.
Source: TIA 2001 in Keefe, 2001

Figure 3.3
Overall Traveller Sentiment Index (2000–2001)

In early 2002, it seemed likely that in the medium term, demand would bounce back to pre-9/11 levels and that in the longer term, there would be a steady increase in demand. These hopes have proved unfounded due to the events in early 2003.

Market segmentation

At the heart of demand for airline travel is the passenger and their needs. From observing Scandinavian Airlines System (SAS)'s operation, Gustafsson et al. (1999) developed a model of hierarchy need fulfilment for airline passengers

(Fig. 3.4). The base level is the fundamental needs of passengers, which are safety, getting the luggage to the right place, and punctuality. In order to become more competitive, the second level focuses on activity support, assisting customers through the process and fulfilling their wants and needs. The third level is to tailor the travelling process for each individual and requires understanding customer motivation, why something is important, or why something is a problem affecting customers. In simple terms, budget airlines provide the fundamentals whilst full service carriers provide activity support, and tailoring for their first-class passengers.

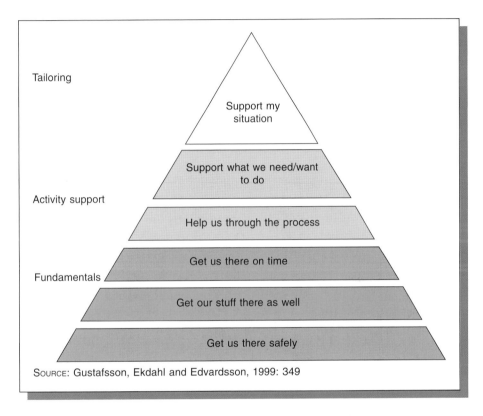

SOURCE: Gustafsson, Ekdahl and Edvardsson, 1999: 349

Figure 3.4
Hierarchy needs fulfilment of flight passengers

Airline companies utilise market segmentation as a means of providing the right product (services) for different subgroups of customers. Once the relevant characteristics of consumer groups are identified they are treated as a target market. The demand for air travel can be divided into four broad customer segments based upon the *purpose of journey:*

1. Business travellers (corporate, independent, conference, incentive)
2. Travelling for leisure purposes (holiday-makers or visiting friends and relations)
3. Travelling for personal reasons (student travel to place of study, visiting sick relations, migration)

4. In addition, there is the revenue earned from the transport of mail and freight

Each of the above segments can also be subdivided into *length of journey* as to whether it is short or long haul; *traveller characteristics* as to whether of a specific age, gender, occupation, income group, household type or education level; *flying experience* in terms of knowledge and background of previous flights, and *length of stay* related to peak versus non-peak travel or any one day or combination of days of the week.

Business travel

Business travel by air is an important segment which can be defined as:

> "A journey made for purposes which would be in conjunction with a person's employment and which is paid for by the employer not the individual" (Gilbert, cited in Jones and Kipps, 1995).

Therefore business trips are related to a need for business activity and as such the purchaser of the ticket is the self-employed business person, the company or organisation. The usual requirements for business travel passengers are those of a fast comfortable journey with a high frequency of flights to enable travel plans to be altered at short notice. The total cost of business travel is substantial and represents on average about 5–6 per cent of a company's total costs for different European countries (O'Brien, 1993) and 2.5 per cent of the European gross domestic product *(Financial Times*, 1993). The business traveller represents the most important area for profit as the ticket price normally represents a higher average value than that of the leisure traveller.

It should therefore be no surprise that given the pressures to remain competitive the individual company is becoming more concerned with the control of travel-related costs. More recently, the realisation of the possibility of achieving major savings for business travel has elevated travel policy decisions to the level of boardroom discussions and led to more bulk buying of business travel related services. However, the business traveller has alternative objectives. Rather than cost, the traveller is more concerned with the overall quality experience of the flight check-in, on-board service, meals, comfort of seats, entertainment, and adherence to time schedules.

While we tend to think of business travel as business meetings, other forms of business travel also exist. These are connected to attendance at a conference, workshop or seminar, or as part of an incentive scheme for the employees.

The business traveller is likely to be around middle age (late twenties to fifties) and male. The *Financial Times* (1993) reported only 13 per cent of European business travellers were female with the highest figures being the 23 per cent women travellers for the UK and 40 per cent for America. Due to the frequency of travel the business travel market contains a narrow band of expert consumers. Because of their regularity of flying, business passengers are more able to make constant comparisons of the standards of different airlines or routes.

Leisure travel

The second type of passenger segment is the one travelling for leisure and paying from their own budget. This market is very important due to its size and the ability of airlines to achieve bookings well in advance of departure dates. This is in contrast to the business travel market where there is a great deal more demand for last-minute travel. The earlier decision-making process of the leisure traveller makes it easier for airlines to operate yield management systems. This segment is more price sensitive than that representing the business traveller and therefore the elasticity of demand is an important factor which airlines have to consider to optimise demand. Economy prices made available through different booking schemes such as APEX or last-minute offers are an important part of the airline marketing mix. As already indicated, the leisure traveller is also likely to utilise a charter flight especially if travelling within Europe.

There are other differences which characterise the leisure traveller. The leisure traveller could be either male or female (as opposed to usually a male business traveller) and represent all ages, stay for longer duration, and require less frequency of operation due to this segment's flexibility regarding departure times. Demand from this segment is seasonal with far greater demand occurring in relation to school holiday periods.

Special reason travel

The final submarket group relates to those who travel for personal reasons and pay from their own budget. The individual travelling for personal purposes is normally travelling at the last moment and has special reasons for travel such as an urgent family matter or illness. Quite often the journey is in reaction to unpredicted circumstances. The trip is often taken with limited time availability and therefore schedule times and availability become important considerations. However, there is also price-sensitive travel such as that of students who journey to their place of study.

In reality, these segments may be more complex than this for different regions of the world or on different lengths of route. For instance, in a case study of air travel market segments (Addnate, 1995), the most significant class of trips are those made by the male business traveller, married with children, educated, and with very high household income. The second largest segment are also composed of men on a non-business trip. The third group is composed of high income, educated, younger, married women on a non-business trip. These segments together were roughly two-third of all air travel trips. (Addnate, 1995).

In another study looking at short haul business travel in the European Union, Mason and Gray (1995) discovered a model of three distinct sub segments based on their behaviour. They were identified as:

The schedule driven business traveller Members of this segment are likely to purchase full-fare tickets from a business travel agent, which offer more scheduling flexibility. Booking the ticket is left with a secretary and set by the directors of the organisation. The traveller with a higher corporate status likely to buy a higher class of travel. The key product elements focus on: flight times, exclusive business class check-in, exclusive business class lounge, and flight frequency, but some products may not be essential to the flight (such as in-flight service, seat comfort, and frequent flier schemes).

The corporate cog segment This segment, who is most likely to have members in the higher social classification (B social grouping), select the flight they wish to take and leave the details of booking, paying for, and collecting the tickets to others within the organisation. The airline seat class is based on the corporate hierarchical level of the traveller. The most important factor is the local airport, but not the price and schedule. Displaying a high element of self-interest, the in-flight service, seat comfort, and frequent flier schemes were valued most highly by this group. Members of this segment tend to work for bureaucratic, cost-conscious organisations and it would seem the results of such a corporate culture is to produce employees who look for areas within their work regime that benefit themselves.

The informed budgeter segment This group displays a good knowledge of the airline products on offer and consequently of the three segments, pays the least fare for their air travel. They are more likely purchasing their airline ticket on their own and directly from the airline than those in other segments. The fare of the lower classes of ticket is fairly restricted in terms of the reservation flexibility and refund capability. With more careful budgetary behaviour, all the elements of the airline product are important.

According to the *1998 survey of Business Travellers*, sponsored by the Official Airlines Guide (OAG) and conducted by the Travel Industry Association of America (TIA), business travellers steadily increased throughout the 1990s from 17.2 million (in 1991) to 19.4 million (in 1994) to 21.2 million (in 1996) to the 21.7 million (in 1998). Each business traveller takes an average of 5.4 business trips a year. Two out of ten travellers (21 per cent) combined business and vacation on their last business trip particularly for women and less frequent travellers. More older people are travelling for business than ever before. Business travellers are earning more than ever before and more likely to work in Health, Legal, and Education services (OAG, 2000). However it seems likely that this market has seen the largest short term decline post-9/11. The strength of the 'bounce back' will depend largely on the behaviour of this segment in the future.

Executive jets and special flights

In addition to schedule and charter flights, caterers also serve the executive jet and special flight market. These are usually owned by large companies or wealthy individuals and transport only a small number of people across the world at a time. Arrivals and departures of these flights are not based on schedules and are often at short notice. The requirements of these passengers are unique in terms of what items are requested and loaded.

Customer expectations

To understand customer expectations we have to be aware of the way in which the customer judges and evaluates the quality of the airline service encounter.

According to Gronroos (1982) this is determined by three dimensions: (1) the technical, (2) the functional, and (3) image.

The technical component is associated with 'what' the customer will receive at the conclusion of a service encounter in a tangible form. For example, it may be the ticket to board, the airline meal, and the use of the CRS to achieve a booking or whether the flight arrives on time.

The functional dimension refers to 'how' the customer will receive it, which includes the way the service provider behaves and interacts as part of the service provision. For example, the flight service should involve politeness, reassurance, appropriate behaviour and dress, and adequate speed of response to passenger needs. The functional and service dimensions in combinations form the customer's experience of the service quality.

The image is made up of the way attitudes have been developed through different marketing communication programmes. This leads to the expectation of a particular service quality in conjunction with the influence of previous experience and evaluation. The reputation or image of an airline is more difficult to communicate if the airline is small or the traveller flies infrequently.

Gronroos was a key figure in the development of the idea that the consumer judges the level of the service gap between expected and perceived service (see Gilbert and Joshi, 1992). The idea of the judgement of service quality being the difference, or gap, between the expected and perceived service was further developed by Parasuraman, Zeithaml and Berry (1985) who developed their own service quality model (Fig. 3.5). The gaps identified in the previous

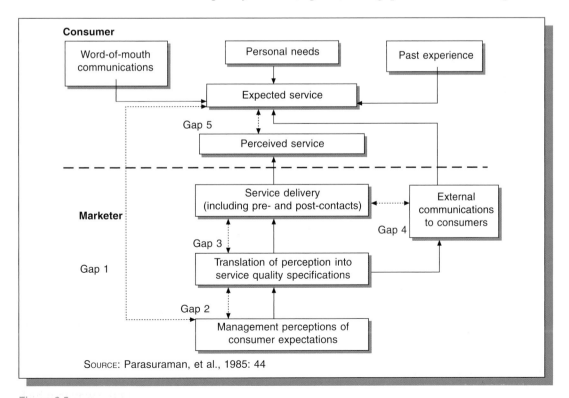

SOURCE: Parasuraman, et al., 1985: 44

Figure 3.5
A service quality model

Parasuraman, Zeithaml and Berry (PZB) model can be reduced by the use of relevant market research to provide the impetus for change.

The gap between consumer expectation and management perception This may result from the lack of an understanding of what the customer expects from the service. As Nightingale (1983) confirmed, there is a disparity between what the service provider perceives as important, and what the consumer expects from a service. British Airways have installed booths at some airports to make it easier for customers to pass on their complaints. This also provides for an outlet and degree of relief from whatever may have been the basis of the annoyance.

The gap between management perception and service quality specifications This gap results when there is a discrepancy between what management perceives to be consumer expectations and the actual service quality specifications established. Management might not set quality standards or very clear ones; or they may be clear but unrealistic. In addition management may not be committed to enforcing the appropriate quality standard. This gap may be even more pronounced where services are contracted out.

The gap between service quality specifications and service delivery Even where guidelines exist for performing the service to certain standards, service delivery may not be of the appropriate quality owing to poor employee performance. Indeed, the employee plays a pivotal role in determining the quality of a service. This is why contracts between airline and caterers (as discussed in Chapter 2) may need to be so detailed, as this kind of gap is highly prevalent when more than one party delivers service to a wide range of different specifications set by different airline clients.

The gap between service delivery and external communications Consumer expectations are affected by the promises made within the service provider's promotional message. Marketers must pay close attention to ensure consistency between the quality image portrayed in the promotional activity and the actual quality offered.

The gap between perceived service and delivered service Customers' perception of their service may be different to the actual service they received. For instance, there is evidence to suggest that people's perception of how long they wait in a queue may be on average at least 40 per cent longer than they actually do (Jones and Peppiatt, 1996).

The PZB model has two main strengths to commend it:

1. The model presents a composite view to the marketing task of delivering service quality. The model alerts the marketer to consider the perceptions of both parties (marketers and consumers) in the exchange process.
2. Addressing the gaps in the model can serve as a logical basis for formulating strategies and tactics to ensure consistent experiences and expectations.

The model has been used as the basis for research into airlines. Frost and Kumar (2000) investigated 'internal service quality', in other words they applied the gap model to operations provided by support staff whose 'customers' were front-line staff. They found that the expectations of these two groups were very similar (no gap 1), but the perception of delivered quality by front-line staff was low (i.e., gap 5 existed).

The customer service encounter

The customer of an airline product has a number of service encounters which make up the overall air travel experience. This involves: obtaining a ticket; travel to the airport; the check-in and wait at the airport; the boarding and flight service; the arrival and collection of luggage; and the travel from the airport. Today's traveller has higher expectations than previously and airlines have to compete by constantly improving passenger comfort and services.

The first influence on this is the **image** created by the carrier airline. The components of BA research into image after its supercare TV campaign were identified by Laws (1991) as being connected to: its world-wide offices, hotels, car hire, travel service, modernity, expensiveness, prestige, safety reputation, business class service, check-in, baggage handling, punctuality, whether well liked, seat comfort, friendliness, meals, and passenger care.

While image is important, the delivery of actual services through **personal contact** is not totally under the control of the airline. An examination of the research that takes place in relation to the assessment of airport-related service provides a clue to what is considered important. This includes the following categories:

- staff who are attentive and ready to help
- politeness of staff
- competence in dealing with any eventuality
- level of tact displayed by staff in difficult situations
- staff that appear to enjoy dealing with people
- availability of airline staff
- response to individual needs
- being treated as an individual
- approachable staff
- staff who are warm and friendly
- being greeted with a smile

The foregoing is based upon personal interactive relationships between the service provider and receiver. This does not take into account the problem of **waiting** prior to boarding. The length of time waiting for a service is an important consideration, as unoccupied time is perceived to last longer than occupied time. According to Maister (1985) the waiting period experience is likely to affect the perception of the quality provided. The perception of acceptability of length of wait is argued to be cultural (Czepiel et al., 1985) whereby different nationalities will demonstrate differential tolerance levels. For instance, it is reported the British 'will join a line when they see one'. The awareness of the elasticity of an individual's perception of time can be decreased by specific strategies. For example, to decrease any complaints about waiting for an elevator in a hotel, mirrors and chairs should be placed next to the elevators. Distraction or comfort are means to allow time to pass more smoothly. Waiting comfort for air passengers is enhanced by the use of lounges for higher value fare travellers.

The lounges are so designed that the passengers can relax, and offer them a tranquil environment away from the noise and congestion of the public areas in the terminal. Lounges are an important 'added value' for business travel as they offer a relaxed place where fax, telephone, refreshments, and even showers are provided.

In the case of airline travel there is also often some **anxiety** about the journey, whether it is due to the lack of control over the arrangements and timing or the boredom associated with the waiting periods. This boredom and anxiety can be amplified due to the recent increases in extra security which lengthen and complicate the airport check-in procedures.

Punctuality is a major concern for airlines as regular delays will weaken the corporate image of the carrier. Some forms of delay can be controlled, but air traffic congestion and missing a slot time are often outside of the airline's control. Some airlines have tried to control the potential technical problems of delay by a regular upgrade of their fleet with new aircraft in order to provide for greater reliability. However, the competitive nature of the current market-place makes this a more difficult option.

Comfort **on board** the aircraft involves both physical and mental considerations. The on-board service requires the need for comfort which may be related to the atmosphere as well as size of the seat, the legroom, the recline angle, and availability of a footrest. The service provision in terms of the aspects listed above in personal contact, as well as the use of meal times to keep the flight customer occupied, create a secure structured environment. Following today's trend towards health-consciousness, airlines now offer menus which reflect this trend. There are low-cholesterol and low-calorie menus as well as better nutritional information for passengers. Following the strong anti-smoking movement, airlines have increased the size of non-smoking areas or banned smoking on flights. The airlines have also increased a range of services. These services include on-board telephone and telex services as well as current video news, and the ability to transfer personal computer data is supplied in order to compete for the business traveller. The choice of entertainment is also being improved with seat-back video systems for films, catalogue shopping, and the ability to gamble while in flight.

The **arrival** is potentially the most likely time that the customer will have anxiety. The problems are associated with fatigue, concern over safety, and collection of luggage, and quite often the passenger is arriving in an unknown destination with only a sketchy idea of the local social and cultural environment. In addition there is the worry of punctuality. As discussed earlier, many airlines strive to ensure they are punctual but the situation is often beyond their control due to the congestion of different air routes.

Service priorities for travellers

While service is a very important factor related to airline choice, technical factors are also of major consequence. The traveller has consistently reported that convenient scheduling is the most important priority when choosing an airline, as is shown in Table 3.4. While the on-board food and drink provision is placed low in the priority list, it is significant in the decision-making process of airline selection. As such it is an important aspect of the passenger's flying experience as customers expect a satisfactory meal and service. If dissatisfaction occurs, a passenger may select another airline. Table 3.4 also illustrates how passenger priorities may change over time, especially in response to changes in external influences. Security was a key issue in the early 1990s due to aircraft hijackings. By 1999 this was no longer such a concern. 9/11 has almost certainly returned this factor to one of high importance.

Factors	1999	1993	1992
Most convenient schedule	1	1	1
Reputation for safety	2	–	–
Good frequent flyer scheme	3	9	7
Extra comfort/legroom	4	6	4
Efficient check-in	5	3	10
Advance seat selection	6	7	11
Reputation for punctuality	7	2	3
Cheapest available fare	8	11	8
Friendly/Helpful cabin staff	9	8	6
Access to lounges	10	10	12
Good on-board food and drink	**11**	**12**	**9**
Know as an award winning airline	12		
Effective security precautions	4	2	
Modern aircraft fleet	5	5	

SOURCE: *Official Airline Guide*, 1993; 1999

Table 3.4
Importance of factors influencing carrier choice

Specifically for catering services, the winning points of the best flight service have included down-to-earth service, food that is consistently reliable, promptness, and efficiency. Examples are Cathay Pacific, Singapore airlines, Swissair, and British Airways. A list has been compiled by 100 experienced hospitality providers about the best airline for food, beverage and service (Table 3.5) (Gostelow 1998).

The debate about how healthy airline food is has gone to two extremes. For example, a spring 2000 study by online health site eFit suggested it is healthier to consume a McDonald's Big Mac, french fries, and a strawberry sundae than to eat most airline dinners. The media has offered a few tips to the travellers about airline meals to work around the system; as examples: order a special meal, bring your own food, eat selectively, or do not eat at all. The belief is that vegetarian meals or fruit plates are healthier and tastier, and have the added advantage of being served first by the cabin crew (Elliot, 2001)

Frequent flier programmes

One of the most important marketing developments in recent times has been the implementation of frequent flier programme (FFP) campaigns. First introduced by American Airlines, these schemes are based upon the objective

Winning points	Worst services
1. Genuine, attentive service, and an attractive range of well-prepared menus that seem to travel well.	1. No distinguishing features
2. Competent professionals	2. Staff do not care at all
3. Good food variety, stylish	3. Terrible food and bad services
4. Attention to detail	4. This airline could not give a damn
5. The only airline adequately to address customer needs for business travel	5. I would not feed this airline's food to a dog
6. Service and choices of meals	6. Sloppy delivery, indistinguishable taste of foods
7. *À la carte* ordering of meals	7. Dirty planes, uncaring attitude
	8. Terrible food
	9. Disinterested service
	10. Cattle car mentality

SOURCE: *Gostelow*, 1998: 23

Table 3.5

Global hoteliers assessment of airline hospitality

of creating customer loyalty. While many believe the schemes are popular due to the benefit of acquiring free flight miles, it is found the schemes have much broader appeal for the traveller. In contrast many companies would like to have them discontinued. This is because the FFP schemes often conflict with company policy on the purchase of air travel as they do not always represent the most competitively priced fare. Table 3.6 indicates the different reasons which have led to the success of these schemes.

Benefits	1999	1993
Mileage points for free air travel	90%	55%
Flight upgrade possibilities	85%	46%
Priority on waitlist for seat availability	85%	72%
Priority check-in	85%	—
Airport lounges available	80%	48%
Recognition of status as a frequent flyer business traveller	78%	36%
Privileged VIP status with partner organisations	70%	—
Points from other schemes	—	25%
Luggage tracing	—	25%
Other rewards	—	12%
Insurance schemes	—	12%
Newsletters	—	3%

SOURCE: *Official Airline Guide*, 1993, 1999

Table 3.6

Traveller's rating of frequent flyer scheme features

Airline operations have been affected by many factors in recent years. Statutory, economic and consumer changes have altered the air travel market-place and made it even more competitive. This has led to industry changes in composition and structure due to the mergers and alliances taking place (identified in Chapter 2). In the struggle for higher load factors airline executives realise that a competitive edge has to be created by paying more attention to the needs of its consumers. The changes taking place dictate that important issues such as scheduling, punctuality, fare structures, safety aspects and standards of customer service and care are given priority. Such changes stress the importance of ensuring pre- and flight catering systems create the highest levels of satisfaction for passengers.

After the terrorist attacks of 11 September 2001, airports have concentrated on searching passengers for sharp objects and scanning luggage for guns or explosive, but the discovery of an Islamic extremist passenger with explosives hidden in his shoes has added a new dimension to aircraft security. The material in the shoes was enough to cause considerable damage to the aircraft and difficult to be detected except by sniffer dogs, yet this low-tech approach defeated airport security. Passengers now may be required to take off their shoes and put them through x-ray machines (BBC News, 2001).

Case study 3.1

Singapore Airlines

Over the last two decades, Singapore Airlines has grown from a regional airline into one of the world's leading passenger and cargo carriers. The company originated in May 1947, when Malayan Airways (MSA) first operated a twin-engined Airspeed Consul between Singapore, Kuala Lumpur, Ipoh and Penang. MSA ceased operations in October 1972, and two new airlines, Malaysia Airline System (now called Malaysia Airlines) and Singapore Airlines, were founded.

In conjunction with its Star Alliance partners, Singapore Airlines now fly to 93 destinations in 42 countries and offer:

- an expanded network
- frequent flyer programme benefits
- seamless checking-in
- access to over 500 airport lounges
- joint fare products, such as the Star RTW Fare

Their hub airport, Changi, is regularly voted the world's best, and serves as a gateway to Asia and beyond. Singapore Airlines has received international awards, such as 'Best Airline' from the Official Airline Guide (UK), travel magazines, and Industry organisations. In 2001, they received 34 different rewards for best services, quality of service, frequent flyer programme, innovation, and crisis management. Singapore Airlines was one of the pioneers of in-flight services such as free drinks and complimentary headsets. It operates its own catering kitchens—Singapore Airport Terminal Services Inflight Catering (SATS). SATS catering attained the ISO 9002 Award for its quality management systems and achieved a 47-year zero-food-poisoning record.

In an examination of benchmarking management practices, Chang et al. (1997) concluded that the critical success factors for SATS were:

- Management with a competitive, customer-oriented approach tied to corporate strategic plan. A most successful product/service brand/differentiation strategy built around and powered by an idea: the Singapore Girl (Chan, 2000).
- Investment in service quality and product innovation by modernising aircraft, airport, and catering facilities. For example, SATS has an automated tray preset line (ATPL) to improve staff productivity and to maintain food quality; the largest automated ware washing system; and an automated waste disposal system).
- Management's dedication to maintain standards.
- Design for market quality as a result of the interplay among suppliers and customers with emphasis on core quality, expected customer services, added value, and potential value against prices. An example is the introduction of flat seats in business class to offer a very good standard of comfort.
- Japanese cuisine the Japanese way. For example, first-class passengers are offered kyokaiseki Japanese services, on specially designed plates featuring bamboo, indicating politeness; pine trees for longevity; and plum for beauty.
- Easy meals to allows the passenger to have his/her meal served at a time of his/her choice.
- Singaporean multi-ethnic cuisine. By employing high-profile chefs as consultants, Singapore Airlines' culinary panels gather celebrity chefs around the world: Yoshihiro Murata of Japan, Nacy Oakes and David Burke of the USA, Dietmar Sawyere of Australia, Yeung Koon Yat of Hong Kong, Georges Blanc of France, Gordon Ramsay of the UK, and Satish Arora of India.

(Chang, Yeong, and Loh, 1997)

Case study 3.2

South West Airlines

Southwest Airlines began service on 18 June 1971 with flights to Houston, Dallas, and San Antonio. Year-end results for 2000 marked Southwest Airlines' 28th consecutive year of profitability and ninth year of increased profits. Southwest was the only major carrier in 1990, 1991, and 1992 to make both net and operating profits, and became a major airline in 1989 when its revenue exceeded the billion-dollar mark. Even after 9/11, Southwest has resumed their full schedule while major airline carriers have been cutting flights and laying-off staff. Despite having only one-tenth of the annual combined sales of American, United, and Delta airlines, Southwest's market capitalisation is almost twice as large as the big three put together (Anon., 2002).

Since 1988 Southwest has won the service Triple Crown five times—(Best On-Time Record, Best Baggage Handling, and Fewest Customer Complaints) and thirty more awards. Southwest was No. 1 (8.62 out of 10) in a survey of customer satisfaction, which recorded nearly 4 million respondents in March 2001 (Kelsey, 2001).

The strategy of Southwest is to operate on a point-to-point schedule, and not a hub- and -spoke system. They fly short-haul, high-frequency schedules, which lead to higher than average passenger load factors and therefore greater cost savings to the passenger and higher profit for the company. As of 31 December 2000, Southwest operated 358 Boeing 737 aircraft and provides service to 58 airports in 57 cities in 29 states throughout the USA. Southwest has no reserved seating, flies only Boeing 737s, and is in the forefront of ticketless travel (Seal and Kleiner, 1999). As a low-cost no-frills airline, the airline offers no meals, no extras, no first class, no wasted time, effort or expense. In-flight movies are not offered to the passengers and nor are headphones for musical listening.

Southwest Airlines' philosophy served as the vision and mission for the organisation are:

- Southwest Airlines is a service organisation
- Employees are No.1
- Think small to grow big
- Manage in good times for bad times
- Irreverence is OK
- It is OK to be yourself
- Have fun at work
- Take competition seriously, not yourself
- Hire for attitude and train for skills
- Do whatever it takes
- Always practice the golden rule—both internally and externally.

(Laszlo 1999)

After examining Southwest with a company excellence model developed by Paters and Waterman in 1982, the success of Southwest Airlines was shown to be due to eight attributes: a bias for action; closeness to the customer; autonomy and entrepreneurship; productivity through people; hands-on, value-driven; stick to the knitting; simple form, lean staff; and simultaneous loose-tight properties (Bunz and Maes, 1998). They also concluded that Southwest's success derives from creating and maintaining a more relaxed working environment in which employees enjoy performing their jobs. While the concept of service has become sterile in the USA, Southwest employees take their performance seriously and are dedicated to service.

Current issues and future developments

The fear of destructive market competition and abandonment of peripheral areas led policy makers to regulate tightly the airline industry on both domestic and international routes in the aftermath of the Second World War. Nonetheless, the resulting financial inefficiency and customer dissatisfaction as well as the presumed low barriers to market entry and exit induced subsequent **liberalisation**, first in the USA (domestic market deregulation in 1978) and then in the European Union (completion of a Single European Aviation Market in 1997). Nonetheless, the process of market liberalisation is far from completed. Although internal markets in many countries now operate freely, the international aviation regime is still based on bilateral agreements which are occasionally very restrictive.

In spite of the tragedy, the events of 9/11 may bring further market developments, as they revealed the inflexibility of the current system to address crises in an effective manner. The European Commission is currently trying to secure the power to negotiate air traffic rights for all its member-states collectively. A potential success will signify the move towards a multilateral aviation framework and perhaps the creation of a Transatlantic Common Aviation Area, following an open-skies agreement between the US and the EU. This will probably have a snowball effect in other countries that will seek to replicate liberal policies. As a result of subsequent privatisation, mergers and acquisitions, a truly global airline industry may then emerge characterised by the prevalence of few transnational carriers. Therefore, the competition authorities should be alert to avoid collusive behaviour or abuse of market power by the dominant airlines (Papatheodorou, 2002).

Deregulation has helped new entrants enter the market, especially the so-called 'no-frills' or budget airlines. For example, Jetmagic, the new Irish airline and Iceland Express Iceland's first no-frills carrier (Momberger and Momberger, 2003b and e). The emergence of this category of travel has created two issues for the full-service carriers. The first is the issue of **seat class**. For many decades the conventional arrangement of seating on a scheduled flight was to have three classes—first, business, and economy (or 'coach' as the Americans call it). Today, that well-established formula is under pressure. Airlines are experimenting with a number of different approaches on different types of route and no clear trend is emerging. In some cases, there is no longer first-class seating. On the other hand, a new category called economy plus by British Airways has also emerged. This category has many elements of the economy experience, but with some of those from the business class. For instance, the economy plus seat on BA has four inches more legroom that the standard economy seat. Virgin Atlantic has provided a 'mid-class' and other airlines have created super economy class travel. These have improved legroom and other features which are attractive to the executive traveller. For example, with Virgin's 'mid-class', travellers can book seats in advance, check in at a 'mid-class' desk, obtain access to express baggage reclaim and utilise complimentary transfer options.

The second issue is **retail sales on board flights**. Traditionally, airlines have provided beverages and food as part of the all-inclusive ticket price. Only duty-free goods have been sold to passengers. However, the budget airlines do not include food and drink in the price. They sell these items from a trolley, just like duty-free goods. For instance, in the first quarter of 2003 United Airlines, US Airways, Midwest and America West all offered passengers the option of purchasing food on their flights to test the concept of selling food on-board flights (Momberger and Momberger 2003a, c and d). Likewise, at least one charter airline flying holidaymakers out of the UK also has separated out the on-board meal price from the rest of the package. Their customers must book a meal if they want one and they pay for this at the time they book their holiday. It may be that this idea of paying for the flight and for on-board service separately from each other becomes very much more common, especially in the economy class.

However, another alternative to the concept of selling food and drink on board the aircraft has emerged—**pre-boarding purchase**. The initiative has been developed primarily by suppliers and airport restaurants and enables passengers to order meals online and have the food ready to be picked up prior to departure. Such a move requires a trade off for airlines between the increased speed of turnover facilitated by the lack of provision of a food and beverage service and the loss of sales generating opportunities from providing such a service.

Conclusion

Air travel has gradually become part of our lives as the numbers of air traffic are increasing more than ever before. Certain areas such as Asia Pacific has generated much attention in developing its capacity in both business and leisure travel sectors. The demand for better service also has increased traveller's expectations. The travel segments have not changed much. Male travellers are still the majority although there are increasing numbers of female travellers. Each segment appears to have different needs and wants. It is up to the flight caterer to design meal services as part of airline products to fulfil individual demands. However, the service encounter involves many aspects of service quality which can be examined through the gap model. Like the big US Carriers, Europe's major airlines—many of which were already struggling before 9/11—have been crippled by the drop in transatlantic traffic and passengers' reluctance to take to the skies. Belgium's Sabena declared bankruptcy and BA had a significant loss for 2001/02. But not all European carriers are struggling. Ryanair, EasyJet, buzz, bmibaby and Go—inspired by the US discounting pioneer Southwest Air—concentrate on short-haul routes, and have been almost impervious to the downturn in transatlantic traffic. Moreover, with the world economy heading toward recession, more employers are pushing their executives onto low-cost airlines.

Key terms

Business travel	Charter airlines	Cost efficiencies
Customer expectations	Demand	Executive jets
Frequent flier programmes	Leisure travel	Market segmentation
Market share	No-frills airlines	Scheduled carriers
Service gap	Service quality	Special flights
Special reason travel	Traveller sentiment index	

Discussion questions

1. What are the key variables in forecasting air traffic?
2. Briefly discuss the characteristics of different types of airline customer.
3. What are the differences from other forms of transport when travelling by air?
4. What are the service priorities for travellers in choosing airlines?
5. Discuss the role of food plays in the airline service encounters (use the case studies as examples).

References

Addnate, E. (1995) "Air Travel Market Segments: A New England Case Study," *TRB Transportation Research Circular*, vol. E-C026, 307–319.

Anon. (2002) "Southwest Airlines Soars with Morningstar's CEO of the Year Award," *PR Newsire*, 4-1

BBC News. (2001) "Shoe Bomb Suspect 'One of Many'", Available from: http://news.bbc.co.uk/hi/english/world/

Bunz, U.K. and Maes, J.D. (1998) "Learning Excellence: Southwest Airlines' approach," *Managing Service Quality*, vol. 8, no. 3.

Bureau of Transportation Statistics. (2001) *Historical Air Traffic Statistics: Annual 1954–2001*, Available: http: www.bts.gov/oai/indicators/airtraffic/annual/

Bureau of Transportation Statistics. (2002) *Fact of the Day*, 4 Jan. Available from: http: www.bts.gov/FOTD/

CAA. (1993) *Airline Competition in the Single European Market*, Civil Aviation Authority, London.

Carter, M. (1994) *European and US Aviation Issues*, Thomas Cook European Forum, 5–6 May, Hotel des Bergues, Geneva.

Chan, D. (2000) "The Story of Singapore Airlines and the Singapore Girl," *Journal of Management Development*, vol. 19, no. 6, 456–472.

Chang, Z.Y., Yeong, W.Y., and Loh, L. (1997) "Case Studies: Critical Success Factors For In-flight Catering Services: Singapore airport terminal services' practices as management benchmarks," *The TQM Magazine*, vol. 9, no. 4, 255–259.

Czepiel, J.A. Soloman, M.R. and Suprenant, C.F. (eds) (1985) "Managing Employee and Customer Interaction in Service Businesses," *The Service Encounter*, Lexington Books, Lexington, Massachusetts.

Financial Times. (1993) "Business Travel Survey," *Financial Times*. 9 Nov.

Frost, F.A. and Kumar, M. (2000) "INTSERVQUAL—An Internal Adaptation of the GAP Model in a Large Service Organisation," *Journal of Services Marketing*, 14, 5, 358–377.

Gilbert, D. (1993) *Study of the Formulation, Control and Implementation of Travel Management Policy*, Thomas Cook Research Centre, University of Surrey.

Gilbert, D. and Joshi, I. (1992) "Quality Management and the Tourism Hospitality Industry," in Cooper, C. and Lockwood, A. (eds) *Progress in Tourism*, Recreation and Hospitality Management, vol. 4, Belhaven, London: 149–68

Gostelow, M. (1998) "Airline Survey Results," *Hospitality Industry International*, no. 19, 23–25.

Gronroos, C. (1982) *Strategic Management and Marketing in the Service Sector*, Swedish School of Economics and Business Administration, Helsinki.

Gustafsson, A., Ekdahl, F., and Edvardsson, B. (1999) "Customer Focused Service Development in Practice: A case study at Scandinavian Airlines System (SAS)," *International Journal of Service Industry Management*, vol. 10, no. 4, 344–358.

Harper, K. and Milner, M. (2001) "Low-cost is flying high," *The Guardian* 2 Nov.

Jones, D. (2001) "IATA Figures Show October Falls," *IATA News* 1 Dec.

Jones, P and Peppiatt, E. (1996) "Managing Perceptions of Waiting Times in Service Queues", *International Journal of Service Industries Management*. vol. 7, no. 5, 47–61.

Keefe, C. (2001) "TIA's Traveler Sentiment Index Improves in Fourth Quarter," *Travel Industry Association of America*, 1–2, 27 Nov. Washington, DC, Travel Industry Association of America.

Kelsey, D. (2001) "Consumers Rate Southwest Airlines Site No.1—survey," *Newsbytes*, 22–24.

Labi, A. (2001) "Cheap Euro Airfares," *The Time Global Business*, Nov.

Laszlo, G.P. (1999) "Southwest Airlines—Living Total Quality in a Service Organisation," *Managing Service Quality*, vol. 9, no. 2, 90–95.

Laws, E. (1991) *Tourism Marketing: Service and Quality Management Perspectives*, Stanley Thornes, Cheltenham.

Maister, H. (1985) "The Psychology of the Waiting Lines," in Czepiel, J.A. Soloman, M.R. and Suprenant, C.F. (eds), *The Service Encounter*, Lexington Books: Lexington, Massachusetts, 113–123.

Mason, K.J. and Gray, R. (1995) "Short Haul Business Travel in the European Union: A Segmentation Profile," *Journal of Air Transport Management*, vol. 2, no. 3/4, 197–205.

Momberger, K. and Momberger, M. (2003a) "Aviation Catering News," *Momberger Airport Information*, 25 May, 4.

———— (2003b) "Aviation Catering News," *Momberger Airport Information*. 10 May, 4.

———— (2003c) "Aviation Catering News," *Momberger Airport Information*. 10 Apr., 2.

———— (2003d) "Aviation Catering News," *Momberger Airport Information*. 25 Feb., 3.

———— (2003e) "Aviation Catering News," *Momberger Airport Information*. 10 Feb., 4.

Nightingale, M. (1983) *Determination and Control of Quality Standards in Hospitality Services*," unpublished MPhil thesis, University of Surrey.

O'Brien, K. (1993) "The West European Business Travel Market 1993–97," In *Financial Times Management Report*, London.

Official Airline Guide (OAG) (1993) "Business Traveller Lifestyle Survey", *OAG*, Dunstable, UK.

———— (1998) "Business Traveller Lifestyle Survey," *OAG*, Dunstable, UK.

———— (1999) "Business Traveller Lifestyle Survey," *OAG*, Dunstable, UK.

———— (2000) "Business Traveller Lifestyle Survey", Reed Elsevier Inc. Available from: http: www2.oag.com/about_oag/market_research/

O'Toole, K. and Ombelet, H. (2001) "Cost Concerns," *Airline Business*, vol. 17, no. 9, 59–62.

O'Toole, K. (2001) "Slow Ahead," *Airline Business*, vol. 17, no. 9, 79–80.

Papatheodorou, A. (2002) "Civil Aviation Regimes and Leisure Tourism in Europe," *Journal of Air Transport Management*, vol. 8, no. 6, 381–388.

Parasuraman, A. Zeithaml, V.A. and Berry, L.L. (1985) "A Conceptual Model of Service Quality and its Implication for Future Research, *Journal of Marketing*, vol. 49, no. 4, 41–50.

Seal, J. and Kleiner, B.H. (1999) "Managing Human Behaviour in the Airline Industry," *Management Research News*, vol. 22, no. 2/3, 1–64.

Passenger appetite and behaviour*

Learning objectives

- Provide an understanding of how the physiology
  of passengers changes when flying
- Develop an understanding of some psychological
  aspects of flying
- Examine the implications of changes in
  passenger behaviour for flight catering

*This chapter was authored by Dr Margaret Lumbers,
University of Surrey.

Introduction

Both taste and appetite change when flying at high altitude. For example, it has been found that the flavour of foods become less distinct at high altitudes and the aromas of wine are reduced. At high altitudes, many people react more strongly to alcohol and caffeine. There are other effects of the cabin environment, such as reduced oxygen levels and altitude effects that produce physiological responses in people, which in turn affect appetite. One of the effects of long-haul flights is dehydration, which has a variety of effects on the body, such as slowing digestion. Combined with a restriction in the amount of movement and the opportunity for taking exercise, heavy foods and meals therefore are best avoided.

In response a number of airlines offer a choice of light and easy to digest meals for their business and first class passengers, for example, British Airways have a 'well-being' menu choice on many flights. Although airlines have invested heavily in improving airline catering and service over the years, passengers have commented that "all food tastes the same" (Kahn, 1995). Furthermore, the timing and nature of cabin service is believed to play a part in countering jet lag. The meals served on westbound flights are designed in relation to the time of arrival so that the flight finishes with a meal that is appropriate for the time of day of the destination. However, this may differ for eastbound flights with evening or late night departures. Although these flights arrive between 11:00 am and 5:00 pm local times at their respective destinations, passengers prior to landing are served breakfast, since lunch or dinner would be inappropriate for them.

In the light of the above it is of interest to explore in more detail those factors that influence the enjoyment of airline food. The following sections discuss the various factors that can affect appetite in general and how they are affected by high-altitude flights, most especially long-haul ones.

Food acceptance—understanding the sensory model

The sensory model of food acceptance described by Cardello (1996) involves four aspects: physical, sensory, perceptual, and hedonic. All foods have attributes of appearance (colour, presentation, etc), and texture (soft/hard, crispiness, etc), flavour (taste and smell), and temperature, depending on their composition and preparation. These attributes dictate the impact on the above and hence the enjoyment or acceptability of food. In other words, the human senses (taste, smell, texture, and vision), singly or in combination, influence appetite and consumption of food.

Studies have demonstrated that flavour (taste and smell) is more important in terms of food acceptance than appearance or texture. However, the relationship varies between both types of food and individuals. When considering taste, it should be noted that there are four basic tastes: salty, sweet, sour, and bitter, although these may only be points along a continuous spectrum. A fifth taste quality has been suggested termed 'umami', described as 'savoury'. Of course, taste and smell are not the only aspects of food and drink that affect its overall enjoyment.

The hedonic component (i.e., the pleasure of eating) is subject to previous experience and learned responses to food, the context, culture, expectations, and physiological status (including appetite, hunger, and thirst). A survey of the sources of pleasure when eating identified 'excellence of taste' as the most important factor for an affluent industrialised area of West Germany, whereas for a less affluent area in East Germany other factors such as 'a pleasant atmosphere' were more important.

Food may be used to define social status and social prestige. For example, particular foods such as caviar, lobster, truffles, or small canapés have come to acquire high status and are normally offered in first class. On the other hand, pies and sausages are highly processed food, far removed from their original state and generally perceived to be for people of lower social status (Bareham, 1995), and may therefore not be served even in the economy cabin.

Some foods are associated with healing powers or illness prevention. Garlic and ginseng are examples well known to contain antibiotics and can contribute to illness prevention. Camomile tea and Chinese tea may aid digestion and are an antiseptic. Other foods can bring comfort and release psychological tensions and stresses for some people when flying, such as milk or alcoholic liquors. Desserts, which are likely to contain a high percentage of fat or calories (for example, a triple chocolate mousse cake), are commonly used to relieve boredom and to reward and comfort passengers, although they carry some guilt. Chicken soup is regarded to be comfort food reminiscent of a mother's caring. Some food can be also linked to special festivals, such as Christmas' roast turkey, traditional Christmas puddings, or 'Mooncakes' for the Chinese dragon festival.

Meeting the challenge of improving sensory quality must take into account the changing nature of the factors involved. Cardello (1996, pp 64) states:

> "The innate sensory preferences that appear to exist across populations will be seen to become less important when compared to the culture-based learned preferences/aversions for foods and the effects of widely varying food/brand contexts across nations."

Airline catering must attempt to account for the influence of the cabin environment on the each component of the sensory model—physical, sensory, perceptual, and hedonic, for example, balancing such factors as the ambience and the taste of food—as well as the socio-cultural contexts.

Appetite

A small region in the base of the brain, called the hypothalamus, in part acts as a regulator of appetite and thirst by producing hormones. The simplest model is of two centres in the hypothalamus, called the feeding and the satiety centres, that regulate food intake. The 'feeding centre' is stimulated by hunger sensations from an empty stomach, while the 'satiety' centre is stimulated when the stomach is full.

Other compounding factors affecting appetite include:

• psychological state of the individual that may affect the production of hormones

- activity level—the appetite control mechanism is less precise in those people who are sedentary or not active physically
- level of glucose and free fatty acids in the blood (chemical stimuli)

Digestive juices, which affect the utilisation and absorption of food, flow more freely when people are hungry, relaxed, and attracted by the appearance and smell of food. Volatile food aromas play an important role in the stimulation of the olfactory receptors (located in the mucus membranes in the nasal cavity). Both olfactory and taste stimulation initiate what is known as the 'cephalic phase response'. The response brings about increased salivation and secretion of gastric and pancreatic juices in anticipation of eating. The extent of the response is thought to be associated with the overall acceptability of foods initiating the response. Learned responses also have a role in that most people have deeply ingrained ideas of what is regarded as acceptable to eat and what is unpleasant.

Another factor affecting the amount of food eaten is called 'specific satiety'. People can only eat a limited amount of the same food whereas a greater amount can be consumed when there are several courses comprising a variety of foods. However, appetite like taste is not simply governed by biological factors. Depression, anger, worry, or apprehension can also have a dramatic affect on appetite, ranging from complete suppression to the excessive consumption of familiar/comfort foods.

The success of flight catering in maximising passenger satisfaction will be achieved by addressing some of these factors, namely:

- the anxiety state of passengers
- the level of hunger—timing of service and previous meals
- the effects of the cabin environment on smell and taste
- the appearance and acceptability of food

Effects of specific foods on mood and behaviour

Many aspects of eating and drinking affect mood and behaviour. Conversely, mood can influence eating and drinking patterns. There is a popular belief that missing breakfast makes people less alert and impairs cognitive efficiency. Heavy lunches are thought to give rise to a 'post-lunch dip'. However, studies tend to be rather inconclusive and in general cognitive performance is not thought to be affected by short-term fasting, although there is considerable variation observed between subjects (Rogers, 1996).

Starchy carbohydrate-rich foods are thought to induce sleepiness (Wurtman et al., 1981). This could be due to a variety of mechanisms including the stimulation of the release of a chemical in the brain—serotonin—high levels of which are associated with sleep inducement, sensory perception, and temperature regulation. The converse is true for protein-rich meals that are thought to inhibit serotonin production and hence make people more alert. Salad dressings and heavy sauces can cause headaches since they are absorbed through the lymphatic system in the neck (Milmo, 2001).

While most passengers do not choose food on the basis of the expected effects on mood, the overall enjoyment of the flight can include the quality of sleep which can be influenced by the nature of the food provided.

Alcohol

Alcohol is offered on most flights and has become an expectation for most travellers. Airlines often appear to encourage alcohol consumption, for example, by supplying miniatures (which are more than a double measure) rather than using a standard optical measure.

Alcohol has a direct effect on the brain and changes behaviour to varying degrees depending on the amount consumed, the passenger's mood as well as on individual tolerance levels. There are profound effects on judgement, emotional control, muscle coordination, and vision. Recent studies show that people who binge drink could be causing rapid damage to their brain cells. Safe limits are 21 units for women and 28 units for men per week. A unit is equivalent to half a pint of beer, one measure of spirits, one glass of wine (120 ml) or one glass of sherry or port. On airlines, some passengers could easily consume a spirit miniature (gin and tonic) followed by two glasses of wine (airline bottle size) with a meal followed possibly with a second spirit miniature (brandy)—all amounting to more than six units, which is well over the average limit for a day.

A general effect of alcohol is to depress appetite, although this varies according to the individual and the circumstances. The high calorific content of alcohol suppresses the appetite of the average person (Polivy and Herman, 1976). Such individuals become unaware that they are hungry, due to the satiating effects of alcohol. However, alcohol can induce eating, particularly when anxiety is experienced. Further, for individuals who have eating problems (dieters, bingers) alcohol and anxiety can remove the self-imposed restraint leading to increased intakes/bingeing. It is also thought that the bitter flavours of some aperitifs such as vermouth and tonic water increase appetite.

Probably, the majority of airline passengers experience some degree of stress and anxiety to which the common response is to seek an alcoholic drink. Stress is reported to be high even among regular travellers (Joseph, 1990). The often cramped conditions, overcrowding, and the sense of lack of control experienced during the flight are likely to increase the already raised levels of stress associated with the process of checking-in and boarding. While passengers often use alcohol on board to relieve anxiety, it may be appreciated that it also acts as a depressant. In addition, the increased potency of alcohol in the air is rarely communicated to passengers and has lead to a number of disruptive episodes on planes leading to high-profile court cases.

Airlines usually offer passengers drinks early in the flight. If the passenger has not eaten for some time, the alcohol immediately diffuses through the walls of an empty stomach and reaches the brain within a minute of being swallowed leading to intoxication. Another effect of alcohol is to increase urine output as it depresses the brain's production of anti-diuretic hormone causing increased thirst. This in turn aggravates the existing problem of dehydration for which the only solution is to drink water. It is important therefore to make water readily available to passengers throughout the flight and indeed to encourage them to drink water. The use of ice and/or water to dilute drinks should be encouraged. Fruits high in potassium are also important (Milmo, 2001).

It is also logical to avoid providing passengers with salty snacks and foods that increase thirst before offering alcoholic drinks. Eating high carbohydrate and high-fat snacks inhibits the absorption of alcohol by slowing peristalsis and keeps alcohol in the stomach for longer.

Hence, the provision of alcoholic drinks on airlines has multiple influences on appetite, mood, the ability to respond to a crisis, and so on. Airlines can avoid some of the associated negative responses in various ways by:

- reducing the stress levels and hence the demand for alcoholic drinks
- managing the quantities offered
- avoiding thirst inducing snacks prior to offering alcohol
- providing water for rehydration
- educating passengers about the adverse affects of in-flight alcohol consumption

Caffeine

Caffeine is the most popular psychoactive drug consumed world-wide (Harland, 2000). The main sources of caffeine are coffee and tea, but it is also found in cola drinks, other health and sports drinks, chocolate, and some medications. Seventy-five per cent of caffeine taken daily comes from coffee; the remaining 25 per cent is equally divided between tea and other products. There is 50–70 per cent more caffeine in coffee than tea and caffeine-containing drinks are in part often drunk for their potential psychoactive effects to improve alertness; conversely, coffee is avoided late in the evening. Caffeine is known to improve reaction time, concentration, alertness, and energy. However, it can lead to increased anxiety, nervousness, irritability, and headaches. As a true stimulant drug, caffeine increases the breathing rate, heart rate, blood pressure, and secretion of stress hormones, and in higher doses it can lead to palpitation and cardiac arrhymias.

In the context of commercial air travel, the psychological and physiological effects of caffeine should be recognised, especially because of concerns regarding deep vein thrombosis, as discussed later in this chapter. Caffeine and alcohol both cause dehydration. Some simple measures that can be taken by airlines include:

- providing the alternative of decaffeinated drinks (which have less effect on dehydration), or herbal teas
- ensuring the ready availability of water and encouraging its consumption
- offering non-caffeine rich drinks before a sleep period

The cabin environment effect on taste and smell

It is well known that the sense of taste and smell are affected by the cabin environment, potentially diminishing the potential enjoyment of meals. The low relative humidity of the cabin (less than 25 per cent) dries the mucous membranes lining the nasal cavity and reduces the sense of smell (Kahn, 1995). Similarly, dryness of mouth can affect the taste receptors.

The inhibition of taste and smell has a consequent effect on the digestion process that is stimulated by these senses. It is worth noting that odorants and the general aromas in the cabin can also mask or distort the experienced flavour of foods provided. As the meal is perceived as being a valuable part of the overall service provided to the passenger, airlines have made considerable efforts to modify dishes so that they have stronger and more robust flavours to improve enjoyment, possibly without a full appreciation of all the influential factors.

Effects of altitude

Flight atmospheric pressure conditions in commercial jet aircraft approach altitude equivalents of 1500 to 2400 m (Allemann et al., 1998). Hence, the observations that have been made regarding climbers at these altitudes apply to airline passengers.

It has been observed that the mild oxygen lack suffered by individuals at high altitudes leads to weight loss due to a change in the water balance, reduced digestive efficiency, and changes in attitudes to eating and drinking. Many individuals experience loss of appetite at high altitudes and have to be persuaded to eat (Westerterp–Plantenga et al., 1999). Another observation in climbers is that leptin values in the blood become elevated (leptin is a discrete protein linked to the regulation of food intake). Hence, the elevated leptin levels found in climbers may in part explain the decreased appetite. The lower cabin pressure and the associated mild lack of oxygen has been suggested as causing a "sluggish effect on digestion and absorption of nutrients" (Kahn, 1995).

In summary, the physiological effects of travelling at altitude are analogous to those observed in climbers. Hence, airlines should recognise and attempt to respond appropriately to maximise passenger satisfaction, for example, by:

- providing opportunities for smaller meals more frequently on demand
- proactively addressing the water balance problem through passenger education and the availability/regular offering of drinking water
- providing meals that are easy to digest and taste good

Dehydration

Serious dehydration can occur insidiously and is easily overlooked by the unwary passenger. The need to drink plenty of fluids, ideally plain water, has reached wider public awareness since the publicity regarding long-haul flights and deep vein thrombosis. However, both alcohol and caffeine intake give rise to dehydration. Similar actions to those previously proposed can help to mitigate the known problems of dehydration.

Case study 4.1

SATS Simulated Aircraft Cabin

In July 2001, SATS declared their Simulated Aircraft Cabin (SAC) fully operational. It is designed to provide a facility on the ground that will reproduce the conditions found in aircraft while in flight. This enables all kinds of food and beverage items to be tasted under these conditions in order to ensure their palatability and acceptance prior to their service on board aircraft.

The SAC consists of two chambers. The main chamber is the cabin itself, which is 3.6 m wide, 2.7 m long, and 2.6 m high. Between this and the outside world is a second chamber, the air lock through which access to the main chamber is gained. The airlock is designed as a safety feature to ensure that there is no sudden decompression in the main chamber. Both the 'hypobaric' chambers have sliding doors which hermetically seal to allow for changes in air pressure as well as view ports (windows). The main chamber is equipped with a dining table and chairs at which food and beverage tastings are conducted, as well as kitchen and galley equipment used for simulating the way in which food is reheated on board aircraft. Up to ten people can be accommodated in the chamber at one time.

Hypobaric chambers alter the air pressure by controlling through valves the amount of air extracted and supplied to the chamber. To simulate air travel, more air is extracted than supplied, thereby lowering the pressure. This system can also control the air temperature and the humidity. When in use, the SAC typically creates an environment in which the air pressure is around 0.75 atm (the equivalent of an aircraft cruising at 30,000 ft), the humidity is between 8 per cent and 20 per cent, and the air temperature is 21°C.

A typical testing or tasting session lasts a minimum of one hour. This is because conditions in the SAC have to be changed relatively slowly in order to ensure the safety and comfort of the occupants. It takes approximately 20 min to change from the normal ground conditions to the simulated conditions, and vice versa (this is similar to an aircraft taking off and landing). There are four trained technicians which operate the SAC, with two on duty when it is in use.

Current issues and future developments

There are two aspects of flying that have led to a high level of interest amongst the media. The first issue is so-called **air rage**. Since the mid-1990s air rage incidents have been increasingly documented in the media. In the period 1994–1997 the International Air Transport association reported a five-fold increase in incidents, from 1132 to 5416 (Behan, 2002a). However, the lack of consistent reporting systems make it difficult to estimate the true extent of the problem. Whilst air rage incidents have fallen on both British and American flights in the wake of 9/11, some aviation analysts believe the fall is merely a blip in a long-term, upward trend (Miles, 2002).

Air rage is commonly but wrongly attributed to alcohol. In fact, smoking was involved in around 70 per cent of the 260 serious incidents recorded by BA last year (Shoesmith, 1998), while drink-related incidents accounted for under a quarter of all incidents (Finn, 1998). Nevertheless, a British judge criticised an airline for selling alcohol to an abusive passenger (Behna, 2002b). Other contributory factors include fear of flying and poor customer service (Bor cited in Behan, 2002a). It has also been suggested that airlines often create expectations they fail to meet, causing stress that can quickly develop into something more profound (Calder, 2000).

The second issue is **deep vein thrombosis** (DVT). A major risk associated with DVT is development of pulmonary embolism. The condition is caused as a result of long periods of immobility which can slow blood flow and lead to pooling. It is also believed that dehydration aggravates the condition as it thickens the blood and can raise the risk of clots (Thrombosis Online, 2002 [online]).

DVT is associated with all forms of long-distance travel, although it is not known whether air travel is an additional risk factor (Perry, 2003). However, some experts believe that long plane trips clearly set the stage for the development of deep vein blood clots (Brody, 2002). Furthermore, Geroulakos argues that the decreased air pressure in the cabin reduces the anticlotting ability of the blood and may also relax the walls of the veins, further enhancing the pooling of blood (Brody, 2002). The condition is also commonly referred to as economy class syndrome due to the legroom often provided in the economy class section of aircraft and where the "hassle of bothering other passengers and stewards to step into narrow aisle dissuades many from getting up and stretching their legs" (Hargrave, 1997). In addition, if dehydration is a contributing factor, "the dry air on planes, consumption of alcohol and caffeine and inadequate intake of hydrating fluids" (Brody, 2002), may increase the level of risk.

Thus, a number of preventative measures have been suggested, such as dressing in loose clothing, getting up to stretch the legs at least once an hour, and wearing an elastic support hose.

However, one solution that would address both issues and perhaps the most significant in relation to flight catering is the avoidance of alcohol. In fact, the first study into DVT among regular business flyers recommended that alcohol be banned on flights (Keenan, 2002). While airlines may be reluctant to implement such a measure due to economic factors and competition, Continental Airlines charges for alcohol in the economy class (Cohen, 2002) with staff reporting that in the three months since this policy began 'air rage' has virtually become a thing of the past (Walters, 2002). Qantas, and German charter carriers have also adopted such a policy (Momberger and Momberger, 2002a and b). Other airlines may decide to implement such a policy in the future. In addition, Virgin was considering trying to educate its passengers about the perils of in-flight drinking (Skapinker, 1998) with many unaware of the effects of alcohol in pressurised cabins. Regarding smoking-related air rage incidents, Austrian Airlines offer nicotine gum to all passengers and nicotine inhalers to premium passengers (Calder, 2000).

Conclusion

There are a number of factors which affect passengers' appetite and behaviour while flying. Sensory abilities such as smell, sight, and taste are affected. Taste buds may function as much as 30 per cent below par. The dry cabin atmosphere dehydrates mucous membranes in the nose, which blunts the sense of smell. A body taking minimum exercise in such a high altitude may require easily digestible meals. The cabin pressure may distort the ability to interpret food flavours, or colour. In the stomach, the pressure in an aircraft cabin also causes gases in the body to expand which may result in a bloated feeling. It would suggest light foods such as fish or salad rather than fatty foods. In compensating for the unique conditions of flight eating, the choice is often for more highly seasoned food and the use of herbs to stimulate stronger taste for passengers.

At such a high altitude, not all wines retain the subtle aroma and bouquet they produce when consumed on the ground. Alcohol acts more quickly in a pressurised cabin and also speeds dehydration leaving passengers both drunk and thirsty. Airlines continue to keep under review their policies in the light of passenger behaviour and experiences.

Key terms

Alcohol	Air rage	Altitude	Appetite
Coffee	Deep vein thrombosis	Dehydration	Digestion
Food acceptance		Sensory model	

Discussion questions

1. Look at a range of airline menus (available on airline websites). How do these reflect how taste changes while flying?
2. What action can airlines take to counteract the effects of flying?

References

Allemann, Y., Saner, H. and Meier, B. (1998) "High Altitude Stay and Air Travel in Coronary Heart Disease," *Schweizerische Medizinische* vol. 128, no. 17, 671–678.

Bareham, J. (1995) *Consumer Behaviour in the Food Industry: a European Perspective,* Butterworth-Heinemann Ltd.: Oxford.

Behan, R. (2002a) "Air Rage Attacks Coming Hard and Fast: Assaults on cabin staff are not only more frequent but more violent, according to a survey conducted on a British airline," *Daily Telegraph,* /02, 5.

Behan, R. (2002b) "Judge says Drink and Flying don't Mix: Virgin Atlantic Criticised in court for selling alcohol to abusive passenger," *Daily Telegraph,* 09/03/02, 5.

Brody, J.E. (2002) "On the Long flights, Take steps, Lots of Them," *The New York Times,* 17 Dec., 8.

Calder, S. (2000) "The Complete Guide to Air Rage" *The Independent.* 18 Mar., 2.

Cardello, A.V. (1996) "Food Choice, Acceptance and Consumption," In *Food Choice Acceptance and Consumption,* Meiselman HL and MacFie HJH Eds. Chapman and Hall

Cohen, A. (2002) "When the Drinks Trolley Hits a Bump: Business travel: Don't take your inflight drink for granted. Air rage and DVT are putting the cork back in the bottle," *The Financial Times,* 11 June, 18.

Finn, G. (1998) "Branson Launches Air Rage Blacklist," *The Independent,* 2 Nov., 5.

Kahn, F. (1995) "Throw a Chicken in the Air. . .," *Financial Times,* 21–22 Oct.

Hargrave, S. (1997) "Sitting Still on Long Flights can Lead to Fatal Blood Clotting," *Sunday Times,* 2 Nov., 18.

Keenan, S. (2002) "DVT Study Calls for an End to In-flight Alcohol," *The Times,* 16 May, 30.

Miles, P. (2002) "Peace Breaks Out at 30,000 ft: Air rage incidents are on the wane," *Daily Telegraph*, 28 Sep.

Momberger, K. and Momberger, M. (2003) "Aviation Catering News," *Momberger Airport Information*, 25 Nov., 4.

Momberger, K. and Momberger, M. (2003) "Aviation Catering News," *Momberger Airport Information*, 10 Aug., 3.

Perry, I. (2003) "Air Travellers Needn't Succumb to Cabin Fever: Perceptions of the health risks we run with air travel often do not fit the facts," *The Guardian*, 4 May, 7.

Polivy J. and Herman C.P. (1976) "Effects of Alcohol on Eating Behaviour: influences of mood and perceived intoxication," *Journal of Abnormal Psychology*, vol. 85, 601–606.

Rogers, P. (1996) "Food Choice, Mood and Mental Performance: Some examples and some mechanisms," in *Food Choice Acceptance and Consumption*, Ed. Meiselman HL and MacFie HJH. Chapman and Hill.

Mandfredin, I.R. Mandfredini, F. Fersini, C. and Conconi, F. (1998) "Circadian Rhythms, Athletic Performance and Jet Lag", *British Journal of Sports Medicine*, vol. 32, 102–106.

Mennell, S., Murcott, A., van Otterloo, A.H. (1992) *The Sociology of Food, Eating, Diet and Culture*, Sage Publications.

Milmo, C. (2001), "Professor with His Stomach in the Clouds and a Tasteless Task Ahead," *The Independent*, 24 Jan., 10.

Richardson, G. and Tate, B. (2000) "Hormonal and Pharmacological Manipulation of the Circadian Clock: Recent developments and future strategies", *Sleep*, vol. 23, S77–S85.

Skapinker, M. (1998) "High Anxiety: Micheal Skapinker looks at whether 'air rage' is really on the increase," *The Financial Times*, 7 Nov., 9.

Shoesmith, I. (1998) "BA gives a Final Warning to Drunken Passengers," *The Independent*, 1 Aug., 9.

Thrombosis Online. (2002) *Fast Facts about Deep Vein Thrombosis and Pulmonary Embolism* [online], Available from: http://www.thrombosisonline.com/dvt_fact_sheet [Accessed 21/05/03].

Walters, J. (2002) "Alcohol Price Tag Puts Paid to Air Rage", *The Observer*, 13 Oct., 4.

Westerterp-Plantenga, M.S., Westerterp, K.R., Rubbens, M., Verwegen, C.R.T., Richelet, J.P. and Gardette, B. (1999) "Appetite at High Altitude," [Operation Everest III(Comex-'97)]: A simulated ascent of Mount Everest, *Journal of Applied Physiology*, vol. 87, no. 1, 391–403.

Wurtman, R.J., Hefti, F. and Melamed, E. (1981) "Precursor Control of Neurotransmitter Synthesis," *Pharmacological Reviews*, no. 32, 315–335.

Young, R. (1995) "Airline Wines are Getting better," *The Times*, 13 July.

Menu planning and food product strategies

- Identify factors influencing the menu planning decision
- Discuss the process of product development
- Identify the different types of special meal provided by airlines
- Understand the need for a crew meal policy
- Identify the requirements for service and product specifications
- Review food product strategies

Introduction

The menu in any foodservice operation, whether it be a restaurant or airline cabin, fundamentally defines the service concept. It has a major impact on customers' expectations with regards to image, value for money, and the nature of experience. Single dishes are easily identified with specific meal occasions or types of operation—eggs and bacon are synonymous with breakfast, the hamburger is associated with fast food, and *pate de foie gras* with fine dining. This chapter is therefore concerned with the menu development process in flight catering, the factors that influence menu decisions, the development of standard recipes and product specifications, and the issue of using branded items as part of the on-board offer.

The menu planning process

There is lack of consensus on defining key terms, such as menu planning, menu development, menu design, menu analysis, and menu engineering. These tend to be used indiscriminately and interchangeably. This is partly because the word 'menu' has two separate meanings—"It can mean the product range that a foodservice outlet offers; *or* the piece of literature or display used to communicate this to the customer" (Mooney, 1994). Mifli and Jones (2001) suggest that the term 'menu planning' be used to describe how the product range is determined at the concept development stage, and the term 'menu development' should refer to the subsequent alteration of the planned menu. The term 'menu design' should be applied to how the menu card or display is created (Bowen and Morris, 1995).

In general terms, at least six stages of new product development can be identified:

1. exploring new ideas
2. systematic, rapid screening to eliminate less promising ideas
3. business analysis, including market research and cost analysis
4. development of remaining possibilities
5. testing the offerings developed
6. launching the idea to the production staff, eventually to the passenger

This general approach can then be adapted for the menu planning process. (Mooney 1994) has drawn up such a model (Fig. 5.1).

The process shown in Fig. 5.1 is made more difficult in the flight catering industry by a number of factors:

- the complex relationship between suppliers, caterers and airlines (discussed in Chapter 2)
- the mixed markets being served, i.e. different classes of passenger and also many different nationalities (see Chapter 3)
- the effect of flying at altitude on passengers appetite and perception of food (discussed in Chapter 4)
- the need to use a technology such as cook-chill or cook-freeze to transport and store food safely on board (discussed in Chapter 7)
- constraints in terms of space and weight on board the aircraft (Chapter 14)

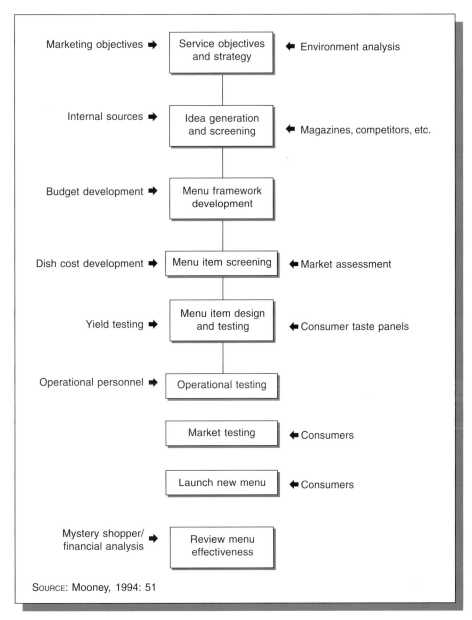

Figure 5.1
Model of the menu planning process

Ad hoc research suggests that in the flight catering industry menu planning has a number of stages as illustrated in Fig. 5.2.

General principles

All menus are planned on the basis of applying some general principles. As far as possible, the menu should offer contrast and variety in relation to a number of factors. These are:

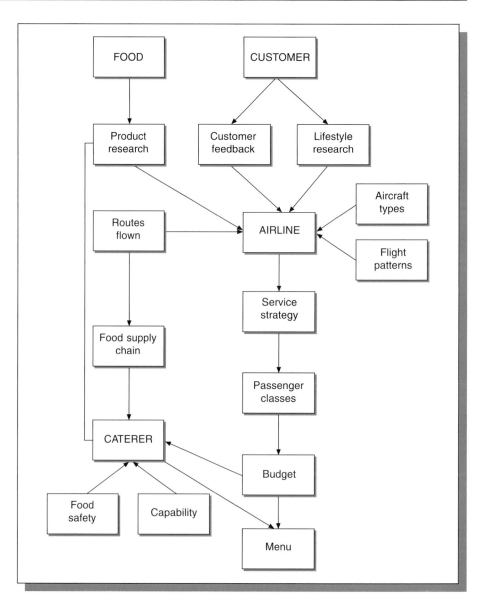

Figure 5.2
The flight menu planning process

- appearance, especially the colour of the food items
- textures such as soft, smooth, crunchy
- taste, i.e. salty, sweet, sour, bitter
- cooking methods, such as steamed, boiled, roast, etc.
- temperature

Food

Types of food and dietary habits vary widely across the world. Suppliers play a key role in influencing menus by assuring the continuity of supply of raw materials and by researching and developing new food products. Part of the job of the menu planning team is to plan menus using safe ingredients. The term 'safe' refers to microbiological safety. The advice given to product development from the microbiology laboratory must be adhered to. The microbiologist will inform the team of foods that are classified as unsafe at the present time or which foods must be continually avoided. Examples may be eggs or certain types of shellfish.

Product research

Menu planning and new recipe development is not just simply creating new dishes but looks more significantly at product performance, i.e. the factors which have to be taken into account when preparing, chilling, holding and reheating on board the aircraft. This often means recipe adjustment—ingredient alternatives and supplements may have to be introduced to stabilise or improve the product. In addition, to alleviate excessive hot food smells on board the aircraft, food may have to be treated in special ways. Product development will also involve experimenting with different pieces of equipment and process methods; examining alternative ingredient suppliers; and experimenting with new ingredients as and when they become available. On occasion it may also mean cost reduction and drawing up alternative recipes and dish specifications. In addition, the airline's product development team in planning the menu would be involved in the organoleptic assessment of food items, dishes and meals (i.e. food tasting).

Customers

Clearly, menus have to be planned so that they appeal to the customer. In order to identify their needs and expectations a variety of methods may be used. Often, lifestyle research is conducted by researching magazines, newspapers, and periodicals to see what concepts and food ideas are being written about. The other approach is to directly ask customers or to monitor their behaviour. There is also some feedback on menu dishes from the cabin crew in terms of customer evaluation. Questionnaires may be used on board the aircraft to assess the popularity of dishes. Records are kept in relation to a two-choice main meal item, stating how much of each was consumed.

Airline routes, aircraft and flight patterns

Establishing what food and dishes are to be served on board the aircraft is one of the basic planning functions. Airlines will very often stipulate exactly what food is to be served. This will include the precise combination of dishes, portions, sizes, etc. for each route. Each airline will, when planning their menus, take into account what the competition is doing and serving. Thought will also be given to the cost of each menu, and parameters will be set for economy, business, and first class.

The basic principles of menu planning also apply to flight catering, except that the starting point should focus on the customers seated in the aircraft with the tray in front of them. Size and scale have an impact on the feasibility of what can be achieved thousands of feet in the air, while at the same time providing an appropriate and comfortable meal for the passenger. For this reason, for best results the planner starts with the tray and works backwards. Therefore, the following are typically taken into consideration:

- the function of the meal in relation to the flight patterns, i.e. which day part is covered (breakfast, mid-morning, lunch, mid-afternoon, evening meal, overnight)
- the size of the tray or bag, overall presentation and dish specification for each airline in relation to the routes being flown and aircraft being used
- the various types of passengers, establishing that adequate provision is made for special diets, religions, ethnic meals, and vegetarians
- the capabilities of the flight kitchen, its labour and equipment in relation to routes flown and flight centres used
- the time of the year
- the number of courses each airline requires, especially applicable to first class

Airline service strategy

Airlines make a choice about their flight service strategy. Catering requirements vary according to whether the service is scheduled, chartered, or low-cost with no frills (Table 5.1). Scheduled airlines have typically viewed catering as a positive influence in retaining business and go to great lengths to keep the food they offer flexible and upmarket.

Flight	Services
Low-cost, no frills	Food not supplied free; Passengers can buy snacks on board, or bring their own.
Chartered	Part of a package with meals supplied, but little or no choice
Scheduled	Wide range of meals supplied as part of ticket price.

SOURCE: Baker, 2000: 31

Table 5.1
Service levels according to the types of flight

Flight type/class

Flight classes (first class/business class/economy class) offer different levels of services. A trend is to move away from a formal dining to a casual service style to meet the customer's needs. The meals used to be very structured in the 1980s and even in the early 1990s in first class. After take-off, one course was served after the other with trolley service at very strict mealtimes. However, this has changed quite substantially. Some airlines have adopted a more modern approach that gives passengers control over what they eat and when they eat it. For instance, in flying with British Airways, passengers have a complete *à la carte* service, and there is no longer a formal meal service in first class. It may looks a little bit like room service in a hotel. The passengers can ask for whatever they would like, whenever they would like it—although inevitably most people seem to want to eat round about the same time. For example, if passengers want to work before they arrive, they might just have a mineral water, some canapes or some savouries for the time being, or a freshly squeezed orange juice, then just a salad or a nice bowl of soup while they do some work, and later on order a main course, or an *hors d'oeuvre* and a glass of champagne. In addition, the services have changed in economy class because the whole style is more fun and more upbeat and the food is also more modern but also with some nice choices, something a little traditional maybe and something slightly more sophisticated (Hafner, 2001).

Caterers

In order to keep abreast of current styles and trends in food and to reflect current practices in restaurants, several of the main carriers and flight caterers have development chef and development kitchens (see also Chapter 8). The purpose of the development kitchen is to create new menus and new dishes, thereby reflecting the carrier's responsiveness to stimulating interesting menus. The regular traveller does not therefore look upon the total package as being repetitive, but can look forward to a continually evolving meal experience on board the aircraft. But provision of dishes and meals can vary from one flight kitchen to another, especially when comparing different regions of the world. Such variation may be based on the nature of the local supply chain and on the capability of any production facility.

Menu design

The menu is often considered to be important in adding to the overall customer experience. The compiling of the menu is one of the flight caterer's important tasks. The content of the menu creates an image which reflects the overall style of the carrier. The printed menu given to the passenger on board the aircraft should match the overall corporate image, incorporating the corporate colours and logo. This printed menu is further seen as yet another way of promoting the airline.

It is clear that there are many factors that influence menu planning. In addition menu planners may develop a particular philosophy of how to plan meals for airlines. For instance, one airline food consultant has suggested a checklist for designing the airline menu (Table 5.2).

Special meals

Special meals have become an important part of the airline food service regime although the percentage uptake is still small. For instance, US Airways has 2.1 per cent of its passenger taking special meals, which translates into about 3,000 special meals served per month in first class and 36,000 meals in economy class (Lundstrom, 2001). Passengers pick a special meal for a variety of reasons, some of them pertaining to religion and health and diet requirements and

Recommended		To be avoided	
Simplicity	Comfort food	Complexity	Traditional hautcuisine
Abundance	All day dishes	Portion controlled look	Formal dishes
Rustic dishes	Treats	Institutionalised dishes	Too much cream
Informal food	Surprises	Structured food	Repetition
Balanced food	Flexibility	Formal menus	Veal
Light dishes	Poultry	Heavy food	Mussels
Fresh look	Fish/seafood	Complicated garnishes	
Variety	Salads	Rigid structure	Peanuts (except Satay)
Uncluttered	Pulses	Crowded	Glace cherries
Vegetarian	Potted poultry/meat	Foie gras	Terrines
Stir fries	Olive oil	Pates	Peanut oil
Mediterranean	British dishes	Wellington	Synthetic cream
Californian	Authentic dishes	Old style hot dishes	Pink peppercorns
Tasty exotic flavour	Fresh fruit	Bland food	Tinned fruit

SOURCE: Hafner, 2001

Table 5.2
Suggested airline menu checklist

others pertaining to something else entirely. For instance, British Airways was a pioneer in introducing a vegetarian main course on Concorde in the 1970s, which was then introduced in their first class, and their Club World class. Now it in also available in economy class (Hafner, 2001). The percentage of special meals is so varied from station to station that it is difficult to pin down an overall figure. Although the numbers are small, the demand is increasing. Overall, all airlines estimated that between 5 and 7 per cent of their passengers request some type of special meal (Anon., 1999). It has also been recognised that people may order a special meal even though they have no special dietary requirements, for example, a non-vegetarian may order a vegetarian meal. The reasons for this are complex and not fully known; it may be that passengers perceive special to mean better than average. Alternatively, they may have noticed that special meals are served first by the cabin crew and thus ordering a special meal can been seen as a way to get quicker service. It could also be due to the experience of special meals; passengers may have tried them and decided they were of superior quality.

When passengers place their order through travel agent bookings or direct reservations, these special meals are generally coded into four letter International Air Transport Association (IATA)'s designations (Table 5.3). There has been a trend towards more standardised and uniform special meal types and the use of common ingredients from country to country and airline to airline. As an example, low fat and low salt meal options are becoming more commonplace

Meal	IATA Code	Description
Vegetarian meals		
Vegetarian meals— Vegan	VGML	These vegetarian meals strictly exclude meat or animal products, including honey, eggs or milk (products).
Vegetarian meal— Lacto-OVO	VLML	This menu excludes meat, fish and poultry and products which feature these ingredients. It does, however, include other animal products such as eggs and milk (products). Soya products and other meat substitutes are used.
Vegetarian meals —Asian	AVML	These meals exclude meat, fish, poultry and products which feature these ingredients. They do, however, include other animal products such as milk (products). This menu has an Indian accent and is prepared with oriental herbs and spices.
Fruit plate	FPML	Naturally, the main ingredients of this vegetarian menu are fruit. However, for extra variety, it may also include ingredients such as vegetables, nuts and cheese.
Medical health-care		
Low sodium meal	LSML	Extremely salty products are excluded from this menu and no salt is added during preparation to prevent high blood pressure.
Low fat/low cholesterol meal	LFML	Featuring limited cholesterol and a high percentage of polyunsaturated fats, these high-fibre meals are suitable for a cholesterol-reducing diet. Their low or limited fat content also make them ideal for any passenger in preventing cardio-vascular disease.
Low protein meal	LPML	Low protein; restrict foods containing high biological value protein (meat, fish, eggs and dairy products); avoid highly salted foods; do not use salt in food preparation.
Low calorie meal	LCML	This menu features increased complex carbohydrates with high fibre foods used wherever possible: low in fat with approximately 1200 calories in a 24-hour period
Diabetic meal	DBML	In the diabetic menu, special attention is given to the balance between proteins, fats and carbohydrates. Meals feature an increased proportion of complex carbohydrates and fibre. A small amount of fat is used, a large proportion of which is polyunsaturated. Products containing sugar feature to a limited extent.
Peanut free meal	PFML	Products exclude any trace of peanut.
Gluten free meals	GFML	Feature exclusively gluten-free products. Products containing wheat, rye, oats or barley are therefore not included.

Non-lactose meal	NLML	The content and preparation of this menu excludes the use of cow's milk protein or lactose.
Bland/Soft meal	BLML	Light, easily digestible meal for stomach/intestinal problems. Low fat food items-low in dietary fibre/residue. Omission of foods or beverages causing gastric discomfort.
High fibre meal	HFML	High nutritious products with water-soluble and water insoluble fibre.
Low purine meal	PRML	Meal without offal products. Prepared to decrease elevated blood and urinary acid levels. Effective in the treatment of gout and uric acid stones.
Seafood meal	SFML	Fish and/or seafood prepared according to local specifications.
Religious meal		
Kosher meals	KSML	All Kosher food is prepared under strict rabbinical supervision and supplied by authorised suppliers. Meals are sealed to guarantee purity.
Muslim meals	MOML	Meals are prepared in strict accordance with the Sharia and therefore exclude pork and alcohol, as well as products that contain them.
Hindu meals	HNML	These meals are prepared strictly according to Hindu directives. They therefore exclude all meat and meat products from the cow. Hindu meals are usually "vegetarian".
Children/Infant meal		
Baby's meal	BBML	Selection of pots of pureed foods for babies between 10 weeks and two years.
Children's meal	CHML	Serve a special fun-box for children aged between two and nine years

SOURCE: IATA, 2001: 122

Table 5.3

Examples of special meal (SPML) codes and their descriptions

in all meals and in some cases airlines have banned nuts completely from their recipes (Sutton and Gostelow, 1997). The airline expects that by combining the components of several dietary regional meals, SPML's should save them some money and cut the amount of labour that currently goes into producing each of the meals. Changing the menu and streamlining the way meals are delivered have been important as airlines work across alliances and borders to please an increasingly diverse group of travellers with a myriad of dietary requirements (Lundstrom, 2001).

The common practice is to cook the most frequent special requirements in a separate area of the kitchen according to each airline's specifications. Vegetarian meals, seafood, and low-fat and low-cholesterol foods are amongst the most frequently requested meals generally prepared by the flight caterer. The remaining SPMLs would be outsourced to specialist facilities for their preparation, especially Kosher, Muslim, and Hindu. A number of religious rituals are involved, particularly with the Jewish faith, involving a rabbi making regular visits to the kitchen, or in some cases being permanently based there.

Once completed, special meals are labelled and loaded into designated meal trolleys. All this translates into higher labour costs and higher food cost. At present nutritional information is not provided to the passenger although some do carry a mark of approval from heart foundations, environmental groups and other institutes. BA, for example, indicates a meal in a 'well-being selection' with an asterisk (*).

Crew meals

In addition to providing meals for passengers, the airline and/or flight caterer is also responsible for developing and providing meals for the crew—both on the flight deck (pilot, co-pilot, engineer) and in the passenger cabin. Airlines have a range of approaches to this. The obvious policy is to allow crew to eat the same meals as passengers, especially, since most flights will have some hot meals left over once passengers have been given a choice. If so, the decision then has to be made as to whether or not the crew meal is the same as the first, business, or economy class meal.

However, there are four problems with this policy. First, if the passenger meal is contaminated with food-poisoning bacteria, the crew will also be affected. They would then be unable to assist passengers who were being ill, as they would be ill too. For this reason, it is the standard policy on all aircraft for the pilot and co-pilot to have completely different meals. Second, the menu cycle for passengers may be several weeks. However, crew fly frequently and they would quickly become bored by having exactly the same meal, every time they worked a flight. For this reason, some airlines develop a special menu cycle for crew meals. Third, the crew, especially the cabin crew, are engaged in physical work. This means that that their energy intake from food needs to be sufficient for them to undertake this work. Typically, this means food items and dishes low in fat and high in carbohydrates. This is another reason for having a crew menu. Finally, in some cases the crew may be working on flights that have little or no food service, but the flight time, or their shift pattern, entitles them to a meal or snack, again to keep their energy levels up.

Menu cycles

Once product development is complete, a menu cycle is then decided for a given period of time. The length of the cycle will be determined by each individual airline, consideration being given to the time of the year and to the different foods available. These menus will be monitored carefully by each carrier. The cycle for short-haul flights must, due to the number of occasions an individual passenger might travel on those routes, change frequently and the cycle may only last for 7–14 days with, for example, four menu cycles within a three month window. On long-haul flights, many airlines now have cycles of one or two months. Due to the increasing number of choice through all classes, even the frequent traveller is granted a different meal while flying more than once during a menu cycle. Too short menu cycles on long-haul flights make it difficult to take advantage of seasonal availability. Procurement is also an important factor, as menus today are much more complex due to the increased number of choices offered, thus increasing the risk of high inventories at the cycle end. It is also easier to calculate and distribute menu cards, along with wine lists, for the same period. For example, the menu for Concorde was changed weekly, whereas charter flight menus are often valid for 12 months.

One example would be a three-cycle system. Cycles A, B and C run for one week on each flight route. For a large airline there can be an average of 300 meals on each cycle, each meal having its own menu specification. This menu specification includes a photograph of the meal and contains information on all ingredients used including any special accompaniments for the meal which may include kinds of crockery (for example, china instead of plastic for different passenger classes).

One of the main problems which restricts greater productivity and reduced wastage is the lack of standardisation among the different airlines. Different airlines that contract with flight caterers to produce meals can differ greatly in their requirements. Some will stipulate every component that makes up the meal. This includes the recipes, where to purchase, what suppliers to use, size of tray, type of cutlery, china, etc., even down to the type of bread roll to serve. Such differences introduce yet further difficulties into the planning process, and the subsequent standardisation of systems of production. Several examples are provided in this chapter, showing flight catering menus and menu specifications (Fig. 5.3).

The menu cycle and flight pattern provide the basic information on the basis of which the caterer can undertake the initial planning of the inputs in areas such as equipment requirements, food and other raw materials, and labour. The initial planning will also include product specifications that might need to be drawn up as also suppliers identified with contracts written to procure these inputs. This outline planning information also provides the basis on which flight production processes can be considered and planned in relation to the inputs and required outputs (see Chapter 8) which details the raw materials to be used.

Service and product specifications

The menu planning team would be responsible for drawing up the dish specifications and standard recipes. They may also have an input into the purchase specification. Furthermore, the foodservice team will naturally focus a great deal of attention on the presentation of food as it reaches the customers. The initial impact is important in creating an impression. It is also possible that the team are involved in cabin crew training as it is essential to develop in the service staff a culture that promotes good tray presentation when handling the total menu product to the passenger. So, at all stages in the catering cycle, there are specifications drawn up to ensure that the customer receives what was originally planned and designed. There are different specifications for

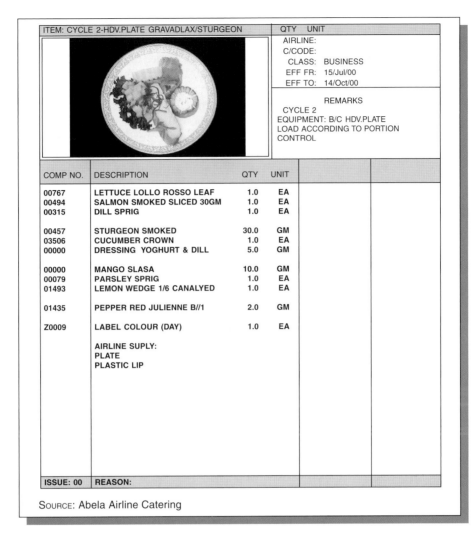

ITEM: CYCLE 2-HDV.PLATE GRAVADLAX/STURGEON		QTY	UNIT

AIRLINE:
C/CODE:
CLASS: BUSINESS
EFF FR: 15/Jul/00
EFF TO: 14/Oct/00

REMARKS
CYCLE 2
EQUIPMENT: B/C HDV.PLATE
LOAD ACCORDING TO PORTION
CONTROL

COMP NO.	DESCRIPTION	QTY	UNIT		
00767	LETTUCE LOLLO ROSSO LEAF	1.0	EA		
00494	SALMON SMOKED SLICED 30GM	1.0	EA		
00315	DILL SPRIG	1.0	EA		
00457	STURGEON SMOKED	30.0	GM		
03506	CUCUMBER CROWN	1.0	EA		
00000	DRESSING YOGHURT & DILL	5.0	GM		
00000	MANGO SLASA	10.0	GM		
00079	PARSLEY SPRIG	1.0	EA		
01493	LEMON WEDGE 1/6 CANALYED	1.0	EA		
01435	PEPPER RED JULIENNE B//1	2.0	GM		
Z0009	LABEL COLOUR (DAY)	1.0	EA		
	AIRLINE SUPLY:				
	PLATE				
	PLASTIC LIP				
ISSUE: 00	**REASON:**				

SOURCE: Abela Airline Catering

Figure 5.3
Example of flight catering dish specification

individual dishes (dish specifications) and whole meal trays (meal specifications). However, the terminology is used interchangeably with the term 'menu specifications' used for both types.

Product (or purchasing) specifications

Specifications play an important part in flight feeding. Different classes of travel demand different foods, menus, and food service styles, and it is therefore essential that the caterer responds and reacts to these requirements. The first step is for the flight provider, often in conjunction with the airline, to draw up the product specifications. These form the basis for supplier selection and procurement action. Once a supplier has been selected, the product specifications assist in controlling and maintaining standards by providing the supplier with a precise statement of the requirement and a mechanism against which the quality and standard of the product can be measured. Should the airline be unhappy with the supplier or his products, then the specification must first be reviewed to ensure that the product meets or continues to meet the airline's exact requirements. If not, it must be amended. If the supplier is failing to meet his contractual obligations, then this should be apparent and the specification can be used as the basis on which to select a new supplier.

In many cases, raw materials are not specified but whole meal 'components'. There are two types of component feeding available: ready to serve (RTS) which are complete bought–in meals, and ready to use (RTU) which require extra labour, not for cooking but for dishing out. While airline caterers have been using component products to some degree for several years, the range of offerings is becoming more sophisticated and their use far more pervasive (Caira, 1995). Hence, the flight provider might need to purchase four or five different sizes of one particular product, for example, beef filet. Under these circumstances, product specifications are essential if the correct supplies are to be procured.

While procuring supplies in the originating country might be relatively straightforward, supplies in overseas countries are less certain. A few large airlines have established catering subsidiaries in countries where they have a substantial interest in terms of the number of flights that land there. However, where the numbers of flights do not warrant establishing a dedicated catering outlet, flight provision must be contracted out to another caterer. This seldom becomes a major issue as the availability of standard or branded supplies does not pose a problem. However, in developing countries or those with different ethnic or religious backgrounds, availability of supplies might be less certain. Under these circumstances product specifications will provide general guidelines for the purchase of foods but non-standard supplies might need to be procured. This is discussed in more detail in Chapter 6.

Standard recipes

The standard recipe is an essential component in flight food production. It is the written formula for producing a food item of a specified quality and quantity. The content shows the precise quantities and qualities of the ingredients together with the sequence of preparation and service. It is essential for control purposes that the standard specifications are adhered to. The objectives are to determine the following:

- quantities and qualities of ingredients to be used, stating the purchase specification
- yield obtainable from the recipe and portion control
- food cost per batch and per portion and hence profit margins
- nutritional value of each dish
- preparation methods required

In addition, the use of standard recipes allows photographs to be used to assist in ensuring quality control at the end point of production, and simplifies the training of new staff, as illustrated in Fig. 5.4. It also provides efficient

Name: Baked red emperor and rudder pie, scented with truffle oil.
Author: Phil Brumby   Created: July 2001

Ingredients	
400 g	red emperor
400 g	rudder fish
4 dessert spoons	white truffle oil
1 kg	puff pastry (see recipe)
500 ml	soubise sauce
Ingredients	Soubise Sauce
	1.2 kg sliced onions
	800 ml cream
	400 ml fish stock
	300 g diced onions
	1 tbsp olive oil
Ingredients	Smoked tomatoes
4	vine ripened tomatoes
50 g	sawdust
50 ml	balsamic
1	clove of garlic

Makes 4 pies. Serves 8 people.

You will need 4 pie dishes, oval dish that is 17.5 cm long, 12.5 cm wide and 5 cm deep.

Soubise sauce
Sweat sliced onions with olive oil and a little salt, cook until the onions take on a very light brown colour, cool then add fish stock and reduce by 1/2. Add cream, and reduce by $1/2$ or until a thick cream consistency is reached, remove from heat.
In a separate pan sweat the diced onion in a little olive oil. Meanwhile blend the onion cream mixture then add the cooked diced onion to this and adjust the seasoning.

Smoked tomatoes
Drop tomatoes into boiling water for a few seconds then plunge into iced cold water and remove the skins. Cut the tomatoes into halves and remove seeds. Place the sawdust into a heavy based pan and heat until smoking. Put the tomatoes halves on a rack, brush them with crushed garlic and balsamic vinegar and place the rack over the smoking pan, cover with a lid and keep smoking for 3 minutes.

To assemble
Roll pastry $1/2$ cm thick and cut into ovals 3 cm wider than the pie dishes. In each pie dish spoon about 2 tablespoons of soubise sauce, lay 100 g of red emperor and 100 g rudder on the sauce. Cover with another tablespoon of sauce and a dessert spoon of truffle oil, cover with the pastry lid and press down the sides. Glaze with egg wash.

Cook pies for 25 minutes at 260°C. Rest for minutes before serving. Serve with mashed potatoes and smoked tomatoes.

SOURCE: Gulf Air

Figure 5.4
Standard recipe for airline hot entree

purchasing, accurate food costs and safeguards against any pilferage and possible errors.

Meal specifications

In addition to having standard recipes for individual dishes, the caterer also needs meal specifications based on the menu cycle. The meal specification identifies what combination of dishes, and the respective equipment that is needed to serve a specific class of passenger on any given flight. In many cases, this takes the form of a photographic illustration of a fully laid-up tray with each item listed separately, as illustrated in Fig. 5.5

Service specifications

In addition to the purchase of tangible products, airlines also need to purchase a number of services. In a similar way to products, a specification is a precise statement of a service to be provided. It would include details such as: the type of service required, the materials and equipment and procedures to be used in the provision of that service, its standard or quality, and the time of delivery, action, and completion. Typically, such specifications may be an addendum to the contract between the airline and the caterer (chapter 2).

In some cases airlines purchase in a number of service provided directly to the airline; in others, the flight provider acts as the intermediary. The type and nature of services provided might range from the provision of a complete catering service to:

- Ready assembled components of the flight provisions: wrapped and packaged cutlery sets, ethnic meals, etc.
- Ready assembled and stocked flight duty-free trolleys
- The provision of transportation services to deliver the flight products to the aircraft
- Laundry service
- Rubbish disposal

Packaging and labelling

In addition to the size of the product, the nature and type of product and packaging must also be taken into account when writing specifications. Packaging requirements are considered in more detail later but, for example, five different flavours of preserves might be required. These could be packed in individual glass jars, 'gourmet' aluminium cups, 'extra cups' and 'mini' cups. Furthermore, the preferred size for flights originating from Belgium is 25 or 30 g, England 20 g, France 30 or 40 g, Germany 25 g and the Netherlands 15 g. Thus, it can be seen that product specifications need to be carefully planned if they are to sustain the organisational requirements.

Closely allied with branding strategies are decisions concerning the packaging and labelling of all products. A number of criteria need to be considered including environmental issues (which are addressed in Chapter 15), but to be successful packaging primarily must also be a physical container for the product. It must

ALPHA
FLIGHT SERVICES

Issue Date
26/10/99

Version Number
0

Menu specification

Customer

Contract Ref
LSAMPLE

Effective Date	Class
01/10/99	**B/C**

Meal/Description

B/C Moslem Meal

Rotation	Product Code
1	**SPSP02**

Loading	Destination

— Ingredients —

Appetiser
142182	Lollo Rosso Lettuce	5	gm
113026	Italian Plum Tomato wedge	2	6th
XWSP02	Fennel and bean salad	25	gm
XWSP03	chick pea chat	50	gm
572349	Cling film 300 mm × 300 m	1	sh
572705	Date Code Label	1	each

Salad
142344	Windsor Lettuce Mix	30	gm
572349	Cling film 300 mm × 300 m	1	sh
572705	Date Code Label	1	each

Entree
XWSP04	Catchcumber rice 2 × 40 gm	80	gm
XWSP05	Beef curry	100	gm
XWSP06	Broccoli and cauliflower curry	60	gm
XWSP07	Mushroom curry	60	gm
660418	Copper Foil	1	each
572705	Date Code Label	1	each
572691	Zs labels multiprint	1	each

Dessert
278033	Ras malai	1	ptn
572349	Cling film 300 mm × 300 m	1	sh
572705	Date Code Label	1	each

Trayset
170518	Margarine Sunflower 10 gm	1	each
516740	Brinjal Pickle	30	gm
511773	Mixed Pickle	30	gm

Bulk loaded items
244430	Plain Naam Bread	2	qtr

— Remarks —

Airline Supply—China Plates/Glass Bowl/Cutlery & Napkin Wrap/Tray/Trayliner
Photograph shows loading arrangements for meal items.
Crew to serve in accordance with normal passenger meal service

SOURCE: Alpha Flight Services

Figure 5.5
An example of meal specification

protect and maintain the product in the best possible condition, and it must also be attractive to the consumer. Wholesale packaging, i.e. the packaging required to transport the product from the producer or supplier to the flight provider, must meet certain requirements. The retail packaging, that is the packaging destined for the aircraft and that will be used by the fare-paying passenger, requires different considerations. These include the following:

Practical Good packaging must work, in that it should provide the right level of protection for the product, while at the same time permit the product to be readily accessible, particularly in the confined spaces of the aircraft cabin. It needs to contain the product in a convenient quantity, i.e. it should be easy to handle by the cabin crew and customer alike, and should satisfy the passengers but at the same time should avoid unnecessary waste. The materials used should have no harmful or sensory effects on the food and be suitable for storage at chilled and ambient temperatures, or for heating, if required.

Inform Besides the legal requirements, the labelling needs to be effective and informative, correctly identifying the product. It should not be misleading and should provide instructions for use.

Aesthetics The products must look attractive and fit in with the overall marketing strategy of the airline. In the economy class, foil containers and tray sets in some cases have been replaced by a more pleasing plastic version in more vibrant colours and oval shapes. Virgin has found that what their customers like to drink with their bacon butties is tea in a mug rather than in a cup.

Emotional appeal The image conveyed by the packaging must conform with the overall image being developed and portrayed by the airline.

Food and beverage strategies

As we have seen in Chapter 3, customers can have ambivalent attitudes towards meals on board the aircraft and airlines can have very different views as to the importance, or otherwise, of on-board service and catering. For those that have a food-focused strategy, one of the key decisions to be made is the extent to which the on board offer includes clearly branded products. More recently, some airlines have also enhanced the reputation of their offer by working with celebrity chefs.

Use of brands

One way to add value to products is to brand the product with the airline's culture, or simply supply passengers with well-known branded products, thereby taking advantage of their quality-recognition factor and wide-spread popularity (Bell, 1997). The decision to brand food service accessories with the brand of the airline or of the food supplier vary from one airline to another, and depend on how branding might fit into the overall thrust of the airline's promotional effort or differentiation strategy.

Various airlines, over the years, have adopted these strategies in the pursuit of their strategic objectives. However, all airlines use a differentiation strategy in which they attempt to promote and identify the benefits and advantage of selected aspects of their own airline. Branding plays an important part in this process where brands are used to associate particular features or attributes, which purport to be advantageous and provide a competitive edge over their competitors and attract international growth. Table 5.4 outlines the main advantages and disadvantages associated with each decision.

	Advantages	Disadvantages
Brand	Better acceptance Better identification and awareness Improved product differentiation Opportunity for brand loyalty	Higher costs: Production/Packaging Marketing Legal
No brand	Low costs: Production Marketing Legal	Lack of market/brand identity Lack of market identity

SOURCE: Terpstra and Sarathy, 1994

Table 5.4
Branding/no brand advantages and disadvantages

The theory behind branding depends on how a **brand proposition** has been defined. The 'proposition' is a set of statements that summarises the combination of positioning and personality and allows the brand to emerge from the fuzziness of the competition. The solution is to build a simple and consistent proposition which consumers can understand, and then to manage it through understanding its intrinsic properties—its core values, added value, image, and identity— and constantly update themselves on consumer concepts of their brand in relation to others (Gilbert, 1999). A brand can be developed as an own-labelled brand, corporate brand, or brand extension. The latter may involve minor product variations to enable sales in different market segments. Virgin Atlantic, for example, pours its own brand of cola and vodka. For first- and business-class service, the trays of many airlines are set with logoed china, cutlery, glassware, and napery to form their own corporate branding.

The advantages and disadvantages of branding can be considered from a number of viewpoints.

Flight catering supplier
- Brand loyalty can be built up thereby ensuring repeat business and some protection from competition
- Opportunity for premium pricing known as *brand equity*

Flight provider (caterer)
- Purchasing is made easier, particularly when purchasing overseas and when buying the same brand
- Consistency and uniformity of quality, content, and performance are assured
- Status and prestige can be derived from using or offering certain brands
- Product improvements are encouraged

Airline
- Branding adds to and helps reinforce the effects of other advertising
- Helps the airline build a reputation for quality
- Consistency and uniformity of quality and content
- Helps facilitate the introduction of new lines or ideas
- Provides prestige value
- Provides visible signals of positional strength in the market place

Airline passenger
- Provides identity and focus for the airline
- Provides the airline passenger with some reassurance
- Prestige value can be attached to products from another class
- A branded product may produce a side effect on a different segment of customers; the hard-sell advertising may put off first-class passengers, but passenger surveys show an overwhelmingly positive response to the recognised brand (Caira, 1995)

Examples include United Airline's emphasis on branding, serving such items as Mrs Field's cookies for first class, Starbucks coffee for all passengers, and Friendly Skies Meals from McDonalds fast food chain. American Airlines serves Pizzeria Uno, Air Canada has Second Cup coffee, while Delta's menu card provides Omaha Steak, and A.1. sauces to give recognition to all of the partners (Henderson, 1998). Some national flag carriers also take the opportunity to show-case some of their country's luxury goods, such as Wedgewood bone-china on BA, and Limoges and Christofle on Air France.

Celebrity chefs

One of the ways in which airlines have been attempting to differentiate is to involve celebrity chefs. Bringing a knowledge of food trends, these culinary advisors have been instrumental in developing dishes that are contemporary and workable within the strictures of containerised galley provisioning (Bell, 1997). Opportunities for variety and fresh preparation attract more chefs to flight kitchens, and the industry has become far more receptive to chefs' ideas. Each of these celebrity chefs brings innovative cuisine from various regions to the airline's passengers (Frank, 2000).

However, such involvement of celebrity personnel can cause a conflict with the product development team who have an in-depth understanding of many of the problems associated with the provision of high-quality food aboard the aircraft. These difficulties and complexities are often not realised by celebrity chefs, who may be narrowly focused when trying to develop speciality cuisine on board the aircraft. However, many such chefs fully cooperate when informed about the implications of serving food and drink at high altitudes in pressurised cabins.

Chefs on board

One strategy is to have a chef on board to cook the food in a restaurant service style. This dates back to the mid-1960s when Lufthansa had certified chefs on board to serve first-class passengers on transatlantic flights. This has made a reappearance with Gulf Air and bmi's business class passengers having all their meals freshly prepared and served by a team of two flight chefs. It claims to focus on the genuine warmth and hospitality of the crew, combined with the efficient, crisp and modern style the customer's demand.

Book the cook

Another method is to order the main course in advance. For example, Singapore Airline's created the "Book The Cook" service with a wide menu selection from Singapore and 10 overseas stations. Through the reservations office or the travel agent, the order can be placed by simply selecting from the list of 'Book the Cook' dishes at least 24 hours before flight departure.

Gate-house service

Pioneered by Germany's Lufthansa and used successfully by Northwest Airlines in Chicago, Delta examines this concept of Gate-house service, in which passengers pick up their food selections, packaged in a branded bag with handles just prior to boarding. The benefit is to save labour and time on board, but some caterers are sceptical about the concept. They found this concept worked most efficiently only when the airline provides only three to four snack items, and stated it can be a costly venture because of the variety of food the airline is required to make available at the gate, the extra personnel required, and the packaging (Caira, 1995).

Meal coupons

This initiative is to offer passengers a discount meal coupon redeemable in their airport concessions, instead of providing a flight meal. This may work well with the emerging no-frills routes when passengers are willing to live with a reduction in services as long as there are corresponding cuts in travel prices (Caira, 1995).

Case study 5.1

British Airways

As part of launching a range of new services and benefits for 'World Traveller' passengers in 1998, BA introduced a total flight meal experience based on:

- New and innovative menus
- Familiar foods and larger servings
- Menu developed with the help of BBC chef—Brian Turner
- New oval shapes of dishes and tray with different colours have modernised the service style and home-like crockery, cutlery and cups have made meal presentation more interesting than ever

Considering the three reasons; that food preferences are subjective, exacerbated by the constraints of travel in a pressurised cabin two miles high, and the importance of food to comfort in the air, British Airways has built their new food style for the millennium. The 'Signature Style' of their flight food strategy used ten menu-planning criteria to reflect the needs and desires of the varied passengers and markets (Table 5.5). In aiming to serve memorable meals in the air, they have summed it up in one phrase: "Understate and over-deliver" when serving the meals, and a question they asked when planning the menu is: "What do our passengers like to eat?"

Criteria	Description
Simplicity: colour, texture, purity	Tastes, colours and textures complement each other. Simple recipes without too many ingredients. . . fish and meat, good quality fruit and vegetables.
Taste: natural, strong, lasting	Tastebuds only respond to four basic flavours—sweet, sour, salt and bitter. Keep tastes natural, strong, and definitive.
Informality: simple, versatile, easy	A new faster pace of life has influenced the way we eat. Simpler, less structured meals have developed into a more varied and versatile food style, offering more exciting choices and combinations.
Suitability: home, comfort, appeal, luxury	Food should offer the comfort and assurance of home anywhere in the world. Every meal should be a celebration.
Visual: appeal, presentation, colour, evocable	Colour and shape is visual pleasure and the natural colours of food skillfully combined in presentation give maximum visual impact.
Authentic: real, honest, pure Health: balance, organic, light	Authentic, genuine and honest cooking has no substitute. Today's lifestyle requires essential commitment to health and well being. Less salt and butter, more olive oil and organic foods offer a better balance for a healthier body and mind.
Seasonal: celebration, freshness, availability	Celebrate each season's bounty. . . Spring lamb, Summer berries and asparagus, Autumn game, Winter root vegetables. Maximise on the tastes and pleasures of seasonal produce.
Variety: choice, exciting, stimulate	Excite the palate and taste buds with a variety of flavours and textures. Balance the menu with choices that avoid repetition in style and ingredients.
Names: kudos, style, quality	Brand names offer the kudos and confirmation of quality and style. They also provide a feeling of comfort and assurance.

Source: BA, 2002 [online]

Table 5.5

Menu-planning criteria for British Airways' Signature Style

The inspiration for Signature Style has come from culinary circles, trends, fashion, and art, and these have been adapted for delivery and presentation

For First Class
(Chicago–London)

BREAKFAST
Freshly squeezed fruit juice

*Our special wake-up energiser drink

*Fresh seasonal fruit

Breakfast cereal with chilled milk

Natural or fruit yoghurt

Warm breads and breakfast pastries

HOT CHOICES
Your choice of freshly scrambled eggs, pork sausage, grilled bacon, mushrooms, tomatoes and rösti potatoes

Mascarpone and cherry crêpe with orange sauce

APPETISERS
*Alaskan crab and avocado tian

Warm herb-crusted goat cheese, marinated mozzarella and tomato salad

Wild mushroom soup

*Mixed seasonal salad served with balsamic oil or parmesan and black pepper dressing

MAIN COURSES
Grilled fillet of beef
With herb garlic butter, mashed potatoes and seasonal vegetables

*Grilled swordfish
with cilantro lime rice and black bean salsa

Stuffed Portobello mushrooms
on creamed garlic spinach and tomato sauce

LIGHTER OPTIONS
Fish pie with flaky pastry crust

Warm olive oil bread
Filled with smoked turkey and Provolone cheese

Freshly cooked pasta
with your choice of pesto oil or clam sauce
Served with freshly grated Parmesan cheese and garlic bread

DESSERT
Warm pear tartin
With vanilla sauce or vanilla ice cream

*Selection of fresh fruit

CHEESE BOARD SELECTION
TO HELP YOU SLEEP

For Club World

BREAKFAST
Chilled orange juice

*Our special wake-up energiser drink of strawberry and banana

*Selection of seasonal fruit
or
Breakfast muesli with fresh milk

Classic British breakfast of scrambled egg, grilled bacon, pork sausage, mushrooms

Breakfast pizza topped with tomato, egg, mushrooms and Mozzarella cheese

Selection of warm breads and breakfast pastries

Nescafe

Decaffeinated coffee, Tea or Chinese speciality teas

Menu
APPETISERS
*Marinated prawn and scallop salad

or

Feta cheese and corn salsa
with Thai marinated zucchini

*Fresh seasonal salad served with vinaigrette

MAIN COURSES
Grilled fillet of beef
with caramelised shallots and red wine sauce

Stir-fried snapper with celery and steamed rice

Roasted red pepper filled with pesto risotto

*Main course char-grilled chicken Caesar salad

DESSERT
Passion fruit mousse

Selection of cheese and crackers

*Fresh fruit

Nescafe

Decaffeinated coffee
Tea or Chinese speciality teas

Chocolates

For Economy Class
(Taipei–Hong Kong)

Light Meal

Barbecued Pork Loin on spicy Oriental Noodle Salad

Almond jelly with fresh fruit

Coffee or tea

Figure 5.6
Examples of BA flight menus

97

in an aircraft environment. Theoretically, it encompasses fresh, high quality, classic, authentic and innovative dishes to suit each destination, and the passenger profiles. They offer a product that is exciting to the palate, comforting to the mind and body, and consistently deliverable in flight. The purpose is to show the pleasure of eating is more than the sum of the menu, to break the routine of flying within an aircraft, and to draw the passengers' attention to the food. Several examples of BA flight menus are provided to illustrate their concepts being put into practice (Fig. 5.6).

Case study 5.2

Emirates

Since its launch in 1985, the Dubai-based Emirates is one of the fastest growing airlines in the world and has received more than 190 international awards for excellence. For the past three years, Emirates has been voted the best airline in the world by the *Official Airline Guide* (UK). They were also awarded the Airline of the Year award in the 2001 and 2002 Skytrax passenger survey, which was a poll conducted by a UK research company.

Emirates also have been certified as a member of the Leading Airlines of the World 2002. Quality standards are audited on an annual basis to ensure compliance with best practice requirements. In 2002, they were given a four-star rating out of a possible five stars in the Skytrax Offical Airline Rating systems for their product and service delivery standards. Their best points in 2002 were their provision of high quality cabin staff service and excellent first-business-class catering.

Figure 5.7 illustrates a sample of their menus. The menus are multi-cultural cuisine on board and designed by skilled chefs of international repute depending on the flight route. The mission of Emirates' menus is to prepare all meats served according to the Halal method. No pork products are used in the preparation of Emirates' cuisine. The business class has been improved to reach the service level of first class (Rouse, 1999). The hors d'oeuvre selection and the salad bowls are served in the same size as the first class offers. The dessert selection moves to be provided on a service trolley offering a choice of cheeses and a selection of fresh fruits.

Current trends and future developments

The growth of outsourcing and the potential increase in retail sales on board, suggests that there will be continued growth in **branding**. Airlines have used highly identifiable branded goods with regards to duty free goods and alcoholic beverages for many years. Increasingly, branded goods are also being used on tray sets. The natural extension of this, combined with outsourcing, is not to use single branded items but the whole meal. For instance, in the USA passengers are being offered pizza meals from the major pizza restaurant chains. Recently, a British airline has developed a range of sandwiches in collaboration with a major food retailer. Such branding may be even more important if meals are sold on board, as suggested in Chapter 3.

With branding and outsourcing, it is very likely that **packaging** will also develop further. It will start to present the same kind of information that retail

First Class Menu

COCKTAILS WITH CANAPÉS
* * * * *

SEVRUGA CAVIAR
served with traditional accompaniments, sour cream and blinis
ARABIC MEZZE
a selection of traditional Arabic mezze, including labneh with sumak powder stuffed in
cucumber, moutabel, shanklish salad, marinated loubieh in tomato cup, cheese sambousik,
sujuk with haloumi cheese, kibbeh stuffed with ratatouille, coated prawns
SMOKED TANGERINE CHICKEN
thin slices of tangerine-marinated smoked chicken breast, served on lentil salad,
accompanied with zaatar dressing
* * * * *

TOMATO AND OKRA SOUP
spicy tomato soup with baby okra slices, served with toasted croutons
* * * * *
FRESHLY PREPARED SALAD
salad prepared by your crew to your liking with a choice of accompaniments
offered with roasted red pepper mayonnaise or Italian vinaigrette
* * * * *

SAMKA HARRA
marinated fillets of hammour, served with orange flavoured sauce, enhanced with
jalapeno pepper
BRAISED BEEF IN COCONUT MILK
shredded slices of tender beef, braised and served in a coconut sauce,
garnished with cilantro and fried red peppers
GLAZED DUCK BREAST
duck breast glazed with wild forest honey, roasted and accompanied with a
mild cherry sauce
AUBERGINE LASAGNE
layers of spinach pasta and grilled aubergine slices, served with creamy
mozzarella sauce, sprinkled with tomato flavoured pesto sauce
* * * * *

VEGETABLES
creamed fennel, broccoli souffle, mixture of turned vegetables, parisienne
potatoes with herbs and steamed rice
* * * * *

BANANA PUDDING
baked banana and pecan nut pudding, accompanied with half whipped cream
STRAWBERRY CHEESECAKE
traditional home made cheesecake with fresh strawberries
* * * * *

INTERNATIONAL CHEESEBOARD
a selection of international cheeses, served with crackers, grapes and crudites
* * * * *

SELECTION OF SEASONAL FRUITS
* * * * *

TEA
Ceylon, China, Earl Grey, Camomile
* * * * *

COFFEE
freshly brewed or decaffeinated

CHOCOLATES

Business-Class Menu

COCKTAILS
* * * * *

HONEY ROASTED CHINESE DUCK
placed on celery and grilled pineapple salad, drizzled with a citrus dressing
MARINATED ASIAN SEAFOOD
scallops, tiger prawns and poached salmon drizzled with oriental dressing
* * * * *

SEASONAL SALAD
served with a choice of caesar dressing or olive oil vinaigrette
* * * * *

FILLET OF GAROUPA
steamed fillet of garoupa topped with julienne of vegetables served with a light basil sauce
accompanied with buttered broccoli, turned carrots and tagliatelle noodles
BEEF TERIY AKI KEBAB
tender pieces of beef, marinated and cooked in teriyaki sauce, accompanied with
grilled vegetables and gratinated potatoes
THAY STYLE CHICKEN CURRY
tender pieces of chicken in a coconut flavoured curry sauce, served with green beans,
cauliflower and steamed rice roll
* * * * *

WHITE CHOCOLATE AND ORANGE MOUSSE CAKE
light and fluffy mousse cake served on a dark chocolate mirror
PEAR STRUDEL
freshly baked pear strudel, served hot, accompanied with vanilla sauce
* * * * *

INTERNATIONAL CHEESEBOARD
* * * * *

SELECTION OF SEASONAL FRUITS
* * * * *

TEA
Ceylon, China, Earl Grey, Camomile
* * * * *

COFFEE
freshly brewed or decaffeinated
CHOCOLATES

Economy Class

SMOKED TUNA
slices of smoked tuna, served with a marinated vegetable salad
* * * * *

SEASONAL SALAD
served with Spanish dressing
* * * * *

CHICKEN BREAST
grilled chicken breast with caramelised plums, served in a cranberry reduction,
accompanied with mashed potatoes, baby spinach and carrot slices
LAMB BROCHETTE
fillet of lamb marinated in Arabic spices, combined with assorted peppers, charcoal
grilled and served with a cinamon scented sauce, accompanied with broccoli, roasted
baby corn and steamed rice
* * * * *

STICKY DATE PUDDING
a delicious home made dessert, served with caramel sauce
* * * * *

CHEESE AND BISCUITS
* * * * *

TEA OR COFFEE
CHOCOLATES

Figure 5.7
Examples of Emirates' Menus

BROOKLANDS COLLEGE LIBRARY
WEYBRIDGE, SURREY KT13 8TT

products provide in relation to ingredients and nutrition. Packaging may also have to be designed to help assure security. For instance, see through materials may be needed so that the contents can been seen at a glance to ensure only the right items are loaded on board. Likewise packages may need to be sealed to show that they have not been tampered with.

A final consequence of these trends is that the **food development team** may no longer be employed by an airline or even the caterer. The greater involvement of large-scale food manufacturers and suppliers now means that they employ flight-catering specialists who develop their products specifically for this market.

Conclusion

This chapter has given an overview of menu planning and discussed potential strategies to overcome the constraints of serving meals at 30,000 feet. Presenting successful meals in the sky to indulge the various passengers is a challenge as it requires thought as to what types of food hold well for several hours and have good taste and texture upon re-heating.

The specifications on meal, menu, or service should be able to clearly define specific elements of each product and service. To some extent, these specifications can be claimed to be the 'Bible' in not only verifying the pricing agreements with the airline but also in quality control providing detailed information for both caterers preparing and cabin crews to serve the flight experience. Innovation and development of the product are necessary for survival in such a competitive travel business (discussed in Chapter 16).

Key terms

Branding	Meal specification	Menu cycles
Menu design	Menu development	Menu planning
Product performance	Product specification	Service specification
Special meals	Standard recipe	

Discussion questions

1. Discuss the menu considerations in planning an in-flight meal and compare them with a current sample in-flight menu.
2. What is the implication of using component feeding with either RTUs or RTSs toward cost issues?
3. Discuss what the process of new product development can bring to a flight operation.
4. Discuss the complexities of the demand for special meals.
5. Identify the advantages and disadvantages of branding strategies with an example of a product.

References

Anon. (1999) "Why SPML? For a Variety of Reasons, Passengers Pick a Special Meal," *PAX International*, Mar./Apr., 18.

BA. (2002) *A New Food Style for the Millennium*, [online] Available from: http://www.britishairways.com/catering/docs/signature.shtml/ [Accessed 17 Mar. 2003]

Baker, J. (2000) "Sky-high Standards," *Caterer & Hotelkeeper*, vol. 188, no. 4131, 30–31.

Bell, P. (1997) "Sky Dining," *Gourmet*, vol. 57, no. 10, 132–145.

Bowen, J.T. and Morris, A.J. (1995) "Menu Design: Can Menu's Sell?," *International Journal of Contemporary Hospitality Management*, vol. 7, no. 4, 4–9.

Caira, R. (1995) "Non-traditional Foodservice: Flying High," *Foodservice and Hospitality* vol. 28, no. 7, 65–70.

Frank, P. (2000) "Sky Meals," *Food Product Design,* vol. 10, no. 1, 107–115.

Gilbert, D. (1999), *Retail Marketing Management*, Pearson Education Limited: Harlow, Essex.

Hafner, K. (2001) Interview with the Food constancy for the British Airways, Unpublished.

Henderson, D. (1998) "Food Trends in the Americas," *IFCA/IFSA Review*, 1[3], vol. 14, no. 46, 11–12.

International Air Transport Association. (2001) *In-flight Management Manual*, 1st edn, International Air Transport Association: Montreal.

Lundstrom, R. (2001) "For a Special Group: US Airways Revamps SPML Lineup," *PAX International*, vol. 5, no. 5, 40–42.

Mifli, M. and Jones, P. (2001) "Menu Analysis in Foodservice Chains," *Tourism and Hospitality Research: Surrey Quarterly Review.* vol. 3, no. 1, 61–71.

Mooney, S. (1994) "Planning and Designing the Menu," in *The Management of Foodservice Operations: An integrated and innovative approach to catering management*, Jones, P. and Merricks, P. Eds, Cassell: London, 45–58.

Porter, M.E. (1990) *The Competitive Advantage of Nations*, Macmillan: London.

Rouse, P. (1999) "Gulf Carriers Seek High-Tech Solutions, Update Menu," *PAX International*, Nov./Dec., 14–16.

Sutton, A. and Gostelow, M. (1997) "Special Meal Appeal," *Hospitality Industry International*, vol. 17, 14–16.

Terpstra, V.C. and Sarathy, R. (1994) *International Marketing*, 6th edn, The Dryden Press: Fort Worth, Texas.

Flight catering supply chain and inventory management

- Understand the role of food and drink manufacturers
- Identify purchasing procedures and supplier relationships
- Understand role of purchase specifications
- Identify how goods are received and stored
- Understand the principles of inventory management

Introduction

The supply chain as a concept is relatively new. But some suggest that the concept is already outdated, for two reasons. First, it is more appropriate from a business perspective to think of these relationships and flows between organisations as a 'value chain' (Porter, 1995). Second, the notion of a 'chain' is too simplistic; in reality, supplier relationships are typically a complex network. In view of this we will consider the flight catering supply chain as an integrated network for the flow of physical goods from suppliers to flight production units, made up of stages which should maximise the value-added content. From this we can identify a number of issues which need to be managed:

- ordering and specification of products from suppliers
- physical handling, distribution, delivery and receipt of products
- identification of value-added elements
- holding of inventory to buffer against uncertainty
- minimising stock levels to reduce storage costs, avoid waste, and help cash flow
- integrating activity and building relationships across a network

A specific aspect of the flight-catering industry is that both airlines and caterers order from suppliers, but that all, or nearly all, products are delivered to the caterer's production facility. It is then the caterer's role to deliver products to the aircraft. So a flight production unit will hold its own stock in stores, as well as stock owned by the airlines for which it has a contract. In many cases, airlines purchase their alcoholic beverage products directly from suppliers or distributors which are then delivered to bonded stores in flight production units. But airlines may also directly purchase other items for use or consumption on aircraft, such as soft drinks, paper products like napkins, and so on.

Increasingly, supply chain management is linked closely to inventory management, as operations try to reduce their stock-holdings and rely on just-in-time (JIT) delivery. This has cash flow benefits for the business and also potentially reduces the capital investment costs in storage facilities. But even with JIT, flight caterers are still required to ensure safe and secure storage of all types of materials in their production units.

Role of food and drink manufacturers

Adapting existing or developing new products

Food and drink manufacturers must continuously seek to develop and expand their business if they are to survive, and this can be achieved in a number of ways. First, they could extend their customer base with additional outlets. Second, they could retain the existing number of customers while at the same time extend the market share of their products offered. Third, they could adopt both courses of action. In the latter two courses of action, food and drink manufacturers must develop new product lines or modify and improve existing product ranges (see also Chapter 16). This they can do in isolation and offer the new or revised products to the flight caterer and airline. However, for the manufacturer this is potentially risky, as the airline or caterer may not like the product; it can also be very expensive. Most manufacturers prefer to work in conjunction with customers to develop jointly a range of new or improved products. In doing so, manufacturers have two distinct customers to whom they need to sell their products. Not only do they need to sell the product to the flight caterer, they must also sell it to the airline. This aspect is perhaps unique in this industry and has evolved for a number of reasons. Airlines, in many instances, wish to use various products as part of their branding strategies and are therefore involved at an early stage in the selection of suppliers and manufacturers. The airlines might also wish to negotiate larger discounts or, where they have other subsidiary interests, ensure that those interests have a higher priority and are used in preference to others. This means that many flight caterers are required to work with products that have been developed and selected by somebody other than themselves, and perhaps would not normally have been preferred or chosen by them.

Manufacturers need then to develop, sell to and keep satisfied two distinct customers—the caterer and the airline—both of whom may have competing or differing interests. In order to achieve this careful balance, many manufacturers need to go to considerable lengths to provide products that satisfy both customers. They might need to develop and offer products which are either unique or perhaps have been branded to provide a degree of product differentiation.

When seeking to develop a new product, manufacturers need to consider a number of additional factors that would not normally be considered in the product development process for other commercial catering outlets. The difficulties associated with flight provision, described here and elsewhere, need to be addressed. For example, the nature and type of the treatment that the products are likely to be subjected to must be taken into consideration. Products need to be able to withstand processing, chilling, transportation, and being held for some time before being reheated and consumed. The product, therefore, must be suitable for the particular process and conditions that it is likely to be subjected to. Commodities that are difficult to transport or that are adversely affected by changes in pressure, for example, would render themselves unsuitable for flight provision. The confined space in which food and drink are held requires that items and packaging conform to specified dimensions. The size of the space available for storage and consumption must also be considered.

Supplier responsibilities and provision

The role of the flight suppliers is to provide the flight caterers with goods and services of a consistent and uniform standard and quality, according to specifications that have been agreed by both the caterers and the airlines. Suppliers have a number of responsibilities that are legal or contractual and also have moral connotations. These responsibilities are applicable to the airline, the flight provider and the fare-paying passenger. Furthermore, suppliers have an obligation to provide and assist in the flow of accurate and timely information which in turn for them makes good business sense.

Many of the responsibilities of the supplier in the provision of goods and services have already been agreed and are contained in the *Airline Catering*

Code of Good Practice (Airline Caterers Technical Coordination Committee, 1990) which requires that:

"All materials must be purchased from reputable suppliers with acceptable hygiene standards. Suppliers' premises and processes should be inspected by competent persons reporting to the catering company, to ensure that satisfactory standards of hygiene are maintained."

A number of other points also addressed in the *Airline Catering Code of Good Practice* include:

"Raw materials should be of specified good quality. As a minimum standard, specifications will detail product attributes that can be checked at delivery:

Essential	Delivery temperature
	Date marking (appropriate to the product)
	General conditions good, no evidence of defrosting or similar deterioration
Recommended	Packaging standards
	Microbiological specifications (particularly for high-risk foods). Agreement of residual shelf-life at delivery
Temperature criteria	
Chilled Group 1	Most microbiologically sensitive. Prescribed temperature 5°C or colder
Chilled Group 2	Microbiologically sensitive. Prescribed temperature 8°C or colder
Frozen Food	−18°C or colder

Purchasing of flight consumables and non-consumables

The volume of food purchases in the international airline catering industry can be quite considerable. In the USA, purchases of food for flight catering operations, excluding alcoholic beverages, was calculated for 1992 as $916 m (£610 m.), a rise in real terms of 3 per cent over the previous year (Anon, 1992). In Europe, purchases of food items are on a similar scale and examples of the airlines' purchases are given in Table 6.1.

When considering the purchasing and sourcing of flight consumables and non-consumables, many factors over and above those associated with conventional catering operations need to be considered.

Indigenous products Passengers flying their own national carriers invariably like and expect to see indigenous foods on those flights. Therefore, German-style food would be expected and usually supplied on Lufthansa flights originating from Germany; Aer Lingus would expect to source 90 per cent of its supplies in Ireland (O'Meara, 1993). Similarly, some passengers fly a national carrier partly because they like or prefer that style of food. Product differentiation within the catering provision in this instance could clearly be used to attract customers to the airline. In addition, it has been suggested that where countries

Food items	Amount	Caterer	
		Gate Gourmet[1]	BA Centre[2]
Beef tenderloin	Kg	90,000	–
Beef sirloin	Kg	34,000	–
Veal	Kg	196,500	–
Lamb	Kg	9,890	127,000
Poultry	Kg	140,115	–
Fish	Kg	90,000	–
Seafood	Kg	57,000	–
Salmon	Kg	–	68,326
Potatoes	Kg	120,000	–
Vegetables	Kg	245,300	–
Butter	Kg	109,500	–
Cream	Kg	116,500	–
Flour	kg	340,000	66,540
Sugar	Kg	–	10,668
Eggs	No.	–	4,121,550
Coca Cola	Cn		2,868,728

SOURCES: 1. Swissair Catering Company (June 1993)
2. British Airways Catering Centre South

Table 6.1
Examples of airline flight catering purchases in Europe

have a major influence over their national carrier, the carrier is obliged, for political-economic reasons, to serve exclusively products from that country.
Sensitive products On some flights the origin and nature of the product must be considered in relation to the flight destination. In general, the airline would be strongly advised to take cognisance of the dominant political, religious and cultural influences of the region in which flights occur.

Supplier relationships

There are certain important factors involved in a successful working relationship with suppliers. Both parties have responsibilities that must be carried out to assure proper food safety and quality.

Reid and Riegal (1988) surveyed the selection criteria and relationships of large-scale foodservice organisations with their suppliers. Most of the 61 organisations surveyed were company-owned retail restaurant chains; hence 60 per cent of the respondents operated more than 100 units. Others were institutional food service operators—both private and government—and hotel food service operators. Nearly three-quarters of the respondents reported average unit sales of over $500,000 per year. The research showed that about 40 per cent of the food service organisations used 100 or fewer suppliers, while 20 per cent used over 500 annually. Operators with larger annual sales had a larger number of suppliers. It made no difference if the organisation was a retail, hotel or institutional food service. There is evidence to suggest that the findings from this study would apply equally well to flight catering firms.

The study investigated the basis on which the foodservice organisations selected their suppliers. Respondents were given a list of 20 supplier characteristics and asked to rate their importance. The six most important characteristics, across all types of organisation, that were identified were:

- accuracy of filling orders
- consistent quality level
- on-time delivery
- willingness to work together to resolve problems
- willingness to respond in a 'pinch'
- reasonable unit cost

Institutional food service operators and the larger firms (probably flight caterers too) were also concerned about:

- reasonable minimum orders
- volume discounts
- frequency of delivery
- payment policies

Good supplier relations take some time to establish. The survey asked operators how many new suppliers they had added in the past year. All the organisations, especially government food service, reported an increase in the use of new suppliers. This is due to a wide range of factors, including the product range and geographical growth of the food service firms themselves. There was also growth in the use of international suppliers, particularly among larger firms and hotel and retail foodservice organisations. Only the largest food service firms—about 10 per cent of the sample—actually visited more than three-quarters of their suppliers. This practice may not be necessary on an annual basis if firms have long-established relationships with their suppliers.

Supplier negotiation

The basis of satisfactory negotiation is that both parties feel happy about the deal they have struck. In Chapter 2, the nature of the tendering process between caterer and airline was discussed and illustrated in Fig. 2.2. A similar process may also be followed between suppliers and caterers or between suppliers and airlines. The negotiation can be formal through a process of inviting tenders and reviewing bids, or informal by simply asking a range of suppliers to quote prices. Successful negotiation gets a supplier to agree on a lower price for a specified quality. Most suppliers' methods of setting price allow some margin for negotiation, but there is always a price below which the supplier will not go.

Suppliers are more likely to negotiate a price if they recognise that the catering manager is really price conscious. This price consciousness is prevalent in the flight-catering sector which operates with very tight profit margins. This supports the caterer's negotiating stance, helping to obtain the best possible price. The high profile nature of the airline business and access to specific market segments also means that suppliers may be keen for their products, especially if clearly branded, to be used by airlines, further assisting the negotiation of a lower or discounted price. Even if suppliers cannot reduce prices further, caterers may be able to negotiate more favourable credit terms or extend payment schedules. Alternatively, discounts may be agreed upon for bulk purchases or prompt payment.

In the Reid and Riegal study (1988), firms were asked how they managed good supplier relations and how they ensured accurate supply and on-time delivery. The most frequently employed practice was through prompt payment, reasonable requests, and shared cost data. As we will see in Chapter 12, the latest internet-based technology is enabling the development of integrated systems that make the sharing of data between suppliers and caterers relatively easy.

Supplier responsibilities during recalls and investigations

Any food safety problem must be notified to the flight caterer as well as possible problems being investigated by regulatory officials. All suspected products under investigation must be immediately recalled. Suppliers, therefore, are expected to have recall procedures in place. Products should have lot numbers that identify specific time periods in processes, or coded in such a way that makes identification easy. In addition to coding on cases, individual packages must be coded where applicable. Open coding systems are preferable, i.e. systems that are simple to understand by anyone, since they can also assist with stock rotation. The supplier typically will have a designated recall officer, who will be the focal point for information during a recall. They also have detailed contingency plans for recalling their own products. These plans identify key personnel and establish appropriate means of communication. All suppliers must have adequate means by which products can be retrieved quickly.

Supplier audits

It is essential that the flight caterers audit their suppliers. Hygiene and sanitation inspections should be both announced and unannounced. The sanitation guidelines used for these inspectors will either be those from the appropriate regulatory agency, e.g. Food Act and Regulations in UK, the Food and Drug Administration (FDA) in the US or the United States Department of Agriculture (USDA), or those sanitary guidelines laid down by the flight caterer.

These inspections should be seen as positive arrangements inviting opportunities to discuss quality aspects of provision and also those aspects of provision, concerns, and requirements the flight caterer has on behalf of the airline. Feedback should also be obtained from the supplier on how the products are being used and how they are performing. The flight caterer may well discover that certain products are not being used to the best advantage. Advice can then be given on the best possible ways forward. Therefore, any inspection should be seen as a friendly exchange of information to improve the understanding of the products being supplied.

A production plant official may well accompany the flight food safety audit and be willing to answer all relevant questions concerning the products they buy. Any sanitation-related documents or records should be made available on request. These should include complaint files, recall procedures, hazard analysis and critical control point (HACCP) documents, and any microbiological test reports. A written report for both parties should follow the inspection (see also Chapter 9).

Purchasing specifications

Purchase specifications determine what is required in relation to purchases. They can vary greatly in relation to the depth of information they contain. This depends on who and where the information is destined to be used. For example, there is little benefit in a back door purchase specification revealing the expected microbiological standard of the product being supplied, as there is no way of checking it. The level of detail required is dependent on numerous factors, such as the country of origin, the nature of the product, the shelf life, the level of risk associated with the product, how the product will be used, and who is utilising the information contained in the specification, for example, is it the manufacturer, the wholesaler, supplier, the airline, the caterer, the receiver, or someone dealing with quality assurance questions.

Purchase specifications come in a number of different forms: food, non-food, contract, and service. Food purchase specifications may contain information on the quality, ingredients, size, variety, condition, weight, packaging, labelling, shelf life, storage conditions, order lead time of a food product, and include technical specification elements that have the most detail including information on microbiological specification, process standards, HACCP limits, and nutritional information. Supplier specifications outline, for example, what the supplier does, products supplied, locations, contacts, order considerations, lead times, safety inventory, whether the product is delivered frozen, ambient, chilled, or fresh, and the delivery schedule, audit results and vendor rating assessments.

The suppliers must be aware of what is expected of the product. They must also make sure that the flight caterers are aware of any food safety limitations associated with the product. These are usually stated on all labelling. Such statements may simply say 'keep refrigerated' or 'keep frozen'; others might well include a graph or chart of the projected shelf-life at different storage temperatures. Some of the expectations of a product's level of quality or safety may be dictated by airline specifications and these are, generally, found in the catering manual for that airline. The responsibility for meeting those specifications is an important factor in a successful catering operation. Some food items may have no listed specifications but might be covered by a federal or local regulatory mandate.

Inventory management

Once goods have been delivered to the flight kitchen they need to be stored safely and securely. McCool (1996) suggests that "inventory management is one of the greatest challenges facing an in-flight caterer". There are a number of reasons for this:

- airlines operate menu cycles (see Chapter 5); so, ingredients and products are changing regularly
- caterers are likely to have contracts with several airlines, each of which is likely to have different product specifications
- product specifications are rigid to ensure airlines have consistent products on all their routes; so, substitution by a similar item is rarely possible
- meeting product specifications will be part of the airline–caterer contract; so, stock-outs may lead to penalty payments or even loss of the contract
- on the other hand, holding too much stock adds costs to the business and is detrimental to the cash flow
- airlines purchase some items directly from the manufacturer and pay the caterer to store them in the flight production unit; so, stock has to be held separately to enable stock checks

Just-in-time procurement

In deciding how to control purchases of materials stocks, three standards need to be established: quality standards, quantity standards, and prices. Quality standards derive largely from the decisions made about the concept and service or production standards. The concept determines the basic cost–price relationship, the technology to be used for production purposes, and the customer expectations about quality. The most basic decision that will be made is whether to 'make or buy', i.e. to produce on the premises or buy-in items prepared elsewhere. Once this decision is made, there are still decisions to be made in regard to grades, brands, degree of freshness, sizes, and method of packaging. Each of these factors may be in the standard purchase specifications.

In addition, it is essential to establish the required quantities of items. The ideal stock level for a specific commodity depends on the nature of the business and the characteristics of the commodity; in particular, the level of sales, the stability of demand, the terms of supply, the costs of stock-holding, cash flow limitations, the shelf-life of the commodity, the storage space available, and market trends in price and availability. The characteristics of the flight catering industry mean that purchase quantities are established in a way which is different from other catering businesses.

In general, the starting point for planning stock levels would be an analysis of the usage rate. Where items are used infrequently (which is often the case with non-perishable commodities), the **periodic order method** can be used. On a regular basis, for instance, once a week or once a month, items will be reordered on the basis of the forecast need plus the buffer stock to avoid stock-out less stock in hand. A more sophisticated approach is based around the idea of **economic order quantity** (EOQ). The total cost associated with a purchase is a combination of the invoice cost, plus the administration cost (postage, clerical time, etc.) plus the storage cost (running the freezer, etc.). These costs will vary, as shown in Table 6.2. Somewhere between the extremes of one large order and very many small orders lies the point where the total cost will be lowest. The EOQs can be calculated using mathematical formulae or by preparing

	Invoice cost	Administration cost	Storage costs
Many small orders	High	High	Low
Few large orders	Low	Low	High

Table 6.2
Effect of purchase order size on purchase costs

cost tables. Either method is laborious and time-consuming, and the useful application of EOQs is limited to very large-scale purchasing.

The quantity ordered can also get affected by concerns about cash flow and storage costs, which in turn are affected by the extent to which items are purchased in bulk. The advantages of buying in bulk are that items may be cheaper because of bulk discount; there may be protection against a sudden increase in demand, protection against sudden shortage in supply, and protection against possible inflation. The disadvantages of buying in bulk include the fact the cash flow position worsens; stock-holding costs increase; deterioration or pilferage may occur; and future demand may decrease. In the case of fresh food the disadvantages obviously outweigh the advantages. With other products the reverse can hold true, for example, wine which can appreciate in value considerably during the storage period.

However, while the flight catering industry is concerned about stock-outs, cash flow, storage costs, and administration costs, caterers now think of inventory as just one part of the total process flow through their production unit. As the system is now being organised on the just-in-time principle (see Chapter 8), inventory management is also operated in this way. In other words, as far as possible suppliers are asked to supply materials as and when they are needed by the operation. JIT is a 'pull system' based on the logic that nothing will be produced until it is needed; which means food production at all stages is firmly linked to a rate determined by the final product assembly schedule, such as the number of trays and choices per flight. JIT production planning for flight caterers equates to 'producing the necessary units, in the necessary quantities, at the necessary time'. Most successful caterers use this technique, in concept, if not in name. The principles to be adhered to are:

- keep down stock levels to an optimum (stockless production) level
- elimination of waste and unnecessary activities
- enforced problem solving
- quality at the source
- clarify process flows
- develop supplier network

Materials (food) delivered 'just in time' are required to be absolutely correct. When the allocation for the day is complete, production stops. Inventory is not built up in order to keep the workers busy. Any spare time is spent at the end of the shift to review the day's production and to develop priorities for action.

The system itself is simple and its objectives easy to understand. Quality must be inherent both in the product and the process and therefore employee commitment is vital for this to happen. By its nature JIT procurement means that the stock held is kept to a minimum, which assists the cash flow. It also means that less storage space is required, storage costs are low, and materials are always fresh. There is a danger of stock-out if a supplier fails to deliver, which means that it is essential for the caterer to forecast their requirements and place their orders accurately, as well as select suppliers that can be relied upon.

Receipt of goods inwards

Usually a separate delivery entry is used to unload goods from delivery vehicles. The bay normally has a high-level platform to allow direct delivery from the back of delivery vehicles (see Chapter 7). This area leads into a goods reception area that allows for the temporary storage, checking and unpacking of all delivered materials before they are allocated either to the appropriate store or directly to a production area.

Universally, the general manager of any flight kitchen is ultimately responsible for assuring that the following responsibilities are carried out:

- All incoming supplies must be checked for hygienic delivery and condition by a trained person
- All supplies not meeting specified minimum hygiene conditions, temperatures, quality, weight, and grades must be rejected. All other discrepancies must be noted and brought to the vendor's attention
- All deliveries must be checked against the purchase and receiving logs. Vendor shipping documents must be corrected to show any discrepancy in quantity
- Upon delivery, all potentially hazardous food must be refrigerated first
- All food items received in cases or in bulk must be stamped so that their receiving dates are known. All supplies must be stored and used with the first in, first out system
- Records must be maintained showing the date of receipt and all other pertinent information such as batch numbers, lot numbers, production dates or use-by dates of items, such as local bakery products, milk products, and other locally prepared foods. These records are important in case of a later problem or recall

Flight food supplies can be subjected to extremes of temperature, time delays, and zero humidity conditions on board before consumption. Therefore, suppliers of potentially hazardous foods should be able to supply upon request such data as:

- the maximum refrigerated shelf-life at 7.2°C
- the maximum allowable time at 12.7°C
- the maximum allowable time at 21°C

These times must be based on the outgrowth of pathogenic organisms that are of significance to their product (see also Chapter 9).

Suppliers of potentially hazardous foods must ensure that any hidden hazards are known to their flight customers. Some examples of hidden hazards are as follows:

- A pop-out meal that contains partially cooked chicken. The on-board cooking of the chicken to 73°C would not be a readily apparent critical control point
- Frozen vegetables that have been blanched but not completely cooked. Possible temperature abuse by employees who might mistake them for raw vegetables could allow the growth of pathogenic bacteria
- Any products containing raw shell eggs as an ingredient. A cooking temperature of at least 73.8°C would be required
- Any gas-packed or vacuum-packed product that can support anaerobic growth of *Clostridium botulinum* if temperature is abused
- Any *sous-vide* product. The suggested refrigeration storage temperature of 1°C is not commonly attainable with existing flight equipment
- Any packaged, potentially hazardous product that will support the growth of pathogenic psychrophilic bacteria at a refrigeration temperature of 7.2°C or below. The time under refrigeration would be a critical control point. For such items as precooked meats that receive no further cooking, the time under refrigeration prior to delivery could be a critical control point if the storage temperature was above 1°C

To enable the storesperson to ensure all of these things, they may be provided with copies of purchase specifications (often in the form of a manual), copies of the original order, price lists, scales (to weigh goods), temperature probes (for checking refrigerated items), a calculator, a jemmy (for opening wooden or cardboard containers), a knife (for cutting into fresh produce such as fruit), and even a bar code reader (if there is a computerised inventory control system). And so that the stores person has time to properly inspect goods, supply is often organised so that deliveries are only made during specified hours and staggered to ensure that only one is dealt with at a time.

The paperwork or documentation that accompanies a delivery is typically of two types. In some cases, goods are delivered with an **invoice** which not only lists the goods but also prices them, in other words it serves not only as a checklist but also as the bill. In the flight catering industry it is more common for the order to be supplied along with a **delivery note**, which is an unpriced list of goods. In such cases, the supplier issues an invoice separately, sometimes on a weekly or monthly basis, often covering more than one delivery. Whichever system is in use, the stores person will be asked to sign a copy for the receipt of the goods. If they are not satisfied, that goods of the correct type or quality have been delivered, they may be rejected. This may mean that the delivery note is adjusted to show goods as returned, or in the case of invoiced delivery, a credit note will be completed by the delivery person to ensure correct invoicing subsequently.

Once the goods have been received and the paperwork completed, it is essential that the goods are moved to their appropriate storage space as soon as possible. Depending on the size of operation, trolleys, carts, conveyor belts, or fork-lift trucks may be used for this purpose. Swift transportation ensures that goods, especially chilled or frozen products, do not deteriorate and that they are placed in a more secure area than the loading bay. In some cases, at this stage, the stores person may also have to date the delivered items (to ensure stock rotation), price items, apply tags to meat, or even add bar codes.

It is important to remove as much outer packaging as possible outside the kitchen area as the packaging can bring soil, bacteria, and insects into the kitchen. Items such as fruit and vegetables are decanted from crates and boxes, and placed in plastic containers. Glass containers are emptied or replaced with plastic containers before storing in the unit to prevent breakage during the cooking process. For operations which produce large amounts of bakery products, flour may be delivered in bulk and transferred pneumatically into storage silos. For frozen items, it is vital, both for reasons of quality and hygiene, that products are thawed in a temperature-controlled environment. Thawing items in a warm room will encourage the growth of pathogens and cause the structure of the items to break down reducing texture and quality.

While it is regrettable, malpractice at this stage is not unknown. There are a great many ways in which fraud or theft can be carried out by an unscrupulous supplier or a dishonest delivery person. A skilled stores operative should check to see that:

- the quality of goods, such as fresh fruit, is as good in all the layers of a box, and not rely on inspecting just the top layer
- tins and packages are undamaged or 'blown'
- product weights have not been increased by adding excess water, packaging, ice, or some other impurity (such as stones in bags of fresh potatoes)
- the delivery person does not illicitly remove items from the loading bay or stores area, especially when goods or packaging (such as empty crates or boxes) are being returned

Of course, some problems may be the result of an unintentional error. Where such problems occur regularly or malpractice is discovered, management are well advised to change the supplier.

Storage areas

Specialised storage areas are required for a wide range of food and non-food materials. Some require a separate temperature-controlled storage area in either a freezer or fridge. Bonded items like alcohol and duty-free goods require a specific area with extra security. Food materials generally include:

- fresh fruit and vegetables
- frozen fruit and vegetables
- fresh fish/seafood
- frozen fish/seafood
- raw meats
- cooked meats
- dairy products
- dry goods
- bonded alcoholic beverages

All storage areas should be cool and well ventilated, screened against insects, and fitted with easily cleaned shelves and bins. The storage of non-consumables is relatively straightforward, as they typically may be stored under normal conditions, at ambient temperature. Some cleaning agents must be stored in well-ventilated areas to avoid the build up of toxic fumes and kept separate from each other to avoid the possibility of a chemical reaction.

Consumables, on the other hand, may require a variety of different storage conditions depending on their perishability or 'shelf-life', i.e. the length of time they may be stored safely without deterioration. Dry goods, such as canned foods, packet items, and jars are stored like non-consumables, under ambient or cool, well-ventilated conditions. Perishable items such as dairy products, fresh meat and fish, and fruit and vegetables need to be refrigerated. Chilling reduces enzyme action and bacterial growth, which either cause the food to deteriorate or allow pathogens or poisons to grow on the food, or both. Frozen products obviously have to be kept in a freezer.

Dry stores

There are three main ways in which dry goods, either consumables or non-consumables, may be stored: shelved, binned, or palletised.

Shelving is used for items that are individually packed in some way, such as packets, jars or cans. There are three types of shelving. Fixed shelving is permanently fixed to the wall or floor; static shelving is self-standing on legs; and mobile shelving is self-standing but on wheels or casters. All types of shelving are made either from wood or metal, sometimes covered with plastic. It is important that these materials are easily cleaned.

Bins are used to store items that may be delivered in paper or cardboard containers but need to be protected from infestation either by insects or rodents. Typically flour and rice are stored in this way. The bin comprises a large metal container, often on castors, with a firmly fitting lid. The term 'bin' is also used to describe how bottled wine is stored.

Palletised storage occurs in very large-scale operations. A pallet is a wooden platform that can easily be moved by a forklift truck on which goods are stored in bulk, usually in boxes or cases. In flight catering this approach is used, linked to decanted bins, ready for use as part of the JIT production process.

Refrigerated storage

Chillers are designed to hold stored materials at a temperature of between 1°C and 3°C, whereas freezers hold frozen goods at a temperature of −20°C.

There are two main types of chiller or freezer unit used for storage (other forms of unit such as display chillers and coolers are discussed elsewhere)- self-standing cabinets or walk-in. **Cabinet chillers** or **freezers** have a front opening door with interior shelving. They are versatile since they can be located anywhere in the storage area (of the food production unit) and are relatively low cost to buy and maintain.

Walk-in chillers or freezers are usually made from urathene foam 10 cm thick sandwiched between two sheets of metal, such as unpainted or painted aluminium, steel or stainless steel. Units are either prefabricated from panels of standard sizes or built in situ. Prefabricated units are less costly to install than purpose-built chillers, but the latter can have a longer working life. The refrigeration system, which comprises a condenser, evaporator and expansion valve, may be mounted on top of the unit, if the ceiling height permits; or on the side of the unit; or remotely, in some other area of the building or the exterior. Remote refrigeration systems are less efficient but have the advantage that the heat and noise of the system is moved away from the working area.

The net capacity of a walk-in unit is considerably less, roughly 50 per cent, than its total cubic capacity, as space has to be left for a person to access stored items. This usually means that items are stored on either side of the chiller, with an aisle down the middle running from the door to the back of the unit. Further space may also be unuseable due to fans, evaporators, lights, and so on. Despite this, large walk-in chillers are considerably cheaper to operate than several cabinet chillers. Borsenik and Stutts (1997) cite an example of one walk-in that stores 900 kg of food, being the equivalent of five single compartment cabinet chillers, but it is over eight times less expensive to operate.

The efficiency of operating and maintaining refrigerated storage is affected by many factors:

- **Amount of insulation** Over time door seals and rubber 'grommets' may wear and lead to tiny but continuous leaks
- **Efficiency of air flow** Fans assist airflow to ensure a consistent temperature throughout the unit
- **Items stored in the unit** Any item placed in the unit that is above the temperature of the refrigerated space will raise the overall temperature in the unit
- **Number of doors and frequency of opening** Normal usage is assumed to be six to eight openings per 8-hour shift. Heavy usage (12 openings or more) increases the heat load by 50 per cent (Borsenik and Stutts, 1997). If units are subject to heavy usage, plastic strip doors may reduce heat gain by up to one-third
- **Surrounding environment** Refrigeration should not be placed near sources of heat, including direct sunlight. Energy savings can be achieved if walk-in chillers and/or freezers are located adjacent to each other (by 6 per cent according to Borsenik and Stutts, 1997) or if access to the freezer is through the chiller (by nearly 19 per cent)
- **Efficiency of the evaporator** As this is cold, air moisture will freeze on it making it less efficient. Most units have an automatic defrost of this component every 12 hours, either using a hot gas defrost system or electric resistance wires

Safe and secure storage

The basic aim of the storage system is to ensure no loss of value in goods purchased. Such losses may be of two types, spoilage or theft.

Spoilage can be prevented by adherence to some basic principles, as follows.

- *Stock rotation*—goods are used in sequence, the older items first, to ensure that they are consumed while still in prime condition.
- *Stock separation*—goods that might contaminate each other, even if just by odour (such as fish tainting dairy products), must be stored separately, if not in their own fridge, at least in sealed containers on separate shelves.
- *Sanitation*—to avoid cross-contamination, both the store areas must be kept clean and stores operatives must comply with good hygiene practices.
- *Temperature monitoring*—the temperature in each main type of storage area— ambient, chilled, and frozen—must be monitored to ensure it is maintained correctly, and if a fault is detected it must be repaired immediately.
- *Safe handling*—items must be handled and transported safely to avoid breakages.
- *Prevention of infestation*—insects and rodents must be prevented from entering storage areas through the maintenance of floors, walls, and ceilings, the closures and screens on windows and doors, and specific equipment such as ultra-violet fly killers.

In the flight catering industry a HACCP system is often adopted to ensure food safety, as discussed in full in Chapter 9.

The **security** of goods can be threatened by anyone who gains access to the stores. The best way to ensure good security is to employ honest workers, select honest suppliers, and design the physical storage area to be totally secure. In most cases, further control systems are put in place in order to deter, prevent or detect dishonest practice (as well as aid financial control of the business and prevent spoilage). Security systems include:

- *Bar codes*—In flight catering, the computerisation of inventory control through the use of bar codes, has made it possible to have a 'perpetual inventory'
- *Stock-taking*—This is the physical alternative to perpetual inventory, i.e. maintaining a physical count of all stock items on a regular basis. The main purpose of this is to calculate the cost of raw materials (and identify any wastage or loss of materials). It also provides information about what needs to be ordered and enables a crosscheck against records and budgets. Physically taking stock can be time consuming and labour intensive. It typically involves one person counting the stock and a second person recording the information on a standard stock record form. Hence, operators have to choose between their need for timely and accurate stock information and the cost of collecting the data. It is typically done at least once a month, and more frequently in high-volume operations or for high-value stock items. In flight production units, stock may be counted by employees of the caterer or by the airline sent in by the airline to check on the stock held in storage for them
- *Locks and keys*—Another obvious security measure is to ensure that goods are stored in a space that is locked when not in use. In many cases, goods are only issued from stores at limited times of the day, say the first thing in the morning and mid-afternoon. This is so that they can be kept secure for the rest of the time. Only authorised individuals should be issued with keys

and locks should be replaced if keys go missing. For a higher level of security, it is now possible to install computerised locks that record who used the lock

- *Rubbish compactors*—Storage areas produce a large amount of paper waste in the form of cardboard boxes and packaging materials. In order to prevent the 'scam' of stealing items, secreting them in waste bins, and then retrieving once the bins have been placed outside the premises, a waste compactor may be used. The also facilitates waste handling and recycling (see also Chapter 15)
- *Employee entrance security*—All flight catering operations should have a single entrance for use by employees. This entrance will typically be staffed by a member of the security team, whose role is to ensure only authorised personnel are allowed access to the building, as well as monitor what is being brought into or taken out of the premises. This is to ensure security for aircraft in flight as well as in the production unit itself
- *Premises surveillance*—While access to storage area should always be limited and controlled, a further deterrent is provided by the use of closed circuit television (CCTV). This provides a 24-hour record of all personnel movements

Stock valuation and stocktaking

Just-in-time inventory management greatly assists in stock control and stock-taking is simplified by the fact that stock levels are kept to a minimum. Stock-taking therefore tends to be applied in this system only to items that are stored in bulk or for relatively long periods, such as alcoholic beverages. Once the stock has been counted, it also has to be valued, in order to reconcile it with the value of goods purchased and sold. The choice of valuation method, particularly in times of rapid inflation, can have significant implications for profit and asset reporting. There are four methods of stock valuation, which can be summarised as:

- FIFO (first-in, first-out)—which tends to give the highest value to stocks and to inflate profits
- LIFO (last-in, first out)—which tends to undervalue stocks, with a more realistic profit valuation
- AVERAGE—which tends to overvalue stocks and consequently overstates profit; it has the advantage of being administratively convenient
- STANDARD—which is a sophisticated technique forming the basis for a comprehensive cost control system

These stock valuation methods can all be used for the valuation of issues from stores. The use of any one of these methods facilitates the preparation of a stores reconciliation which will accurately identify any loss (possibly through pilferage) from the stores. Computer-based stock control systems can utilise one or another of these methods.

There is an alternative method of stock valuation which is administratively far simpler and which is commonly used in many foodservice businesses. This is to value stock using the most recent price paid for a commodity—also known as the current price. There is a significant disadvantage associated with the use of this current stock valuation method, namely that it does not permit an accurate stores reconciliation to be prepared. Managers can choose a more complex method of stock valuation which permits accurate measurement of stores losses or a simpler (and cheaper) method of valuation and forfeit an accurate control over the stores.

Investigating stock control problems

Stock-taking serves a number of purposes. First, it establishes the value of stock according to one of the methods described above. Second, stock-taking compares the actual value of the stock held with the value of the stock calculated from the stock record system. This enables the actual food cost or profit percentage to be established for comparison with the target, if necessary. If there is a discrepancy between the target food cost and the actual food cost, but no physical stock discrepancy, this is likely to be a policy variance or a production control problem. The manager needs to carry out a systematic investigation into the causes of the problem (see also Chapter 8).

If there is a difference between stock records and actual stock, this is a **stock variance**. Stock shortages may be due to 'ghost' supplies, poor stock rotation, breakages or usage, unauthorised consumption on the premises, or theft. The so-called **'ghost' supplies** refers to goods for which the operator is charged but which are never received. This can occur in a number of ways—the supplier can supply the correct stock but overcharge, the supplier can charge the correct price but undersupply, the delivery person can deliver less than the full order, or substitute inferior goods for those specified. **Poor stock rotation** leads to wastage, as perishable items may deteriorate before they are used, and tins or jars may be held onto beyond their 'use-by date'. New deliveries should always be stored behind existing stocks to ensure the older items are used first. **Breakages** also create losses. Management should ensure that the staff are trained in the safe handling of materials and that proper equipment is provided for transporting items. Obviously, if goods are stolen, there will be a stock discrepancy. **Theft** may be carried out by trespassers on the premises who do not have the authorisation to be there, or by dishonest employees. Employees, in particular, can engage in one specific form of theft, namely **unauthorised consumption**, i.e. eating or drinking items that have not been provided to them.

Outsourcing

Traditionally, flight production units have been called 'flight kitchens'. However, throughout this book we prefer to use the term 'production unit' as the 'kitchen' is only one small part of the unit as a whole. Moreover, it is getting smaller, as a major trend in the flight catering industry is outsourcing production of food items to food manufacturers, such as Birdseye, Nestle, or Kraft.

There are many reasons for this trend. The main reason is that these manufacturers have developed an ever wider range of cook-chill or frozen-meal products, usually for retail distribution, through supermarkets to the domestic consumer. However, such products can equally be used by the flight catering industry. The large-scale manufacture of these items, based on economies of scale, often means that their unit price is lower than that achievable by caterers if they produce them in-house. In addition, by purchasing cook-chill entrees, vegetables, desserts, and so on, there is less need for investment in blast chillers, kitchen equipment, and other related infrastructure, and less need for skilled labour.

This policy is also consistent with trends in the airline industry in general, which has been adopting the general business principle that a firm should concentrate on its core business. For airlines, this is transportation, so they have tended to outsource a range of non-core activities, such as IT, ramp handling, sales and marketing, and of course catering (Pilling, 2002). For flight caterers, their core business is increasingly being seen as logistics rather food production (as discussed in Chapter 11).

However, the pattern of outsourcing can be very complex. One study at the University of Surrey, of outsourcing at Heathrow, found that six different caterers had each adopted a unique policy in this area. For instance, the production of kosher meals was outsourced by them all, but some caterers produced halal meals in-house while the others outsourced them. Five caterers purchased bread products from suppliers, but one had their own in-house bakery. Indeed, there was one 'caterer' in the sample who engaged in no food production at all, and outsourced all food production, in some cases actually buying cook-chill entrees from another flight 'caterer'.

Given this complex picture, it is difficult to be certain what factors influence the outsourcing decision, but these are likely to be:

- the availability of suppliers with the expertise and scale of production to supply the necessary product
- the volume of demand (high demand is often outsourced)
- the age and efficiency of the caterer's own plant and equipment (often outsourcing is costed against plans for refurbishing or replacing existing equipment)
- product characteristics ('complex' products that require specialist equipment, skills or conditions—such as kosher foods, halal foods—are most likely to be outsourced)
- Lower unit cost of outsourced product
- Branding (putting a labelled branded product on the tray set may 'add value')

Clearly all of the above will vary from location to location, facility to facility, and airline contract to airline contract. Hence, it is entirely logical for ICL at Heathrow to produce their own Japanese meals, as their major contracts are with Japanese Airlines. But for other Heathrow-based caterers outsourcing is adopted, as their volume of production is low, and they do not have the expertise.

Clearly the outsource decision has implications for all aspects of flight catering—supplier relationships and inventory management (discussed here), production facility planning (Chapter 7), and production operations (Chapter 8). As far as supplier relationships are concerned, outsourcing means that caterers (and sometimes airlines) will have more contracts with food manufacturers rather than growers and distributors of raw materials. Traditionally, growers and wholesalers are relatively small-scale operators and have little power in the marketplace. But some food manufacturers are global firms with a great deal of negotiating power. Thus outsourcing may require caterers to apply their expertise in negotiating purchasing contracts to the securing of the best contractual terms with their suppliers.

Outsourcing also affects the nature of the inventory being supplied. This is entirely consistent with the shift to JIT, as cook-chill entrees, desserts, bakery goods, and so on by definition have to be used as soon as possible after they have been delivered to the unit.

Case study 6.1

Abela flight kitchen, London Heathrow

The Abela unit at Heathrow averages 16,000 meals a week. The stores area comprises four main areas—the receiving dock (loading bay), dry stores and bonded store on the first floor, and production stores on the ground floor.

The receiving dock is 6 m by 12 m with space for one vehicle to unload. There is an office for the Receiving Clerk, a temporary chilled storage area of 60 sq. m, and a dry store of 220 sq. m. All goods are checked and weighed on arrival, then transported directly to the main stores or production stores. They are only stored in the temporary storage if capacity is unavailable elsewhere. All fresh produce arriving at the dock is taken directly to the production stores on the same floor. There are two 300 cu. m capacity freezers for frozen goods, and three 200 cu. m chillers for fresh vegetables, dairy produce, and meat.

The dry stores and bonded store are approximately 800 sq. m, with the latter taking up one third of the total space. Most goods are stored in bulk on pallets and moved by fork-lift truck. There are two 250 cu. m freezers for holding frozen foods in this main store. A feature of a flight catering unit is the bonded store. This is an area for stock items, mainly alcohol, cigarettes, and perfume, on which no British sales tax, i.e. VAT will be paid as they will be served or sold to airline passengers as duty free items. This area has to be physically separated from the other stores and be totally secure. British customs and excise officers can inspect the bonded stores at any time. At Abela there are three shelves, the top and ground level shelves hold pallets, and the middle shelf holds individual stock items. These are arranged by airline rather than by item, as in effect the stock is owned by the airline and Abela is providing warehousing for it. Stock-taking is carried out by Abela at least once a month, and may also be carried out by any of the airlines at any time.

Abela has approximately 120 separate suppliers ranging from mainstream bulk suppliers of dry goods to specialist suppliers of ethnic speciality foods. In some cases the airlines nominate suppliers of specific items. As menus may change once a month for each of the different airlines, items are not stocked to par. There may be as many as 4000 separate commodity items stored. There are a total of 18 staff employed in the stores function.

At the loading bay, food and equipment are separated. Food is kept on the ground floor while equipment goes to the first-floor storage area, either taken up in the goods lift or lifted to an upper door with a forklift truck. The unpacking area is substantial because all foods are taken out of their boxes and packed into plastic containers on arrival. All food is checked for temperature and weight. Packaging is examined to ensure that it is undamaged. Foods in glass jars, such as pickles and relishes, are decanted into plastic packs to avoid any chance of glass getting into the food.

Before preparation and cooking, the food is stored in coldrooms on the right-hand side of the main corridor, which runs the length of the building. Each cold room is for a different type of commodity—vegetables and fruits, meat, fish, dairy, and so on. The next stage in the flow takes place on the other side of the corridor. Food that will be cooked goes into separate preparation rooms for vegetables and salad, meat and fish, mezze and general use. Beyond these rooms are cold stores with doors at the front and back. Food from the preparation room goes in one door and out through the other into the hot kitchen, so that there is no backtracking in the flow. The flow of cold food is similarly well organised. It also progresses from cold rooms to a kitchen on the other side of the corridor. Separate from both the hot and cold kitchens is the pastry kitchen, complete with its own portioning area and cold stores.

Current issues and future developments

There are three issues that are leading to a growth in the concept of **upstream storage**. This is the idea of reducing the amount of goods that are stored in the flight production unit by only ordering supplies just before they are needed. Goods are therefore delivered 'just-in-time', often less than 24 hours before they are needed. The first reason for this is outsourcing (discussed as a trend in Chapter 2). If goods are purchased in a fully prepared state from suppliers, the amount of raw materials and items for processing is reduced. The second reason is that this approach is consistent with the process re-engineering that is taking place (see Chapter 8). The third reason is the further development of information technology that makes it possible to keep and order inventory in this way.

Indeed **computerisation** and **bar coding** are a significant trend in the industry. By using scanners and conveyor belts, some production units have been able to almost completely automate their handling and storage processes.

Conclusion

The flight catering industry has a complex supply network, due to the international nature of the industry, frequent changes to output due to menu cycles, and the role of several stakeholders (discussed in Chapter 2). The adoption of just in time production and outsourcing is tending to make the flow of materials from supplier to flight production unit 'seamless'. Underpinning this integrated philosophy and approach are highly effective planning and forecasting systems, as well as good communication and collaboration between the different parties.

Key terms

Dry stores	Just in time	Outsourcing
Perpetual inventory	Purchase specification	Refrigerated storage
Storage	Supplier audits	

Discussion questions

1. What are the fundamental characteristics of developing good supplier relationships?
2. What are the advantages and disadvantages of purchase specifications for flight caterers, airlines, and fare-paying passengers?
3. Flight caterers commonly serve multiple airlines. What implications can this have on inventory management?

References

Airline Caterers Technical Co-ordination Committee. (1990) *Airline Catering Code of Good Practice*, Hygiene Services: Heathrow, London, 2–3.

Anon. (1992) *Restaurant Business*, 20 Sept., 75.

Birchfield, J.C. (1988) *Design and Layout of Foodservice Facilities*, Van Nostrand Reinhold: New York.

Borsenik, F.D. and Stutts, A.T. (1997) *The Management of Maintenance and Engineering Systems in the Hospitality Industry*, John Wiley & Sons: New York.

Katsigris, C. and Thomas, C. (1999) *Design and Equipment for Restaurants and Foodservice*, John Wiley & Sons: New York.

Ley, S. (1980) *Foodservice Refrigeration*, Van Nostrand Reinhold: New York.

McCool, A. (1996) "Pricing and Cost management for the in-flight Foodservice Industry," *The Bottomline*, Oct. Nov., 14–19.

O'Meara, A. (1993) "Aer Lingus—A Winning Team," *Hotel & Catering Review*, vol. 23 Apr., 16–19.

Pilling, M. (2002) "Drive to Outsource," *Airline Business*, Jan., 38–42.

Porter, M. (1995) *Competitive Advantage: Creating and Sustaining Superior Performance*, Free Press: Boston.

Reid, R. and Reigel, C. (1988) Foodservice Purchasing: Corporate Practices, *Cornell HRA Quarterly*, May, 25–29.

CHAPTER 7

Flight production facilities and systems planning

Learning objectives

- Examine the factors to be considered in designing the kitchen layout
- Understand the work flow in a production kitchen
- Understand alternative systems for holding food safely
- Identify alternative approaches to tray assembly and trolley loading

Introduction

A catering system has to be designed and organised to produce the right quantity of food at the correct standard, for the required number of people, on time, and using the resources of staff, equipment and materials effectively and efficiently. A central constraint is that in flight catering, production is separated from service by distance and time.

Because of the complexity of the operations in terms of numbers and meal components, catering and process engineers have become heavily involved in the design of the operation. Such an approach to design provides:

- in-depth analysis of functional requirements
- integrated thinking
- enhancement of knowledge base
- effective flow
- balance between all stages of the process

The design application should cover a logical sequence of the planning procedure while considering the delivery of total quality management.

Principles of flight production unit design

As the costs of space, equipment, fuel, maintenance, and labour continue to rise, thought has to be given to production facility design in order to achieve the integration of process, organisation, and systems. The requirements of the system have to be clearly identified with regard to the type of service that is to be prepared in the production unit and served on board the aircraft. Since the early 1990s concepts developed in the manufacturing industry have begun to be applied to flight catering units. Three key concepts all relate to improving unit productivity. These are:

- decrease in the volume of in-process materials (just-in-time approach)
- improving labour productivity
- waste reduction

Planning and design plays a key role in achieving these goals. Systems are typically designed so that:

- the plant layout is process-driven
- material flow is simplified
- materials are automatically delivered to the operators on request
- materials are handled ergonomically
- inventory material flow control is constantly updated
- equipment is automated
- fault recording providing utmost transparency in the system

The following factors are likely to influence the design of a flight production unit:

- the size and extent of the operations in terms of the maximum number of flight meals to be produced
- capital expenditure available
- cost and availability of skilled labour in the region
- policy on outsourcing and the use of pre-prepared products
- the use of latest technology
- hygiene and food safety legislation
- proximity to airport

In addition, the management must have easy access to the areas under their control and have good visibility in the areas that have to be supervised.

The method by which food and associated items may be handled or processed varies from unit to unit depending on their production system. The three main production philosophies are:

- Batch production
- Continuous (flow) production
- Cell production

In flight catering, all three of these may be found, as discussed below.

Batch production

Batch production is based on the premise that a small quantity is produced at one time and only when required. Speed and consistency are the advantages. However, the side effects are a lot of double/triple handling, which can result in poor staff utilisation (especially if one item runs out) and higher wastage. This is typically the process type adopted for the production and tray assembly of first-class meals and preparation for special flights and special meals.

Continuous (flow) production

Continuous production is based on high volume utilisation of equipment. Identical meals are produced in large numbers and then allocated to flights afterward. The benefits are low wastage, consistency, and good staff utilisation in each department. However, the speed of production can be very slow and bottlenecks can appear at busy times of the day. The system cannot cope well with small or highly variable volumes, particularly for first-class, business, and special meals. If one department falls behind schedule, the rest of the departments may have to stop to wait for the flow to resume. This process works best in flight production units producing very large numbers of meals for only one airline.

Cell production

Many flight production systems design is based on the cellular manufacturing principle, which is the grouping of machines and equipment into configurations related to each family or each part, i.e. a collection of cells each dealing with separate but related families within a production process. In effect this combines both elements of the batch and flow-process types. The essential concept is that set-up time is reduced within the whole process because the family and the machines and equipment are matched. Modern equipment employed in flight catering, such as combination ovens, high pressure steamers, Bratt pans, and food processors, are good examples of multi-purpose equipment. These pieces of equipment can not only be used in individual cells but by a number of cells. The extent of this is dependent on the scale of production required; therefore large-scale production leads to more single-cell usage and equipment being designated for a particular intensive use.

The procedure can accommodate small volumes and eliminates much double handling so as to be flexible with the demand. The staff can be rewarded with some feeling of ownership of quality. However, the quality of product can vary depending on the individual and it requires a high level of supervision and planning. The risk of cross-contamination can be higher than with other production methods.

Scale and scope of production facilities

As an example, a large production unit may produce 10 million meals per annum, which is equivalent to 27,000 meals per day. In making this estimate, a meal is considered to be the contents of an individual tray served to a customer and, as such, it can be anything from coffee and biscuits to a full meal. In a typical day, this large operation may produce all of the materials required for up to 200 flights. In order to produce this quantity of food and other supplies, over 1,000 employees may be needed. Table 7.1 give the volumes of product

Product	Tonnes	Product	Amount	Units
Sausages (assorted)	33.5	Milk	602,250	pints
Fresh salmon	67.25	Double cream	46,397	pints
Fillet steaks 4.5 oz	9.75	Chocolate boxes (club)	557,507	box of 2
Bacon	15.0	Bread loaves	20,930	loaves
New Zealand lamb	125.0	Lettuce	182,736	lettuce
Chicken breasts	40.5	Melons	38,950	melons
Carrots	75.0	Tomato sauce	9,552	bottles
Cream cheese	3.5	Cornflakes	77,150	packets
Live lobsters	39.0	Tea	1,983,240	bags
Frozen lobster meat	30.0	Fresh eggs	2,700,000	eggs
Prawns	31.0	Hard-boiled eggs	1,421,550	eggs
Caviar	6.0	Biscuits	50,154	tins
Flour	66.5	Strawberry jam	274,464	portions
Sugar	10.5	Lemonade	1,204,752	cans
Smoked salmon	22.0	Coca-Cola	2,868,828	cans
Fresh strawberries	44.5	Orange juice	1,101,400	cuplets
Fresh tomatoes	126.5	Orange juice	170,000	litres

Source: British Airways Catering

Table 7.1
Annual volume of products used in a flight catering unit

used in a typical large flight kitchen per year. In the case of a facility supplying as many as 30 different airlines to their own specifications, the management of multiple contracts increases the complexity of the planning and control of the operation.

Process flow

Food preparation should be planned to allow a 'work flow', whereby the food is processed through the flight kitchen from the point of delivery to the point of assembly on the tray ready for distribution to the aircraft with the minimum of obstruction. The various processes should be separated as far as possible and food intended for human consumption should not cross paths with waste food or refuse. Staff time is costly and a design that reduces wasteful journeys is both efficient and cost effective. Figure 7.1 illustrates a schematic example of workflows in a typical flight kitchen.

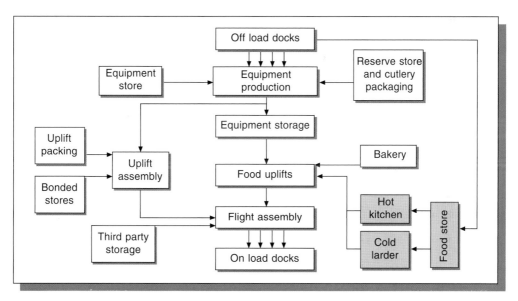

Figure 7.1
A workflow chart of a typical kitchen

The overall sequence of receiving, storing, preparing, holding, serving, and clearing need to be achieved by:

- minimum movement
- minimal back-tracking
- maximum use of space
- maximum use of equipment
- minimum expenditure of time and effort

The detailed layout of the production units vary depending upon the process type selected (batch, flow, or cell), the scale of the operation, and the nature of flights serviced, but all systems share some degree of similarity in the kitchen system design. Coherent links between departments and the planning of production capacity are crucial to the successful working of the operation. The layout and design of storage areas has been discussed in the previous chapter. This chapter will focus on the layout and design of food production and tray assembly areas.

Production kitchens

Flight catering companies normally use a modified cook-chill system for the preparation and storage of cooked items. For some flights, frozen meals may be required, for example, where an aircraft is carrying food for the return leg. The production areas may be in operation 16–23 hours per day, with a short close-down for cleaning operations. Flexible cooking technology based on high-capacity cooking equipment (Bratt pans, combination ovens, convection ovens, pressurised steamers, etc.) allow a range of hot entrees to be produced from the same processing plant. After foods are cooked, they are rapidly chilled to below 5°C and then stored below this temperature until required for packaging. Processes are designed to comply with guidelines of good practice for cook-chill operations.

The basic elements of the flight kitchen can be arranged on the basis of Cold Wet Areas, Hot Wet areas, Hot Dry areas, and Dirty areas (Table 7.2).

Cold Wet Areas	Vegetable and fruit preparation, butchery (if used), poultry preparation, seafood preparation
Equipment	Washing machines, peeling machine, vacuum tumbler, meat grinder, high speed cutter, juice machine
Cold Dry Areas	Cold meat slicing, terrine and pate cutting, garnish production, salad production
Equipment	Slicing machine, cutting machine, MAP (modified atmosphere packaging) machine, vacuum machine
Hot Wet Areas	Blanching, boiling, poaching, steaming
Equipment	Steam jacket/electrical boilers/kettles, pressure/atmospheric steamer, combination ovens
Hot Dry Areas	Roasting, baking, grilling, sauteing, cooking, braising, gratinating (surface browning of cooked food), frying, emulsifying
Equipment	Roasting/convection ovens, low temperature ovens, continuous cookers, tilting frying pan, induction or infra-red cooking ovens/range, slalmander, rice cooker, grills and char broilers, griddle plate
Dirty Areas	Refuse, small equipment cleaning, dish washing

Table 7.2
Basic elements of a kitchen unit

The production area is divided into a number of segregated areas, each with its own temperature-controlled storage to hold materials that have been processed and are waiting for the next processing operation. All production areas have strict hygiene requirements in relation to floor and wall coverings, which must be non-porous and easy to clean. In addition to this, floors must be constructed with a non-slip surface. The design must minimise the possibility of access by insects and rodents and must eliminate the possibility of there being inaccessible voids that can act as breeding grounds for these pests. Door and window openings must be designed to prevent the ingress of birds and flying insects.

Fruit and vegetable preparation

This area requires sinks for washing vegetables together with stainless steel tables for manual operations, a wide range of vegetable preparation machinery, including peeling, shredding, cutting/dicing machines and vegetable-washing machines, spin-drying machines, tomato-slicing machines, and facilities for the disposal of waste. Prepared materials are packed into plastic boxes ready for transfer to the hot or cold kitchen. With the trend towards the purchase of ready prepared vegetables, space allocation required for vegetable preparation is decreasing.

Meat preparation

This area requires similar equipment to the vegetable preparation area, with specialised preparation equipment including mincing machines, bowl choppers, and dicing machines. Many of the raw meat items used in the preparation of meals are bought in pre-portioned servings, such as steaks and cutlets, reducing the amount of space required for meat preparation. Meats may be seasoned in this area. Weighed quantities of meat are mixed with precise amounts of seasoning and oil. This mixture is then placed in a vacuum tumbling machine for anything between 1 and 10 minutes. The meat is then cooked conventionally by any required method. The resulting product shows an increase in yield, more consistent seasoning, and lower cooking oil consumption. Once raw meats have been prepared, they are transferred to plastic storage boxes and held in refrigerated storage until required by the hot kitchen.

Fish preparation

This is very similar to the meat preparation area in terms of the basic requirements. Fish products will include raw fish (fresh and frozen), smoked fish, and cooked fish products. It is essential to ensure that the preparations of raw and cooked items are completely separated. For good hygiene practice, separate colour-coded, impervious, hard rubber chopping boards are required to avoid bacterial cross-contamination.

Hot kitchen

This area makes use of large-scale batch production equipment, such as boiling pans, Bratt pans, pressurised bratt pans, convection ovens, and combination

Figure 7.2
Photograph of hot kitchen
Source: *Gate Gourmet* © Copyright 2003

ovens. Additionally, some continuous equipment may be used in the larger operations, for example continuous frying equipment. Sophisticated ventilation systems, which incorporate automatic cleaning and energy recovery systems, are often installed. In addition to this large-scale equipment, which is used for the majority of the production, there may be a small area of the main kitchen (or a separate kitchen) which is used for producing special items and for individual VIP/first-class requirements.

Cold kitchen/larder

This kitchen is used for the preparation of hors d'oeuvres, cold meats, sandwiches, salads, and other larder items. In addition to preparation tables the area requires items such as slicing machines. Cooked meats may be delivered (chilled to below 5°C) or they may be purchased ready cooked in Cryovac packs. A sophisticated slicing machine is used to control the weights of cold meat per serving; prepared items are held in refrigerated storage until required for tray assembly. The shift to bought-in, pre-prepared, products was covered in Chapter 6 but essentially these products mean that the cold kitchen work has possibly moved to assembly.

Bakery/pastry

This part of the preparation area covers the making of all desserts and baked goods. A decision regarding the buying-in of ready-made bakery produces or an in-house bakery would depend on each unit requirement. The basic requirement is for mixing machines, moulding machines, proving ovens, and baking ovens. In an operation which has a large bakery department flour may be stored in silos and transferred pneumatically along pipelines directly to weighing hoppers located over the mixing machines. With mass production, a computer-controlled machine can be used to weigh all ingredients for a specified recipe automatically into the mixer. Once a dough is mixed, it is divided and shaped. Large-scale operations can use computer-controlled machines for dividing and shaping a wide range of breads, bread rolls, and other yeast-based bakery products. These machines can be pre-programmed to produce up to 100 different shapes and sizes of product. Typically, a bakery can produce 4,000 rolls per day. Pastry products, such as cakes, pastries, quiches, puddings, and fruit salads, also require preparation space and equipment, such as dough mixers, kneading machines, programmable ovens, pastry-rolling machines, cream-whipping machines, and refrigerated storage for holding raw materials and finished goods. Finished goods are loaded onto trolleys for transport to the tray assembly area. Special attention is needed for ventilation ducts and cleaning since items such as flour, sugar, and fat encourage various insect pests to thrive.

Utensil washing

Large commercial utensil-washing machines are required to wash pots, pans and food containers used in the stores and production kitchen areas. This facility is totally separate from that used to handle flight returns (see Chapter 15). Often, the cleaning system is designed into the building to allow for spray jet or foam cleaning breaks in production. All production areas require hand-washing sinks and hand-drying equipment at their entrance. The specific production areas used relate to the nature of flights served and the methods used to organise production. Whatever method of organisation is used, each area is self-contained in terms of space, production tables, sinks and storage for prepared items. Typically, a flight kitchen will need areas for the preparation of vegetables, salads, meat, and fish, a hot kitchen for cooking and chilling main course items, a cold kitchen/larder for the preparation of cold meat dishes and sandwiches, and a bakery for bread products and baked desserts.

Test kitchen

A test kitchen may be required in order to evaluate new recipes and to carry out routine testing of dishes. In the test kitchen, foods can be produced on a small scale, but using the same types of catering equipment as used in the main production kitchen. The test kitchen also has a range of galley ovens to simulate the galley reheating of dishes. Most galley kitchens have forced convection ovens, but there have been trials of combination ovens (steam and forced air convection) by some airlines.

Beverage preparation

Some smaller or older aircraft do not have facilities for making hot beverages on board and there may be a need for a beverage section which prepares hot water and fresh coffee, which is loaded into specialised heat-retaining containers.

Holding systems and facilities

Because food is prepared on the ground and consumed by passengers in the air, there has to be some way of 'holding' foods under safe conditions between their preparation in the production facility and their service in the aircraft. There are three main ways this might be done – cook-chill, cook-freeze, and *sous-vide*. The most common of these used in flight catering is cook-chill.

Cook-chill

Cook-chill is a catering system based on the full cooking of food followed by fast chilling and storage in controlled low temperature conditions just above the freezing point (0°C to + 3°C) with subsequent thorough re-heating close to the consumer before consumption. In order to preserve the appearance, texture, flavour, nutritional quality, and safety of the cooked food, **blast chilling** should commence as soon as possible after completion of cooking (and portioning if it is done after cooking) and in any event within 30 minutes of leaving the cooker. In order to achieve the recommended chilling process, the chiller used should have a performance specification showing its capable of reducing the temperature of a 50-mm layer of food from 70°C to + 7°C or below in a period not exceeding 90 minutes when fully loaded. Theoretically, the quicker the freezing process the smaller the ice crystals that form within the cells of the product will be. The smaller the ice cells the better the quality and structure of the product when it is thawed. The frequent opening of doors would cause unacceptable temperature fluctuations in the product. With the risk of contamination the storage should be used solely for the products of the cook-chill process.

The capacity of the blast chiller should be sufficient to match peak production scheduling to ensure that rapid chilling can commence within 30 minutes of completion of cooking. The speed of chilling of a foodstuff is affected by the following:

- size, shape, weight of food and construction material of the container
- food density and moisture content
- heat capacity of the food and the container
- thermal conductivity of the food
- the design of the chiller will affect chilling speed
- temperature of the food entering the chiller
- whether the container is provided with a cover (Department of Health, 1989)

To facilitate cooling after cooking, it is recommended that joints of meat or packs of meat products should not exceed 2.5 kg in weight and 100 mm in thickness or height, and that large poultry carcasses should be broken down into sections not exceeding these parameters.

Figure 7.3
Photograph of a blast chiller
Source: Abela Airline Catering

Three typical methods of chilling are employed:

1. The use of clean, high velocity re-circulating air at low temperatures in mechanical apparatus; special mechanical chillers for liquids are available but these require appropriate cleaning and disinfecting between batches
2. The use of cryogenic apparatus involving the use of non-oxidising gas at low temperatures
3. The immersion of packed products in a safe and suitable refrigerated liquid

With chilling techniques, recipes or ingredients can be applied to a wide range of both pre-cooked and uncooked dishes, although there may be some trouble with the sauce stability. Care should be taken to avoid excessive contact between the sauce and the base of the containers to prevent overcooking during re-heating. Cooling does thicken sauces and care should be taken to ensure that the viscosity of the sauce after cooking is slightly thinner than normal. For example, concasse or croute bases may be used to insulate the sauce from the hot container.

Reheating of chilled food should begin as soon as possible and no longer than 30 minutes after the food is removed from the chill (either bulk chill, secondary chill, or chilled trolley). For reasons of safety and palatability, the centre temperature of the food should reach at least 70°C and be maintained at not less than 70°C for 2 minutes. Once the food has been heated properly, the service of the foods should commence as soon as possible and within less than 15 minutes of reheating. The temperature must not be allowed to fall below 63°C. Any meals not consumed should be destroyed and not reheated or returned to chilled storage. Chilled food can be saved for 48 hours for cold food and 72 hours for hot meals (Kang, 2000).

Cook–freeze

Cook–freeze is another catering system based on full cooking followed by fast freezing and storage at controlled low temperature conditions well below freezing point (−18°C or below). As long as this storage temperature is maintained, micro-organisms cannot grow. This is subsequently followed by thorough re-heating close to the consumer before prompt consumption. The food should reach a centre temperature of at least −5°C within 90 minutes of entering the freezer and subsequently should reach a storage temperature of −18°C. The shelf-life of pre-cooked frozen food varies according to the type of food but in general it maybe stored for up to 8 weeks without any significant loss of nutrients or palatability. After that time rancidity may develop in foods with a high fat content, but other foods can be satisfactorily stored for longer periods. In addition, a clear system of coding the containers with product identification, batch production, and expiry dates should be used so that stock can be rotated on a first-in/first-out basis.

These two systems of catering have a number of similarities in their basic design and the choice on which to use would depend on the balance of benefits to be obtained for the caterers' needs, as illustrated in Table 7.3. The preservation of food in cook-chill operations is of a limited nature, after which it should be destroyed. Since the storage life is relatively short, the linking of production to service is much tighter than what is needed in cook–freeze operations. In general, the production unit would generally produce food for a known predicted demand 2–3 days in advance, working consistently to the predicted daily requirements. Unpredicted variations in demand will tend to produce either much higher wastage or greater shortages in the catering system than might be encountered in a cook–freeze operation.

Sous-vide

This allows sauces and entrées to be produced in batches up to 14 days in advance and stored (Gehrig, 1990). Food is bulk chilled and packed in vacuum sealed bags. Typically, a production run may be sufficient for four flights. The benefits are said to be that productivity can be increased through the use of

Benefits	Cook-chill	Cook-freeze
Increased labour productivity	***	***
Improved working conditions	**	**
Take advantage of seasonal prices	***	-
Microbiological control and hygiene	***	**
Reduction of service kitchen floor area	**	***
Reduced energy requirements	*	**
Ensured quality control	***	**
Range of dishes handled	**	***
Optimise capital investment	***	**
Improved portion control	***	***
Food service wastage control	***	**
Stock control capability	***	*

Note: *starred rating
SOURCE: *Electricity Council*, 1982: 59

Table 7.3
Benefits and comparisons of Cook-chill and Cook-freeze

larger batches, better production planning and resulting in production smoothing. In addition, there are yield gains and improved control over hygiene, the latter being extremely important.

A separate kitchen area is required for *sous-vide* production. High-capacity production equipment is used and thought needs to be given to efficient and fast materials handling. This includes the use of combination ovens which are loaded directly from trolleys. Precise production control is required, with strict adherence to recipes, production times, and control temperatures. It is very important that high-quality raw materials are used in the process and these should all have low bacterial counts, including minor ingredients such as herbs and spices.

Sauces are produced in batches of 200 litres. After cooking, in a jacketed pan or Bratt pan, the sauce is then cooled and packed in Cryovac containers with a capacity of 1.5–2 litres. These are then heated in a combination steamer, at a temperature of 95°C, until the product has a core temperature of 78°C. The packs are then cooled in a salt-ice bath to a core temperature of 5°C and stored at temperatures between 0° and 2°C (Gehrig, 1993).

Meat products can be produced in a similar way with raw meat, vacuum-packed in Cryovac bags, which are then cooked in a steam oven, combination oven or water bath to a core temperature that ensures pasteurisation of the particular product. The product is then rapidly chilled and stored as for the sauces.

Sous-vide products are manufactured in batch sizes sufficient to meet the needs of 14 days' consumption. Individual packaged items can be taken out of chilled storage as required, prepared for meal assembly (i.e. slicing of cooked meats, portioning of sauces). The whole of these post-storage activities should be carried out in a temperature-controlled environment (10–15°C) and the foods returned to storage as quickly as possible. Strict quality control procedures are required because of the potential microbiological hazards.

Tray assembly

This area of the operation is responsible for putting together all of the requirements for a meal tray, based on the specifications provided by the airline (see Figure 5.7). The detailed tray setting varies, depending upon the carrier, the type of meal and the passenger class. In order to accommodate a number of variations, this area must be designed in a flexible way so that it can be easily and quickly modified to suit the specific requirements of the tray being assembled. Capacity demands may be in excess of 1,000 trays per hour and may require, for example, a full set of trays for a Boeing 747 to be assembled in less than an hour. The activities carried out in this area include assembling the requirements for special meals.

For small operations or flights with limited requirements, long tables can be used for tray setting. Larger operations may use a conveyor belt, with a number of stations for the addition of all cold food items, crockery (plastic or china), cutlery sets, condiments, and other requirements. Where the meal is to include a hot meal, a space is left on the tray where the heated container will be placed during the flight and after it has been reheated in the galley oven.

Conveyor belt

Tray assembly areas normally have a number of conveyor lines, with assembly points located on either side of the belt. The assembly points can be flexible, allowing for changes to be made to suit the specific requirements of the meal service. Each assembly point has a container holding a specific tray component and a staff member places this item onto the tray in a specific location. At the end of the belt, trays are loaded directly into the appropriate type of trolley for the flight and labelled, showing the type of meal, the flight number, the day of the flight, and the stowage position. Once they have been loaded into trolleys, they are kept in refrigerated storage until they are required for assembly. At that stage, those trolleys which contain foodstuffs are loaded with dry ice in order to minimise the temperature rise between the time they leave the refrigerated store and the time that they are loaded into the galley. The trolleys have a shelf at the top of the tray compartment to allow for the storage of blocks of dry ice. The number of blocks used depends upon the ambient temperature, the duration of the flight and when the meal is served on board. More modern equipment can 'shoot' dry ice on to individual shelves, so distributing the cooling more evenly in the trolley.

Work stations

An alternative way to assemble trays is to adopt the concept of JIT and merge the 'make and pack' procedures at the same work location. Normally, one person or two people working together as a team assemble the items to set trays in the trolley. The benefits are:

- mistakes and carelessness are easily traced
- increased empowerment
- less need for supervision

Figure 7.4
Tray assembly by conveyor belt

- less hold-up of production
- less storage and handling
- less wastage

However, the labour remains the same and the staff may have some resistance to training in this new working procedure. Equipment and workspace may be required to be adjusted to fit in the flow. This process works effectively with small quantities of meals such as for first or business class.

Trolley and container loading

This area of the operation is responsible for loading containers with equipment for the flight—glassware, crockery, cutlery, holloware, plastic glasses, and so on. Here again there are significant developments in automation, such as cutlery-packing machinery, because of the emphasis on a fast turnaround of equipment.

Final assembly of flight requirements

Assembly starts about 2–3 hours before the scheduled flight departure. The many individual items which go to make up the full inventory for a flight are grouped together in a defined physical location within the assembly area. Sufficient space is required to allow materials for each flight to be marshalled separately. The area also requires a loading bay at the correct height for offloading onto flight transportation (see Chapter 10).

All trolleys and containers are checked in terms of quality and quantity against computer-generated inventory lists. The temperature of the marshalling area is maintained at 4°C in order to prevent any risk of food poisoning.

Case study 7.1

ALPHA flight kitchen–Airport Gate London Heathrow

The In-flight production unit for Alpha Flight Services at Heathrow was the amalgamation of three existing operations which, while not providing any additional capacity, had the benefits of improved process flows and logistics, consolidating stores and office operations to cater to an average 15,000 meals per day, with a capacity of 25,000 meals per day.

The total floor area is 5,250 sq. m, which consists of three existing steel-framed warehouse units rather than a purpose built site. Land at Heathrow, as at any other international airport, is difficult and expensive to obtain, and the Airport Gate site is within half a mile of the runways.

Of the three units, one was solely designated for offices and staff facilities including a large canteen to cater to the 450-strong staff. In the remaining two units a suspended concrete floor was installed at a height of 1.5 m to create a loading dock.

Mezzanine areas were installed in two locations to house the plant rooms to leave the main ground floor free for production. A third mezzanine was installed in the first unit to create additional office floor space. The mezzanine areas also afforded the designers to incorporate some Manager/Supervisor offices with viewing windows to oversee the operational areas under their control. The majority of internal walls and ceilings in the production areas were created out of coldroom panels with a 1-hour fire resistance to maintain compliance with current building control regulations.

The actual total production area of 3310 sq. m then breaks down to:

- Food Stores 84 sq. m
- Refrigerated Stores 260 sq. m
- Preparation 78 sq. m
- Hot Kitchen 196 sq. m

- Japanese Kitchen 44 sq. m
- Assembly 425 sq. m
- Despatch Coldroom 265 sq. m
- Dishwash & Potwash 630 sq. m
- Equipment Stores & Packing 985 sq. m
- Loading Dock 340 sq. m

The bond store is housed in a separate adjacent building with completed trolleys collected when required for the various flights. A separate 'Presentation Kitchen' is incorporated into the design, in part to act as a kitchen to prepare separate small batches for presentation to potential new clients, but also to act as a test kitchen for new concepts.

As the facility largely caters for scheduled flights, with a particular bias toward long-haul flights and business-class customers, the production system favoured is that of Cell Production. Alpha utilises two-tier stainless steel benches, each staffed by one operative, which can hold every requirement needed for a passenger's tray. The completed trays are then loaded straight on to airline trolleys, avoiding double-handling. A small amount of Batch Production is utilised when first-class meals and some special dietary menus are required.

Goods are received and dispatched from the long raised dock area, two-thirds set aside and delimited for dispatch with one-third for receiving and returns.

From goods in, which takes place 7 days a week, food follows a path through dry stores holding to coldroom storage (see Figure 7.4). Food then follows a horse-shoe shaped flow to preparation, hot kitchens, blast chilling, tray assembly, and despatch chiller. Great attention has been paid to prevent back-tracking and cross-contamination from areas; for example, the hot kitchen preparation area has one door in from the food storage area and a second door out to the hot kitchen.

(a) Fruit and vegetable preparation   Most vegetables are bought-in ready-prepared, although fruit is prepared on site in the cold prep area. A salad wash machine is utilised to avoid labour costs. Separate chillers are designed into the scheme to hold prepared fruit and vegetables and raw fruit and vegetables to limit any potential cross-contamination. Waste disposal units are not utilised in the cold preparation areas as it has led to historical local drainage problems.

(b) Meat preparation   Daily meat deliveries are dated and temperature recorded upon arrival and are mostly part or fully prepared, limiting the need for mincing and chopping machinery.

(c) Hot kitchen   Situated around a central cooking island, the unit has two bratt pans, one pressure bratt pan, one wok cooker, two boiling kettles, one salamander, one boiling table, two griddles, a bank of three fryers, and one solid top boiling table. Separate banks of five floor-standing combination ovens are wall-sited under a separate canopy to allow ease of trolley access. Additional gas and electrical capacity is designed into the scheme to allow for future expansion.

(d) Cold kitchen   The kitchen has some shared facilities with the cold preparation area with ease of access to the cooked meat chiller and fruit and vegetable chiller, but the majority of this work is carried out in the assembly.

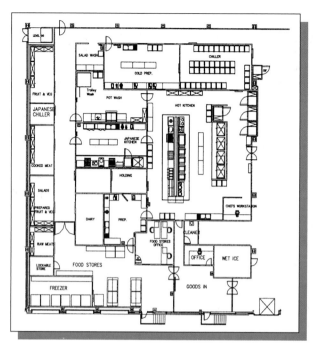

Figure 7.5
Plan of Airport Gate stores and kitchen areas
Source: Hepburn Associates

(e) Japanese kitchen   This separate kitchen adjoining the main hot kitchen is designed to produce very specific menus with manual preparation. Specialist equipment, such as high capacity rice cookers, wok cooker and water-cooled salamanders are used to create authentic cuisine.

(f) Potwash   A large automatic utensil washer and trolley washer are situated off the hot kitchen and cold preparation areas, suitable to handle the volume of items used by the chefs and kitchen assistants, complete with extraction to make the area more amenable to work in.

(g) Presentation kitchen   Set somewhat further afar from the rest of the kitchen unit, this area is designed not only for testing menus, but presenting them within the nearby meeting rooms and boardroom.

The Alpha unit is designed to operate a blast-chill system, and incorporates a bank of three blast chillers on the north east wall of the hot kitchen. Each unit capable of chilling 80 kg of produce in 90 minutes from + 70° to + 3°C. There is also a smaller blast-freezer. The walk-in chillers are all floorless to allow ease of trolley access and designed with sliding doors to limit any hindrance to corridors and lobby areas.

This modern unit is designed with flexibility for future expansion, while utilising the most hygienic building finishes for ease of operation and durability. Even though a number of items of existing equipment were transferred from existing units, the fit-out still had a final cost approaching £ 6 million.

Case study 7.2

Airline Services Limited—Nigeria

Airline Services Limited wanted to expand and improve their operations in Lagos. They provide an assembly operation only, buying in all their requirements to run a tray-set service. The facility largely caters for scheduled flights, aiming to gain additional business from airlines presently back-catering when travelling via Lagos.

The total floor area of their new production unit is 3,730 sq. m, which is fitted into a purpose built unit designed over three floors. A basement area is included within the design for storage of airline equipment and future expansion, with the ground floor given over to production operations and a first floor area largely given over for offices. The facility is designed to produce 5,000 meals a day at present with areas set aside for some future expansion. The new facility is within half a mile of the runways at Lagos.

The ground floor is suspended at 1.25 m above ground level to create three distinct loading docks for goods-in, goods-out and returns respectively. The majority of internal walls and ceilings in the production areas are created out of concrete blocks and tiled for a hygienic finish, with a resin floor finish throughout. Standard cold-room panels are used in temperature-controlled areas and chillers.

The actual total production area of 750 sq. m. breaks down to:

- Food Stores 23 sq. m
- Refrigerated Stores 75 sq. m
- Preparation 96 sq. m
- Hot Kitchen 104 sq. m
- Assembly 177 sq. m
- Dispatch Coldroom 80 sq. m
- Dishwash & Potwash 21 sq. m
- Equipment Stores 68 sq. m
- Loading Dock 107 sq. m

A separate 'test kitchen' is incorporated into the design on the first floor, in part to act as a kitchen to prepare separate small batches for presentation to potential new clients, but also to act as a staff feeding facility to gain maximum usage.

The ASL unit carries out ray assembly on work stations comprising stainless steel benches; each staffed by two operatives completing an individual passenger's tray.

Goods are received and dispatched from separate raised dock areas; and an additional distinct dock area is created for returns. From goods in, food follows a path through to decant and into dry stores holding or coldroom storage. Food then follows a straight-line flow along a central processing corridor to preparation, hot kitchens, blast chilling, tray assembly, and the dispatch chiller. The design has been examined carefully to prevent backtracking and cross-contamination from areas.

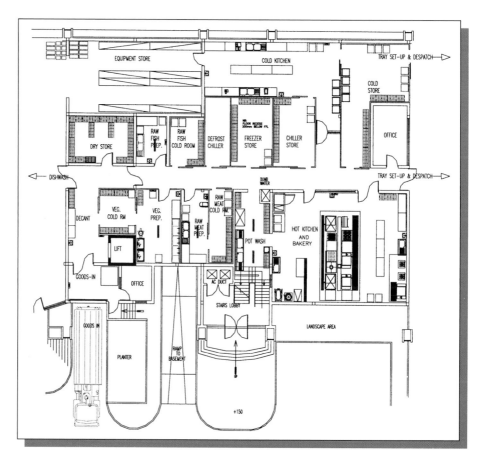

Figure 7.6
Plan of Airline Services Limited stores and kitchen areas
SOURCE: Hepburn Associates

There are a number of different sections:

(a) Fruit and vegetable preparation   Most vegetables and fruit are sourced locally, when available and in season in a raw state. As labour is more cost effective in comparison to European operations, most processing will be manual. Only produce that cannot be sourced locally will be brought in from abroad, some of which will be in a ready-prepared state. The fruit and vegetable preparation room benefits from its own walk-in chiller.

(b) Meat preparation   Daily meat deliveries are dated and temperature recorded upon arrival and is mostly part prepared. Some on-site butchery takes place and items such as a band saw and mincer are incorporated in the raw meat preparation room. An adjacent walk-in raw meat chiller is designed into the scheme.

(c) Fish preparation   Daily fish deliveries are dated and temperature recorded upon arrival and are mostly un-prepared. A separate fish preparation room with adjacent chiller is included for the operation.

(d) Hot kitchen   Situated around a central cooking island, the unit boasts 2 bratt pans, 2 boiling kettles, 1 salamander, 1 boiling table, 1 griddle, a fryer,

1 solid top boiling table and 220 grid floor-standing combination ovens. Additional gas and electrical capacity is designed into the scheme to allow for future expansion. A separate wall-sited section incorporating a bratt pan and 2 stockpots has been included to assist with staff feeding.

(e) Bakery Situated just off the hot kitchen is a small-in house bakery area so that consistency can be maintained, and incorporates a 40 litre mixer, small dough divider and prover. The bakery staff will utilise the hot kitchen combination ovens to bake-off an average of 5000 rolls daily. Some additional products such as Danish pastries and fruit puddings are also produced.

(f) Cold kitchen This has some shared facilities with the cold preparation area with ease of access to the cooked meat chiller and fruit and vegetable chiller. It leads via its cold store directly into assembly.

(g) Potwash A large automatic utensil washer is situated off the hot kitchen and bakery areas. A hot-rinse triple bowl sink unit is also included as a back-up to operations.

The ASL unit is designed to operate a blast-chill system, and incorporates a bank of two blast chillers on the north west wall of the hot kitchen. Each unit capable of chilling 80 kg of produce in 90 minutes from + 70°C to + 3°C. The walk-in chillers are all floorless to allow ease of trolley access and designed with sliding doors to limit any hindrance to corridors and lobby areas.

Airline Services Limited of Nigeria have kept in mind the fact that the majority of their potential customers will operate to European and North American standards and as such have ensured that the finished unit reflects these standards. The designers have incorporated the flexibility for future expansion and included hygienic building finishes for ease of operation and durability. They have also taken into account the fact that the area benefits readily from an inexpensive source of labour, so that the basic raw preparation takes place on site, allowing the unit tight control over the quality of much of its output from a very early stage. There is even an area incorporated in the design for an in-house laundry operation to be situated in the basement. While the unit may be far less automated than European or American operations, the processes of design remain very similar.

Current issues and future trends

The trends in previous chapters suggest that the **design** of flight production units may change over time. Upstream storage means that the scale and type of storage areas may change as less raw material and more finished product is used. Outsourcing also means that the size of the hot kitchen will decrease, if not disappear altogether. The adoption of bar coding also suggests that transportation within the production unit may be automated. The Gate Gourmet facility in Zurich has adopted this approach. All equipment items and most consumables are stored in bins or on pallets that are bar coded. Bins are transported to and from their location in the storage area on conveyors and lifts, with scanners reading the bar codes in order to direct them.

Clearly many of the operations, especially that of the tray assembly, are labour intensive. So some companies and equipment manufacturers are looking at **automating processes**. Investing in robotic machines for tray setting may well improve the productivity rate and efficiency, but needs to be coordinated within the context of the company's overall capabilities. For example, there may be insufficient funding to finance the capital investment, or automation might well have an unwelcome adverse effect in staffing and labour relations. While there are many potential applications of robotics in the food service industry, there are only a few tried and tested applications (Phillips, 1991). In theory, the scale of a flight operation makes the use of robotics an attractive proposition. Trials are taking place of the use of robotics as part of the tray-setting line. The robots are used to place items in the correct location on the meal tray.

An automated system such as the Building Maintenance System (BMS) is also important in monitoring the core food product temperatures, refrigeration temperatures, and the cooling system temperatures. The system should link to an independent computer system with an alarm warning. The idea is to have a simple and manageable system to prevent incorrect and false information, which can have an even greater detrimental effect.

Automation is also being adopted in response to the increased concern about terrorism. Flight production units are designed to ensure that only authorised personnel are given access. Typically photographic identity cards are issued. But at least one flight kitchen at Heathrow now has a machine that reads the handprint of people seeking access, thereby increasing the level of security.

No layout or design of a catering facility is ever permanent. New technology may become available that changes how processes are carried out. Labour costs may change due to external economic and social circumstances. In the flight catering industry especially, changes in the volume and variety of output will be affected by the winning (and losing) of airline contracts. Also, outsourcing decisions will affect what is produced in-house. So, catering organisations must spend time on planning and replanning their operations. This is often referred to as **process re-engineering**.

Conclusion

The nature of flight catering is changing constantly, driven by a number of factors such as developments in computer and catering technology and changes in the approach to production management and quality management. A number of trends can be recognised such as outsourcing of materials to reduce the number of activities taking place at the operation and just-in-time (JIT) inventory to control and reduce the level of stockholding and wasted materials.

The overall objectives of the flight caterer are likely to be broad based, such as increased market share, improved profit margins, and introduction of new products. It is the primary responsibility of the manufacturing manager or the director of flight catering to develop a detailed strategic plan for the food production unit to support these objectives. The person responsible must constantly take several factors into account, but there are often some very important, specific areas which should normally be reviewed: production management, plant engineering, quality control, and labour relations. He/she must ensure that maximum output is produced for minimum cost by keeping the workforce and equipment as fully occupied as possible since the production costs form a large part of the total operational costs. There should be a plan for regular maintenance and cleaning to ensure that the plant and its equipment are consistently kept up to standard and that predictable problems are avoided.

There are, of course, always unpredictable equipment breakdowns. In very large operations which are partially or fully automated these breakdowns can be extremely expensive if not corrected immediately. For this reason, most establishments have stand-by engineers. The plant engineering department is also responsible for ensuring that the layout and production flow are planned to give maximum efficiency and for utilising new technological advances as and when they become available to improve the manufacturing process.

Key terms

Batch production	Cell production	Cook-chill
Flow production	Production capacity	Sous-vide
Tray assembly		

Discussion questions

1. Design a flow of an in-flight kitchen and discuss which stages of the process can provide added value. What are the challenges?
2. Discuss the relative advantages and disadvantages of each different type of production method.
3. Debate on the pros and cons of assembly method with either *make and pack* or *conveyor belt*.

References

ACTCC Hygiene Services. (1990) *Airline Catering Code of Good Catering Practice*, ACTCC: Hounslow Middlesex.

Department of Health. (1989) *Chilling and Frozen: Guildelines on Cook-chill and Cook-freeze Catering Systems*, HMSO Publications: London.

Electricity Council. (1982) *Planning for Cook-chill*, The Electricity Council's Project Planning Unit (Catering): London.

Gehrig, B.J. (1990) Prinzip and Einsatzmöglichkeiten des Sous-Vide Verfahrens, *Mitteilungen aus dem Gebiete der Lebensmittelunter-suchung und Hygiene*, vol. 81, no. 6, 593–601.

Kang Y. (2000) "Safe food handling in airline catering", in J.M. Farber and E.C. Todd (eds), *Safe Handling of Foods*, Marcel Dekker New York.

Flight catering operations and organisation

- Explore the complexity of production scheduling
- Identify how meal production is managed
- Understand tray assembly and flight assembly processes
- Understand how flight production units are organised and staffed

Introduction

This chapter focuses on how food, beverages and equipment are prepared and assembled on a daily basis, prior to their transportation and loading onto the aircraft. There are three main elements to this—the preparation of materials (hot and cold food, beverages, equipment), tray assembly, and flight assembly. The following explains how each of these processes may be carried out, based on the typical practice across a number of flight kitchens operated by many different companies. For any specific operation, there will be local variations because of a number of factors, such as:

- the size of the operation
- the complexity and/or sophistication of the flight service
- the number of airlines handled by the facility
- the number of flights serviced during the day
- the duration of the flights serviced

Organisation of production unit

Before looking at production planning and operational activity, it is necessary to understand how a typical production unit might be organised. The traditional approach to this is to organise the unit so that under the unit general manager there would be managers responsible for different parts of the operation. Thus, there would be operational managers in charge of food production (often called Executive Chef), purchasing and stores, equipment handling (concentrating on offloading and ware washing), and transportation. In addition there would be functional managers responsible for human resources, accounting, and sales and marketing. This is shown in Fig. 8.1. The logic for this is that many organisations are organised in this way—based on 'work disciplines'— so that managers can be trained and given expertise in these areas. Furthermore, in the operations area, the physical plant is divided into separate areas, with

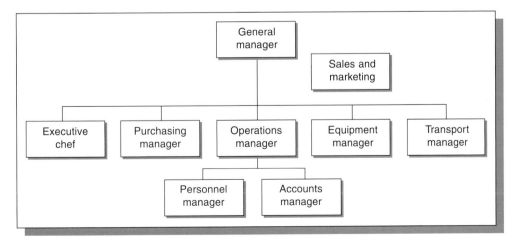

Figure 8.1
Traditional organisation chart of flight production unit

specific staff assigned to work in those areas, so it is clear who has the responsibility for the area and for the staff.

However, some firms are looking at their organisation in new ways, often influenced by what is called **business process reengineering** (BPR). BPR advocates the concept that the organisational structure should reflect the core processes undertaken by the business, with a manager given responsibility for each process. Under the traditional structure, if there is a problem with servicing a flight, no one manager would be responsible—the fault might lie with the purchasing manager for not ordering supplies, the equipment manager for not having the right equipment, the production manager, or the transportation manager. So, some caterers have now organised their production units based on core processes. For instance, Gate Gourmet in Geneva (Emad, 1997) identified these as Equipment Handling, Customer Management, and Goods Supply and Preparation. An example of an organisation chart based on this approach is shown in Fig. 8.2. Equipment handling involves all those activities related to the handling of equipment—unloading and loading aircraft, transportation, ware-washing, recycling—as well as those activities that involve handling standard equipment loaded onto the aircraft independent of passenger numbers. Goods supply and preparation clearly covers all aspects of hot and cold food preparation and production, as well as the supply of non-food items in relation to the specific needs and passenger numbers of any flight. Customer management involves all aspects of dealing with the airline and the management of the contract from the initial tender process, invoicing and billing, and all aspects of customer relations.

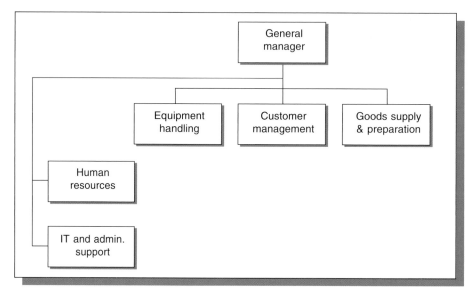

Figure 8.2
Organisation chart of flight production unit based on core processes

Given the diversity of flight production units and different management approaches in different countries, it should be noted that in addition to these two ways of organising a production unit, there can be other ways that combine the two approaches. However, whatever way the unit is organised, operational activity will have to be planned and executed.

Production planning and scheduling

Flight catering is very complex. Table 8.1 shows the uplift for a 747 'jumbo jet'. It is made up of more than 40,000 separate items. In production units handling many flights, literally millions of items have to be handled, processed and assembled in order to service that unit's airline contracts each day. Production planning and scheduling are essential if this is to happen efficiently and effectively. In one respect, this is straightforward as the number of flights to be serviced each is usually known well in advance. After all, aeroplanes fly to a timetable and the caterer will have a contract to supply these agreed often months in advance.

Contents	Number
Food items	
First-class perishable items, soups, garnish etc.	63
Food portions for 18 pax	312
Club World items packed on 2.5 trays service	2,963
World Traveller items packed on 2 trays	10,894
Flight and cabin crew trays, equipment, food items	226
Plus bread rolls, milk, butter, bar fruit, oven racks, etc.	3,029
Total for all food items	17,487
Catering equipment	
Dry stores, holloware, glasses, china, headsets, menus	18,204
Bonded items	
Liquor, wines, beer and duty free items, etc	4,203
Major equipment to contain the items	
for transporting and stowage on the aircraft	256
Total items supplied by catering per aircraft worldwide	40,150

SOURCE: British Airways Catering

Table 8.1
Contents of a typical 747–400 uplift

However, planning and scheduling may be disrupted for a number of reasons:

- Loss of airline contract—this is rarely sudden, but can be significant
- Re-scheduling of aircraft due to bad weather—this often affects several flights at the same time
- Re-scheduling of flight due to mechanical failure—this may mean recatering a flight if a replacement aircraft is different to that planned
- Servicing unscheduled flights i.e. private, executive aircraft

Production planning

The production plan is an overall guide to the operations activity over the forthcoming period (week or month). The purpose of the production plan is to balance the meal requirements for each airline against the resources available (labour, materials (food) and equipment) so that the plant operates at maximum efficiency. A backward flow scheduling system is required, starting with the link with ground transportation and working backwards through materials handling, processing and storage to the procurement of materials.

The first action required to formulate a production plan is to sort out the meal requirements. The orders are then broken down and sent to the suppliers. From this the production manager determines what food, labour, and equipment will be needed. This is a crucial process as circumstances can alter from day to day, hour to hour, and being short of one component or ingredient can affect the efficiency of the whole production.

In drawing up a plan it is important to realise that consideration must be given to total plant loading; unless each section is working flat out, resources may be wasted by paying premium rates for overtime in some areas, while in others, people and equipment stand still. For such reasons it is important to plan a flexible workforce.

The key elements of planning are:

- putting the orders into a sequence according to the date the airline requires to be loaded with the meals
- breaking down the orders into constituent details
- balancing mix between production lines
- batching orders for different airlines together if possible to achieve economies of stock

In any production process, it is usually impossible to state precisely what can be produced with the given equipment, food, and labour. However, computer software is available which is able to formulate the base production plan, according to a wide range of possible resource allocations against a sequence order plan. Smaller operators may have to rely on simpler systems, coupled with the experience of their individual managers. Within the priorities of the order plan, managers should plan to ensure where possible that downtime is kept to a minimum.

Using available labour to the maximum is a complex issue for the production planner. Particular equipment may require specialist skills that are limited to a few operatives. The workforce may also resist changes in shift patterns or levels of overtime working. In some cases the flexibility of labour is also dependent on the prevailing state of industrial relations.

Production scheduling

The production schedule is a more detailed plan that outlines what will be done each day. It is based on the production plan, plus the most recent available data about expected passenger numbers and so forth. Based on the flight data, a schedule is prepared for each of the production areas—cold kitchen, butchery, hot kitchen, pastry, bakery. Plans are developed based on loading times for a flight. From this time slot, all other activities are planned in a reverse sequence —container loading, tray assembly, pastry, cold kitchen, bakery, hot kitchen, butchery, stock issue. In this way, all the requirements are planned on a JIT basis to minimise food-holding stages.

This information forms the core of the system, since it is used to coordinate inventory requirements, kitchen schedules, assembly schedules, staffing requirements, and so on. The system calculates the requirements per flight for food and non-food items based on aircraft configuration, crew requirements, and advanced reservations data.

Pre-printed labels are prepared for each flight, showing the flight number and the contents of the trolley. Key elements of production scheduling are:

- food component requirements in place according to the priority of the number of meals to be produced
- minimisation of equipment downtime
- food requirements planning based on accurate stock recording systems
- maximum use of available labour hours

Production control

Production plans and schedules are rarely, if ever, carried out completely. Equipment breaks down, staff fall sick, suppliers fail to deliver, and so on. The function of production control is to ensure that production is maintained in line with the production plan wherever possible and secondly, to respond to the things which do go wrong and rework the plan to get back on schedule.

The food production managers monitor the supply and production process to ensure that there is always up-to-date information on what has been achieved and what further actions may be necessary to maintain the production flow. Where deviations from the production plan are spotted, corrective action is then taken to overcome any shortfalls in the production:

- Regular checks must be made on food availability, and alternative suppliers must be identified in cases of emergency where a designated supplier fails to deliver on time or to the exact quantity
- All food production managers and supervisors must be aware of what labour hours are available and how the operation is performing in terms of quality and productivity
- Procedures and plans must clearly identify alternative production strategies if equipment breaks down or if there is a shortage of labour
- The process of checking, reworking and rescheduling must be continuous to be effective. The original plan must remain the key objective. Changes should only be made if they are totally unavoidable

Meal production and packing

Cold kitchen

Most food served on board the aircraft is not hot. Aircraft have limited oven capacity, and handling hot food adds to the service complexity. So starters and desserts are usually cold, snack items are typically sandwiches and so on, and even main course items may be salads. In this case, food can be prepared at ambient temperatures or in a chilled room. The type of equipment used in this area of the production unit will be washing machines, peeling machines, vacuum tumblers, high speed cutters, slicing machines (Table 7.2).

Hot kitchen

All foods are cooked in batches, following the standard recipe. All the equipment in a production kitchen is designed for this scale of production—ovens, continuous cookers, tilting frying pans, grills and char broiler, steamers (Table 7.2). Most types of cooking can be adopted, although deep fat frying is rarely adopted. This is because food cooked in this way is no longer crisp if it is chilled and reheated, due to the water in the food turning to steam during the regeneration. Manufacturers who specialise in making food products of this kind are looking at ways in which they can overcome this problem.

Once cooked, food is transferred to bulk storage containers (colour coded with the day of production) and rapidly chilled in blast chillers (mechanical or cryogenic) to safe storage temperatures. A probe thermometer measures the temperature inside the food. Chilling from cooking temperature to around 2°C usually takes in less than 90 minutes There are strict rules about discarding any materials which have passed their 'use-by' date, which is typically 2–3 days for cook-chill products. In fact, with JIT systems in place in flight kitchens, most food is served within 24 hours of production.

Bakery

A particular type of hot kitchen, which specialises in making bread and other baked goods, is the bakery. This area has specialist equipment such as mixers and proving and baking ovens. The bakery in the Gate Gourmet kitchen in Geneva baked 54 different types of bread and bread rolls each week. Such a specialist facility tends only to be found where there is strong demand from airlines for a wide variety of bread products, and where the production unit has sufficient space to accommodate this facility.

Special meals

As we have seen, the production of special meals may be outsourced. However, if not, many types of special meals are prepared separately in a special kitchen devoted to that activity.

Crew meals

In addition to providing meals for passengers, the flight caterer is also responsible for providing crew meals. Given the importance of ensuring that at least the pilot and co-pilot have different meals, to avoid them both being subject to food-borne illness, production units have to ensure that there is no cross contamination between the food items prepared for these two meals. This applies to the ingredients used, as well as their production and subsequent handling.

Dish packing

Chilled food items are packed into appropriate containers, which may be foil, plastic or china. Chilled entrees are covered with foil that has been labelled to show the type of meal (fish, meat, hot breakfast, vegetarian, crew, etc.) and the day of production and the flight number. They are then held in refrigerated storage until they are required for packaging.

Packaging of hot breakfast and main course items may be carried out using large tables, or there may be a conveyor system which transports empty containers (foil or china) past a filling station, as shown in Fig. 8.3. Here, food is dispensed into the containers using a variety of techniques including the manual transfer of solid foods (plastic disposable gloves or tongs), manual ladling of liquid/semi-liquid foods such as stews and sauces (or the use of semi-automated dispensing hopper). The conveyor system is rarely used—usually only when there is a high volume to be packed and more than one item is placed in the dish, such as meat, vegetable, and potato for a main entrée.

This operation is usually conducted in a chilled environment. Once filled, the dishes are placed in oven boxes, which typically contain 20 or 40 dishes.

Figure 8.3
Dish-packing conveyor belt

Such boxes are not chilled, which is why this needs to be done in a chilled environment and the boxes be stored subsequently in cool conditions.

Tray and trolley assembly

All flight requirements are packed into appropriate trolleys and containers for aircraft type. This includes chilled meals, trays, drinks, tableware, linen, toiletries, newspapers, magazines, children's games, duty-free/sales items, baby food, first aid kits, accessories (slippers, blindfolds, headsets), toiletries, pillows, blankets, face towels, napkins, and printed menu cards. In order to identify what needs to go into each trolley, every type of trolley has a layout diagram, as illustrated in Fig. 8.4.

Tray assembly

The items to be assembled onto trays are likely to come from a number of different areas within the kitchen—chilled storage for the cook-chill meals, special meals and cold dishes, bakery, equipment store, and cutlery wrap area. The standard approach to loading this wide variety of items is to place as much as possible onto the tray that will eventually be presented to the passenger on the aircraft. As Fig. 8.5 illustrates, there tends to be a standard approach to this for main meal trays. The hot entrée is placed at the bottom of the tray (nearest the passenger), with the cutlery pack alongside it (to the left or right or across the top). Adjacent to the hot entrée (often on the left, but sometimes the right) is either the starter or cheese and biscuits. Then across the top of the tray from left to right, is either the dessert, cheese and biscuits or bread roll, and cup, or the starter, dessert and cup. In some cases there is a separate glass, in other cases a disposable water carton is placed inside the cup.

Just as for dish packing, tray assembly can also be carried out on a batch or flow basis (see Chapter 7). In batch assembly, a single worker at a workstation assembles everything onto trays and puts these into a trolley. This is illustrated in Fig. 8.6. This is sometimes known as 'make and pack'. In line assembly, the tray moves along a conveyor belt and different workers each put on different items until the completed tray reaches the end of the line and is again placed in a trolley. Since the line assembly requires the coordination of up to six or seven different workers, this tends to be used where only a large number of trays need to be assembled. In addition, it is really only efficient if the line is 'balanced', that is, all assembly workers take the same time per tray to complete their task, since the conveyor can only move at the speed of the slowest worker.

Increasingly, flight caterers are adopting ideas and techniques from manufacturing industries that are also involved in assembly-type operations. Many of these originated in Japan. For instance, at the heart of the just-in-time (JIT) approach is the use of 'kanbans'. Although this Japanese word means 'card', it refers to a container in which parts or components are moved from one work area to another. Each kanban is large enough to hold a small and fixed number of identical items. Kanbans are now in use in combination with work stations (see Case study 8.2). Likewise, 'poka-yokes', which is Japanese for a fail-safe device, are also used. Some poka-yokes can be incorporated into machinery to ensure their proper use, but others are simple check-lists,

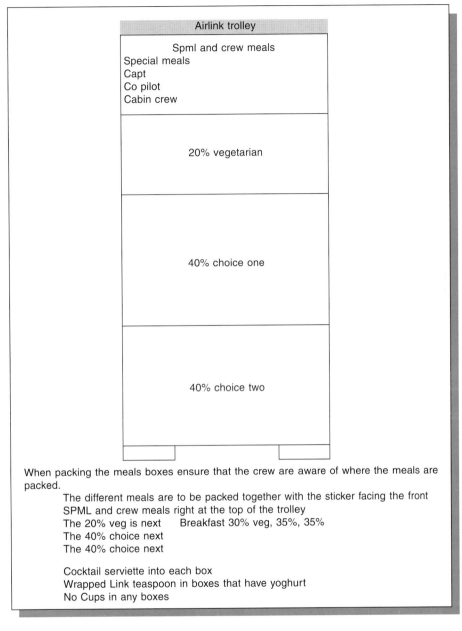

Figure 8.4
Trolley layout diagram
SOURCE: Ground Crew Catering Company

photographic illustrations or 'flags' to help workers do things in the right way. For instance, trolley brakes are coloured red and green to help employees know which brake pedal to press when parking or moving the trolley.

Figure 8.5
Examples of tray layups

Bar and duty free trolleys

Bar trolleys tend to be equipped with drawers rather than trays. Each drawer is of sufficient depth for the storage of the different types of item stored in it—miniature, half or full-size bottles of spirit, wine bottles, beer bottles, cans of soft drink, and glassware of all types. Most bar trolleys must be packed in the secure bonded store area, as the trolleys will have a mix of duty-free alcohol and other items in them. The duty-free trolleys with retail items for sale, such as perfume, watches, and so on, will also be packed in this area, for the same reason. Once these trolleys have been packed, they are sealed. The seal must

Figure 8.6
Work station layout
Source: Alpha Flight Services

remain unbroken until the trolley is on the aircraft and has been handed over to the cabin crew.

Other equipment trolleys

Other trolleys will typically be packed in the area where equipment for that airline is stored in the flight production unit. Such trolleys will have not only such things as headsets, first aid boxes, blankets and so on packed into them, but in addition any 'dead-head trolleys' will also be packed here. As explained later in Chapter 11, in order to ensure all the equipment needed by an airline is located at the right station, in some cases trays, crockery and cutlery are transported in trolleys on a flight even though they are not needed for that flight. This is referred to as 'dead-heading'.

Flight assembly

Trolleys from the tray assembly area, bonded store, and equipment stores are then moved into the flight assembly area, where all of the trolleys for a specific flight are marshalled. The contents of trolleys are checked by inspectors against the inventory of the flight. Food trolleys may be packed with dry ice in order to maintain a chilled temperature. In some cases, trolleys now have electric refrigeration units to keep them chilled. These must be plugged in during this assembly stage, as well as once they get onto the aircraft. Oven containers for meals that are to be reheated are kept in chilled storage until the last minute, and/or stored in insulated boxes. Each flight has its own checklist against which the assembly is monitored, as illustrated in Fig. 8.7.

The next stage after this is the transportation and loading process, which is discussed in Chapter 10.

Staffing

The process of preparing and cooking meals, assembling equipment, laying trays, and assembling the trolleys together for each flight clearly involves a large number of staff of different types. In addition, each production unit will also have staff in the stores (Chapter 6), drivers and loaders for the transportation of these meals (Chapter 10), and operatives in dishwash and cleaning (Chapter 15), as well as administrative staff engaged in production planning, scheduling, invoicing, sales and marketing and personnel. In addition, there may be some highly specialist staff such as laboratory technicians to monitor food safety, halal or kosher chefs, and so on. A large production unit might employ up to 1,000 workers, although these are likely to be divided across two or three shifts per day.

Given the great diversity in policy and practice between production, it is almost impossible to give any detailed breakdown of staffing levels. Some production units may employ a large number of skilled chefs, pastry chefs and bakers, whereas others that rely on outsourcing may employ none at all. However, in order to give some idea of the relative importance of staff in different areas of the production unit, a unit located off airport producing 6,000 meals per day, to 40 flights for several airlines, might employ on one shift the following:

- 10 employees in the dry stores and bonded stores
- 10 chefs in the hot kitchen
- 10 cooks or workers in the cold kitchen
- 5 workers in the equipment store
- 15 employees on dish and tray assembly
- 5 flight assembly workers
- 40 drivers and loaders
- 20 workers in dish-wash and recycling
- administrators

This list, while only approximate, highlights some key issues. First, in production units that are off airport and need to use public roads to transport trolleys to aircraft, drivers and loaders are up to one third of all the staff employed on a shift (see also Chapter 10). Second, in the production area itself, the two main areas that need high levels of staffing are those areas with a great deal of manual handling—tray assembly and dish-wash. Third, the number of unskilled staff is high. In the production area, the only staff that may have a high degree of training, skill, and expertise will be chefs.

Gulf air CDN GF—002/004 New Menu Cycle 1
Eff   01 july 01
Day/Date   Flight No GF 00

	BOOKED	UPDATE	FINAL FIGURE	T.O.B.
F/C				
B/C				
E/Y				

F/C	F/C Continued	E/Y
FULL LUNCH DINNER	**STANDARD UPLIFT**	**FULL LUNCH DINNER**
Canapés-100%	Butter Portions × 6-1 STD	Traysets—95%
Butter Medalions-100%	Fresh Orange Juice LTR-1-12 (a.m. fits)	Bread Roll on Trayset-100%
Bread Rolls × 20-1-12	Fresh Orange Juice-LTR-1-12 (sld)	Asian Veg Trayset-5%
White & Brown Arabic Bread 1-12	Gulf Pitted Dates-1 Box STD	Chix biryain 45%
Garlic & Herb Baguette-1-12	Orange Slices-Quarters-1-15	Chix Top Off-20%
Salad Bar Items × 4-1-12	Lemon Slices-Quarters-1-15	Lamb navarin 30%
Mixed Lettuce Leaves-1-12	Fresh Skimmed Milk-Pints	Asian veg curry 5%
Herb Vinaigrette-1-12	Gulf Champagne Bottle-1 STD	*Bulk Bread 120%*
Yogurt/Blue Cheese 1-STD	Sparking Mineral Water-1-4	*SPMLS*
Garlic & Herb Mayo-1-STD	Alcove Arrangement-A340 Only	
Cold Mezza × 6 Cycle 2-1-12	Gulf Flower Arrangement-1 std	
Hot Mezze Choice 1 m/foil 1-12	Wet Ice-Kgs	
Hot Mezze Choice 2 m/foil 1-12	**B/C**	
Tahini Sauce in Bowl 1-12	**FULL LUNCH DINNER**	
HDV Prawn sushi 1-6	Trayset-100%	
Flask of Arabic Coffee-1 STD	Butter Medallions-100%	
Soup green pea × 1ltr 1-STD	Vinaigrette dressing 18 ml 100%	Fruit Pieces—Trays-1-30
Soup Garrish-Croutons-1-12	Salad Bowls	
ENTREES: rack of lamb/sauce	HDV chaud froid 100%	
Chix biryani	Bead Rolls × 8-1-12	
Salmon/sundried tom	White & Brown Arabic Breads 1-12	**SECOND SERVICE**
Spaghetti primevera	Garlic & Herb Baguette-1-12	Fruit Scone Plates
Roast potatoes 1-6	Entrees: Chix biryani 60%	*SPMLs*
Basmati rice 1-4	Salmon/sundried tom 30%	
Green Beans & Mixed Veg 1-6	Lamb navarin 30%	
Broccoli & Cauliflower 1-6	*SPMLS*	
Ratatouille 1-6		Wet Ice-Kgs
		Fresh Milk-Pints
SPMLS	Chocolate torte 1-18	Lemon Slices-Quarters-1-50
	Pot of Double Cream-1-12	
UMALI 1-12	Fruit Tray-1-12	
Custard Sauce 1-12	Cheeseboard-1-18	KIDS PACKs
Double Cream Pint 1-12	Cheese Biscuit-1-18	
Pistachio/Vanilla ice cream 1-6	Gulf Chocolate Box-1-18	
Ice cream biscuits 1-12		
	SECOND SERVICE	

SOURCE: Gulf Air (Need Authorisation)

Figure 8.7

Flight assembly checklist

161

Flight catering chefs

An interesting feature of the flight catering industry, compared with other foodservice sectors such as restaurants or contract catering, is that there may be two kinds of chef employed. The first type is the production chef, who is responsible on a daily basis for hot and cold meal production. The second type is the 'development' or 'research chef'. These chefs specialise in developing and trialing new dishes for use in flight catering. As we have seen in Chapter 4, food and drink when consumed at an altitude may taste very different to what it does on the ground. Moreover, some airlines are highly proactive, as part of their strategy, in terms of being at the leading edge of consumer tastes in food. Thus, there may be a great deal of dish and recipe development being conducted in flight kitchens. Research suggests that production chefs and development chefs need different sets of skills or competencies to each other in order to perform these two tasks, although this may vary from country to country (Hayama, 2002). This research surveyed flight catering chefs in the UK, USA and Japan, and found eleven 'essential competencies' for *all* chefs:

- time management
- knowledge of culinary fundamentals and production systems
- knowledge of kitchen functions and pressures
- knowledge of quality assurance and food safety
- ability to work in multi-task environments
- ability to distinguish levels of quality in food product
- ability to make decisions
- general communication skill
- understanding food testing
- knowledge of culinary uses and applications of products and ingredients
- skilled at food presentation

The first five of these eleven competencies may be particularly important for production chefs, and the last three particularly important for development chefs.

Scheduling and rostering staff

Staff rosters are usually planned and organised by the head of each of the operating departments. In many cases, the roster is planned by them and then checked (by computer) against the production plan and schedule, in order to see whether each section of the production unit will be working efficiently. In other words, for any given number of meals, tray assemblies, or flights there will be an estimated number of work hours.

Depending on the nature of the airlines and the contracts being serviced, flight production units may have weekly or seasonal peaks and troughs in activity. Many units therefore employ a proportion of core staff on a full-time basis throughout the year, and then use part-time or casual non-skilled staff for periods of high demand. In some cases, these temporary workers are supplied through employment agencies.

Case study 8.1

Air Fayre, London Heathrow

Business Process Reengineering (BPR) has developed different ways of organising the structure of a flight-catering unit but perhaps the most far reaching of all has been that of Air Fayre at London Heathrow. They decided that the skill of the flight caterer was focussed on the logistics of an operation rather than the production of food and therefore they eliminated the requirement for food production within the operation. As such, it has become a pure logistically focussed business, which has helped considerably to reduce operating costs. All food product is purchased from recognisable manufacturers, 'pre plated' and ready to use, thereby removing the often cost inefficient functions of Hot Kitchen, Bakery, Food Production and Preparation. While HACCP and Health and Hygiene continue to be rigidly enforced, it has reduced the amount of time and controls that have to be in place in more traditional flight kitchens.

At the assembly points, the operation is similar to that of a more conventional flight catering operation, with the exception that short haul flights are transported in bulk, in fully refrigerated vehicles, to a Forward Catering Facility, on the airport, from where they are distributed to the aircraft. This removes the need for catering high-loaders to make numerous trips from the catering centres, which are often a few miles from the aircraft. Perhaps most importantly is that the chill-chain can be completely secure from unit to aircraft.

The increased flexibility of 'finalising' the flight later into the delivery process allows for adjustments in passenger figures to be made, both increases and decreases, ensuring the correct amount of meals are on board and minimising wastage.

A clear change in direction has been signalled by this style of operation, to one of a logistics-based approach rather than a food manufacturing and delivery concept. There is clear opportunity for this to be encouraged further, in other areas of the supply chain, which would challenge the fundamental aspects of the flight catering industry.

Case study 8.2

LSG Skychef, Stockholm

Work stations are now used for almost all the tray assembly in this unit. It has been found that this has significantly improved labour productivity. Each work station comprises a tray slide, above which there are two sloping shelves on which bins can be placed. The height of the station can be adjusted so that each worker can work at a comfortable height. Some prefer to stand, others may sit on a stool. Each bin contains one separate item for that particular tray layup, such as milk jigger, sugar sachet, and so on. The bins are 'balanced', that is, each bin contains approximately the same number of items. This is so that all the bins run out at the same time, rather than individual bins needing replacing at different times, as this would waste time and effort. The bins are also laid out along the top and bottom shelf in a predetermined order designed to facilitate the tray layup. Each worker also takes items from these bins in a specific order, typically starting at the top right and moving in an anti-clockwise direction. Trays are laid up two at a time because the worker picks up one item *in each hand* from the first bin to put on each tray, and then takes from the second bin and so on. Once laid up, trays are put into trollies. These may be on a trolley lift that adjusts in height to the level of the tray slide. This minimises movement and also reduces strain on the employee.

The work stations are organised into rows of three which are placed back to back with another row. Between the two rows, there is an aisle which allows access between them. This allows the operation of the 'kanban' system. When a bin becomes empty it is placed on a low shelf beneath the work area. An employee, called a 'runner', has the job of checking along the aisle between works stations for any empty bins. These are removed and replaced with full bins collected from the stores. To keep things simple and avoid mistakes, each 'empty' bin has one item left in it so that the runner knows precisely what to get. This is a good example of a 'poka-yoke' (fail-safe device).

Another poka-yoke in use on the work station is a 'flag' above the top shelf. In this case it is cards that are either red or green. When the employee is working normally the green 'flag' shows. But if there is a problem, the flag is changed to red. This alerts a supervisor who should come to the work station to see what the problem is, without the worker stopping what they are doing. Another poka-yoke is a labelled photograph showing how to lay out the work station correctly.

Management has found that both productivity and quality have increased since introducing this system. All kinds of 'waste' have been removed from the process—wasted time, wasted movement, wasted stocks, and so on (see the next section below). Quality has been improved through the systematisation of the process so that fewer mistakes are made. Employees have also found the approach satisfactory. Their work is less strenuous and they have responsibility for the whole assembly process rather than some part of it.

Current issues and future developments

One of the implications of the growth of large firms in the flight catering industry is that there is a significant increase in 'benchmarking' that is comparing the performance of one unit against all the others. When top-performing units are identified it is possible to examine what they do and then adopt it across all units. Likewise, it is possible to trial new ideas and new processes in one unit to test them, prior to spreading this 'best practice' to all the others. Both Gate Gourmet and LSG SkyChef have been engaged in **process reengineering**. This refers to looking at all the processes within the unit and looking at ways in which the process can be made more efficient and effective. Often this involves removing so-called 'waste' from the system. The Japanese guru Taiichi Ohno, one-time Chief Engineer for Toyota, has identified seven types of waste:

1. Doing too much
2. Waiting
3. Transporting
4. Too much inflexible capacity or lack of process flexibility
5. Unnecessary stocks
6. Unnecessary motions
7. Defects

An implication of upstream storage, process re-engineering and outsourcing is a change in the structure and skill base of **employment** in flight production units. If less food is stored and processed in the flight production unit, fewer skilled chefs will be required. On the other hand, if processes are automated, one or two more IT professionals may be needed.

Finally, all processes need to incorporate appropriate **security** measures. For instance, the trolley assembly process now includes the sealing of each trolley with a secure tab which should only be broken by cabin crew once loaded onto the aircraft. Even back-of-house processes may be involved. For instance, when employing new staff, firms are likely to adopt tighter screening and vetting procedures than a few years ago.

Conclusion

Although flight production units are often called 'flight kitchens', as this chapter has demonstrated, only a small part of the operational activity in the unit is concerned with cooking and meal production. The hot kitchen itself may be less than 10 per cent of the total floor area and employ relatively few staff out of the total. Production staff generally work to a well-established routine, which only varies in terms of the number of passengers forecast for each flight. Sometimes, this routine may be disrupted, by bad weather or a defective aeroplane, in which case emergency procedures are adopted in response to this.

There seems to be a trend towards allocating tasks to production workers so that they have full responsibility for an activity. Hence, they are organised by workstations to assemble trays. Many managers believe that this is not only more efficient but also more motivating. Employees like to be involved in the total process. Moreover, in the event that there is a defect with the dish or tray or trolley, it is also possible to identify the employee responsible for that and to retrain them to ensure that it does no re-occur. In the next chapter we go on to look in detail at a system for assuring quality standards and food safety.

Key terms

Business process reengineering (BPR)	Downtime	Flight assembly
Kanban	Make and pack	Poka-yoke
Production planning	Production scheduling	Tray assembly
Trolley assembly		

Discussion questions

1. Design a production schedule within 24 hours to supply a flight of Boeing 747 aeroplane flying to a destination of your choice with departure at 10:00 a.m.
2. How might the location, design, layout and process choice of a production unit affect the organisation of staff?
3. What would happen in a production unit if a flight was delayed for more than six hours?

References

Emad, S. (1997) *Gate Gourmet Geneva*, International Institute for Management Development: Lausanne, Switzerland.

Hayama, M. (2002) *"Investigation of the Job Roles and Competencies of Airline Catering Chefs in the UK, USA and Japan", unpublished dissertation* , University of Surrey.

Food safety management*

Learning objectives

- To identify hazards to food safety in flight catering
- To identify best practice in food safety and food handling practices
- To describe the Hazard Analysis and Critical Control Points (HACCP) system

*This chapter was written by Dr Anita Eves and Panagiota Dervisi.

Introduction

Flight caterers and airlines have an excellent record for food safety, especially considering that the business is characterised by a number of challenges—cook-chill production, time delay between production and consumption, and large-scale operations. Over the years, however, there have been a small number of outbreaks of food poisoning amongst passengers and crew. Clearly, the implications of a food poisoning outbreak to a business can be significant. Costs could include tracing the source of the outbreak, loss of business through loss of contracts with airlines, and paying compensation to airlines and/or passengers. It is a sad fact that most outbreaks of food poisoning are the result of a breakdown in good hygiene practices and could have been avoided. Patrick Wall, when Chief Executive of the Food Safety Authority (Ireland), encapsulated this beautifully when he said, "Food poisoning is not bad luck, it is bad management."

This chapter defines safety hazards, reviews the nature and control of micro-organisms, gives a brief account of major food pathogens (micro-organisms causing illness), including examples of food poisoning cases associated with the flight catering industry, and concludes with a discussion of Hazard Analysis, Critical Control Points (HACCP). HACCP is the method widely advocated as the food safety management system of choice in the food industry, including the flight-catering sector.

Nature of hazards

A number of factors can influence the safety of food, and these hazards can be categorised as biological, chemical, or physical.

Biological hazards include microbiological organisms such as bacteria, viruses, fungi, and parasites. These organisms are commonly associated with humans and with raw products entering a food establishment. Most are killed or inactivated by cooking, and numbers can be minimised by adequate control of handling and storage practices. This chapter focuses on microbiological hazards, because this type of contamination is likely to not only affect a single passenger, but all those that consumed the product, perhaps more than 100 passengers on a 747.

Physical hazards include foreign objects (e.g. glass, metal, stones, wood, plastic, and pests), resulting from contamination and/or poor practices at some point along the food chain. Practices such as avoiding the use of glass, including glass thermometers in production areas, aim to minimise such risks. Although physical contamination of food usually affects only single passengers, it accounts for a fairly large proportion of customer complaints, with insect contamination the major concern followed by glass and plastic. A survey by the British Airways Food Safety & Environmental Health Team carried out in the late 1990s indicated that some 11 per cent of total passenger complaints related to foreign bodies found in flight meals. Furthermore, unlike microbiological contamination and any consequent illness sustained by the passengers or crew, there rests an element of proof that is required before the airline or caterer can be held responsible or proven to be guilty. In addition, the stress and discomfort such incidents may cause the passenger do nothing for the reputation of the airline or caterer, and possible compensation claims from passengers can be high. Thus, looking for possible physical contamination in the food safety audit has become a high priority with caterers and airlines.

Chemical hazards can occur at any stage of production. They include cleaning chemicals, pesticides, and toxic metals (Mortimore and Wallace, 1994; Loken, 1995; Hobbs and Roberts, 1993). The effect of chemical contamination on the consumer can be long term (e.g. carcinogenic) or short term (e.g. burns).

It is also worth including allergens here, as they have had an impact on flight-catering practices. Over 170 foods have been documented as causing allergic reactions. For practical purposes attention should focus on the 'major serious allergens' (MSAs), including the 'big eight'—milk, eggs, soy, wheat, peanuts, shellfish, fruits, and tree nuts—which account for the majority of food allergies (Taylor, 1992 in Institute of Food Science and Technology (IFST), 1999 [online]). Many airlines no longer offer peanuts as flight snacks, to avoid potential allergic reactions, as the smell of peanuts being consumed by another passenger may be enough to trigger a potentially fatal response for those with severe allergies.

The nature of micro-organisms and their control

Micro-organisms comprise a group of very small organisms including bacteria, yeasts, moulds, and viruses. Bacteria and viruses are most often linked to food poisoning. Yeasts do not usually cause illness, and the presence of moulds is usually more evident than that of bacteria or viruses. Moulds can lead to either acute (immediate) illness or chronic illness. A good example of the latter is a mould that grows on peanuts and forms a poison known as aflatoxin. The toxin is carcinogenic. The remainder of this chapter will focus on bacteria and viruses.

Bacteria and viruses are not visible to the naked eye. Their presence or otherwise cannot therefore be determined by visual inspection, and all food should be handled as if they are present. Indeed, with the exception of foods that have been sterilised, all foods will contain some micro-organisms. In order to grow all micro-organisms require moisture, food, an appropriate temperature, and time. The growth of micro-organisms can be controlled by limiting access to one or more of these factors. In addition, some organisms require air to grow, while others are killed by oxygen. In optimum conditions, micro-organisms can multiply at an alarming rate, reaching levels that will lead to food poisoning within a few hours. Control measures aim to reduce the rate at which organisms multiply, or to destroy them.

Key pathogens

Some of the key food poisoning organisms are discussed briefly below, although not all have been linked, yet, to food poisoning outbreaks in flight catering. Where they have, examples are given (these originate from Kang, 2000). Some food poisoning organisms are major contributors to food poisoning world-wide, others tend to be prevalent in individual countries owing to particular food consumption patterns (for instance *V. parahaemolyticus* is particularly problematic in Japan owing to the consumption of raw fish). However, with flight caterers preparing foods for flights going to a myriad of world-wide destinations, occurrences of food poisoning from a wide variety of organisms or sources is possible.

Salmonella sp Salmonella sp are major pathogens world-wide, and have been implicated in a number of outbreaks of food poisoning associated with flight catering. Salmonella is an enteric pathogen, meaning that it is associated with the digestive tract (of either humans or animals). It finds its way into food either through contamination of raw ingredients, or by cross-contamination from food-handlers carrying the organism (usually the result of poor personal hygiene). Food handlers can carry the organism for many months after themselves suffering with illness, or can carry it without showing symptoms (known as the carrier state). Food handlers who contract Salmonella food poisoning must not return to work until faecal samples show that they are no longer carrying the organism.

For illness to occur, a person usually needs to consume a large number of organisms of salmonella. This means that in most cases the organism must grow on the food to reach high enough numbers to cause illness. This usually occurs as a result of prolonged storage of the food at temperatures supporting the growth of the organism (for instance, storage at room temperature of 20°C in the UK, but potentially much higher in the Southern hemisphere). Salmonella is controlled by heating foods to a minimum of 70°C for 2 minutes (which should kill the bacteria) and by storage of foods below 5°C (which slows the growth rate of the organism). These are minimum requirements, and individual company guidelines can be more stringent. When heating foods, it is important that all parts of the food satisfy this temperature–time requirement. The illness usually manifests itself 12 to 36 hours after consumption of the infected food—thus, in most cases illness will not be apparent until some time after the passenger leaves the aircraft. Flight foods that have been implicated include cold salads, hors d'oeuvres and sweet desserts. Other foods with which the organism has been linked include eggs (and products containing raw eggs) and poultry, but also chocolate, orange juice, and diced tomato. There has been widespread advice to use pasteurised eggs in dishes that do not receive a heat treatment (such as mousses and mayonnaise), and that if shell eggs are to be used in cooked dishes, they should have sanitised shells.

Campylobacter sp These are also enteric, and to date have not been implicated in food poisoning originating through flight catering. Although less well-known than Salmonella, it is thought to be responsible for more cases of food-poisoning in the UK, although more recently there has been question over how many of the cases are actually foodborne, rather than contracted through other activities. A key issue with Campylobacter is the very low infective dose. Thus, if a food becomes contaminated, it remains a risk even if the food is stored at temperatures that do not support bacterial growth. It is, however, very sensitive to heat and is destroyed by normal cooking. Post-process contamination of foods that will not subsequently be reheated, however, presents a significant risk. The organism has been associated with undercooked poultry and unpasteurised milk.

Shigella sp Shigella sp have been linked to a number of outbreaks associated with flight catering. It is an organism that is very similar to salmonella, with similar control requirements. Seafood cocktail was implicated in a case of Shigella food poisoning on a flight in 1971.

E.coli 0157:H7 This organism is an increasingly important food pathogen. It is again enteric and although to date has caused relatively few food poisoning outbreaks (none involving flight catering), its notoriety is the result of the high mortality rate associated with those who contract the illness (and some who survive will go on to develop unpleasant kidney conditions). Like Campylobacter, the infective dose is low. Major outbreaks have occurred relating to meat products and to bean sprouts (one outbreak in Japan affecting 10,000 people). Organically fertilised salad vegetables have also been implicated. Cross-contamination from raw to cooked meats and undercooking meats have both been identified as risk factors.

Staphylococcus aureus This has been implicated in at least four outbreaks of food poisoning associated with flight catering. The illness, which results in abdominal pain, acute cramps, vomiting, and often spontaneous diarrhoea, has an incubation period of 1 to 7 hours. This can have disastrous effects in the air depending on the level of toxin, the severity of symptoms and number of passengers and crew affected. Experience indicates that this can result in large numbers of people becoming ill with limited sanitary facilities on board resulting in possible diversion, or danger to the aircraft if the crew are also involved. The organism usually finds its way onto food as a result of contamination by food handlers, as the main reservoir of this organism is human (including the hands and nose). Major contributors are coughing and sneezing, including contamination of hands through the use of handkerchiefs, and handling foods with septic cuts (uncovered). The illness is the result of the organism growing on the food and producing a toxin. It is the toxin that causes the illness. Thus, to cause illness the food has to become contaminated, and the organisms must have sufficient time in appropriate conditions to grow and produce enough toxin to result in illness. The toxin is also heat stable, thus subsequent reheating cannot be assumed to remove the problem. Avoidance of contamination through good personal hygiene on the part of food handlers and storing the food below 5°C (preventing both growth and toxin production) will minimise the risk of this type of food poisoning. In addition, food handlers with infected cuts on their hands must not be allowed to work with foods until the infection has cleared. The foods implicated in flight outbreaks include ham, eclairs (containing whipped cream), and custard. Cured meats are often implicated as this organism is not controlled by the salt (sodium chloride) in these products, and where whipped cream has been implicated, this has been linked to contaminated cream passing through a whipping machine, which is then not properly cleaned and sanitised thus contaminating subsequent batches. This highlights the importance of training staff to clean and sanitise the equipment that they are using properly.

Some bacteria produce spores, which are highly resistant forms of the bacteria that can survive most common control measures, and then grow when conditions become favourable again. The most important are Bacillus sp and Clostridia. Clostridia sp are also anaerobes.

Bacillus cereus This organism is linked to food poisoning from rice or meat products (leading to vomiting or diarrhoea respectively). The spores formed by this organism will survive normal cooking. If conditions allow, they will germinate after cooking and produce toxin. If the product is not subsequently reheated or not reheated to reach a high enough temperature, the toxin will cause illness. Thus cooked rice and meat products should be cooled rapidly after cooking and stored at refrigeration temperatures, which will then not allow the spores to outgrow. Reheating must be at a high enough temperature for a long enough time to destroy the toxin. It should be noted that airlines throughout the world use rice as a basic ingredient of many menu cycles.

Two Clostridia sp are important in food poisoning, *Cl perfringens* and *Cl botulinum*. *Cl perfringens* has been implicated in a case of food poisoning associated with flight catering (in Turkey), but, thankfully *Cl botulinum* has not, as this organism produces a powerful neurotoxin and is fatal in a relatively large number of cases.

Cl perfringens   This organism is mainly associated with large-scale production of joints of meat (particularly rolled or boned meats where the contamination on the surface of the meat ends up in the centre of a large joint) or meat dishes. Large volumes take a long time to cool, and spores that have survived cooking will outgrow. The organism is controlled by rapid cooling and storage below 5°C. It may be necessary to separate the joint/dish into smaller portions to facilitate this. Thus a product should be cooled to below 5°C within 2 hours. The spores will not germinate within 2 hours, and will not grow below 5°C.

Cl botulinum   While *Cl botulinum* poisoning is rare, circumstances in which cases have arisen serve as cautionary tales. A significant feature of this spore-forming organism is that it will survive and grow at 3.3°C, below refrigeration temperatures. The types of food with which cases have been linked are canned and vacuum-packed food. The canning process is designed to destroy *Cl botulinum* spores and involves complete sterilisation. Acid foods (e.g. canned fruits) require a lower time-temperature combination as the acid sensitises the spores to heat. Problems arise if the cans are underprocessed, or if contamination occurs after processing. A case involving hazelnut yoghurt in the UK was found to be the result of underprocessing of the hazelnut puree used to flavour the yoghurt, as the same time–temperature combination was used as for the fruit (acidic) purees usually produced. Consequently, some spores survived and subsequently grew. When the organism grows it produces gas, so a good indication of contamination is a can with blown ends. This was the case here; however, the puree was used, and food poisoning resulted. This shows the importance of people working at an operational level being adequately trained to recognise problems and understand the need for their control.

Viruses   Viruses can also cause food poisoning, the most common being the Norwalk-like viruses. These are most often passed on from food handler to food. One of the largest outbreaks of food poisoning associated with flight catering was the result of viral contamination of orange juice. The outbreak affected more than 3,000 people, including non-travellers. It was traced back to contamination at the manufacturers, and whilst it did not then directly implicate the flight caterer, it shows the importance of having suppliers who follow good hygiene practices themselves. One of the problems with viral illness is its very sudden onset. Thus, a person working within a processing/kitchen environment may feel perfectly well when arriving for work, but then suddenly be taken uncontrollably ill.

Food safety and handling practices in flight catering

An important starting point is to *minimise contamination of food*, either as purchased or during the production process. Especially important is avoiding contamination of foods that will not subsequently be cooked. Ensuring suppliers are operating hygienically is an important management role, and could involve setting specifications, requiring that suppliers have a HACCP system in place or inspecting premises. Preventing contamination during production means ensuring that the staff behave in a hygienic way—including supplying appropriate clothing, facilities, and training. It also means ensuring that pests, and other creatures, cannot enter production or storage facilities. In addition, separate areas and equipment should be designated for raw and cooked foods and effective cleaning regimes must be in place. Staff training should include the ways in which foods can become contaminated and how to avoid this.

Measures to control or remove micro-organisms

While the measures above will minimise their presence, measures will still be needed to prevent any micro-organisms present multiplying or to remove them. The main control measure open to all food producers is temperature. Other measures include manipulating atmosphere, the use of anti-microbial ingredients, and reducing moisture and irradiation.

Temperature

Bacteria multiply most rapidly at around 37°C. This is close to ambient temperatures in some countries and also a temperature to which badly ventilated kitchens can rise. Most bacteria will not grow below 5°C, but they will survive. Indeed, freezing will not kill most bacteria. Most bacteria are killed at temperatures above 65°C. Keeping bacteria out of the 5–65°C zone—*the danger zone*—will optimise chances of controlling microbial growth. This is achieved by adequate refrigeration, heating to high enough temperatures or cooling hot foods rapidly. Some bacteria, however, form spores which require complete sterilisation (120°C) to destroy (e.g. Bacillus sp and Clostridia sp) and others are able to survive and grow, albeit slowly, at temperatures below 5°C, notably *Cl botulinum* and *L monocytogenes*. When heating foods, it is important to satisfy the time—temperature combination prescribed, as the time the food is held at a high temperature is important in achieving the desired lethal effect.

Atmosphere

Some bacteria are aerobic—require air to grow (e.g. Salmonella sp), while others are anaerobic and cannot survive in air (e.g. Clostridia sp). If the organism that requires control is aerobic, its growth can be retarded by reducing or removing air/oxygen from its packaging. This may include vacuum packing to remove all air. It must be remembered, however, that in removing the growth requirements of one group of organisms, the conditions become more favourable to another—in this case anaerobes. In addition, as soon as the pack is opened, conditions once again become aerobic.

Anti-microbial ingredients

A number of ingredients are added to foods to make the environment less favourable to micro-organisms. Some have a duplicate effect of reducing available water—notably salt (sodium chloride) and sugar. Anti-microbials include acids (e.g. acetic acid in vinegar) and additives such as sodium nitrite used in the production of cured meats.

Moisture

Different organisms require different minimum amounts of moisture in order to grow. Removing moisture by drying will preserve foods, but most bacteria will survive dry conditions, and will grow when moisture is again introduced. It is also important to draw a distinction between moisture content and available water. The latter is the factor limiting microbial growth, and this is not always reflected in the moisture content. As intimated above, sugar and salt will limit the available water in a product, despite it having a high moisture content.

Irradiation

Irradiation is a method of reducing the number of bacteria and, at higher doses, bacterial spores. It involves exposing food to gamma rays from a radioactive source or beta rays from an electron beam generator. The food never comes into contact with the source, and thus does not become radioactive. The dose is determined by the length of time for which the food is exposed, with low doses killing insects or preventing sprouting of vegetables; intermediate doses controlling bacteria and higher doses controlling bacterial spores. Irradiation is not suitable for use on all food products, particularly those containing a lot of fat (which become rancid) and those with a delicate cell structure (which can become unacceptably soft). Other changes to taste and texture are generally small when appropriate doses of irradiation are used. One major advantage is the potential to treat complete plated meals, thus removing post-processing contamination that may occur during the plating process. However, it is generally viewed unfavourably by environmental and food safety experts within the flight catering industry. It was reviewed some years ago by British Airways and it was agreed that while it had some advantages for removing post-processing contamination it might leave an avenue for suppliers/manufacturers to irradiate poor quality food products.

Potential causes of food poisoning

A number of factors have been identified as contributing to catering-related food poisoning outbreaks, the relative frequency with which different factors are recorded being dependent on data collection methods and classification. None-the-less key factors include preparation of food too far in advance, inadequate heating or cooling and cross-contamination (Griffiths, 2000; Guzewich, 2000). Usually more than one factor is implicated—for instance, food that has become contaminated being held for too long at a temperature that allowed microbial growth. Practices implicated in flight outbreaks have been very similar. Flight catering has more potential than most catering businesses to fall foul of these factors, given the inevitable delay between production and consumption. In addition, the extensive handling of foods (adequate automation of meal construction has yet to be achieved) gives an opportunity for post-process contamination. Airlines allow 48 hours between preparation of foods and delivery to aircraft for cold foods and 72 hours for hot meals (Kang, 2000). Once on board, foods may be stored for a number more hours before being served to passengers, especially if the flight is delayed. It should be noted that these storage times assume adequate temperature control during the holding period and also (for hot items) adequate regeneration of the meals on board.

An important issue in relation to flight catering is the number of people who may receive a contaminated item. A single flight may carry 350 or more passengers, receiving a very narrow range of food options and an infected item may go on to several flights. Thus one contaminated food item can affect a large number of people. For instance, an outbreak of *St aureus* poisoning in 1975 (traced back to ham), affected 196 out of 343 passengers, and an outbreak of *S typhimurium* poisoning in 1976, affected 550 of 2500 (on several flights) passengers (Kang, 2000). While these outbreaks were traced back to flight catering, if passengers do not become ill on the flight they will travel to disparate destinations and thus the true source of the illness may not be determined. For instance, one case, ultimately attributed to flight catering, only came to light because it affected a professional football team (*Shigella sonnei* affecting 30 of 725 passengers eating sandwiches on 13 flights—Kang, 2000). By comparison, some forms of food poisoning may manifest themselves within 30 minutes of consumption of the affected food. Thus an airline could find themselves with a large number of sick people on board (as was the case in the outbreak of *St aureus* poisoning in 1975). It is worth noting here also that food poisoning can be fatal, particularly to the elderly, the very young and the immuno-compromised. For instance, in 1992 seafood salad originating in Lima, Peru, was implicated in a case of cholera affecting 75 passengers, ten of whom were hospitalised and one of whom died (Kang, 2000).

Training

It has been suggested (Mortlock et al., 2000) that the benefits of hygiene training need to be more widely promoted in order to encourage managerial commitment to staff training. Managers must be made aware of the inherent risks involved in their business practices and the contribution training makes to minimise these risks.

Training should be viewed as one part of a broader food hygiene control strategy. Adequate training for all personnel, including those whose duties take them into manufacturing areas or bear on manufacturing activities, is essential (e.g. those concerned with maintenance, services, or cleaning). Integrating food safety into training curricula is the key to reaching the diverse audience that makes up the food service operations workforce. Particular attention should be given to overcoming language or reading difficulties. Training should begin on the first day an employee comes to work with an introduction to food safety (Seward, 2000). This initial training must be reinforced, matching the level of training with individual responsibilities. More advanced training for managers, dealing with food hygiene in greater detail and covering management and systems is considered good practice (Worsfold, 1996). HACCP training may also be included here. Periodic assessments of the effectiveness of training programmes should be made, and checks should be carried out to confirm that designated procedures are being followed (IFST, 1998).

A study conducted by Mortlock et al. (2000) indicated that variations exist in food hygiene training delivery and qualification levels across the food industry, which raise ongoing concerns about the adequacy of the training being delivered. The problems associated with the training of the large number of food handlers working in catering include high staff turnover and large numbers of part-time or temporary workers (Griffith, 2000). When it is necessary to employ temporary staff through agencies, their food hygiene qualifications should be checked (Worsfold, 1996).

Microbiological testing of foods

Many flight kitchens have in-house laboratories for quality control and quality assurance purposes. Others will sub-contract such work to other agencies. The laboratories will sample incoming supplies to ensure that they meet specifications, and complete products to verify that hygiene management systems and production processes are operating correctly. Periodic environmental sampling may also be undertaken to ensure that personal hygiene, cleaning and sanitation regimes are effective.

Items will be sampled, meaning that not every item will be tested, but just a representative number. The proportion of items tested, and the frequency of testing, will depend on the severity of the risk posed by the micro-organism of interest or the process. Sampling should, however, cover all times of the day, as problems could be unique to the actions of a particular operator, which could be missed if samples are taken routinely at one time in the day. Care must be taken when taking samples (including methods of taking samples and labelling of samples) and, where it is necessary, in the transportation of samples to the laboratory (e.g. temperature control).

Records of test results over time should be maintained, as these may show a gradual deviation towards unacceptable levels of micro-organisms. This allows action to be taken before unacceptable levels of micro-organisms are reached. As mentioned above, it also allows identification of personnel or processes contributing to rising levels of micro-organisms.

The results of microbiological tests can take some time to derive, especially those designed to identify specific organisms. This has implications for decisions made on the basis of such data. There is ongoing work into rapid methods of microbiological testing.

End-product testing is important to verify the safety of product and the effectiveness of hygiene management systems. The preferred approach, however, is to ensure that potential hazards are predicted and controlled prior to them causing a problem. The current method of choice to achieve this is the application of Hazard Analysis Critical Control Points (HACCP).

Hazard Analysis Critical Control Points (HACCP)

HACCP is widely recognised in the food industry as an effective approach to establishing production, sanitation, and manufacturing practices that produce safe foods (Pierson and Corlett, 1992). It has been applied in flight catering since 1993 (Lambiri et al., 1995).

HACCP systems establish process control by identifying points in production that are most critical to food safety, and determining how these should be monitored and controlled. HACCP has often been expanded to include quality parameters. This can lead to a large number of extra controls and can be difficult to administer, producing a system that is unwieldy, time-consuming to audit, and one that detracts from the essential safety aspects of food production (Wallace and Williams, 2001; Mortimore, 2001).

HACCP's preventive approach is seen as more cost-effective than end-product testing (ICMSF, 1988), and means control being exerted on a day-to-day basis rather than merely being carried out at random points (Mortlock, 1999). Evidence of improved safety of foods produced under the HACCP system is beginning to be reported (Hernandez Torres, 1998; Gillespie et al., 2001) including within the flight-catering sector (Lambiri et al., 1995). Airlines require their suppliers to provide evidence that HACCP is being complied with on a day-to-day basis. Normally this means going through an inspection or audit process (Panisello and Quantick, 2001). Suppliers that have been asked to comply with HACCP may be encouraged to pass their disciplines back through the supply chain to their suppliers.

The key to successful HACCP is proper preparation and planning, including gaining commitment at senior level and ensuring proper allocation of resources (Mortimore, 2001), including for HACCP-specific training. Training will ensure the correct application and maintenance of the system. The key elements needed to set up an effective management system are:

- Transfer of ownership of HACCP plan to operatives, supervisors, and managers
- Training of operatives, supervisors, and managers to implement HACCP plan
- Maintenance of HACCP plan (Khandke and Mayes, 1998)

Thus, product safety and the HACCP system are team efforts. All employees must be involved in HACCP development and training and they must understand that they play an important role in using the HACCP system, and making safe food (Pierson and Cortlett, 1992). Support and commitment of senior management is an essential prerequisite during development, implementation and maintenance of a HACCP system. The management is responsible for establishing a product safety policy, for defining the objectives to meet this policy, and for implementing these through appropriate programmes (Jouve, 2000). Food safety must be communicated by the senior management as non-negotiable (Armstrong, 1999).

The development of a HACCP system involves a number of stages, the first of which is to set up a team of relevant people.

Formation of the HACCP team

HACCP should be carried out as a multi-disciplinary team effort (Mortimore and Wallace, 1994; Jouve, 2000). The HACCP team should comprise a number of persons from different departments, and should include line operatives and supervisors working in the front line in the decision-making stages to ensure that they feel involvement and commitment towards the plan (Khandke and Mayes, 1998).

The team should consist of people who have knowledge of raw materials, products, processes, and hazards. One person can fulfil more than one role, provided that the team is capable of obtaining and using relevant information to identify the hazards potentially associated with a particular production operation, to assess their significance, and to control them (Anon., 1992; Mortimore and Wallace, 1994; NACMCF, 1992; WHO, 1995). If in-house expertise is not adequate, it can be sourced externally. Access to such expertise is vitally important if the HACCP study is to be meaningful (Mortimore, 2001).

Pre-requisites

The plant or kitchen layout must be designed to achieve the smooth flow of operations, and equipment should also be designed to facilitate cleaning, maintenance and inspection (Chartered Institute of Environmental Health, 1998).

It is unlikely that a HACCP system can be effectively implemented in the absence of some existing management programmes—pre-requisite programmes. These are considered as support programmes, providing foundations for HACCP (Wallace and Williams, 2001). Mortimore and Wallace (1998) have described a HACCP Support Network (Fig. 9.1), which shows the inter-relationship of

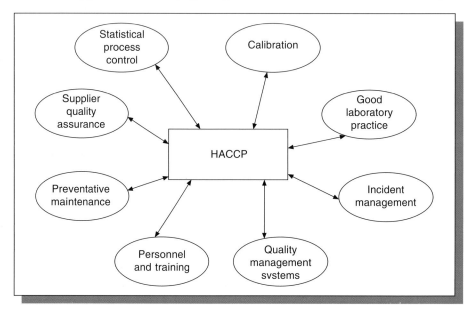

Figure 9.1
The HACCP Support Network
SOURCE: Mortimore and Wallace, 1998

management systems and procedures in any food business for the production of safe, high quality products. In essence, pre-requisite programmes design out more generalised hazards, leaving HACCP to focus on product-process hazards (Mortimore and Wallace, 1998).

Good manufacturing practice (GMP) This includes mechanisms in place to prevent cross-contamination through, for instance, cleaning, operator and environmental hygiene, plant and building design, and preventative maintenance (IFST, 1998).

Supplier quality assurance Having systems in place that allow confidence that suppliers are producing safe foods consistently, based on criteria set by the purchasing company. Criteria may include specifications of acceptable levels of contamination or that the supplier also operates a HACCP system (Engel et al., 2001), and routine audits of suppliers.

Statistical process control Assessment of whether a process is capable of consistently achieving the control parameters necessary for control of safety. This approach also enables process control managers to determine whether deviations observed in control measures are inherent variability or represent a significant deviation from the norm that requires investigation.

Calibration A system in place that ensures regular calibration of equipment, including monitoring equipment (e.g. temperature probes), to ensure that such equipment is operating correctly.

Good laboratory practice This can include the accreditation of systems used in the laboratory—whether the laboratory is internal or external to the company. Other issues may include training of staff, monitoring of staff performance, and building controls into sample testing procedures.

Incident management The existence of systems to be followed in the event of a serious incident. Such a system would specify the actions to be taken and by whom. For instance, what should happen to affected product, who should be informed and the procedures for investigation of the cause of the incident.

Quality management systems These may include systems such as total quality management, conforming to BS5750/ISO 9000. Such systems aim to ensure the production of products that consistently meet a specified level of quality.

Personnel and training Policies relating to the nature of the staff who should be employed to certain positions, the competencies that they will need, and the training programmes available (either in-house or from training providers) to develop, refresh and update such competencies. A policy may also include ways in which training needs are identified, including encouraging personnel to identify their own needs, mechanisms for establishing the effectiveness of training and maintenance of training records (see also previous section on training).

Preventative maintenance A system in place that ensures regular preventative maintenance of premises and equipment. This may include contracts with pest control agencies to regularly audit premises for signs of infestation, as well as ensuring that such pests are not able to enter premises.

HACCP Principles

The information here derives from an Food and Agriculture Organisation of the United Nations (FAO) (1998) document unless stated otherwise. The seven principles, which are involved in developing and operating a HACCP program are described by NACMCF (1992) and Codex (1997).

Principle 1: Conduct a hazard analysis *Prepare a list of steps in the process where significant hazards occur and describe the preventative measures*
A process flow diagram is constructed detailing all the steps in the process, from incoming raw materials to finished product. The HACCP team then identifies the hazards that could occur at each stage and describes measures for their control. Both the likelihood of occurrence and the severity of that hazard must be considered (Fig. 9.2) (Mortimore, 2001).

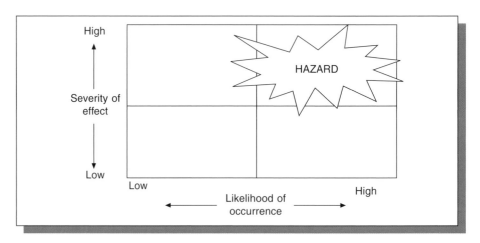

Figure 9.2
Hazard analysis
Source: Mortimore, 2001, p. 212

Principle 2: Identify the Critical Control Points (CCPs) in the process
When all hazards and preventive measures have been described, the HACCP team establishes the points where control is critical to managing the safety of the product. These are the critical control points. A control point is critical when if an operation is faulty and/or monitoring is inefficient at this point, this will result in a major concern and a high probability that a severe, direct health hazard or a high level of spoilage will occur (Jouve, 2000). It is likely that there will be many controlling steps in the process, some of which are not directly associated with control of safety, i.e. not CCPs. Decision trees have been used as an aid to the selection of CCPs. They take into consideration hazards, the effect of actions exercised at the operation in question, whether control actions should be taken at this or subsequent operations and whether the CCP will be monitored (Bryan, 1996).

Principle 3: Establish critical limits for preventative measures associated with each identified CCP

At each CCP, critical limits are established and specified. These represent the boundaries that are used to judge whether an operation is producing safe products. Critical limits may be set for factors such as temperature, time (minimum time exposure), physical product dimensions, water activity, and moisture level (Pierson and Cortlett, 1992). These parameters, if maintained within boundaries, will confirm the safety of the product. The critical limits should meet requirements of government regulations and/or company standards and/or be supported by other scientific data. It is therefore essential that the person(s) responsible for establishing critical limits has(ve) knowledge of the process and of the legal and commercial standards required for the product. If the information needed to establish critical limits is not available, a conservative value should be selected or regulatory limits used.

Principle 4: Establish CCP monitoring requirements; establish procedures from the results of monitoring to adjust the process and maintain control

The HACCP team should specify monitoring requirements for management of the CCP within its critical limits. The monitoring procedures must be able to detect loss of control at the CCP. Therefore, it is important to specify fully how, when and by whom monitoring is to be performed (Mortimore, 2001; Jouve, 2000). Monitoring is the process that provides the producer with accurate records enabling them to show that the conditions of production comply with the HACCP plan (Jouve, 2000; Pierson and Cortlett, 1992; Mortimore and Wallace, 1994). Ideally, monitoring should provide information in time to allow any adjustments to the process, thus preventing loss of control of the process and critical limits being exceeded. In practice, operating limits are often used to provide a safety margin, which allows extra time to adjust the process before the critical limit is exceeded (Table 9.1). Managers should be aware of the limitations of their operations and realistically design monitoring procedures and schedules commensurate with their operations (Panisello and Quantick, 2001).

Process	Critical limit	Operating limit
Acidification	pH 4.6	pH 4.3
Drying	0.84 A_w	0.80 A_w
Hot fill	80°C	85°C
Slicing	2 cm	1.5 cm

SOURCE: FAO, 1998 [online]

Table 9.1
An example of critical limits versus operating limits

Principle 5: Establish corrective actions to be taken when monitoring indicates a deviation from an established critical limit

Loss of control is considered as a deviation from a critical limit for a CCP (Loken, 1995; Mortimore and Wallace, 1994; Jouve, 2000). Corrective action should be taken following any deviation to ensure the safety of the product and to prevent recurrence (Pierson and Corlett, 1992; Mortimore, 2001). This will include action to bring the process back under control and action to deal with product affected by an out-of-control process. Actions taken should be documented. Process adjustments should also be made when monitoring results indicate a trend towards loss of control at a CCP, to bring the process within the operating limits before a deviation occurs.

Deviation and corrective action procedures should be prescribed so that employees are able to understand and perform the appropriate corrective action(s). The producer's corrective action programme should include investigation to determine the cause of the deviation, effective measures to prevent recurrence of the deviation and verification of the effectiveness of the corrective action taken (modifying the HACCP plan if necessary).

Principle 6: Establish effective record keeping procedures that document the HACCP system

Records must be kept to demonstrate that the HACCP system is operating under control and that appropriate corrective action has been taken for any deviations. This will demonstrate safe product manufacture and support any "due diligence" defence (Mortimore and Wallace, 1994).

Documentation covering the complete HACCP process and other quality management systems should be assembled into a user-friendly manual, easily accessible for reference. This should include a record of the decisions taken during the HACCP exercise and forms for recording monitoring procedures. Targets and tolerances should be included on the record form where practical, to be readily available for reference by operatives and management. Similarly, working procedures and the specific roles of each operative should be readily available (Mayes, 1999).

Principle 7: Establish procedures for verification that the HACCP system is working correctly

A system of verification will confirm that the HACCP procedure is working correctly. This may involve internal audit, additional microbiological or other testing of finished or intermediate product, or more detailed testing around specific CCPs. Review of the nature and frequency of the occasions where the process has been out of control is also valuable in this process, highlighting weakness either in the process, or in the control measures in place. HACCP plans should be regularly reviewed and continually improved and updated to reflect changes in the company (Armstrong, 1999).

Implementation of the HACCP system

At this stage responsibility for HACCP passes to the personnel within the day-to-day operation (Mortimore, 2001; Jouve, 2000). The successful implementation of HACCP requires training, monitoring of CCP's, taking actions when required and recording results. Unless the HACCP plan is properly implemented its real benefits will not be realised.

In the food industry as a whole the catering sector has been found to be much slower at adopting HACCP than other sectors (Ward, 2001). However, wihin the catering industry the flight-catering sector has probably been the earliest adopter of the HACCP approach. Traditional HACCP systems reduce hazards for relatively stable, repetitive and predictable manufacturing processes. Foodservice HACCP systems, however, must have flexibility to accommodate changing products and procedures, diverse employee capabilities and inconsistent production volumes (Seward, 2000). Also, in manufacturing, typically a thermal process is applied to a finished product. In the catering environment, food handling after cooking is very common practice and the potential for recontamination exists (Adams, 2000). It has been suggested (Griffith, 2000) that a generic HACCP approach to similar groupings or categories of products may help caterers (Fig. 9.3). A number of professional organisations associated with flight catering, including The International Flight Catering

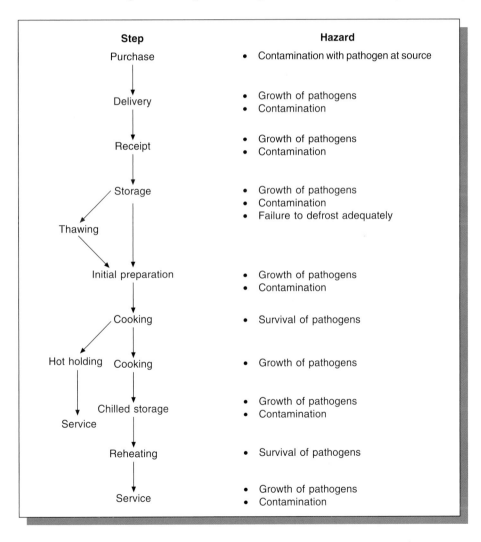

Figure 9.3
Generic flow diagram for catering operations
Source: Griffith, 2000: 248

Association have produced HACCP-based manuals relating to food safety (Anon, 1994).

HACCP implementation problems in the UK food industry

A number of factors may hinder wider acceptance and practical implementation of HACCP. These problems have been observed worldwide and throughout the food industry (Bernard, 1998; Boccas et al., 2001; Engel, 1998; Kvenberg et al., 2000; Ropkins and Beck, 2000; Hathaway, 1999; Untermann, 1999; Mossel et al., 1999) but some are particularly pertinent to the catering sector.

HACCP is often perceived as an additional regulatory burden (Unnevehr and Jensen, 1999; Motarjemi and Kaferstein, 1999; Ehiri et al., 1995) and a complicated system requiring much documentation and paper-work (Motarjemi and Kaferstein, 1999; Ward, 2001; Engel, 1998). However, research has shown that companies that already have good manufacturing practices in place find the transition to HACCP less problematic (Eves and Dervisi, Personal communication). HACCP has also been perceived to require a large amount of resources (Motarjemi and Kaferstein, 1999; Unnevehr and Jensen, 1999). In the initial stages additional resources are required for training, technical support and equipment. However, in the long term, the invested resources will be rewarded by a decrease in recalling contaminated food, improved safety of the food, greater confidence of the customer and less consumer complaints. The major problems perceived by managers relate to lack of knowledge and training, staff turnover, and the large variety of products (Adams, 2000; Ward, 2001; Panisello et al., 2000).

Managers, without appropriate training, may think that as long as the product looks normal and there is no evidence of spoilage, the product is all right to distribute. They may, however, be unaware of the risks involved with the handling of their raw materials and processing operations (Panisello and Quantick, 2001).

The application of HACCP to catering operations presents unique challenges. This is due to the lack of a well-defined product flow, a diverse workforce, the constant turnover of employees, with varying levels of education and language ability, the diversity of foods served, and methods of food preparation and service, and variation in potential demand and workloads (Bernard et al., 1994). Lack of resources such as time and manpower, as well as the difficulty of training staff are the main barriers affecting the use of HACCP.

Caterers face special problems regarding HACCP, such as different menus and equipment, different system of drinks dispensing, and different methods of food preparation and service (Panisello et al., 1999; Adams, 1995). Designing food safety into products, procedures, equipment, facilities and training can reduce the hazards that need to be addressed in a food service HACCP plan, e.g. using products that are precooked and pre-prepared (Seward, 2000).

Some problems relate to personnel. For instance, some managers take the view that there is no reason to change their current procedures when those procedures have worked well for many years and enabled them to produce 'safe' food products (Panisello and Quantick, 2001). In a fast-moving environment, such as a catering establishment, time is always limited. Thus, employees although adequately trained, might ignore some of the procedures because of the limited time available (Panisello and Quantick, 2001).

Staff motivation is an important element in maintaining the HACCP system 'alive'. Many authors (e.g. Tompkin, 1994; Mortlock, 1999; Mortlock et al., 2000; Mortimore, 2001; Wallace and Williams, 2001; Panisello and Quantick, 2001; Motarjemi and Kaferstein, 1999; and Khandke and Mayes, 1998) have noted that plant personnel must be 'active participants', giving them a sense of ownership of the work at hand. Doyle (1999) also found that the attitude and commitment of catering staff to food safety depends on the leadership given by management.

Audits

Most airlines and recognised auditors use the Association of European Airlines format for audit purposes. Medina (Case Study 9.1) uses the AEA format for the food safety aspects of their audit. Members of the AEA food safety committee are recognised environmental heath and food safety experts from the airline and flight catering industry with years of field experience.

This audit system has recognised the principal critical controls required to be in place and to be seen consistently correct. These are given a score of four points.

Alongside these are what are described as standard operating procedures and these are given a score of one point. A critical control if not correct or seen to be consistently incorrect is a food safety issue and total points should be subtracted Similarly standard operating procedures are either right or wrong. IFCA/IFSA have just completed four years work on standardisation of food safety procedures. This was documented and published this year.

This inevitably will help to standardise audit procedures within the flight catering industry, as they are not at this time. In reality, what we are have witnessed is individual airlines and independent auditors using the 'framework' of the AEA system. They are changing the score systems and interpretation of the critical controls that have been identified and agreed by the AEA, customer airlines, and the caterers. This results in many variations which are not only confusing for caterers but can lead to alarming results with major food safety issues being missed or unidentified. IFCA plan to carry out Theoretical and Practical Audit training on completion of the updated AEA Audit Sheet.

The caterer needs to be in a position where total traceability is possible of food and beverage products from the point of supply until it is delivered to the passengers on the aircraft. For this to be achieved successfully, supplier hygiene audits must be undertaken or sufficient information be made available to prove that source and distribution of food and beverage is of good quality. It also requires fulfilling international and local food safety specifications.

The caterer is required to prove that a planned HACCP programme is in place and that this plan is subject to regular review. This plan must indicate that all major food safety hazards have been recognised; that appropriate critical controls have been put in place; and these controls are being regularly monitored. This in practice means that quality control and food safety systems have to be fully documented. They will be required to be used in proof of due diligence in any investigation or allegation of food contamination or food borne illness.

A typical audit consists of:

- A pre planned action plan
- A briefing meeting prior to the audit
- An agreed time and date for the audit
- Specified HACCP team members involvement during the audit

There are two types of audit—full adequacy audits and physical audits. In a full adequacy audit the auditor will look at all documents related to food safety and quality control including details of suppliers; food safety training; company hygiene policy documents and food safety procedures; personal hygiene and health controls; building maintenance; cleaning procedures and chemical specifications; pest control; and temperature and quality control records of food and beverage and equipment.

This can be a lengthy process, but the aim is to see that all the records are accurate and have the correct information in place. The advantage of the external auditor is documents and processes can be viewed in a different light. The auditor will advise where discrepancies are seen or documentation does not follow a logical flow, and will seek agreement for upgrading or change. The auditor should be considered to be a team member to ensure that total value from the audit is achieved.

The Physical Audit consists of an examination of the catering unit by departments and this is usually from 'goods in' through to 'dispatch' and similar with equipment flow lines. The purpose is to identify potential hazards and to determine that they have been recognised and dealt with correctly. Technical data reviewed initially will be checked against what the auditor is witnessing during the physical review. Any food safety or environmental hygiene discrepancies obviously will be noted and taken into account in the final analysis.

A final debrief meeting will be held which should be minuted but often is not for operational reasons. An action plan is agreed and a score will be awarded. This will be followed up by a fully documented report from the auditor within seven working days.

Measurements, sample sizes as well as frequency of measurements activities need to be reviewed in order to comply with evolving food safety legislation.

There is adequate information to prove that two audits a year are not sufficient to provide assurance of quality consistency. However, in the current context of the food safety World Standard, which means all caterers and all food suppliers use common guidelines these two audits could be used as a validation of food safety internal audits. The number of self-audits performed by caterers and or food suppliers should be statistically sufficient to correlate with twice-yearly food safety audits (validation) performed by external auditors.

The traditional model for compliance measurement no longer adequately responds to the changing environment of airline catering and food handling/preparation methods. The mission of caterers in many cases has changed to an assembler of third party products dictating a new approach in the food safety auditing process.

Severe limitations on airlines' financial resources are dictating a substantial change to current internal audit cost structures; therefore, reassessing the value and need of an objective, cost-efficient, third-party quality management process. This will also drive the need for a streamlined approach to in-flight quality standards similar to the current food safety world standard which could enable airlines to share the cost of quality management audits.

Case study 9.1

Medina International

Medina International is a company that specialises in conducting third-party audits for flight-catering production units. In 2002, the company conducted 316 audits, in 123 units, on behalf of four different airline companies. In 2003, Medina will extend its auditing process through the supplier chain using a new online software application (ASP) for food suppliers. A total of 22 years experience in auditing gives Medina International Inc. a considerable knowledge base in the areas of auditor selection processes and audit procedures as well as technology developments to ensure rapidity of information and research projects related to in-flight food safety and catering standards.

The actual audits include four different modules, namely Food Provisioning, Food Safety, Inventory and Catering specifications.

Medina has found through experience that auditors cannot audit more than three stations a month as extensive travel can alter their work efficiency and audit quality. Furthermore, **auditor rotation** is essential in order to maintain the integrity of the audit. The same auditor cannot visit the same station twice within a year.

The audit process includes a questionnaire, which ensures auditor objectivity. For example, a question could need a numeric answer such as four or zero but not in between as leaving a person to express a judgement call will create inconsistencies in the audit response. This questionnaire must relate to specific guidelines, which should be part of a monthly follow up training with auditors. Medina audit software integrates the guidelines for each question ensuring that each auditor understands the issues in the same way therefore guaranteeing objectivity. All guidelines are based on the airlines quality standard expectation from caterers and/or food suppliers.

Each audit should take the necessary time to cover all issues in a professional manner. It takes an average of 2.5 days to complete a Medina audit. A basic visit includes areas such as the receiving area, storage areas, pre-preparation area, hot and cold kitchens, special meal areas, tray set-up area, dishwashing area, waste collection station, holding area, dispatch area, as well as a verification of HACCP logs and SOPS documentation. Medina also assesses catering specifications (weight checks and procedures), commissary, inventory, and in some occasions environmental issues. A typical audit report provides information on all observations and highlights areas of improvement, new non-conformities, and on-going non-conformities.

The reporting process to airlines as well as the debriefing of the audit with the caterers or food suppliers is important in the audit process. Rapidity of information is essential so that any major food safety discrepancies can be addressed as fast as possible. Value for money, optimum customer satisfaction, consistency and safety of catering products is the basis of auditing process so all audit reports should be transferred 24 hours after completion and an action plan to correct non conformities should be submitted, a maximum of 5 days after the audit. The third-party quality assessment company should be responsible for monitoring corrective measures in order to notify its clients on a regular basis. Current technology enables clients to access rapidly their food safety audits at any time anywhere in the world so that they can be use to follow up action therefore limiting potential food safety liabilities.

Audit information is essential to assess the auditing process and auditor performance. Each Medina audit is transferred into a central database, which is currently used for research on different aspects of the catering audit procedure such as auditor consistency during audits and assessment of in-flight quality standard. The database includes 4,000 audits and is classified according to continent, country, station, etc.

Current issues and future developments

The **outsourcing** of food processing and production may appear to shift the responsibility for food safety from flight caterers to suppliers. This is especially the case if food and drink is received and processed in sealed packaging. However, the flight production unit will still have to ensure that these items are stored at safe temperatures, as well as ensure stock rotation so that items are consumed by their use-by date.

In addition, in the UK under the Food Safety Act 1990, the Food Standards Agency (FSA) with government support reviewed the powers of entry to ships and aircraft. While at the time of writing the industry had no idea what impact this would have on the airlines, it was advised that food safety training should be implemented for cabin crew in order to prove due diligence. In this regard, British Airways had already adopted a voluntary code of practice with all cabin crew undergoing a minimal module of training on food safety and galley hygiene. Other airlines are likely to follow.

Conclusion

Flight catering has an excellent record for food safety. There have, however, been cases of food poisoning traced back to flight caterers. The nature of the business—notably the delay between production and consumption of food—means that those involved in producing meals must be constantly vigilant to prevent contamination of foods and to ensure appropriate temperature control. One lapse in good hygiene practices could result in a large number of people being affected, with consequent effects on the business implicated. The method of choice for managing food safety is hazard analysis critical control points (HACCP), a proactive system that aims to predict possible hazards in food production and built in controls and monitoring procedures to prevent or minimise them. Evidence is starting to emerge confirming that this system does result in foods of a higher microbiological quality. It is important that everyone involved in flight catering, from chief executives to line operatives, understands the importance of maintaining good hygiene practices and that managers communicate this to their employees.

Key terms

Allergens	Audit	Contamination	Cross contamination
Food poisoning	HACCP	Hygiene training	Micro-organisms
Pathogens			

Discussion questions

1. Identify the main hazards to food safety in flight catering.
2. Discuss the implications of poor food safety management to both flight caterers and airlines.
3. Discuss the ways in which production unit personnel can bring benefits and challenges to the development and implementation of a HACCP system.
4. What is the difference between a HACCP system and an audit?

Further reading

Anon. (1994) *An introduction to Food Safety in Airline Catering Based on HACCP*, International Flight Catering Association: Surrey, England.

Kang Y. (2000) "Safe food handling in airline catering," in J.M. Farber and E.C. Todd (eds), *Safe Handling of Foods*, Marcel Dekker Publications: New York.

Mortimore, S. and Wallace, C. (1998), *HACCP: A Practical Approach*, 2nd ed, Aspen Publications: Gaithersburg, MD.

References

Adams, A. (1995) "Food Safety: The final solution for the hotel and catering industry", *British Food Journal*, vol. 94, no. 4, 19–23.

Adams, C. (2000) "HACCP Applications in the Foodservice Industry", *Journal of the Association of Food and Drug Officials*, vol. 94, no. 4 22–25.

Anon. (1992) CFDRA (Campden Food and Drink Research Association) *HACCP: A Practical Guide. Technical Manual no. 38*, CFDRA: Chipping Campden, UK.

Anon. (1994) *An introduction to Food Safety in Airline catering Based on HACCP*, International Flight Catering Association: Surrey, UK.

Armstrong, G.D. (1999) "Towards an Integrated Hygiene and Food Safety Systems: The Hygieneomic Approach," *International Journal of Food Microbiology*, vol. 50, 19–24.

Bernard, D. (1998) "Developing and Implementing HACCP in the USA", *Food Control*, vol. 9, no. 2–3, 91–95.

Bernard, D., Gavin, A. and Scott, V.N. (1994) "The Application of the HACCP System to Different Sectors of the Food Industry," in: *The Use of HACCP Principles in Food Control*, Report of the FAO Expert Technical Meeting, Technical Manual no. 58, FAO: Rome.

Boccas, F., Ramanauskas, A., Boutrif, E., Cavaille, P., Lacaze, J.M. and Pilipiene, I. (2001) "HACCP « Train-in-action » Programme in the Lithuanian Dairy Industry," *Food Control*, vol. 12, 149–156.

Bryan, F.L. (1996) "Another Decision Tree Approach for Identification of Critical Control Points," *Journal of Food Protection*, vol. 50, no. 11, 1242–1247.

Chartered Institute of Environmental Health, (1998) *Food Safety for Supervisors*, Chadwick House Group London.

Codex Alimentarius Commission, (1997) "Hazard Analysis and Critical Control Point (HACCP) System and Guidelines for Its Application," 2nd ed, in: *General Requirements* (Food Hygiene), Supplement to Vol. 1B, FAO/WHO.

Doyle, P. (1999) "Hygiene for Caterers ... The New Ballgame," *Hotel and Catering Review*, Jun. 1999, 18–20.

Ehiri, J.E., Morris, G.P. and McEwen, J. (1995) "Implementation of HACCP in Food Businesses: A Way Ahead," *Food Control*, vol. 6, no. 6, 341–345.

Engel, D. (1998) "Teaching HACCP: Theory and Practice from the Trainer's Point of view", *Food Control*, vol. 9, no. 2–3, 2137–139.

Engel, D., MacDonald, D. and Nash, C. (2001) *Managing Food Safety*, Chadwick House Group: London.

FAO. (1998) *The Application of Risk Analysis to Food Safety Control Programmes*, [online] Available from: http://www.fao.org/docrep/w8088E/w8088e07.htm [Accessed 01/07/01].

Gillespie, I.A., Little, C.L. and Mitchell, R.T., on behalf of the LACOTS and PHLS, (2001) "Microbiological Examination of Ready to Eat Quiche from Retail Establishments in the United Kingdom," *Communicable Disease and Public Health*, vol. 4, no. 1, 53–59.

Griffith, C. (2000) "Food Safety in Catering Establishments," in: Farber, J.M and Todd, E.C. (eds), *Safe Handling of Foods*, Marcel Dekker: New York.

Guzewich, J.J. (2000) "Safe Preparation of Foods at the Foodservice and Retail Level: Restaurants, Take-out Food, Churches, Clubs, Vending Machines, Universities, Colleges, Food Stores and Delicatessens," in: Farber, J.M. and Todd, E.C. (eds), *Safe Handling of Foods*, Marcel Dekker: New York.

Hathaway, S. (1999) "Management of Food Safety in International Trade," *Food Control*, 10, 247–253.

Hernandez–Torres, D. (1998) *Role of Government Agencies in HACCP Audit*, Background document for the FAO/WHO consultation on the Role of Government Agencies in Assessing HACCP, Geneva, 2–6, June.

Hobbs, B.C. and Roberts, D. (1993) *Food Poisoning and Food Hygiene*, 6th ed., Edward Arnorld: London.

ICMSF. (1988) *Application of the Hazard Analysis Critical Control Point (HACCP) System to Ensure Microbiological Safety and Quality, Microorganisms in Foods 4*, Blackwell Scientific: Oxford.

IFST. (1999) Food Allergens, [online] Available from: http://www.ifst.org/hottop19.htm [Accessed 14/02/03].

IFST. (1998) *Good Manufacturing Practice. A Guide to Its Responsible Management*, 4th ed., IFST: London.

Jouve, J.L. (2000) "Good Manufacturing Practice, HACCP and Quality Systems." in: Lund, B.M., Baird-Parker, T.C. and Gould, G.W. (eds), *The Microbiological Safety and Quality of Food*, Vol. II, Aspen Publications Inc: Maryland.

Kang, Y. (2000) "Safe Food Handling in Airline Catering." in: J.M. Farber and E.C. Todd (eds), *Safe Handling of Foods*, Marcel Dekker: New York.

Khandke, S.S. and Mayes, T. (1998) "HACCP Implementation: A Practical Guide to the Implementation of the HACCP Plan," *Food Control*, vol. 9, no. 2–3, 103–109.

Kvenberg, J., Stolfa, P., Stringfellow, D. and Garrett, E.S. (2000) "HACCP Development and regulatory assessment in the United States of America," *Food Control*, vol. 11, 387–401.

Lambiri M., Marridou A. and Papadakis J. A. (1995) "The Application of Hazard Analysis Critical Control Points (HACCP) in a Flight Catering Establishment Improved the Bacteriological Quality of Meals," *J. Royal Soc. Health*, vol. 115, no. 1, 26–30.

Loken, K.J. (1995) *The HACCP Food Safety Manual*, John Wiley and Sons: New York.

Mayes, T. (1999) "How can the Principles of Validation and Verification be Applied to Hazard Analysis, *Food Control*, vol. 10, 277–279.

Mortimore, S. (2001) "How to Make HACCP Really work in Practice, *Food Control*, vol. 12, 209–215.

Mortimore, S. and Wallace, C. (1998) *HACCP: A Practical Approach*, 2nded, Aspen Publications: Gaithersburg, MD.

Mortimore, S. and Wallace, C., (1994) *HACCP: A Practical Approach*, Chapman and Hall: London.

Mortlock, M.P. (1999) "Barriers to the Implementation of HACCP System in the UK Food Industry," *Concord-Cardiff*, vol. 9 no. 2, 15–20.

Mortlock, M.P., Peters, A.C. and Griffith, C.J. (2000) "A National Survey of Food Hygiene Training and Qualification Levels in the UK Food Industry, *International Journal of Environmental Health Research*, vol. 10, 111–123.

Motarjemi, Y. and Kaferstein, F. (1999) "Food Safety, HACCP and the Increase in Foodborne Diseases: A Paradox?," *Food Control*, vol. 10, 325–333.

Mossel, D.A.A., Jansen, J.T. and Struijk, C.B. (1999) "Microbiological Safety and Assurance Applied to Smaller Catering Operations World-wide. From angst through ardour to assistance and achievement, The facts, *Food Control*, vol. 10, 195–211.

NACMCF, (1992) "Hazard Analysis and Critical Control Point System, *International Journal of Food Microbiology*, vol. 16, 1–23.

Panisello, P.J. and Quantick, P.C. (2001) "Technical Barriers to HACCP," *Food Control*, vol. 12, 165–173.

Panisello, P.J., Rooney, R., Quantick, P.C. and Stanwell-Smith, R. (2000) "Application of Foodborne Disease Outbreak Data in the Development and Maintenance of HACCP Systems," *International Journal of Food Microbiology*, vol. 59, 221–234.

Panisello, P.J., Quantick, P.C., and Knowles, M.J. (1999) "Towards the implementation of HACCP: Results of a UK regional survey," *Food Control*, vol. 10, 87–98.

Pierson, M.D., and Cortlett, D.A. (1992) *HACCP: Principles and Applications*, Van Nostrand Reinhold: New York.

Ropkins, K., and Beck, A. (2000) "Evaluation of Worldwide Approaches to the Use of HACCP to Control Food safety," *Trends in Food Science and Technology*, vol. 11, 10–21.

Seward, (2000) "Application of HACCP in the Foodservice," *Irish Journal of Agriculture and Food Research*, vol. 39 no. 2, 221–227.

Tompkin, R.B. (1994) "HACCP in the Meat and Poultry Industry", Food Control, vol. 5, 153–161.

Unnevehr, L.J. and Jensen, H.H. (1999) "The Economic Implications of Using HACCP as a Food Safety Regulatory Standard," *Food Policy*, vol. 24, 625–635.

Untermann, F. (1999) "Food Safety Management and Misinterpretation of HACCP," *Food Control*, vol. 10, 161–167.

Wallace, C. and Williams, T. (2001) "Pre-requisites: A Help or Hindrance to HACCP? *Food Control*, vol. 12, 235–240.

Ward, G. (2001) "HACCP: Heaven or Hell for the Food Industry," *Quality World, Mar.*, 12–15.

WHO (1995) *HACCP System: Concept and Application*, Report of a WHO consultation with the participation of FAO, Geneva, 29–31 May 1995 WHO document WHO/FNU/FOS/95.7, WHO, Geneva.

Worsfold, D. (1996) "Training Caterers for the New Hygiene Regulations," *British Food Journal*, vol. 98, no. 6, 27–32.

Transportation and loading

- Identify the different types of uplift
- Examine staff capacity in matching the complexity of dispatch
- Discuss the issues of loading

Introduction

This chapter describes the processes and procedures by which supplies, or 'catering uplift', are transported to and from the aircraft, and how they are loaded and unloaded. It concentrates on the technical aspects of these transportation movements and operational activities, as also discusses the control mechanisms that can be used to ensure the satisfactory completion of the task. There are a number of safety and security issues related to transportation and loading, as well as implications for logistics, profitability, contractual and legal liability, and strategic issues.

The organisation of the transportation and loading and the equipment used in the process depends on a number of factors. These include the nature of the contractual relationship between the caterer and the airline; the type of aircraft and its configuration; the airport at which this activity is being carried out; and the route the aircraft is flying. In some cases, an airline may have its own production unit located close to its own dedicated airport terminal, operating a fleet of aircraft with a standard configuration, into and out of destinations with similar facilities. This tends to be the case for 'national' airlines flying out of their home base, such as Singapore International Airlines in Singapore, or for airlines flying out of their 'hubs'. On the other hand, a flight caterer may be contracted to load a wide range of dissimilar aircraft, on stands spread throughout an airport, for routes to destinations that have little or no flight production facilities. For instance, ALPHA Flight Services supply a large number of charter flights out of London Gatwick to tourism destinations such as the Gambia and Crete. In this second case, it is apparent that the supply of aircraft is much more complex and requires considerable operational control over activity. It makes it less likely that last minute adjustments in passenger numbers and/or requirements can be accommodated, while delays or changes in aircraft type can too cause major problems.

In addition to the number of airlines being catered for, another major factor is the location of the flight production facility relative to the airport. Approximately 50 per cent of the world's flight kitchens are located on the airport perimeter. This means that supplies from manufacturers can be delivered to a 'land-side' loading bay directly off the public highway; whilst high loaders delivering to aircraft can depart from 'air-side' loading bays. This tends to be the case for newer airports, especially in Europe and Asia, such as the Gate Gourmet facility in Zurich. However, at other stations, the flight kitchen will be located off the airport, often on an industrial estate, sometimes several kilometres away, such as for all the caterers at Heathrow and Gate Gourmet's facility in Sydney. This type of location requires a longer lead-time to ensure trucks reach the aircraft on schedule, especially when they have to travel along the public highway. Longer travel times in turn require more trucks and more staff.

Types of uplift

Loading and unloading procedures vary, depending upon the contract that the caterer has with the airline. The minimum procedure is to attend to the aircraft and make sure that the cabin crew do not require any top-up supplies, of such things as coffee, soft drinks, and so on. On some small aircraft a supply of hot water may be required. The other extreme is the full service procedure, which entails a full strip down and resupply of all cabin service items. The strip down and resupply may be done during the same trip to the aircraft, or it may involve two separate trips.

Figure 10.1 is a basic representation of the product flow in a loading and transportation system. It is important to recognise that other systems are also involved and must be integrated with this. For example, the meal production and assembly systems and the number and location of aircraft galleys are intricately connected with loading and transportation.

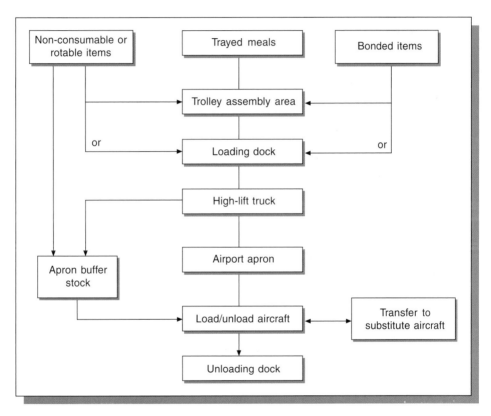

Figure 10.1
Flight catering transportation and loading system

The various types of service can be listed; however, service upgrades on long-haul flights have taken place during the past decade, while short haul service has been increasingly reduced. Therefore, it is necessary to differentiate between the types of service. However, it should be noted that no consensus exists regarding the use of terminology.

Long haul

Full uplift involves loading all the food and catering equipment and usually includes a complete new cabin as well, e.g. blankets, pillows, headrest covers, seat-pocket supply, and toilet items. Cabin refurbishments are seldom done by caterers, but by service companies or the departments affiliated to the airports. However, the caterers, even through outsourcing, may provide services such as laundry.

Full galley uplift includes an exchange of meals, beverages and dry goods, but no cabin supplies, and this is performed mainly at stopovers. As long-haul flights are becoming increasingly non-stop, galley uplifts have diminished.

Return catering may exist in two different ways. One way is to provide the **complete load**, where all food and beverage items are loaded in the hold, sometimes in LD3 containers with cooling facilities. The loaded items are off-loaded at the destination and taken to the flight production unit to be processed and are then returned to the aircraft. This method takes less space as items can be packed in bulk. The other possibility is the **return load** on a second leg (short, 1–3 hours), where no further processing is wanted or needed at the turnaround port and items are simply moved from one location on the aircraft to another. The reasons for this could be quality, cost (price level, double transport, and loading), or logistics (double stock-keeping). Return catering is also discussed in Chapter 11.

Top-up service might take place when the actual passenger number exceeds the amount of return meals loaded. In this case a limited amount of equipment might be stocked.

Short haul

Full uplift includes cabin items, and usually takes place for the first departure after the night stop. Beverages, dry goods, and other standard loads are often designed to last several legs.

Food or meals only are then uplifted at subsequent destinations, with top-up items loaded subject to requests from the cabin crew (e.g. soft drinks or ice cubes during the summer).

In addition to the general loading, some airlines require availabilily of last minute adjustments of meal numbers. This can be achieved by providing a small refrigerated vehicle with a variety of meals on the apron. Meals can then be transferred from this buffer stock to the aircraft up to the time that the doors are closed.

Each type of uplift would usually be accompanied by the equivalent amount of strip down. This is an important part of ensuring that adequate supplies of company-specific, non-consumable equipment is maintained. Another aspect of this would be that a considerable amount of 'dead-heading' occurs to ensure equipment 'balance', as explained in Chapter 11.

In addition to the food and the items necessarily associated with the food, its service and consumption, a number of other items may be included in the load. This would include duty-free items on flights where this service is available. Some airlines include newspapers with the catering uplift, and most if not all, include blankets, headsets, and free gifts where they are provided as part of the cabin service. This is more likely to occur with long-haul flights. These additional items will usually be assembled as part of the load and picked up with the catering uplift. The exception to this would normally be the duty-free goods which are normally collected from the bonded store. Non-alcoholic bar items are often provided from the same area as duty-free goods, although they may be supplied from the catering stores.

Transportation vehicles and staffing

Loading is usually carried out using high-lift vehicles or high-loaders, although typical commercial trucks are also used in some circumstances. These comprise a rear storage compartment which can be hydraulically raised to the level of the aircraft to a maximum height of 6 metres, along with a loading platform over the cab of the vehicle which serves as a 'ramp' to the aircraft, as shown in Fig. 10.2. This allows trolleys to be wheeled directly from the vehicle onto and off aircraft. In addition, a 'loading bridge' consisting of a bridge type piece made of steel which allows trolleys to go over the rubber protection of the truck platform and the bottom frame of the aircraft door without shock or damage to both. Various types of high-lift vehicle are available, but they generally fall into two categories relating to the height off the ground of the aircraft. 'Universal' trucks have a low-level cab for the servicing of smaller to medium-

Figure 10.2
Photo of high loader
SOURCE: Gate Gourmet © copyright 2003

sized aircraft, while 'jumbo' trucks, as their name implies, have a standard cab for use with the larger aircraft. Obviously greater extension is required to service a Boeing 747 and other wide-bodied aircraft, whereas smaller aircraft require the body to be able to adjust to a low level. These vehicles are all equipped with stabilizers for use when the vehicle is in the raised position at the side of the aircraft. Operators may also use a number of high-lift vehicles that also have tail lifts. These are particularly useful for carrying out hold transfers of fully stocked bar carts or trolleys.

The vehicles are generally not refrigerated except for those used for the buffer stock for last minute adjustment of meal numbers and these are normally vans without the lift facility. Refrigerated trucks are not only more costly, but due to the insulation in the walls of the vehicle, also tend to have a smaller interior capacity. However, refrigerated versions of high-loaders are available and may be necessary for some circumstances, for instance loading operations at airports in the tropics where there may be high ambient temperatures, or alternatively, where there are long distances between the assembly facility and the aircraft. Refrigerated trucks also allow some operational flexibility. For instance, during peak periods, these trucks can be loaded ahead of time as they are in effect an extension of the cold storage area in the production unit.

The number of trucks needed by a production unit to transport their meals varies quite widely at different airports, as it is affected by the location and proximity of the production unit to the airport apron, aircraft turnaround times, flight time slots, and the types of truck available.

Vehicles are designed to allow the safe and secure transportation of a range of different materials and trolleys without damage to either the trolleys themselves or their contents. However, the technology is not sophisticated. For instance, loads inside the vehicle are often secured by simple straps hooked onto sockets in the walls. Some vehicles may also have drop-down shelves to allow for the transportation of box containers. These are at a height to allow trolleys to be placed underneath on the floor of the vehicle compartment. The vehicle door is constructed in such a way that will allow sealing for security reasons, usually a plastic seal through the rear door lock.

Vehicles are normally crewed by a driver and a loader. In many operations, the crew take the assembled load from the loading dock and secure it in the vehicle, transport this load from the central production unit to the aircraft on the apron, and unload the supplies onto the aircraft securing them in the respective galley compartments. In some cases the vehicle crew can collect their loads from the assembly/dispatch area in the production unit. Prior to departing from the loading bay, a dispatcher will normally check to see that the load corresponds to the specification. In addition to the crew actually completing the loading on board the aircraft, it is common practice to have another member of staff involved for checking purposes. This representative or agent is responsible for checking that the load is correct and has been correctly loaded, and for signing it over to a member of the cabin crew representing the airline. This person may also be responsible for meeting any last minute supply requests from the cabin crew and where appropriate arranging for meals for passengers checking in late. Similar handing-over arrangements are made for off-loading and at the points where used trolleys are returned for cleaning and refilling, such as the bonded store.

Transportation control and staffing

Transportation control is normally carried out from a loading control room or dispatch office located near to the loading dock. This is typically equipped with a computerised materials handling system, as well as information systems related to aircraft arrivals and departures. In addition to the information typically shown to passengers in the airport terminals, these handling agent systems also identify aircraft stands, estimated times of arrivals, and so on. These same displays are also fed to the caterer's central production units and utilised by the dispatchers. The control office will also have radio links with each of the vehicle crews, as well as a video and intercom link with the loading dock. The number of staff engaged in transportation control will vary widely according to the number of meals produced and vehicles used for transportation. For instance, ALPHA Flight Services at London Gatwick have a dispatcher along with two operations clerks, when handling a peak of around 14,000 meals a day, and 15 trucks.

An important part of the control system is that which allocates the various loads to the vehicles and staff. A forward plan is produced using provisional data supplied by the airline(s). This plan allocates vehicle crews to service specific flights at specific times on a daily basis. If computerised, this scheduling system permits the effective allocation of shift times and staff breaks, as well as calculating the efficiency or productivity of each of the vehicle crews. Shift patterns for loading crews will vary according to the level of demand, as illustrated in Fig. 10.3. On this day in August 1994, 16 crews are scheduled, of which three start work at 05.00 hours, six at 05.30 hours, and others at 07.30, 08.00, 08.30 and 09.30 hours. The length of the shift varies from between 8 and 12 hours and each crew loads between three and five aircraft in a shift.

Loading and unloading of vehicles

Vehicles are operated on a cyclic basis. A typical system would be that the loading crew collects the appropriate load from the loading bay according to the allocated worksheet. The load is 'handed on' to them by the dispatcher or load supervisor. Any additional load items are collected as required as noted on the worksheet. This typically would be the bar-trolleys and duty-free items, which may be located in a bonded store in another location.

Worksheets can be made out for each loading crew and vehicle which provide the relevant information on the type of aircraft and its registration, flight number, destination or origination, and stand number. As this information would usually appear on the label on each item of the uplift, it allows the loading crew to check to reduce errors.

The order in which the items are put onto the loading vehicle correspond to the aircraft design, access arrangements, and galley and hold configurations. There are few set procedures for loading, each crew tending to use its own way of working:

- For very large aircraft, with sufficient turnaround time, the aircraft may be stripped down on to one truck and then loaded up from another
- For larger aircraft with short on-ground time, it may be necessary to replace

Crew names	Roster	Shift times	Task allocations						
Driver 18 Loader 18	18	500 1700	610 UK509 700	UK511 855	UK483 905	Break 30	Break 30	1500 BA2838 1630	
Driver 5 Loader 5	5	500 1330	510 AMY801 700	BA2820 730	Break 30	850 BA197 1055			
Driver 12 Loader 12	12	500 1300	530 AMY801 700	Break 30	835 CP97 1130	Break 30	1055 SPP718 1210		
Driver 24 Loader 24	24	530 1730	635 EAF2042 800	AMY831 900	Break 30	Break 30	1555 CNB135 1645		
Driver 26 Loader 26	26	530 1730	610 AMY821 725	BA2380 825	Break 30	1010 BA199 1215	Break 30	1530 AMY837 1700	
Driver 7 Loader 7	7	530 1400	615 HV600 725	HV602 825	BA2640 900	Break 30	1005 BA2828 1130	Break 30	
Driver 14 Loader 14	14	530 1500	540 QTR002 635	740 BA2004 915	Break 30	1045 UK515 1225	UK487 1245	IG574 1420	Break 30
Driver 13 Loader 13	13	530 1330	620 BA2412 750	BA2016 830	BA3202 830	Break 30	945 EAF2086 1110	AEA242 1155	Break 30
Driver 19 Loader 19	19	530 1730	600 BA2002 730	Break 30	905 BA2328 1040	BA2560 1130	Break 30	1530 AMY803 1700	
Driver 16 Loader 16	16	730 1930	750 BA3128 830	Break 30	935 BA2378 1100	1145 HV604 1250	Break 30	1425 SUSHI 1845	
Driver 22 Loader 22	22	730 1930	810 BA2824 940	BA2695 1010	BA2006 1100	Break 30	1245 BA2414 1415	1525 UK491 1640	UK521 1650	Break 30
Driver 28 Loader2 8	28	800 1900	840 BR062/R 1225	Break 30	1555 HV606 1700	SPP716 1800	Break 30		
Driver 1 Loader 1	1	830 2030	855 IG3532 955	Break 30	1235 BA2382 1405	Break 30	1600 BA2840 1730	BA2420 1900	BA3206 1855	BA247 1950
Driver 21 Loader 21	21	830 1900	910 AAN215 1035	EAF2090 1115	1150 BA3204 1230	Break 30	1510 AMY803 1700	AMY879 1745	Break 30
Driver 8 Loader 8	8	830 2030	915 BA195 1120	Break 30	1355 AEO103 1600	Break 30	1730 BA2641 1900	BA2698 1945	
Driver 27 Loader 27	27	930 1830	950 CK302 1215	BR062/F 1225	1200 BA2832 1330	Break 30	Break 30	1525 BA2008 1700	AMY879 1745
	20	1230 2130	15 1310 BA2018 1445	930 BA2836 1530	IL702 1630	1700 Break 30	Break 30	1840 UK525 1945	UK497 2035	UK524 2200
	3	1400 2100	1430 BA2418 1600	Break 30	Break 30	1745 BA2020 1920	BA2844 1955	HV610 2030	
	17	1630 0	1720 BA3120 1815	BA2010 1930	CNB191 2015	Break 30	Break 30	2155 ALO104 0	

Figure 10.3

Staffing rota for aircraft loading crews

Source: Alpha Flight Services

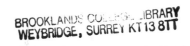
BROOKLANDS COLLEGE LIBRARY
WEYBRIDGE, SURREY KT13 8TT

trolleys on a one-for-one basis, that is remove a returning trolley from the aircraft and replace it with a new one
- For smaller aircraft, it is usual to load the truck with the supplies at the front, and keep space for the returning trolleys and stock at the rear. The aircraft would then be stripped down completely before the new load is put on board

In the case of aircraft requiring more than one loading vehicle, such as Boeing 747s or A340s, appropriate subloads are assembled and allocated to specific loading crews who will access the aircraft at different points and load particular parts of the aircraft. The use of more than one loading vehicle may be influenced by the airport authorities, as well as the airlines, aircraft layout, and other ground services. If the 'on ground time' is short, it may be necessary to use two vehicles even for a medium-size aircraft. The servicing of the aircraft with on-board products and meals usually takes longer than those other activities carried out, such as refuelling, unloading and loading passengers, and security and safety checks.

Correct location of load

There is a detailed load plan which is followed by the loading crew. An example is given in Fig. 10.4. This loading plan varies for different aircraft, and can vary with different flights and different airlines (Chapter 13). Aircraft are often constructed in several configurations according to the wishes of the original purchasing airline and the date of manufacture. Some airlines may have a mixture of these various configurations in their fleet. This may extend to having similar aircraft needing differing types of trolleys or carts. Although this is primarily an issue for the load assembly area, it can also affect the way in which the aircraft is loaded.

Each stowage area is numbered and where necessary the items of the load are appropriately numbered with the stowage area to be used. The plan may include loading of the ovens where hot food is to be served on the outward flight. The use of this system, besides being generally more efficient, also avoids the need for labelling of container contents. The exception to this is when special meals are included, as the container is then labelled appropriately to assist the cabin crew. The order of loading can be an important part of the load plan. Sometimes, some trolleys are stowed behind others as, for example, the rear ones will not be needed until the return flight. The loading crew are responsible for not only placing each trolley in its specified location, but also ensuring that they are secure. On aircraft with refrigeration systems, the loading crew also connect the trolleys to this system.

Operational issues

The key issues that face flight caterers supplying aircraft are responding to aircraft delays, changes to aircraft type, microbial safety, and security.

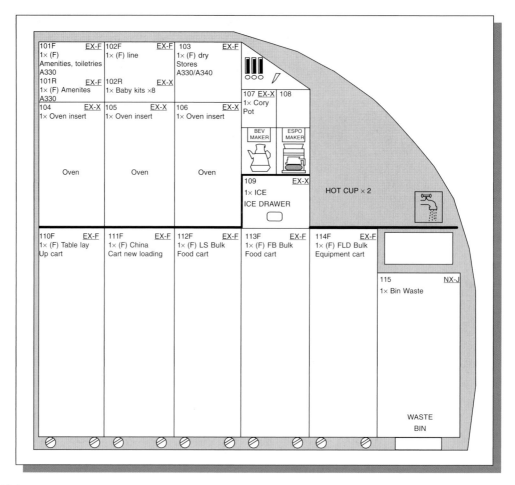

Figure 10.4
Example of a galley loading plan
SOURCE: Gulf Air

Delays

Every effort is made to prevent delays in view of the cost and loss of goodwill that can result. If a delay does occur, it is necessary to pinpoint the cause; hence careful record-keeping is important. A note is made by the loading crew of the time of arrival and departure from the dispatch area, and of other relevant times such as completion of loading. Other significant factors are also noted. These include whether any other ground services were still attending the aircraft, and whether any of these services delayed loading, such as baggage handling or cleaning. Also important is if any loading delay did actually hold up the aircraft or if, for instance, refuelling or maintenance was still taking place.

Aircraft changes

The impact of a change in aircraft depends upon the change that is made and when it occurs. A substitute of the same type of aircraft before loading would normally cause no problems. If the substitution is made after loading, it would require a crew and vehicle to download the original aircraft and reload on to the new one. Temperature checks may be necessary to ensure that the delay has not compromised the microbiological integrity of the food.

If a different type of aircraft is substituted, it may be possible to use the original load as originally packed, or more likely, it may be necessary to return the load to the catering unit for repacking into the correct configuration for the new aircraft. Good communication and following of procedures are essential when any changes occur so that sufficient time is allowed for the recatering before the delay is blamed on the catering operation.

Microbial safety

Microbial safety is of great importance in relation to transporting and loading perishable food items, especially in view of the inevitable time delay between production and consumption. The person responsible for assembling the load should ensure that the food is at the correct temperature and should arrange for appropriate procedures to be carried out. Since neither loading vehicles nor galley compartments on aircraft are usually refrigerated, it is usually trolleys which are cooled to a temperature of below 5°C. This is achieved by either dry-ice packs stored in a compartment in the top of the trolley or a blast from a carbon dioxide 'snow gun'.

As the system is designed around specific timings of aircraft movements, microbial safety is most threatened in the event of aircraft delays. Catering suppliers will check the temperature prior to dispatch and upon loading onto the aircraft. Once a member of the aircrew has signed for the meals, the responsibility for microbial safety becomes the airline's. If the aircraft is delayed on the ground, the airline may request the caterer to return to the aircraft to recheck the temperature and possibly restock the entire aircraft.

If the catering is being provided by a contractor, the caterers may have no power to force an airline to recater because of a delay, even if microbial safety is threatened. However, contractors may insist on a liability disclaimer if their advice is not followed. Similar tensions may develop between departments of an airline when in-house catering is being provided. Other hygiene issues may result from the particular circumstances in certain countries. For instance, some airlines may prohibit certain foods or not allow the uptake of water at certain destinations, while the fumigation of the off-load is the routine from some originating countries.

Security

In view of the considerable amount of vehicle movement on the airport apron and the direct access to aircraft, catering has to operate systems which conform to an acceptable standard of security. Regulations are imposed by the airport authorities and additional procedures may be required by various airlines. In addition, bonded stores may be subject to regulation by the customs authorities. After assembly some airlines require that all trolleys are visibly sealed. This is achieved by a variety of plastic seals designed so that tampering would be evident. A person is made responsible for checking and sealing the trolleys.

The seals used must themselves be controlled in such a way as to prevent unauthorised access. All trolleys issued by the bonded store must be sealed and locked.

Once the load has been put onto the loading vehicle, the vehicle may also be sealed and this is noted by the loading control. This then allows access to the apron. Any vehicles apparently not sealed are examined by airport security before being allowed access to the apron and this can cause a significant delay.

On the apron, procedures are specified with regard to vehicle movements and only approved personnel are allowed to drive. The general rule is that aircraft have absolute priority. Any collisions with aircraft must be reported immediately so that liability and cost can be assessed and, more importantly, checks can be made to ensure that the aircraft is still airworthy. Furthermore, to reduce possible damage to aircraft, high loaders approaching or leaving the aircraft must be directed in or off by a second person from outside.

On return from the aircraft to the catering unit, the bonded goods and other drinks carts are deposited at the bonded store. Containers that are sealed go into stock, while the rest of the load is taken to the dirty trolley off-load area.

Case study 10.1

Abela—London Heathrow

Abela at Heathrow in 2002 had contracts with 26 different airlines. Their production facility has 28 high loader trucks and a number of smaller refrigerated vehicles; and to provide all-year service, 60 drivers and 40 loaders are employed.

Abela organises its contracts and uplifts into three main categories. The **full catering uplift** refers to each aircraft being completely stripped down and reloaded with completely new items for the next flight. This will comprise tray sets in food trolleys based on passenger numbers, as well as a 'standard uplift' which includes:

- Bar cart with fruits and ice
- Dry stores, such as ketchup and vinegar
- Lit packs (blankets, pillows, etc.)
- Duty free items
- Headphones
- Flowers
- Printed materials

Abela conducts this type of uplift on flights operated by Gulf Air, Air Emirates, and Singapore Airlines.

Similar to this is the **turnaround uplift**. The main difference is the shorter time period in which to conduct the work, thereby requiring a higher number of vehicles and/or staff to attend the aircraft. For instance, Abela's contract with Air India includes servicing their Delhi to Chicago flight, which is on the ground at Heathrow for under one hour.

Abela's third category is the **partial uplift**. For instance, on contracts with Egypt Air and Royal Air Maroc, Abela load trolleys for first and business class passengers only, as economy class is back-catered. On other contracts, such as Air Malta, Abela provide top up meals on request, usually using small vans to do these 'run outs'.

Air Fayre—London Heathrow

There is one potential development that may greatly affect how aircraft are loaded, especially where flight production units are outside the perimeter of the airport.

Air Fayre at London Heathrow have developed an approach to loading based on having a low cost 'assembly facility' off airport and a logistics holding facility, for completed flights 'air side' on the apron. The advantages of this style of operation are that flight uplifts can be transferred in larger numbers from the main unit to the forward holding facility. The completed uplifts are customised at the forwarding unit to ensure that they accurately reflect the number of passengers travelling and the individual requirements of the uplift. The tangible benefits from this style of operation are as follows:

- Lower unit operating costs at the assembly facility
- Greater efficiency in transportation between the assembly unit and the airside logistics facility, particularly the avoidance of traffic congestion, which is an increasing problem around airport approach roads
- Reduction of wastage levels for the airline, as flights are managed and coordinated much closer to departure time and can be matched to the fluctuating passenger requirements of short-haul airlines
- Increased accuracy of uplift
- Improved punctuality performance, due to the greater flexibility and proximity to the aircraft stands for delivering the final uplift
- Integrity of the Chill Chain for food products, right through to final departure

The approach is unique in its simplicity and looks set to lead the way in which short-haul airlines are handled in the future, in an environment of ever increasing cost pressures and the requirement of flexibility.

Current issues and future developments

The transportation and loading of on-board products and meals onto aircraft is not a technically sophisticated operation. There are therefore few *significant* changes likely to take place to the technology. Four developments are occurring.

First, there is a trend towards the use of more **refrigerated vehicles**. The cost differential between non-refrigerated and refrigerated trucks is becoming less, and the additional microbial safety offered by refrigeration is recognised. For instance, ALPHA Flight Services had a fleet of vehicles of which 20 per cent were refrigerated. As trucks are replaced, this company intends to increase the percentage of refrigerated vehicles to 60 per cent.

Second, the **high-lift trucks** are becoming more technically sophisticated with regard to their handling characteristics. For instance, Norquip Edbro have developed a truck that incorporates ultrasonic and infra-red sensors to prevent damage occurring to aircraft or the truck itself while being raised. The truck also has a device for controlling the height of the loading platform once the truck is in position, so that if the aircraft settles during loading the platform moves down with it, preventing damage to aircraft door sills. Closed circuit television can also be used to monitor the raising of the truck body or while reversing the vehicle.

Third, the **scheduling** of trucks, and hence of loading crews, is becoming more sophisticated as a result of the integration of information systems. IT systems, which use data generated by the airlines concerning reservations to develop meal production plans, are being extended to control the efficient and effective assembly and dispatch of meals.

Finally, one trend that is related to **technology** is the development of systems to track delivery trucks in real time. This enables caterers to respond to delays and unforeseen requests thus improving overall efficiency. In addition, the system can address the important issue of security on vehicles when in transit between flight production units and the airport. The system is able to 'activate an alarm if a vehicle is detoured, if it stops for too long at suspicious points or if a door is opened outside loading/unloading areas (Momberger and Momberger, 2002).

Conclusion

The loading and unloading of the aircraft are normally part of the contract between the caterer and the airline. Precise loading and unloading arrangements are specified along with the level of service required, including the access arrangements and the relationship with other ground services. The required turnaround time is specified as well as arrangements for dealing with such events as notification of adjustments to meal numbers, the level of over ordering, and so on. The procedure to cope with delays is also detailed. It may be necessary for some of these features to be the subject of negotiation at an early stage so that realistic time slots are allocated.

These factors, as well as those having a bearing on the cost of the contract, need to be integrated with all the other activities of the organisation. This will ensure that arrangements can be made to optimise the use of resources while delivering the agreed level of service. The supplying of each aircraft with the correct load is a matter of careful organisation with effective control and monitoring. Information management is important so that coordination can ensure that the correct load is put on each aircraft taking into account late changes, etc. It is equally important that unloading is carefully monitored because of the critical part off-loaded items play in the logistics chain. Meticulous record-keeping will enable accurate cost and liability apportionment as well as providing reliable data for analysis with the object of improving the overall performance and prevention of the recurrence of errors. In the next chapter we examine the overall logistics implications of aircraft movements around the world.

Key terms

Aircraft changes	Back-catering	Dead-heading	Delays
Dispatch	High-lift truck	Lead-time	Loading
Security	Uplift		

Discussion questions

1. Identify the reasons why tight security is imposed on the transportation and loading of flight services.
2. What are the advantages of utilising refrigerated trucks?
3. Discuss the factors which affect the organisation of the transportation, loading and equipment used in this stage of the flight catering process.

Reference

Momberger, K. and Momberger, M. (2003) "Aviation catering news", *Momberger Airport Information*, 25 Oct. 2003.

CHAPTER 11

International logistics

Learning objectives

- Identify the nature and role of logistics in flight catering
- Identify the key logistics issues
- Evaluate the key logistics decisions
- Review the major logistics activities

Introduction

As we have already seen in this book, flight catering is mainly logistics and very little cooking. When the very large numbers and variety of items which must be loaded for passenger service during a flight are considered, together with the need for them to be loaded at widespread locations, the complexity of logistics is obvious. Logistics is concerned with adding value and reducing waste across the entire flight catering system. It is particularly concerned with non-consumable or non-disposable stock items (crockery, glassware, trays, etc.), although increasingly it is addressing other types of inventory too (particularly alcoholic beverages and duty-free items).

In order to use these stocks effectively and efficiently, logistics is concerned with:

- material demand forecasting
- equipment sector (or shelf) life
- sourcing of products
- contracting suppliers
- managing purchase contracts
- transportation of stocks
- warehousing of stocks
- inventory management of stocks and 'dwell time' (time not in use)
- stock balancing across the network
- galley and trolley planning

Given the importance and scale of logistics in flight catering, it might be argued that this whole book is really devoted to this topic. In fact, logistics as a 'boundary-spanning process' (i.e. a process that goes across traditional boundaries of firms or within firms) has only relatively recently been recognised within the industry. One of the reasons that logistics has been relatively uncoordinated to date is that the information systems to manage this complexity have not existed in an integrated format, especially since airlines, caterers, and suppliers have often used different platforms for their IT. This lack of integration has also meant that it has been difficult to monitor the logistics function, since without integrated data, it has been difficult to establish the key performance indicators.

The principal objectives of a logistics system are based around getting the *right products/materials* to the *right place(s)* at the *right time* and at *least cost*. This chapter attempts to deal with the complex issue of the logistics of flight catering by first addressing the particular characteristics of the logistical problems faced in this industry before analysing the problem from the standpoint of a typical logistics approach. The issue of having effective and integrated information systems is left to the next chapter (Chapter 12).

Logistics issues in flight catering

The logistics issues of flight catering are affected by a number of important features of the airline industry, the most important being the basic features of the business, the specifics of route scheduling, the impact of actual passenger loadings, and the 'product' mix.

International airline business activity

The basic features of the industry are that it has global dimensions, it is highly competitive, and profitability depends largely on maximising revenue in the face of variable demand. The airline business is increasingly competitive and most airlines in considering their competitive edge take account of the quality of the 'service package' offered to customers. For instance, there are strong pressures in some cases to use quality non-disposable items, such as china crockery, rather than cheaper disposable equivalents. The reinforcement of brand image also causes most to require that several items bear the company livery and logo. This has strong implications for the logistics problem since it could prevent local supply of these items.

Demand can be highly variable both in the shorter (across a week) and longer (across a year) cycles. Profitability is highly dependent on maximising revenue for which the technique of yield management was devised. The basic aim of this is to maximise passenger loading while as far as possible ensuring that the average fare paid by customers is also maximised. This may result in a wide variation in the passenger mix. At 'peak times' when seat sales are relatively easier there may be a high proportion of first-class passengers, while at off-peak times there is a higher proportion of sales in the economy class. Thus, the logistics system must be capable of adapting to variations not only in passenger numbers but also in the mix of passenger service requirements. For instance, outbound flights from Paris to European destinations will carry a high proportion of business people, especially in the morning, whereas the return flights will have a higher proportion of leisure travellers. Likewise, over the long cycle, flights into Switzerland carry a very different mix of business and leisure travellers in the ski season than at other times of the year.

Route scheduling

Routes and schedules operated by airlines will have a significant impact upon the overall organisation of the logistics system. For many scheduled operators, the service offered on a particular flight may well be influenced by the following:

- route served
- length of haul
- number of intermediate legs
- sector times
- customer revenue class
- aircraft configuration

In the drive to maximise seat occupancies, flights often have intermediate stops so that tickets may be sold not only for an entire flight but also for parts of it, that is one leg of the journey. This may present the additional logistics complication of restocking aircraft at intermediate stops. For instance, although it is technically possible for an aircraft to fly non-stop from Europe to the Far East, many flights have a stop-over in the Middle East or India in order to improve seat occupancy levels.

Long-haul flights present special problems in terms of coordinating the logistics function. This is particularly the case where airlines have full traffic rights and seek to maximise revenues from each sector of a multiple leg flight. For catering uplifts this means that logistical arrangements can be quite varied. For example, long-haul economy meals, being high volume and relatively standardised products, may be supplied from the place of origin and an intermediate port of call. However, on the same flight first- or business-class meals offering extensive customer choice and menu flexibility may be catered throughout from the place of origin. Maintenance of a consistently high standard of service may leave this as the only viable option. Additionally, it may prove advantageous to uplift other items such as liquor elsewhere on the journey. Table 11.1 illustrates how the uplift has been devised for a flight from London Gatwick (LGW) to Bangkok (BKK) via Abu Dhabi (AUH). At each airport, items may be changed (X), added (A), off-loaded (O), replenished (R), or deleted (D). For instance, bulk food trays in stowage position 924 are changed in all three places: the hot jug is added at London Gatwick on the outbound leg and changed at London Gatwick on the inbound; and ice cubes are replenished at all three stations.

Passenger loadings

Passenger factors are major drivers which test the responsiveness of the logistics system on a day-to-day basis. Passenger numbers affect the size of uplifts for meal trays (but not for bars, which are normally stocked to par stock levels). In order that balance is maintained within the system, equipment levels will have to remain relatively constant. For short-haul flights, which fly to a destination and return directly to point of origin, there should be no major problem. If the aircraft flies out with a full set of equipment, it should return with a full set. But even on short haul, in aircraft with a flexible cabin that allows the size of business class relative to economy to increase or decrease, some equipment imbalance can occur. On long-haul flights, however, especially those with intermediate stopovers and more than one-meal service, equipment taken off the aircraft at one point may not automatically be reloaded at the same point. To overcome this problem, airlines have adopted **dead heading**. This involves loading aircraft with equipment items sufficient for the maximum number of passengers irrespective of meals required, thereby ensuring that equipment exchanges at intermediate or final destinations can take place without excess stocks developing in some parts of the system and shortages occurring elsewhere. Thus, it is a logistics requirement that equipment exchanges take place satisfactorily under conditions where, for example, outward flights may be carrying low occupancy but return legs the opposite. Unless massive stocks were to be held at each catering supply point it is easy to imagine a situation where differences in passenger numbers could lead to much of an airline's equipment ending up in one place (Case study 12.1). Even for charter business where passenger loadings are less volatile and **return catering** more common, this type of arrangement tends to hold for equipment items.

Many airlines operate aircraft dedicated to particular routes and with fleets conforming to identical configurations. Therefore, any change of aircraft for whatever reason, such as maintenance overhauls or traffic delays, should have little impact upon the logistics function. Where aircraft variations do exist,

Loading order sheet
Maximum catering configuration 12/56/336

Flight Number: GA.880-881
Type of Aircraft: B-747
Configuration: 10/52/330

900A

X = Change
A = Add
O = Off

R = Replenish
D = Delete

Heading	CM Page	Load Unit	NMB	Stowage Position	DPS	CGK	BKK	AUI	LGW	AUI	BKK	CGK
F C1 1/1 Bulk food trays	109A	T11	1	924	A	X		X	X	X	X	
F C1 1/1 Bulk food trays	109A	T11	1	925	A	A		X	X	X	X	
F C1 Oven	100A	OIS	1	915	A	X		X	X	X	X	
F C1 Oven	100B	OIS	1	916	A	X		X	X	X	X	
F C1 Meal trans. container	100A	STC	1	9E	D							
C C1 1/ Trays trolley	114A	T11	4	221-227-421-422	A	X		X	X	X	X	
C C1 1/ Trays trolley	114A	T11	4	323-328-929-930	A	A		X	X	X	X	
C C1 Oven 1	103A	OIS	2	211-411	A	X		X	X	X	X	
C C1 Oven 1	103A	OIS	2	212-412	D	X						
Y C1 2/3 Trays	120A	T23	8	425-425-621-622- 623-821-822-823	A	X		X	X	X	X	
Y C1 2/3 Trays	120A	T23	8	524-525-526-625- 626-724-725-726		A		X	X	X		
Y C1 Oven	105A	OIS	12	413-417-418-611- 612-613-617-618- 811-812-818	A	X	X	X	X	X		
Y C1 Meal trans container	106A	STC	12	409-451-459-505- 601-609-651-659- 807-808-857-858	D			X	X			
Crew trays main dish	121B	STC	2	303-506	A	X		X	X	X	X	
Crew trays main dish	121B	STC	2	555-556		A		X	X	X	X	
Crew trays main dish	121B	STC	2	362-353	D							
Y C1 Juice cups		CUP	1	Work top galley	A	X		X	X			
Y C1 Juice cups	180A	STC	3	551-702-752	A			X				

(Continued)

Item	Code	Type	Qty	Serial						
Hot jug	172A	HJG	1	917			A		X	
Ice cubes	170C	SPC	1	911	R	R	R	X	R	R
Ice cubes	170D	SPD	1	214	R	R	R	R	R	R
Ice cubes	170A	SPC	6	311-361-511-561-711-761	A	X	X	R	X	R
Linen/silver ware	150D	T11	1	921			A			
Linen/silver ware	152	LOT	1	B1			A			
Y C1 St steel container	154B	STC	2	401-501			A			
Y C1 St steel container	154A	STC	2	502-701			A			
F & C C1 Hot towels	156A	STC	2	472-473			A			
F C1 Porcelain/glass	111A	T11	1	922	X	X	A	X	X	X
C C1 Glass container	118B	T11	2	475-476	X	X	A	X	X	X
F C1 Alc beverages (Cold)	500A	T12	1	923A	X	X	A	X	X	X
F C1 Alc beverages	500C	STC	1	9D	X	X	A	X	X	X
F C1 Alc beverages (Cold)	510A	T12	4	228A-228B-321A-321B	X	X	A	X	X	X
F C1 Alc beverages	510B	STC	2	312-313	X	X	A	X	X	X
F C1 Alc beverages (Cold)	520A	T12	8	521A-521B-522A-522B-721A-721B-722A-722B	X	X	A	X	X	X
F C1 Alc beverages	520B	STC	4	513-514-713-714	X	X	A		X	X

AUTHORITY: JKTCIGA ISSUED: 11.10.1993

ISSUED BY: JKTCHGA EDFECTIVE: 31.10.1993   SERIAL NBR: INT/CHB/WTR/10/93

Table 11.1
Uplift for flight from LGW to BKK
SOURCE: ALPHA Flight Services, 1993

problems with equipment supply may arise. In turn equipment variations can force changes in other areas such as food items served.

Product mix

Typically a 'service package' is taken to include 'tangibles', that is goods provided for the customer, and 'intangibles', relating to the quality of service provided to the customer. The flight service package includes both. Logistics tends to focus on the provision of just the tangible elements. The problem to be addressed is the need to ensure that any flight, whatever its place of origin and destination, is fully stocked with the physical items contained within the service package, together with clean and functional equipment requested by cabin crew for providing service. Broadly, these goods fall into four categories:

1. Food items (including drinks to be consumed on the aircraft)
2. Non-food items (this is an extensive list which may include newspapers, blankets, toilet bags, headsets for aircraft sound or video systems, and so on)
3. Duty-free goods for passengers to purchase on the aircraft
4. Equipment required by cabin crew for providing service (service equipment including tea- and coffeemaking equipment, first-aid kits, and so on)

Many of the items used are consumable not only in the direct sense, such as food and paper items, but also because it is expected that passengers will retain them after use. In such cases it is essential to arrange fresh stocks for each flight. Some items are 'rotable', implying they may be used more than once. However, it will be necessary to service them between uses. For instance, blankets need to be washed, according to procedures issued by the manufacturers, and headsets sterilised. Even with rotable items it will still be necessary to replace defective items or make good 'shrinkage'. Shrinkage arises from items being broken, damaged, lost, misappropriated, or mistakenly retained by passengers.

For each category of goods, there is also likely to be a variety reflecting the different seat classes, and possibly cultural factors. The different types of equipment used for tray lay-ups have already been discussed in Chapter 8. It is essential for the logistics system to restock the aircraft adequately with items of the right quality as specified by the operating standards of the company and not simply topping up from local stocks to the adequate quantity level.

A network of providers

The diversity of the materials and products consumed on the aircraft means that there are a number of interrelated distribution systems needed to service the aircraft. One is the conventional distribution of non-food consumables and some dry goods for the stocking of warehouses and/or stores. This kind of distribution is obviously carried out by suppliers to central production units or bonded stores. But it may also be carried out by airlines, or their agents, for the distribution of goods or materials from their central stockholding facility to satellite units. For instance, BA transports stocks by road from Heathrow to the other UK airports at which they operate, and cargo freight by sea and air for stocking stations outside the UK. The second type of logistics system is that relating to the stocking of aircraft with prepared meals, and a third relates to the transportation of rotable equipment from one airport to another to ensure that equipment is 'balanced'. It is these latter two interrelated systems, unique to flight catering, that this chapter is focused on.

Some airlines operate their own flight catering service, based around flight production units owned and operated by the airline. This is particularly so in the case of countries where costs are lower, whose monetary exchange rates are disadvantageous, or which have restrictions on the use of hard currency. In such cases, it is common for them to attempt to stock the aircraft not only for the outward flight but also for the return flight except when other considerations prevent this, such as food shelf life. Most others contract out to caterers. Such airlines, therefore, use agents for outward and return flights. The problem is compounded by some flights having intermediate stops. This may be required for refuelling or to maximise seat occupancy, adding passengers for each 'hop' of the flight to those travelling the whole distance. In such cases, some restocking may be necessary or desirable for each leg of the journey, which might be done by different agents in each case. The growth of LSG Sky Chef and Gate Gourmet has potentially addressed this problem as they have such an extensive global network of provision.

This network may be further extended by subcontracting. It is increasingly the case that flight production units are concentrating on tray and trolley assembly, and subcontracting out meal production to specialist suppliers (Chapter 8). In some cases, these may be very small businesses undertaking small steps in the process such as sorting out cleaned cutlery and packaging complete sets which are returned to the main agent for incorporation into meal trays.

An example of one airline's 'network or providers' and its logistics activities are illustrated in Fig. 11.1 and Table 11.2. In summary, BA currently restock European, African, Middle Eastern, Far Eastern, South American and Caribbean airports from their bases at London Heathrow, while they use agents from a depot in Newark, New Jersey for North American flights, and Asian/ Australasian agents from Singapore for some aspects of supply.

Key logistics decisions

A major airline operating on a global scale will, therefore, need to operate via an extensive network of agents with attendant subcontractors in some cases. Not only will these need to conform to the standards expected by the airline (with all the attendant contractual and control issues) but may need to be supplied with at least some items that they cannot source themselves. This can result in a complex distribution network ensuring that the supply agent at each and every airport has adequate stock levels of a wide range of products ranging from small consumable items bearing the airline livery to replacement rotable items. This can be done directly from the home base or via regional depots.

There are basically three key logistics decisions that need to be made by an airline. These are the extent to which return or 'back' catering will be carried

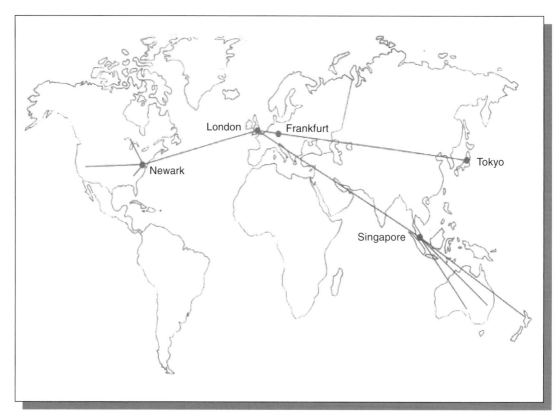

Figure 11.1
Map of airline's logistics network

out; whether to utilise the flight service facilities of those airports into which flights are routed; and whether to use local suppliers.

The return catering decision

There are basically two options in arranging provision for return flights. **Return catering** entails carrying provisions for the return flight on the outward flight. Alternatively, the return journey can be restocked through a local agent, or less commonly from an airline outstation. In most cases, there is a mixture of these two options, some items being back catered and some being provided by local agents. Factors governing which of these options to adopt are:

Hygiene On longer flights, it may be impossible to guarantee the safety of back catering. On the other hand, an airline may consider that there is no local agent who can meet the specified hygiene and/or quality standards.

Cost It is in the interest of airlines in low-cost countries to use back catering as extensively as possible (especially if the alternative requires payment in precious hard currency). Conversely, airlines from high-cost countries may find it attractive to restock locally as far as possible.

Payload space The potential cost advantages of return catering can be

Location	Logistics infrastructure	Logistics activity	Responsibility
London Heathrow	Warehousing and distribution handling centre for Europe	Bulk storage of equipment, liquor and dry goods	Contract distributor
	Long-haul production unit	Meal production and loading	Contractor
	Short-haul production unit	Meal production and loading	Contractor
	Long-haul bonded store	Bar packing	Contractor
	Short-haul bonded store	Bar packing	Contractor
Newark	Warehousing and distribution handling centre for USA	Bulk storage of equipment, liquor and dry goods Some local purchasing of wines/non-branded goods	Contract distributor
Singapore	Warehousing and distribution handling centre for Australasia	Bulk storage of equipment, liquor and dry goods	Contract distributor
Tokyo	Production unit	Meal production and loading to long-haul specifications	Contractor
	Bonded store	Bars exchanged	Contractor
Frankfurt	Production unit	Meal production and loading to short-haul specification	Contractor

Table 11.2
Part of the logistics activity of one airline

offset by the space or weight requirements of the items for the return journey. The additional weight increases fuel used by the aircraft and the additional volume may reduce freight capacity if carried in the hold or reduce seating space if galleys are enlarged for carriage there.

Security   Some items may be highly desirable and easy to pilfer if stocks are provided for local resupply. For this reason such items as coffee pots and headsets are usually 'back catered'.

Control   Back catering may be preferred in some cases since it offers greater control than may be possible with local agents. In some cases it may also avoid security problems such as drug smuggling or the planting of terrorist devices, as containers are sealed at point of origin.

Quality assurance   Airlines try to avoid overstocking and go to great lengths to load just sufficient meals for the number of passengers on the journey, even topping up at the last minute (Chapter 7). At the outset of an outward flight it may be difficult to predict the number of passengers on the return flight. Local resupply is more flexible and allows a better match to passenger numbers. On charter flights, passenger loading is more predictable than is sometimes the case with scheduled flights and back catering is less likely to lead to over or under provision.

Local availability   Some items may not be available locally and if perishable, must be carried out on the outward journey, for instance newspapers.

Airport capabilities

Maintenance of customer service levels and cost control will, for all airlines, be influenced by the servicing capabilities of airports visited. The impact of this factor can be significant even for major international airlines operating on the most lucrative scheduled routes. From a logistics perspective, tightest control exists when an airline operates from its 'home base' or hub. Major international airlines usually service flights internally through their own catering facilities when operating from their main base or another major domestic centre. In many cases airline-operated catering facilities will have sufficient capacity to supply other airlines flying to that centre. For instance, Singapore Airlines has an extensive flight production unit in Singapore capable of serving not only its own needs but all airlines using that airport.

Airlines operating away from their home base will, because of scale economies, normally use the services of a local caterer. In some cases this may simply mean using different units owned by the same company. Thus, it may prove possible to maintain the important understanding that underpins any successful relationship between airline and caterer.

At major international airports, such as London Heathrow, airlines may be able to derive benefits from a competitive marketplace. However, in heavily regulated aviation markets these benefits may prove illusory if access to gates is denied or jealously guarded in favour of a home carrier. Even within the European Union it is possible to find a monopolistic catering situation at a major international airport, for instance in Rome. Being a major player in the global aviation market offers no immunity from the resultant loss of control or higher charges levied with respect to catering facilities. Scheduled airlines operating into and out of regional centres will, in the majority of cases, have access to only one caterer. For charter services, some remote and/or minor destinations may offer few or no catering facilities. Thus it may be necessary to operate on a fully catered basis from the airline's home base. Scheduled operators can face this problem in varying degrees. Just as airlines 'shop around' when refuelling on certain routes, catering services may be declined in part or whole if deficiencies are seen to exist at a particular airport.

While traffic volume is a principal determinant of an airport's capabilities, the adequacy of catering facilities is dependent upon a number of other factors. Airlines may not use services on offer for reasons ranging from poor transportation and loading arrangements to fears concerning the safety of basic supplies such as water. The pivotal role of equipment exchange alone dictates that airlines find equal players at destinations served by their aircraft.

Market growth achieved through the opening up of new routes and new destinations may be checked by the speed at which support services such as catering develop. For example, on some of the new long-haul routes in Australasia it is difficult to overcome non-existent catering facilities through the use of return catering, because of hygiene and product freshness. As a consequence it is not uncommon for airlines and caterers to collaborate in joint ventures aimed at producing the required infrastructure. New services developed in the mid-1990s to destinations such as Vietnam illustrate this spirit of co-operation.

International and local supply

Procurement decisions will, more than any other factor, determine the complexity of the logistics function. Arrangements between airlines and caterers vary considerably, giving rise to wide differences in contractual and operational obligations. At one extreme, an airline may leave sourcing of products and materials entirely to the caterer. This tends to be the case with most charter businesses. Alternatively, sources of supply may be identified and specified by the airlines themselves. For most scheduled operators some intermediate position holds.

The major international airlines are often large corporations capable of wielding significant purchasing power. Therefore, it may be the case that supplies of materials to the caterer are organised through contacts negotiated by airlines themselves. This is most likely where an airline operates a centralised purchasing system or is part of a much larger holding company. It has to be recognised that some caterers, such as Gate Gourmet and LSG Sky Chef, are also global organisations possessing comparable purchasing power. However, some airlines do not simply make purchasing decisions on unit cost grounds alone. They are influenced by their position as a national carrier, strategic alliances formed with other multinational companies, the brand image they are trying to create for their flight catering, and so on.

Where airlines specify the use of 'own branded' products, supplies will often come to the caterer via the airline's home base. For the contracted caterer this may result in high inventory levels and warehousing costs. Meeting the tastes of its home customers abroad may also result in supplies being shipped from home base, if no local supplier can be found. For other products, such as liquor, handled by the caterer, an airline operating a centralised purchasing system may source items themselves, and ship them to the home base before distribution takes place to end users. Given that this practice is widespread for items such as wine and bearing in mind the shipment involved, many wines must be robust to travelling!

Even where systems are heavily centralised caterers are still given scope to utilise local supplies. Frequently, this can result in higher product/material quality and lower costs. For instance, countries such as Sri Lanka and Indonesia offer high-quality fresh produce at very low prices. In such countries, the relatively low volume of purchasing may mean that these low unit costs do not make significant cost savings when the total cost of procurement is taken into account. Other factors will also influence the decision to use local supply. For example, meat sourced from the UK may not be regarded as acceptable if fears over BSE disease command the attention of passengers. Also, it has to be recognised that many national airlines literally fly their country's flag, generate valuable export earnings, and employ thousands of citizens. Moreover, where the airline is state owned, preferential status may be given to home-produced goods. Thus national interests may take precedence over purely commercial considerations.

Logistics activities

The opening section of this chapter has drawn attention to the distinctive characteristics of flight catering logistics. Some of these issues have been dealt with in other chapters, as follows:

- Demand forecasting and flight scheduling (Chapter 8)
- Sourcing from suppliers (Chapter 6)
- Contracting (Chapter 2)
- Stock and equipment balancing (Chapter 12)
- Galley planning (Chapter 13)

This section therefore focuses on the traditional perspective of logistics as a distribution function, with its principal components of warehousing, transportation and inventory management. It is around these areas that some of the key conceptual and theoretical concepts are now discussed.

Warehousing

In many distribution systems, warehousing and transportation perform key roles in support of the marketing function. Therefore, the development of an effective system will focus upon issues such as the number, size and location of warehouses. In turn, these factors together with routes operated, influence the choice of transport. In the flight industry, the 'warehouse' is often in the same location as the central production unit. Of the four kinds of goods identified above, food items are highly perishable with a shelf life of only a few hours, whereas the non-food items, duty-free goods, and equipment are not perishable.

With flight service, the warehousing function is of major importance but has a different orientation compared with, for example, retailing. There are three main differences. First, flight warehouses tend to stock raw materials rather than goods available for final consumption; with the exception of items such as duty-free goods very few products are actually supplied to a marketplace. Second, stock-holding and supply of equipment are just as important as product/ materials (food retailers do not normally have to supply cutlery and crockery as well). Finally, location of warehouses tends to be fixed, usually within close proximity of an airport. Assembly of meals and of aircraft total service loads is usually on or near the aircraft boundary where space is at a premium: stocks may be held some distance away. Therefore, the warehousing function in the context of flight catering bears a closer resemblance to the network of supply points operated under a military logistics system than that operated by supermarket retailers. Although the main warehouse operated by an airline or caterer (often at a 'hub' airport) may hold non-food stocks as finished goods in case quantities (as in retail distribution), the production of meals and location of equipment at distribution points in a network around the world create a military style logistics system.

The amount of space relative to the production capacity of the kitchens varies widely. For example, the total size of the KLM production unit at Schipol, Amsterdam is 9,500 sq. m, of which 4,000 sq. m is racked warehouse storage. This unit stocks over 3,000 different non-perishable catering items and has a maximum capacity of 25,000 meals. Where the caterer is a servicing agent potentially more warehousing space will be required. Some of this will be geared directly to the caterer's production facility, the remainder to supplies specified by each of airlines with whom the caterer has contract. The range of

Figure 11.2
Photograph of a flight catering warehouse
SOURCE: LSG Sky Chefs

items and the number of airlines serviced by some caterers mean that stocking policies will have a profound effect upon distribution costs.

Transportation

Chapter 10 has explained in detail how goods are transported from the central production unit to the aircraft. Unlike other distribution systems, the transportation centres around scheduling rather than routing. Most retail supply chains necessitate applying routing algorithms in order to establish the most efficient and effective way of supplying a number of outlets spread over a wide geographic area. In flight service, trucks basically travel between the flight unit and the airport apron. Even though the aircraft being serviced may be located at different stands around the airport, this does not present significant routing difficulties. However, airlines and caterers that have a main distribution centre and make road deliveries to production units at a number of airports, will adopt the same kind of routing algorithms as retail distributors.

Inventory management

In providing the desired level of service, warehouse stocks provide an important buffer between supply sources and demand which may at times be variable and uncertain. The stock levels sustained in flight warehouses and production units are very large. Ad hoc research indicates that both airlines and caterers would generally agree that stocks may be greater than needed, thereby tying up capital in underused equipment. In the past, the philosophy has been 'better safe than sorry'. Often, the cost of trying to devise and implement a system of stock control that would achieve higher levels of utilisation was greater than the savings to be made. With the development of just-in-time (JIT) systems, bar coding, and materials handling systems, it seems likely that this will be a major area for significant development in the future. At least one major international airline believes that it could save several million pounds per annum through reducing stock-holding levels.

The function of inventory management is to maintain some kind of balance between the cost of investments in inventory and the benefits bestowed in terms of better availability of materials/products. Combined inventory costs can be quite substantial and comprise storage costs, handling costs, interest charges, shrinkage, wastage, and insurance costs. Ultimately, it is the opportunity cost of capital tied up in inventory that has to be justified. Lowering inventory levels simply to reduce these costs runs the risk of incurring stock-outs. For many inventory systems, this leads to other costs in the form of lost or delayed sales. For flight catering this will show up as lower customer service levels and perhaps for the caterer a risk of losing contracts.

Stock replenishment and inventory policy, whether based upon classic economic order quantity (EOQ) models or a JIT-based approach, will be influenced strongly by the distinctive nature of flight service. For instance, European airlines purchasing products from the Far East, such as cutlery or amenity kits, would tend to adopt the EOQ approach and bulk purchase in container loads. On the other hand, high-value items such as gifts or high-volume items with regular, shorter distance delivery are more likely to be sourced on a JIT basis.

Operations spanning national boundaries and the possibility of restocking stop-over or return flights add degrees of complexity seldom found in many logistics systems. Given the scale of the warehousing and supply function, stock levels may be a source of tension between agents and airlines. It is in the airlines' interest to minimise stock levels, since they bear capital investment costs, and in the agents' interest to maximise stock levels, since they bear much of the stock-out inconvenience, storage and handling cost.

Information systems

A logistics system geared up to supplying a complex service package to the required standard first time and every time wherever an airline operates, places heavy demands upon managers in terms of information handling. This is discussed in more detail in Chapter 12.

At one level it is necessary to collect 'hard' data for control purposes. For example, the stocks of rotable equipment if not tracked carefully may not be utilised in the most efficient manner. Some airlines such as Qantas use sophisticated computerised systems to monitor allocation and use of equipment items. The system is designed in such a way that automatic replenishment from the airline's home base in Sydney keeps stock held and required by caterers at appropriate levels. Airlines such as Cathay Pacific, operating a centralised purchasing and supply system, also maintain tight control through their home base.

Aircraft movements and the primary business of passenger airlines create a need for information suitable for planning purposes. Catering contracts with airlines tend to operate over a relatively long time period and require some degree of long-range planning from the position of supplies. Seasonal and daily demand fluctuations in passenger numbers will transmit themselves through to the logistics system. It is usual for caterers to monitor passenger numbers 48, 24 and 12 hours prior to departure. Although many may plan their production around this lead time, the logistics system may need to be more proactive in terms of forecasting. As logistics have become more and more important, many caterers now ask for at least weekly forecasts to support JIT delivery of raw materials.

Many airlines optimise passenger revenues through the application of sophisticated yield management systems. These use a wide variety of forecasting methodologies and generate forecasts for passenger numbers well ahead of departure date. Just as this facility may ultimately protect the airline's revenue position, so it may come to be used to enhance the logistics planning function.

It is interesting to note that one European airline serving 13 destinations in the US, generated and regularly updated forecasts for passenger numbers, which were given to a supplier of frozen hot entrees in the US. This supplier stated after some years of contract that no other airline had ever given such reliable forecast figures, thus alleviating the problem of high inventory at the end of a menu cycle.

Case study 11.1

Delta, e-gatematrix and Kuhne & Nagel*

E-gatematrix, a member of the Gate Gourmet Group, and Kuehne & Nagel have agreed on a ten-year partnership in the field of inflight logistics. As logistics supplier to Jetlogistics AG, an affiliated company of e-gatematrix, Kuehne & Nagel has been providing customised inflight logistics services for Jetlogistics' airline customers like Air New Zealand, Aeromexico, SWISS, and South African Airways for some years. From 2002, Kuehne & Nagel, who are already providing sea freight activities for Delta, will cover all Delta services for 20 European destinations.

By agreeing on a ten-year partnership, e-gatematrix and Kuehne & Nagel highlighted their intention to extend their inflight logistics business globally. Due to the trend that the airlines increasingly outsource activities outside of their core competencies, the field of inflight logistics is a promising market for worldwide operating companies offering logistics and supply chain management solutions. "We have high confidence in the capabilities of the Kuehne & Nagel Group. Their innovative and flexible logistics solutions complement our airline know how ideally. This strategic partnership will strengthen the market position

---

*This case is based on a press release from the companies concerned.

of both companies and will generate competitive advantages," said Niels Smedegaard, President & CEO, e-gatematrix.

While e-gatematrix calculates the demand for the required inflight logistics articles and coordinates the flow of goods, Kuehne & Nagel is in charge of handling integrated services—warehousing and distribution, customs clearance, sea, air and overland transports—as well as other value-added services. The Kuehne & Nagel Group is one of the world's leading logistics companies with 17,000 employees at 600 locations in 90 countries.

Current issues and future developments

In previous chapters, **outsourcing** has been identified as a major trend. Not only can food production be outsourced, but also many aspects of the logistics function. For instance, global logistics companies already have warehousing and transportation fleets in situ for handling all kinds of manufactured and retail goods. Rather than manage the logistics of ensuring wine is always available for loading at every station this could be outsourced in its entirety.

Second, the trend towards **process re-engineering** in flight production units is creating a short-term logistics problem for many airlines. By adopting JIT inventories and reducing waste and process cycle-time, many units have found they are over-stocked with equipment, such as trays, crockery, and cutlery belonging to their clients. They have therefore been returning this unwanted stock to airline warehouses. This has led to a significant increase in equipment held centrally and will take some time for airlines to adjust their stocks to appropriate levels reflecting the more streamlined operations now being developed.

The next logical step is for airlines to **lease** all their equipment rather than own it. This would enable them to respond very much more flexibly to change in demand, adapt their equipment to reflect a new branding strategy, or respond to new technology. Leasing equipment is common in many other industries as it greatly assists cash flow management and reduces perishable assets on the balance sheet.

Conclusion

The core activities of a logistics system—distribution, warehousing, transport, and inventory management—may be viewed as forming part of a complex mosaic; the supply chain spanning the objectives and constraints of diverse functions such as marketing and procurement. Measurement of system performance may well lead to attention being focused upon operating costs and resource efficiency. However, in addition to these largely quantitative indications, customer service levels and overall effectiveness require serious consideration. Indeed, it would seem entirely appropriate to view the contribution of logistics from a 'value analysis' perspective. Logistics, like marketing, is now recognised by many companies at a strategic level for the competitive edge it may bring in today's market-place. Thus, any review of performance must consider the impact of logistics upon the whole system and not in terms of optimising individual components of a complex network.

Flight service does not present a unique problem in terms of logistics requirements. However, as outlined previously, it does carry certain distinctive characteristics. Pressure to deliver customer service levels 'first time and every time' will be an exacting task in any system operated through a network of participants whose activities are open to varying degrees of control. The character of flight logistics is mixed. The scale of operations and geographical dispersion make it similar to a military support system, but the end objectives are purely commercial. From the customers' perspective, the impact from logistics and the catering system in general may seem indirect. For airlines, the impact of logistics upon core business activities is direct and measured in terms of passenger numbers. Ultimately, this translates into the difference between profit and loss. While passengers may have the freedom to choose between one package and another, airlines are constrained to provide the customer with a package of services. Logistics ensure that the package is delivered at least cost to the airline and to the service level demanded by the customer.

Key terms

Dead-heading	Distribution	Intermediate stopovers	Short-haul
Logistics	Long-haul	Rotable	Warehousing
Shrinkage	Traffic volume	Transport	

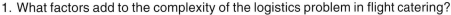

Discussion questions

1. What factors add to the complexity of the logistics problem in flight catering?
2. What considerations need to be made when deciding whether or not to back-cater?

Flight catering information systems

Learning objectives

- Examine information flows from airlines to flight providers
- Identify the requirements for service and product specifications
- Understand the use of e-business strategies

Introduction

It is clear from previous chapters that flight catering depends upon a great deal of information. Airlines were early adopters of computers and IT to handle their reservations and ticketing processes. Now IT is used in every business sector to handle information needs, including flight catering. However, a major problem has been that many IT systems were originally developed to handle specific and different aspects of the operation, and developed by different software companies or user groups. This has meant that until the late 1990s most systems were not integrated. It is only now that we are beginning to see the emergence of fully integrated management information systems.

This chapter looks at information systems and examines their use and purpose within the flight catering industry. The significant flows of information are identified, along with the communication channels that are used to disseminate it. In addition, we will examine why there is a need for information systems in flight catering and investigate the benefits they can offer. In addition to these current uses of, and trends in, information systems in flight catering, we will look at how businesses in the industry are adopting e-business strategies.

Information systems

An information system is a mechanism that assists a decision-making process. To be more specific, it is seen as a work system whose business process is devoted to capturing, transmitting, storing, retrieving, manipulating and displaying information, thereby supporting other works systems. Information systems can vary widely in type, from a simple manual hardware device such as a pen and paper or an informal communication channel such as word-of-mouth, to computer-based information systems that use computer hardware and software or telecommunication networks. The use of information systems and other forms of information technology enable businesses to transform data resources into valuable information that can assist their decision-making processes.

What is information?

Information can be considered as data that has been gathered, processed and presented in such a way that it is meaningful to the person receiving that information; but in order to be meaningful it must have a number of attributes (Table 12.1).

Why use information systems?

The fundamental roles of information systems in any organisation are to support business processes and operations, decision making by managers and employees, and strategies for competitive advantage.

Flight catering processes and operations create data that needs to be captured and prepared, with which useful information can be derived and upon which decisions can be based. The data that is captured needs to be inputted by some means in to the information system, after which point it is then subjected to

Attribute	Explanation
Accuracy	Not only is it true or false, but does it accurately portray the situation?
Breadth	Does the information provide the scope required?
Completeness	Is the information complete enough to make a decision?
Consistent	Is it consistent with other factors?
Form	Has it been presented in a usable format?
Frequency	How often is the information needed, collected and utilised?
Impartial	Information which has not been 'corrupted' by other influences
Relevance	To be relevant the information must be needed
Reliable	Is the information reliable
Time horizon	Is it oriented towards past, present or future activity?

Table 12.1
Attributes of meaningful data
SOURCE: Senn (1990)

processing activities. The processing of data typically includes activities such as calculating, comparing, sorting, classifying and summarising. These activities convert the captured data into useful information for end-users (those that will be using the information). This information is known as the output of an information system.

The objective of any information system is to produce appropriate information products for end users. For flight catering, common information products include things such as passenger numbers, new menus, tray layups, galley configurations, aircraft type, routing, and so on. The information produced is routinely used by a business to optimise performance of their processes and operations.

When looking at the flight catering industry in particular, products and services must be delivered in a timely manner, which means than any delays in decision making can be detrimentat to the efficiency of the procedures. In addition, it must be understood that the industry is fragmented and international in nature, which means that communication is essential for the success of the business.

This industry has millions of daily transactions on a global basis, between passengers and airlines, and millions of business-to-business (B2B) interactions among airlines, caterers, and suppliers. This volume of 'connectivity' across national boundaries is higher than almost any other industry.

The impact of using information systems

Any business using information systems to handle and manage their data does so to improve business efficiency and to help streamline and organise all their day-to-day operations. The successful use of information systems and software solutions can be rewarding to all those involved in the flight catering process. It can lead to better planning, the production of accurate documentation, access to vital information as and when needed, and improved customer service. Airlines can also attain reductions in cost, complexity, inefficiency and errors in the supply chain. An airline can obtain all the information they need to inform the supply chain of what to do, how much to do, how to do it, where to buy it and how well it was done by the successful use of information system applications. This information can then be exchanged and used to build relationships between customers and suppliers of the airline and also enable them to increase competitive advantage over their business rivals.

However, it cannot be assumed that the benefits highlighted above will arise automatically. Research suggests that there is actually limited evidence that IT of itself improves productivity or business performance. Studies have looked at industry sectors, firms, and operating units with mixed results. Any link between the amount of money a firm invests in IT and its performance is tenuous. In some cases it has been found that performance has fallen with the introduction of IT. It seems that the reason for this is that firms must ensure that they fully exploit the opportunities that IT provides rather than simply 'automate' existing processes. In Chapter 8, the concept of business process re-engineering (BPR) was discussed. IT often is a key to making BPR successful, and it is BPR that actually leads to improved performance. In this sense IT and integrated information systems are not an end in themselves, but the means to an end.

Information flows and requirements

The interface and passage of information between those who provide goods or services and those who receive or use them are important in any business operation. Flight catering is no exception, but the nature and immediacy of the catering product require that the information be both accurate and timely if it is to be of any value in the decision-making process and the continued success of the operation. Information needs to be passed between three major players: the airlines, or their various representatives; flight providers, in this case caterers and other suppliers; and those using the airline's services, that is the fare-paying passengers (Chapter 2).

However, the passage and smooth flow of information are not easy, and in the airline industry it is compounded not only by the immediacy of the products and services involved but also by the fragmentation and international nature of the business. In addition, it is difficult at times to know who the customer really is; who therefore influences and affects the information being received and processed and, in consequence, the relative importance of these influences in the decision-making process. When addressing the interface between the airline and flight provider, it is first necessary to consider who, within the airline industry, the customer actually is. It is perhaps assumed that the customer is the flying passenger who purchases the ticket, or in the case of the business traveller, the company who ultimately pays for it. In many cases, when viewed from the perspective of the supplier, the real customer might be the caterer who uses the product, or possibly the airline who pays for the caterer's product and on many occasions, influences purchasing decisions.

Information flow from airline to flight provider

In looking at the flow of information, the relationships between the airline and the flight provider can be considered as a system, that is, a set of interrelated parts that function as a whole to achieve a common purpose. The common purpose in this case is the provision of food to fare-paying passengers. Information therefore flows not only forwards in the system but also backwards, providing feedback as diverse as meal requirements and performance.

The provision of integrated information systems for all aspects of flight catering are still at a relatively early stage of development. This is because it is only recently that the IT industry itself, and software developers, have had common platforms on which to develop their systems. The most obvious common platform that most people are familiar with is the internet or world-wide-web. But other developments, such as Windows, have also helped to facilitate the integration of systems that hitherto had been almost impossible to link together.

In the flight catering industry, the scale and scope of such systems often reflects the particular orientation of the IT provider or software developer. Some systems are based on airline reservation systems and have integrated 'backwards' along the supply chain to add on related software programmes. Other systems are based originally on software developed by caterers for managing the production processes in flight kitchens. In another case, the original software was developed to facilitate galley planning, from which further programmes were developed to address issues of forecasting, scheduling, loading, and equipment balancing.

Due to the variety of sources of IT solutions, there is no one agreed information systems 'map' or schema which shows *all* the information requirements for flight catering. Indeed there may never be a single such map, as different airlines and/or caterers may have very different needs. Information, and the systems that communicate and analyse this, costs money. There is no point in having a Management Information System (MIS) more sophisticated than the business requires. Hence no frills or budget airlines are almost certainly going to have a system that looks and behaves in different ways to a system that supports a full-service carrier. Furthermore, the system in use may reflect the age of the firm, or at least the last time a major investment was made in IT systems. Some airlines may have so-called 'legacy' systems, that is to say hardware and software that they are left with, and which are far from state-of-the-art. Nonetheless, Table 12.1 attempts to list all the different types of information that might be included in an integrated system.

The planning and flow of information initially commence with the airlines when they draw up flight routing procedures. Although no hard and fast rules apply, a general planning consideration for economy class is that, if the flight lasts less than 1 hour, simple refreshments are served; if the flight lasts between 1 and 2 hours, a snack or light meal is served; and if the flight lasts between 2 and 3 hours then either a hot or cold main meal is served. Thereafter the type and combination of meals served is a function of many factors including the length of the flight, the origin, intermediate and final destination airports, take-off and arrival times and the total budget allocated for the catering.

Type of information	Principal source of information
Routes flown and flight schedule	Airline timetable
Aircraft type	
Aircraft configuration	
Aircraft tail number	
Flight number	Airline timetable
Service provision for each route	
Menus and meal specification for each class	Specification manuals
Dish and recipe specifications	Specification manuals
Raw material requirements	Specification manuals
Menu rotation sequence	Airline policy and/or contract with caterer
Equipment and tray lay up specifications	Specification manuals
Equipment inventories	Stock-taking and inventory records
Passenger numbers (pax.)	Reservations systems
Classes of passenger	Reservations system
Hot meal production	Pax × class × route
Tray assembly data per flight	Pax × class × route
Trolley assembly per flight	Pax × class × route × aircraft type
Equipment balancing	
Galley plans	Stowage plans
Aircraft loading	Loading sheet
Budgets	
Actual operating costs	
Invoice reconciliation	
Labour scheduling in flight production unit	
Meal pricing	
Profit margins	
Local tax information	

Table 12.2
Information needs for flight catering

Routes and flying patterns

Information on the number and types of meals available and to be served on each flight is then generally published in the time table (Fig. 12.1) which forms the basis and the start point for the information flow process. The information which the flight provider now has available could still be considered as raw data that have allowed commencement of planning, but at this stage are far too crude for him/her to base or even to begin the process of food production. Information is therefore needed on which production planning can commence.

Airlines, in gathering and using passenger information on which to base their flight production, work differently.

```
1AIRLINE STANDARD SCHEDULE DATA SET      1
000000000000000000000000000000000000000000000000000000000000000000000000C
000000000000000000000000000000000000000000000000000000000000000000000000C
000000000000000000000000000000000000000000000000000000000000000000000000C
000000000000000000000000000000000000000000000000000000000000000000000000C
2GCA      8      31OCT9925MAR0028JUL99CAT-W99                       28JUL9
000000000000000000000000000000000000000000000000000000000000000000000000C
000000000000000000000000000000000000000000000000000000000000000000000000C
000000000000000000000000000000000000000000000000000000000000000000000000C
000000000000000000000000000000000000000000000000000000000000000000000000C
3 CA   0020101J31OCT9924MAR00 23 5 7 LHR10001000+0000   BAH164 01640+030C
3 CA   0020201J01NOV9920MAR001        LHR10001000+0000   BAH164 01640+030C
3 CA   0020202J01NOV9920MAR001        BAH17401740+0300   AUH18501850
3 CA   0020301J04NOV9925MAR00    4 6  LHR10001000+0000   BAH164
3 CA   0020302J04NOV9925MAR00    4 6  BAH17401740
3 CA   0030101J01NOV9922MAR001 3      BAH095000
3 CA   0030201J04NOV9923MAR00    4    BAH
3 CA   0030202J04NOV9923MAR00
3 CA   0030301J05NOV9924
3 CA   0030302J05N
3 CA   00
```

Figure 12.1
Extract from SSIM (Airline Timetables)

Passenger numbers

Most airlines use computer-based passenger reservation systems which provide accurate and timely information on passenger numbers and flights involved. This information is readily available to the flight providers who, with limited access, are themselves often linked into the computer system. In areas such as charter flights, the number of passengers to be fed and the meal requirements are not only known some time in advance, but the requirements are contractually agreed, with the numbers unlikely to change. This provides a firm planning figure for the flight provider. On other flights, the numbers of meals required, by class of traveller, is likely to change quite considerably, right up until the departure of the flight. This provides more of a challenge in forecasting the numbers of meals required.

Generally speaking, airlines adopt two different approaches to overcome this. In the first approach, exact figures based on the number of passengers who have checked in for each flight, may be supplied to the flight provider, 24 hours, 12 hours, 6 hours, and 2 hours prior to the flight's departure; the last figure is just before the food is dispatched from the production centre. These timings will vary according to local conditions. The alternative approach is to adopt one of the standard forecasting techniques and use the figures produced for the entire planning process.

The major problems in the first approach—waiting for and relying on figures based on passengers booking in for the flight—are that in many cases, passengers need only turn up and check in less than 1 hour before departure, and flights can easily be delayed, diverted, or cancelled. In events such as this, it is too late for the caterer to respond to the requirements in the normal planning process. An alternative planning process, favoured by some airlines, is to adopt a forecasting technique that has some proven degree of reliability. One airline, for example, has a well-established and reliable system that bases the numbers to be catered on figures from the same flight, 13 weeks ago, 4 weeks ago and

1 week ago, modified for known discrepancies and events such as bank holidays and delayed flights. Another airline makes decisions on how many meals to order based on a percentage of seats on a given flight (Pedrick et al., 1993). These figures are used until just before the departure of the flight. Historically, it has been claimed that these figures have proven to be so accurate that little amendment is normally required. Where some change is necessary, either more meals are required or a surplus has been provided. This change is made by a 'forward kitchen' which has been strategically sited near to where the aircraft are parked, allowing last minute changes to be made with a minimum of inconvenience, fuss and security complications. This of course is dependent on how close the catering unit is to the airport and what facilities are available to caterers at each port. Alternatives include a mobile kitchen or storage based in the embarkation pier where the aircraft is parked.

Flight type/class

Catering requirements vary according to whether the service is scheduled, chartered, or low-cost with no frills. Scheduled airlines view catering as a positive influence in retaining business and go to great lengths to keep the food they offer flexible and upmarket.

Menus and product specification

The menu is often considered to be important in adding to the overall customer experience. The compiling of the menu is one of the airline or flight caterer's important tasks (Fig. 12.2). The content of the menu creates an image that

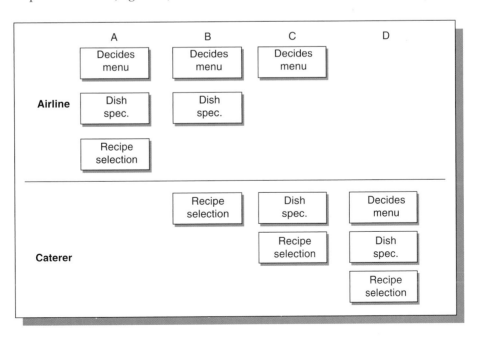

Figure 12.2
Alternative models of the role of airlines and caterers

reflects the overall style of the carrier. The printed menu given to the passenger on board the aircraft should match the overall corporate image, incorporating the corporate colours and logo. This printed menu is further seen as yet another way of promoting the airline. However, it is also costly to design, print and distribute, as well as adding to the waste stream from aircraft. In future, in economy class especially, passengers may be given information about the meal offer on the seat-back video screen in front of them.

Having established the basic feeding requirement and ideal meal configuration, the airline, in conjunction with their caterers, must then agree how this requirement can best be satisfied in terms of the menus provided and food served. Where the flight provision is undertaken by a contractor, the airline would traditionally have in place their own employee, the 'airline catering supervisor' who provides the link between the flight provider and the airline. This trend is declining and few airlines will employ a staff member at each catering station, however at key stations some constant supervision may exist. Together the airline and the flight provider decide upon and draw up a series of menus that would be suitable, and this is normally developed into a menu cycle (Chapter 5). Once menus and meal requirements are agreed, these are then confirmed in an internal letter of agreement between the parties concerned. With large airlines menus are determined by head office and passed to contractors.

The development of integrated IT systems has been one of the factors that have affected the extent to which the airline decides on and controls the level of specification. A number of different 'models' now exist, as illustrated in Fig. 12.2. The trend is moving from A towards D. These range from the airline deciding on the menu, the dish selection and the actual recipe for preparing this dish and requiring the caterer to conform to their specification, across to the airline devolving complete responsibility to the caterer for determining these three things with their agreement. The rationale for doing this is the idea that catering is not the core competence of an airline, but it is for the caterer, and that caterers have more expertise now than ever before. But what makes this possible and gives the airline the confidence to devolve responsibility, is an integrated IT system that enables the airline to monitor the caterer's activity at all levels within the operation.

The menu cycle and flight pattern provide the basic information on which the caterer can undertake the initial planning of the inputs in areas such as equipment requirements, food and other raw materials, and labour. The initial planning will also include product specifications, which might need to be drawn up; suppliers identified with contracts written to procure these inputs. This outline planning information also provides the basis on which flight production processes can be considered and planned in relation to the inputs and required outputs.

Operational systems

At the centre of most flight production operations is a computerised production planning system which assists in the management of ordering, stock control, production control, and flight marshalling. This is similar in many ways to the types of computer systems used routinely in catering operations (Braham,

1988), but it is unique in terms of its links to flight data systems. The production unit may utilise either an integrated computer system or separate linked systems to perform these functions. These systems take their inputs from a number of other systems, through links between the various computer systems, which may be automatic, semi-automatic or manual. The data, held by the computer systems, are stored in the form of linked databases which include information on the following.

- **Recipe files** Details of ingredients and quantities for each menu based on inhouse airline specifications or contract data
- **Aircraft data** Specific details of configuration data for each type and configuration of aircraft (as configured for a specific airline), in terms of types of storage, type of containers and trolleys, maximum passenger capacity and crew requirements
- **Flight schedule** Data on flight times, routing, menu plans, capacity per class, specific crew data; detailed specifications in terms of meal requirements, cabin requirements, crew requirements, duty-free, dry stores, beverages, holloware, glasses, china, headsets, menu cards, and newspapers
- **Advanced reservations data** Current booking data for a flight, including requirements for special menus and other individual requirements
- **Check-in data** Data on actual passengers checked on to flight, based on information from the check-in system of airport
- **Production plans** Data on the issuing of materials, food quantity and variety to be produced in each production area, plans for tray assembly and trolley-loading areas, together with marshalling times and full inventory lists for each flight

All of this information is used to prepare the basic production plan for the forthcoming planning period. These data are based, in the first instance, on projection of requirements, (Chapter 8), based on previous flight histories. Twenty-four hours before departure, more precise data on a specific flight are loaded from the advanced reservation data of the airline and these are updated by data from the check-in system. These adjustments may be made right up to the close of check-in for the flight, by using a rapid transport system taking materials from emergency stocks.

In a typical large-scale operation there are linked computer systems at the heart of the production planning process. For example, one system covers the supply of materials, including ordering, costing and stock control. The second computer system is used for production planning. It is linked directly to the airline reservation computer. It generates plans for each department so that all of the materials needed for a flight can be prepared ready for assembly and marshalling.

The basic production plans are drawn up 2 or 3 months ahead, based on flight schedules and projections of demand based on historical data. Actual demand is calculated through the link to the airline reservation system, and 2 or 3 days before the flight the production plan is fed into the inventory computer system. This calculates material requirements on recipe quantities and estimates of number of meals, in order to calculate total material requirements for each day.

Production schedule Estimated quantities for each specific individual ingredient are aggregated to give a total requirement for each material. This then gives a total requirement for all materials, including fresh foods, beverages, dry stores, disposables, toiletries, packaging materials, containers, and other cabin requirements. Based on this information, orders for fresh foods are generated through the consolidation of all production plans for a day. In addition to this, stock item requirements are checked against existing inventory levels, and any necessary orders generated. In some situations, it is possible to set up on-line automatic links to suppliers which can be used to trigger the goods ordering cycle.

Flight assembly The system provides a checklist of all trolleys required to service a particular flight. It may also provide the labels with which to mark and code each trolley.

Transportation The system can be used to develop timing and routing schedules for the vehicle fleet based on production plans.

Loading diagrams Loaders can be provided with detailed plans to ensure trolleys are correctly placed in each galley.

Procurement system The inventory system also maintains stock records for all items of dry goods, packaging materials, etc. in order to control stock utilisation and to order replenishment of stocks, based on the economic delivery quantity of each item. Trends towards JIT production management are being used to minimise inventory levels and to bring suppliers into much closer contact with the production planning system.

Cost control Costs of raw materials data are used to produce reports on yields of recipes, levels of wastage and cost variances. This data is used for the day-to-day management of the operation, but is also of value when bidding for new contracts and preparing budgets for control purposes.

Implications of integrated systems

The major benefits of information systems to the flight catering industry can be seen in the improvements made to the way information is communicated and decisions are made.

Information systems can help to improve communication in flight catering processes by enabling communication that otherwise would not be possible. Time is spared by eliminating the need for person-to-person communication; instead, it is made available by other means such as via the web. By reducing the double entry of data, through integrating systems, data accuracy is increased and systems errors reduced.

Information systems ensure not only the smooth flow of data, but also the speed at which it is transmitted. Consequently, the flow of communication does not cause delays in the carrying out of tasks and it is made more widespread and accessible. This in turn affects decision-making processes; as information is more readily available, decisions are more informed. Consistency of communication is improved and repetitive decisions are made in a more consistent manner. Productivity is increased as more communication can occur with less effort. In terms of security, using information systems ensures that only the intended recipients will receive communications, and that decisions are made and controlled only by those authorised to do so.

The stages/processes involved in meal planning have already been covered, so we will now look at the benefits that information systems can bring to each of these main activities.

Scheduling

- Automatic calculation of required meal types on the schedule based upon rules by class, flight length, time of departure and route
- Determination of the tray service requirements based upon appropriate rules
- Ability to determine a service order for distribution to crew

Meal planning and control

- Allows airline to define/specify meals
- Ability to pass information directly to and from caterers
- Ability to create 'what if' scenarios and evaluation of different unit prices
- Electronic distribution of meal specifications to caterers and crew
- Forecast catering costs for a given period or flight and calculate average cost per passenger
- Ability to change meal specifications and see effect on budget
- Closer inspection of quality control and performance monitoring

Inventory control/logistics

An airline needs to know how much equipment it must take aboard each flight according to either the amount of passengers onboard or a full load. At present, airlines may lose anywhere between 10 and 20 per cent of their equipment each year as a result of unequal balancing of equipment at catering stations. The process is therefore very time consuming and expensive. The successful management of inventory levels can result in drastic cost savings. This can be seen by the reduction in equipment needed, and also by a reduction in the transportation and warehousing costs. The airline can also minimise stock levels taken on board the plane as a result of improved forecasting and trolley tracking.

With the correct tools, the airline can achieve greater efficiency in tracking the entire equipment process. With the aid of an adequate software solution, the airline is able to forecast, plan and control their entire equipment supply chain much more effectively:

- Forecasting equipment needs for new products and schedules
- Prediction of catering equipment needs based on passenger numbers

- Balancing equipment within the system based schedule
- Using web based interfaces to maintain inventory counts at stations
- Compare forecast consumption with actual consumption
- Reduce overall stock inventory

Procurement

The benefit to an airline of using a software solution to handle the procurement of supplies means that all purchasing processes can be made using a single workstation, which can be made accessible via the web. One provider of such software estimates that their product could save an airline up to 70 per cent on transaction costs.

As already established, lack of standardisation between the airlines can restrict productivity and increase wastage. Implementing a suitable procurement solution standardises products, purchasing processes and communication across the supply chain.

One flight business solution provider offers software that can support all the processes that are necessary in order to run a flight services department. Their web-enabled solution enables the airline industry to work together and share relevant information, standardising the supply chain between airlines, caterers and suppliers, tackling the issues that were raised earlier regarding restricting productivity.

It need not be costly to invest in implementing an information system solution. As a result of the standardisation of products, processes and communication, airlines, caterers and suppliers do not have to develop exclusive systems to meet their requirements, therefore eliminating major operating costs. This is further discussed in looking at the trend towards e-business (below).

Meal finance

- Simplifies creating and checking catering invoices
- Saves time and money for the caterer and airline
- Reduces errors and complexity of invoice procedure
- Provides defined procedures and processes for reconciliation of invoice discrepancies
- Create invoices based upon agreed meal and handling and uplift costs when actual passenger numbers are known
- Analysis of meal wastage

Galley planning

- Easier, faster and more accurate
- Definition of standard components reduces caterer confusion
- Accurate weight calculations—maximises payload versus fuel burn
- Clearer instructions to caterer—contributes to improved and consistent onboard product
- Accurate information to flight crew improving safety standards
- Generate high quality catering manuals and distribute them electronically
- Faster implementation of product changes

- Access to all aircraft loading details
- Web publishing reduces printing costs

Case study 12.1

Continental Airlines Catering Equipment Control System

Continental Airlines, in conjunction with Jetlogistics and Calibre, have developed an integrated system for managing their catering equipment. The system was designed to achieve a number of objectives:

- Provide accurate knowledge of flight equipment requirements in relation to menu specifications and provisioning codes
- Identify equipment movements between stations
- Forecast passenger numbers
- Provide accurate aircraft configurations
- Enable the reporting of regular equipment stock taking by caterers in all stations
- Provide data about equipment sector life
- Enable forecasting of equipment needs for any new products or schedules
- Reduce overall stock of equipment
- Integrate all of the above information in order to deliver equipment 'just-in-time', monitor performance, identify problem areas and help to eliminate them

This involved setting up an information system with four key elements, illustrated in Fig. 12.3.

The Continental Master Food Schedule (CMFS) identifies the provisioning codes for each flight, approximately 4 weeks before the flights are due. These codes can be sub-divided into regional categories, such as domestic, international, and intercontinental, as well as aircraft type in order to establish the specific equipment requirements and tray set ups. The type and quantity of equipment is essentially made up of three types:

- Equipment need to respond to the forecast passenger numbers on this aircraft type and route (i.e. pax related provisioning codes)
- Specific bulk equipment need for that aircraft type or route (non pax related provisioning codes)
- Core galley equipment by aircraft type and route (bulk loaded equipment)

This information was then processed by the 'analyser equipment forecasting routines' in order to develop a network analysis of the flow of items in and out of any selected catering station. In order to achieve this, each type of equipment was defined as disposable or rotable, and given a sector life (by definition disposable items have a sector life of 1, i.e. they are used once and thrown away). For instance, in this system the sector life of a trolley was designated as 200. Hence this part of the system enables Continental to calculate for any given day what equipment should be held at any station (stock held = equipment coming in plus any par stock, less equipment at end of sector life and equipment going out).

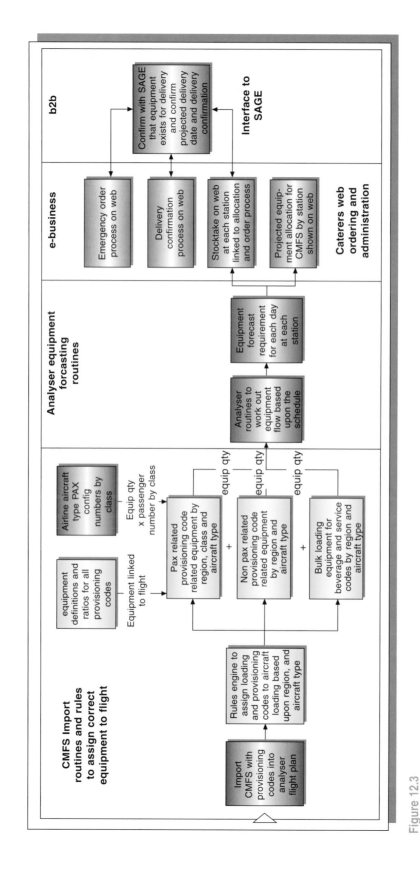

Figure 12.3
Information system flow of Continental's equipment control system
Source: Calibre

However, the system also enables the caterer at each station to order and administer their own equipment requirements via the internet. They can access order forms, place orders and check delivery confirmation via this system. This e-business solution was an improved version of the old 'pull based' inventory system used previously (the 'pull system' refers to the idea that it was caterers that requested equipment based on their estimates of need).

The e-business solution was designed to interface with SAGE, which was Continental's existing information system for managing their equipment warehouses worldwide.

By developing this integrated information system, over time Continental were moving from a 'pull system' based on caterer's estimates to a 'push system' based on their forecast of what was needed using their network analysis software. To start off with stations could continue to order equipment via the web and could over-ride what the forecast provided by the Analyser. However, to do this the caterer had to provide a reason for doing this. This enabled the airline to investigate the extent to which caterer's were holding unnecessary par stocks, mishandling equipment and so on. Likewise, as the system developed and caterer's gained more faith in the Analyser they tended not to over-order stock.

Current issues and future developments

The Internet has transformed the way in which businesses operate and people work, and how information technology supports business operations and end user work activities. This is because the internet enables anyone, anywhere, to use a common interface to access shared data. Some industries, such as retailing, banking and education have been radically changed due to this. Amazon.com has revolutionised book retailing, Lastminute.com is having a significant impact on the travel industry, and online reservations are playing an increasingly significant role in the airline industry.

E-business is the practice of performing and co-ordinating critical business processes such as designing products, obtaining supplies, manufacturing, selling, fulfilling orders, and providing services through the extensive use of computer and communication technologies and computerised data (Alter, 2002). It has been argued that e-business is not simply speeding up how a business operates by 'computerising' it, it fundamentally changes how business is done. Processes may be completely redesigned and interactions between suppliers and customers transformed. Davis and Meyer (1998) call this 'blur'. Transactions in this 'connected economy' are blurred because communication is two-way, information is shared, processes are interactive, activity can occur anywhere and any time (24 hours a day, 7 days a week), and due to this sharing and interaction, the exchange may go beyond the simply economic and engage people emotionally as well (many customers become very loyal to internet-based companies, such as Amazon, due to the customised nature of the communications they receive from such companies).

Given the complex supply chain that exists in flight catering (Chapter 6), it is not surprising that e-solutions are also being developed for this industry. The disparate locations of airline ports make web-based information systems an attractive proposition; the only investment at each catering station is a generic computer system with access to the Internet. Many software providers now offer web-based software to assist managing the airline catering process. The Worlds' largest airline caterers LSG Sky Chefs and Gate Gourmet have fuelled this trend by starting their own spin-off organisations (eLSG.SkyChefs and e-gatematrix) designed to make full use of the Internet to assist airlines manage their entire catering department. These companies offer partial and full out-sourcing of the catering function and have made full use of the latest information systems technology since their conception. By running all software applications over the Internet, both companies can remotely manage large operations, with reduced overheads. This trend towards remote software application deployment is due to continue as traditional software suppliers join with service providers to offer out-sourcing to airlines.

A major trend, which is affecting all classes of meal service, is the trend towards allowing passengers to **pre-book** their meal. Of course, this has always been the case with special meals, but now a number of carriers have developed this for standard meals too; buzz, the low-cost carrier were doing this; Air Tours surcharged their charter passengers who order a meal when they book their holiday package; and Air-India allow first- and business-class passengers to pre-book their meal up to 24 hours in advance of their flight. In many respects this is an ideal situation as the customer has directly ordered what they want, which eliminates the need to forecast demand and sales mix, and also reduces waste. One reason why this is now being introduced is that technology, in particular the internet, now makes this relatively simple to do. Indeed, with the way that mobile telephony is developing it may be possible, in the near future, for passengers to look at a copy of the menu on their way to the airport, and to order their meal only two or three hours prior to departure. However, loading a wide-body aircraft is complex and aircraft and trucks are may be loaded three hours prior to departure. In addition looking at the deterioration of airfares this 'special service' may be limited to business- and first-class passengers. Nevertheless, these meals are more complicated than an economy class tray. Therefore, it may be that the main course could be ordered within the 3-hour frame, while all other menu components are already in trolleys, cooled down properly and loaded and secured on high lift trucks.

Conclusion

The emergence of common platforms and e-business has revolutionised the way the way IT can be utilised by industry. Consequently, integrated management information systems have the potential to optimise business processes and operations and in many cases to change the very way business is done. This is particularly true for the flight catering industry, due to its fragmented, international nature.

In the flight catering system, information and its quick and accurate communication across global operations and complex supply chains, are vital in maintaining competitive edge and efficiency in an increasingly cost-conscious business environment. Of particular importance are the benefits integrated IT systems can bring to the logistics function, given that flight catering is estimated to be mainly logistics (Chapter 11). Such systems can lead to better planning and equipment allocation and control, reductions in supply chain errors and waste and can lead to better decisions that are based on up to the minute, accurate information. The development of integrated systems also has many direct advantages to the fare-paying passenger, with developments occurring, such as pre-booking meals, that add to the overall service package provided.

However, the development of MIS is still in its infancy, and thus its full potential to flight catering is yet to be realised. What is clear is that end users need to fully exploit the benefits that IT can bring, understanding it's purpose within the operation and what advantages it can bring, and this will differ according to the particular business and its needs. End users need to recognise that if IT is to be used to its maximum potential, optimising processes and operations, then it must be viewed as the means to and not the end in achieving this.

Key terms

Common platforms	e-business	Efficiency
Information flows	Integrated information	
Software solutions	systems	

Discussion questions

1. Identify the advantages to flight caterers of using integrated information systems.
2. How might 'blur' occur in the flight catering industry?

References

Braham, B. (1988) *Computer Systems in the Hotel and Catering Industry*, Cassell: London, 59–106.

Davis, S. and Meyer, C. (1998) *Blur—The Speed of Change in the Connected Economy*, Capstone: Oxford.

Pedrick, D. Babakus, E. and Richardson, A. (1993) "The value of qualitative data in quality improvement efforts," *Journal of Services Marketing* vol. 7, 26–35.

Senn, J. A. (1990) *Information Systems in Management*, 4th edn, Wadsworth: Belmont, California.

CHAPTER 13

On-board stowage and regeneration

Learning objectives

- Understand different levels of service
- Identify the arrangement of galleys
- Understand the complexity of galley design
- Examine the operation procedures
- Discuss the issues of stowage

Introduction

As we saw in Chapter 1, the galley started off as a simple storage area for equipment needed on the flight. Today, these areas have been systematised through the use of trolleys and innovative equipment so that they provide the maximum of utility in the minimum of space. In line with the terminology used in the transportation sector the storage of goods is commonly known as 'stowage' as items are not simply placed in storage units but also made secure to protect their movement during transportation.

In this chapter we will consider aircraft configuration and galley design, the service requirements to such galleys, and then consider storage issues. The various groups of activities to be carried out to provide a meal service, and their associated equipment, will be described, and the chapter will conclude by looking at possible and planned future developments. The service of food and beverages to passengers is considered in Chapter 14.

Service level and galley provision

Service levels on aircraft vary widely, on the basis of the level of competition, routeing, flight time, and aircraft type. A survey of 6,800 airline passengers in the USA (Ott, 1993) reported that on long-haul flights, customer service levels were very important, and that half of customers' satisfaction from such flights was achieved through the elements of food, comfort, staff helpfulness, and roominess. Short-haul passengers, on the other hand, gave priority to amenities such as ground transportation, convenience at gates, and comfort of waiting areas.

More recently, research undertaken by SITA/Inflair which surveyed 1010 consumers in Great Britain found that most people will search for flights based price and reputation (75 per cent and 62 per cent respectively) (SITA and Inflair cited in Momberger and Momberger, 2003). However, the research also found that a quarter of respondents felt that the quality of food served on both long and short-haul flights is a major factor influencing the decision of which airline to fly with (SITA and Inflair cited in Momberger and Momberger, 2003). In addition, on short haul flights food was 39 per cent more important than in-flight entertainment and on long haul flights it ranked 25 per cent higher (SITA and Inflair cited in Momberger and Momberger, 2003).

As we have seen, airlines are constantly trying to compete with their rivals, for instance, Continental Airlines are a full service carrier but they have recently instituted some 'peanut fares' services in Florida—reduced fares on short flights. These flights do not include a full meal—simply snacks and beverages. They feel that on short flights meal services are not a priority among passengers. Thus on flights of less than one hour only beverages are served. On flights over 90 minutes for first class and two hours for economy class, beverages and a complimentary meal or snack are offered during appropriate meal or snack times. On flights over three-and-a-half hours in first class beverages and an entrée are served and in economy beverages and a snack basket are offered (Continental Airlines, 2003 [online]). Southwest Airlines take a very similar view. They believe that by offering a no-frills service, their customers save money on their flights which they can then spend on hotel accommodation, and suggest, "Who can't go an hour without a meal?" On the other hand, several airlines now offer sleeper seats on long-haul flights. Continental, on their 'business first' class, feature a service which enables customers to dine at the most convenient time for them, rather than fit the established pattern of meals throughout the flight.

All these developments have impacts on flight service levels and on galley configuration and design. As catering requirements fall, and the proportion of economy class passengers increases, this will impact on the space allocated to special catering equipment. Thus more space should become available for passengers, something that would be encouraged by the airlines. Future aircraft and galley design will also take this trend into account.

Aircraft configuration

Aircraft carry passengers paying different fare structures in separate parts of the aircraft. British Airways, for example, still offer first-class service, in addition to business class (Club World) and economy (World Traveller); some airlines now offer only two levels of service but others have added a fourth, for example, 'economy plus'. This style of service provides a standard seat with extra legroom and economy class products and services. Many short-haul charter airlines only offer an economy-class service. As passengers in different sections of the aircraft may receive different types of food on different-sized trays using different types of cutlery and crockery, the sections of the aircraft are often separated from each other. This may be simply by the use of a curtain, but often a galley structure will form part of this differentiating barrier. The mix of different customers (business class and tourist class) will vary considerably according to the time of day and destination. Some flights, for example those from London to Lagos, have a very high demand for business-class seating. To facilitate this, some changes of seating arrangements can be achieved within a few hours. Some airlines will simply fold down each alternate seat in a row of economy-class seating to give the business-class passengers more space. From a flight catering standpoint this may simply mean that more business-class meals have to be stored in and served from the rear galley area of the aircraft, with the necessary changes in trolley requirements being carried out by the contracted flight caterer.

Service trolleys or carts

All specifications for trolleys are determined by the Association of European Airlines, based in Brussels. A technical data sheet for an ATLAS meal trolley supplied by 'Jet' is shown in Table 13.1; and a typical trolley is illustrated in Fig. 13.1. Due to the nature of flight service all trolleys have to be capable of being locked into position in the galley, and all carry foot-operated braking systems so that they do not represent a hazard during normal flight manoeuvres.

Trolleys are subject to quite severe handling during the processes of loading and unloading, and therefore are likely to get damaged. The nature of the construction therefore becomes important as the airline will already have sets that are in the aircraft, have been off-loaded at the arrival airport, and are waiting to be loaded at the destination airport. This is a large capital investment,

Criteria	Specification
Sizes	Height 1.030 mm Length 0.810 mm Width 0.305 mm
Capacity	28 ATLAS trays 14 ATLAS drawers
Structure	Aluminium sandwich panels of phenolic resin with insulation foam. Laminates in agreement with the internal decoration of aircraft. Aluminium frame with rounded corners to avoid injuries.
Door latches	1 up to 3 fixing points or basic
Brake system	Push 1 or 2 pedals actuated and released on both sides of trolley

Table 13.1
Technical specification of ATLAS meal trolleys

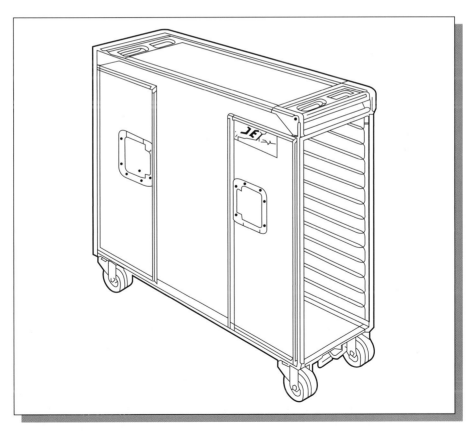

Figure 13.1
A typical service trolley
SOURCE: Jet Equipment

and any time out for repairs will mean further investment in spare trolleys. Reparation can be slow as trolleys are usually of a riveted construction. To attempt to overcome this problem some manufacturers are now producing trolleys using alum joint as the construction method, and can be supplied in 'knock-down' kits and flat packed. In this way trolleys can be repaired quickly, and flat packing facilitates transportation at lower volumes.

Some hybrid trolleys have been developed in recent years, and good examples are special rubbish compactors, trolleys designed specifically for retail sales (transparent), and those which have been combined to act also as the heating source for a hot entrée.

All galleys are designed to receive modular trolleys and equipment according to the specifications of the airlines. There are two common standards known as KSSU and ATLAS. British Airways have a customised standard known as ACE, and North American airlines too tend to favour customised systems. The systems adopted by the major European airlines are illustrated in Table 13.2.

KSSU	ATLAS
Swiss	Air France
KLM	Alitalia
SAS	Brussels Airlines
Austrian	Lufthansa
	TAP/Air Portugal
	Iberia
	bmi

Table 13.2
Airline adoption of modular trolley systems

Galley location and design

The main galleys are usually located in the tail of the aircraft, with a further one located in the centre, and a smaller, possibly drinks only, galley at the front. Very large aircraft, such as a Boeing 747-400, may have as many as seven galleys on the main deck, a further three on the upper deck, supported by a further understairs stowage area. Normally, galleys are located at suitable points throughout the aircraft to facilitate ease of service and located on the deck on which the passengers will be served. However, on some DC-10s the central galley is actually located immediately below the cabin area, effectively in the cargo hold. Cabin crew then obtain their customer requisites and trolleys from this galley and access the main cabin using a small elevator. When loading galleys, access points from the exterior are usually adjacent, but some aircraft configurations mean that some galleys can only be supplied by wheeling trolleys along the aisles. The location of the galleys on an Airbus 330–200 is illustrated in Fig. 13.2.

Weight is a critical factor for the operation of aircraft, as it will affect fuel operating costs. In addition, any saving in the weight of basic equipment

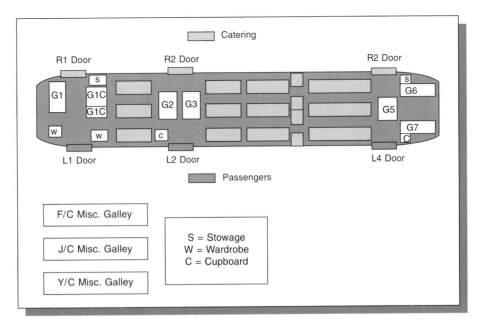

Figure 13.2
Location of galleys on an Airbus 330-200
SOURCE: Gulf Air

means that additional cargo could be handled. The total payload limit of an aircraft is ultimately determined by the thrust creation of its engines, hence to save weight, galleys are built of a honeycombed design by specialist manufacturers to the specific requirements of individual client airlines.

Aluminium is used widely in their construction, but a major part of any galley are spaces for inserts to receive items such as food trolleys, coffee machines, ovens, and possibly refrigeration. The manufacturers of such equipment therefore will ensure that their products are as light as possible, while offering the durability required by aircraft, and meeting the design and safety standards set by the Civil Aviation Authority (CAA) in the UK or the Federal Aviation Authority (FAA) in the USA.

Safety is a vital factor in the operation of equipment within aircraft which could be travelling at typical altitudes of 6 miles. Particularly important is the need to prevent possible electrical fires, the use of fire-retardant materials, and the need for equipment to operate safely at high altitudes. A major area for problems in the aircraft is corrosion due to moisture emanating from the galley. Spillages in particular can be a problem, as this affects the main cabin floor. Immediately below this floor are the cables which run from the cockpit to the rudders, and hence control the aircraft. Each subsection of a galley has a predetermined and carefully marked maximum load capacity and these will be considered when the airlines brief suppliers on their requirements.

A typical aircraft galley will act as a focal point for the delivery of service to the passengers by the cabin crew. These areas, therefore, will have to provide storage of food items, holloware, liquor, retail goods, entertainment items, customer comfort items and amenity kits. A galley is a combination of storage area, regeneration kitchen and servery area for the use of the cabin crew. Like any kitchen, a galley has to provide the following:

- storage areas for holding food at safe temperatures
- regeneration ovens (for all but the smallest aircraft)
- cold storage for minerals, waters and beers, etc.
- water boilers and beverage machines
- stowage for customer items such as crockery, cutlery, and glassware
- stowage of waste products

Individual airlines will take decisions about what goods they wish to carry. If, for example, an airline operating holiday charter flights wished to increase its revenues by offering duty-free goods, then it would have to compromise on space elsewhere, perhaps by cutting down on flight entertainment equipment, meal tray sizes, or other customer products. Alternatively, as considerable space had to be used in the past for stowage of waste materials, an airline may decide to invest in a waste compactor to reduce the space requirements for this essentially useless by-product. This can allow it to carry more retail goods.

Electrical power on most aircraft is standard at 115/200 V three-phase, but in the aircraft design there needs to be some flexibility to allow power supplies to be picked up in situations other than normal. Also, any movement of a galley will necessitate a link to the galley waste system. This galley waste escapes via a small outlet outside the aircraft. Contrary to popular belief, all toilet waste is normally channelled to tanks and emptied into the sewage system at the aircraft's destination. Water for the toilets and general use in the aircraft is stored in tanks in the outer wall void of the aircraft. Water supply and toilet servicing are usually provided by ground handling companies.

A typical galley is illustrated in Fig. 13.3. As a normal uplift of a 747-400 comprises over 40 000 items, stowage is a major function of all galleys. To facilitate this stowage, and subsequent delivery of products to passengers, a system of trolleys or carts form the basis of the service system. Such trolleys are loaded with food and other customer requisites by the supplying outlet, and the trolleys are then transported to the aircraft and stored in special insert bays in the galleys. The trolleys are subsequently removed from these bays by the cabin crew. This cuts down the amount of handling of the food and beverage items. Other storage containers support the trolleys, and they too are located in special compartments within the galleys. Some equipment, such as sinks, water boilers and ovens, may be permanently installed, but in other cases an airline may choose to adopt a modular system which will give some potential flexibility of use.

The specific galley design in each aircraft is determined by the purchasing airline. It will be based on factors such as the passenger capacity of the aircraft, the aircraft's range, its intended use, and the catering policy of the airline. For example, a typical ATLAS standard single-width oven will accept 32 entree dishes, and therefore a 90-seater aircraft would need three such ovens if a hot meal service were being provided. Meal trolleys have a capacity determined by the tray size. A small snack may only require a one-third sized tray, while half- and full-sized trays would be used to accommodate full meals.

Thus, galleys within particular types of aircraft for particular airlines will

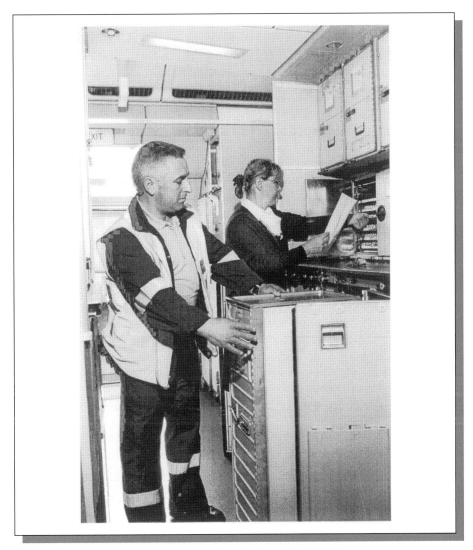

Figure 13.3
Photograph of an airline galley
Source: Gate Gourmet © copyright 2003

have essentially standard galley design. However, first-class galleys would have more stowage space per customer due to the requirement for stowage of more articles for customer convenience, usually a choice of food items, and also additional requirements for crockery and glassware. For example, the eighteen passengers on a BA 747 could be supplied with a total of 237 glasses.

As it is the airlines who determine which standard of insert they will use for their galleys, a particular aircraft type, such as a Boeing 747-400, could have different galley systems according to the client needs. This has posed some problems for airlines who buy second-hand aircraft. For example, one small national airline operates three Lockheed Tristars purchased from three different airlines. Unfortunately, all three used different standards for their trolleys. As a result, the aircraft servicing companies have a difficult task in packing meals and other customer items, as they require to know the individual aircraft used on a particular flight rather than a simple aircraft type. This of course adds logistical problems for the flight caterers.

Hence major airlines will work with aircraft and galley manufacturers to produce bespoke systems. British Airways use a fleet of aircraft that is predominantly based on Boeing aircraft, hence they have been working closely with this manufacturer on new Boeing aircraft. This has resulted in a redesigned, flexible galley system which will take up less space, and hence allows the aircraft to carry more passengers. This flexibility will also allow more speedy reconfiguration of an aircraft to meet the mix of passengers on particular flights.

Galley equipment

To eliminate safety risks, all equipment has to be approved by the CAA or FAA before it can be installed in aircraft. Anything which could be a potential hazard to the aircraft must be eliminated. Also, in the operation of equipment there are special safety features which arise as the result of the nature of air transportation, with its steep angles of take-off and landing. For example, coffee makers and water boilers have an incorporated brew handle to secure the liquid container and a written warning on the machine. Some airlines will incorporate fixed equipment into their galleys; typically ovens for the regeneration of entrees and water boilers or coffee machines. A recent trend, however, is to use flexible modular systems which will allow equipment to be interchanged for specific flights.

Cold storage

The need to hold protein foods at low temperatures is even greater within an aircraft environment than in any other catering establishment. The duration of long-haul flights is sufficient for passengers to suffer the effects of an excess intake of harmful micro-organisms through their food consumption. Hence such foods have to be held at safe temperatures. Most caterers will supply foods at or below 5°C, and then a variety of methods will be used to hold the food at or below this temperature. This can be achieved in a number of ways.

A simple cooling agent An example is solid carbon dioxide ('dry ice'), which can be located within the trolley or cart. Foil capsules of this item can be located in small trays at the top of each trolley which is packed with its 'tray sets'. As cold air falls, the chilled air will then circulate throughout the insulated trolley.

A dry ice 'snow' machine This alternative can be used to pack dry ice around the tray sets within the trolleys. This can either be achieved by a snow gun or by locating an open trolley against a machine with injectors at several heights which will dispense dry ice to a variety of locations within the trolley simultaneously.

A chiller unit This can be incorporated into the galley design which will then circulate chilled air around the trolleys when they are located in their bay in the aircraft. Such 'cassette' systems will typically incorporate fan-assisted chiller units which will refrigerate compartments up to 12 cu. ft in capacity. The advantage is that they eliminate the need for a cabinet section of a conventional refrigeration unit. It is suggested therefore that a saving in weight of 40 per cent can be achieved with such a unit.

Refrigerators   Some galleys, particularly those used on long-haul aircraft, have refrigerators built into them, or they form part of an interchangeable modular system. Thus, a refrigerator could, for example, be exchanged with a standard ATLAS oven. As the unit would have the same interface connector and spigot location as the oven, no physical or electrical modification would be required, although the refrigerator would require less electrical current. Such refrigerators could be conventional in design, but one innovation has been the introduction of air circulation refrigerators. As with most galley equipment, this equipment operates at 115/220 V. The most common use of such items would be to chill down beverages to a serving temperature as quickly as possible, although the unit could also be used for the refrigerated storage of entrees perhaps for the second meal on a long-haul flight, or for storage of special presentations of food, such as that required for first-class service. They would also have use in corporate aircraft. These have been initially designed to fit the current standard systems, such as ATLAS, although the manufacturers can produce tailor-made versions. For additional flexibility, many of these units are also designed to operate at freezer temperatures.

Regular ice packs   In some regions dry ice is not available, in this situation regular ice packs can be utilised which keep trolleys cool. For example, two ice packs can keep a trolley cool for more than 14 hours (Momberger and Momberger, 2002).

A unit which was interchangeable with a standard ATLAS oven would have a capacity of 1.4 cu. ft and be designed to accept up to 48 lb (22 kg) of loading, but a full trolley size would provide 5.3 cu. ft of storage (110 lb, 50 kg load). It would typically be constructed from aluminium with a stainless steel interior, thus balancing the need for the lightest construction possible while being easily cleaned. It would be insulated by a foam sandwich between two skins and an insulating gasket on the door.

Use of low outside air temperatures   A final system, still being considered by airlines as it has implications on the aircraft design, is the use of the low outside air temperatures experienced at high altitudes. Thus a modified heat exchanger using ducted air from the exterior of the aircraft could produce an energy-efficient and hence ecologically friendly system of cooling. At the time of writing such a system is being considered by Lufthansa for new additions to the fleet.

Regeneration ovens

The centre of any hot meal provision is the regenerating oven. These usually use a system of forced air circulation. As service levels have generally been designed to offer a service to all passengers simultaneously, the passenger capacity of the aircraft determines the oven capacity required. A standard ATLAS oven holds 32 entrées. As all meals are served together, this determines the oven number requirements. For instance, a 747-400 series operated by KLM, due to its size and mix of passengers, requires 24 ovens. As a general rule each entrée heated requires approximately 100 W of power. An oven will normally take 25–35 minutes to raise an entrée to the service temperature, dependent on whether the product is chilled or frozen. It can then be set to hold at that temperature until required. Cabin crew receive detailed galley information sheets from the caterers including the required regeneration times for foodstuffs. Air crew would only operate on certain types of aircraft, for example, 747 for long-haul or 737 for short-haul. This would enable them to become familiar with particular types of galley equipment.

Not all aircraft will be equipped with ovens, especially the smaller ones. In this case the food will either be provided hot by the supplier and served soon after take-off, or alternatively a combination trolley can be used provided that there were the appropriate services available. A modified low-temperature oven is used by some airlines in an attempt to improve the palatability of its bread rolls. Such rolls are usually supplied in foil packaging or clear plastic material which is capable of being subject to heat treatment. Such systems should help retain moisture and prevent the drying of the bread product.

Waste storage and compaction

Waste is stored either in specialist trolleys, or in some cases, it is placed in bags in convenient locations throughout the aircraft or placed in the void under the floor of the main cabin. Traditionally, waste, such as paper, plastic and metal cans, has been removed by cleaners, who often then compacted it at their own base. However, space is most at a premium on the aircraft itself and therefore compactors are increasingly being used here. These are available in full- or half-trolley sizes and come in two main types. First, those in which all types of rubbish are put and then compacted by a single hydraulically operated compacting plate. The compacted rubbish is stored in special liquid-proof containers and can be reduced to one-tenth of its original volume. Special-sized trolleys locate under the compaction unit in the normal trolley space in the galley. The second type of compactor allows for recycling as well as compaction in that rubbish can be sorted into three separate sections, such as cans, glass and plastic, as the trolley is wheeled along the aisle during the collection of passengers' waste. In this case the galley compression plate which is fixed to the galley can move backwards and forwards to compress each section of the trolley load in turn. Normally, ground service personnel may have to collect waste in up to eight different locations within an aircraft, and hence compacted systems can help to reduce the turnaround time for aircraft. Like all other equipment, such systems have to undergo a thorough testing and approval system, and there are special requirements for fire containment, flammability and heat release, in addition to requirements for public health bodies such as the USA's Food and Drug Administration.

Operational procedures

Because of the complex and varied nature of their requirements, airlines will provide detailed plans for caterers and air crew indicating the location of different items to be stored within the galleys in the aircraft. Each section of the galley is numbered, and the supplying caterer will number its boxes and trolleys to correspond to these sections to facilitate the loading of the aircraft.

This labelling of the trolleys will also indicate to the aircrew what is being stored in each section. Short-haul flights, such as those ferrying holidaymakers to and from the UK to European holiday destinations, will often carry outward and inward meals from the base in the UK.

If there is insufficient capacity within the galleys, then inward meals may be carried within the cargo hold of the aircraft. Similarly, such flights may carry a large bar service, and again this will limit the volume of food that can be stored in the galleys. For example, a galley layout plan was illustrated in Fig. 10.4. This shows a heavy concentration on bar service, as five out of the eight trolleys on board are designated for drink and duty-free goods storage. Here, 100 entrées are stored within the two ovens in which they will be regenerated and the accompanying tray sets are stored in the left-hand aisle galley. All in-bound tray sets and entrees are loaded in the forward hold of the aircraft.

As trolleys have to be wheeled around the cabins, they are located at floor level. This location for storage of foodstuffs would not be ideal in a traditional kitchen, but mobility is the key issue. Cabin staff therefore have to do much bending to dispense food trays to passengers. The trolleys will usually be loaded with individual tray sets of a number of food items and appropriate cutlery and crockery or alternatively with multi-portioned items, such as cheese-boards. The entree of a hot meal will usually be loaded separately, and put into the ovens in the galley, which also double as storage areas.

Stowage is carried out in accordance with the specific requirements of individual flights as determined by the airlines. Hence, the precise content of stowage trolleys will be determined by factors, such as the time of day, duration of the flight, class of customer, and country of origin of the flight. Major airlines will produce detailed loading diagrams for servicing agents, indicating the precise insert slot in which particular items are to be stowed. It also shows that some aircraft which are making return trips to their base will often also carry the food for the return trip ('in bound'). Hence, they will not be fully serviced at their next destination. This food could be located in spare galley bays, or alternatively packed into the cargo hold. In this example both methods are used. In addition, some flights will use a system of dead-heading in which essential equipment is transported to other servicing airports to top up their supplies of trays, crockery, glassware, etc.

Current issues and future developments

At the time of writing, Boeing are the major producer of high-capacity wide-bodied jets. In mid-1995 the new Boeing 777 started in service. A mid-size (313 passengers) wide-bodied aircraft, its final design has benefited from help at the planning stage from some of its major customers. This means that the aircraft has design features which gives the carriers some of the features they have been looking for in order to improve their operating efficiency. The carriers have insisted on interior flexibility. On long-haul flights, galleys and toilets are traditionally used as dividers between first class, business class and economy. The problem with this approach was that it fixed the configuration of the aircraft at the time at which it was ordered from the manufacturer. This gave the operators a problem as the mix of demand for different classes varies according to route, day of the week, and evolves over a period of time. What the airlines want is the ability to have a different mix of numbers of passengers per class on each flight. The airlines therefore asked the manufacturer to produce an aircraft with flexible plumbing, galleys and toilets so that they could move their position in the cabin. The new 777 has three sliding galleys which can move along the fuselage up to a distance of 22 ft. In addition, a major redesign of the rear galley allows the installation of a further twelve seats, a significant advantage to the airlines and their quest to improve profitability.

The next generation of aircraft will have two decks (the full length of the fuselage). Airbus are in the process of such an aircraft, the A380, which was launched in December 2000 (Airbus, 2002 [online]). The A380, which will enter airline service in 2006, was designed in close collaboration with major airlines and will seat 555 passengers in a typical three-class interior layout (Airbus, 2003b [online]). The A380's twin aisle twin-deck passenger cabin claims to provide more space regardless of class of ticket (Airbus, 2003d [online]. Furthermore, the lower deck can be used by the airlines for lavatories, sleeper cabins, crew rest areas, business centres or a bar (Airbus 2003d, 2003g [online]). It can also be anticipated that the new Airbus will reflect the flexibility offered by their other aircraft which allow galleys, lavatories and stowages to be located in different numbers, groupings and locations (Airbus 2003 a, 2003b, 2003c [online]). Another advantage for flight catering of the new A380 is that the aircraft will comprise two sets of doors which will reduce the turnaround time (Airbus, 2003e [online]).

During the pre-launch period of the A380, Boeing stayed in the superjumbo game saying that it would launch a programme if orders were forthcoming (Field, 2001). However, "Boeing has twice floated higher capacity versions of the 747 but neither has flown in the market" (Shifrin et al., 2002). Thus, "for now Boeing is leaving the superjumbo market to Airbus preferring to dream of speed rather than size with the futuristic Sonic Cruiser" (Field, 2001) which Boeing claim could be up to 15–20% faster than current aircraft (O'Toole et al., 2001).

As discussed in Chapter 12, the internet provides many opportunities for the future of flight catering, such as ecommerce. However, the internet also makes it possible to exert **control over galley equipment** from the ground. Currently, equipment, such as ovens, are switched on and off by cabin crew. These may be automated too, with timers to ensure they reheat chilled entrees for the right time and with thermostats to ensure this is at the right temperature. It is now possible to remove all control from the cabin crew and have ovens switched on and off from the ground, as well as be monitored. This would enable the caterers to exert control over all aspects of the food, and let cabin crew concentrate on serving passengers.

Conclusion

Flight catering depends on the effective design and operation of galleys and galley equipment. This 'back-of-house' area performs the functions of an equipment store, regeneration kitchen, still room (hot beverage preparation area), dispense bar and waste storage area. Since it performs these functions in a very confined space, the system depends on using modular equipment and trolleys and adopting clearly laid down procedures for stowage and flight service. The design of the galley and its equipment also has to take into account issues relating to safe and secure storage while the aircraft is in transit and the availability of energy sources while airborne. The whole system is based on space available to passengers for dining while in their seat. This 'table space' determines the size of the tray; the size of the tray determines the dimensions of the trolleys; the trolley size determines the size of stowage space in galleys; the stowage space determines the type of equipment needed in that galley. While the equipment used in flight catering is not unique in terms of its function, it is unique in terms of how it has been designed to meet the specific context of being installed on to an aircraft.

Key terms

Aircraft configuration	Cargo hold	Galley design
Regeneration	Stowage	

Discussion questions

1. Identify the factors that influence galley configuration on an aircraft.
2. Identify the factors that influence storage requirements on an aircraft.

References

Airbus. (2002) *A380 Double Deck Family-Flagship of the 21st Century*, [online], Available from: http://www.airbus.com/media/a380_family.asp, [Accessed 17/03/03].

Airbus. (2003a) *A300/A310 Family-Cabin Layouts* [online], Available from: http://www.airbus.com/product/a300_cabin_layoute.asp, [Accessed 18/03/03].

Airbus. (2003b) *A320 Family-Cabin Layouts*, [online], Available from: http://www.airbus.com/products/a319_cabin_layouts.asp, [Accessed 18/03/03].

Airbus. (2003c) *Airbus A330/A340 Family-Cabin Layouts*, [online], Available from: http://www.airbus.com/products/a330_a200_cabin_layouts.asp, [Accessed 18/03/03].

Airbus. (2003d) *A380 Family-Cabin Layouts*, [online], Available from: http://www.airbus.com/product/a380_cabin_layouts.asp, [Accessed 17/03/03].

Airbus. (2003e) *A380 Family-Economics*, [online], Available from: http://www.airbus.com/product/a380_economics.asp, [Accessed 18/03/03].

Airbus. (2003f) *A380 Family-Introduction*, [online], Available from: http://www.airbus.com/product/a380_backgrounder.asp, [Accessed 17/03/03].

Airbus. (2003g) *A380 Family-Passenger Comfort*, [online], Available from: http://www.airbus.com/product/a380_comfort.asp, [Accessed 18/03/03].

Continental Airlines. (2003) *Dining within the United States*, [online], Available from: http://www.continental.com/travel/inflight/dining/domestic/default.asp, [Accessed 22/01/03].

Field, D. (2001) "The Tortoise and the Hare" *Airline Business*, May, 33.

Momberger, K. and Momberger, M. (2002) "Aviation Catering News," *Momberger Airport Information*, 10 Aug. 4.

Momberger, K. and Momberger, M. (2003) "Supplier News," *Momberger Airport Information*, 10 Mar. 3.

O'Toole, K. Pinkham, R. and Pilling, M. (2001) "Fast Talking in Paris", *Airline Business*, Jul., 72–74.

Ott, J. (1993) *Aviation Week and Space Technology*, 1 Feb.

Shifrin, C. O'Toole, K. and Pinkham, R. (2002) "The Contest Continues," *Airline Business*, Apr., 46–50.

On-board service

Learning objectives

- Understand different cabin design and services
- Examine cabin crew staffing levels and training
- Discuss the in-flight policy and service procedures
- Discuss issues of customer feedback

Introduction

On-board policy starts with the service concept adopted by each airline, as discussed in Chapter 3. Essentially, this encompasses all aspects of customer comfort during the flight and must also include all regulatory and other processes that the airline is obliged to follow. Policy, then, determines the procedures that will be followed during any flight. There are a great many areas to consider with regard to customer comfort. In this respect, meals and drinks on board are just one item within a long list, and need to be seen within the total context of the service concept, with an appreciation of the many constraints under which the food and beverage services have to operate. In essence, every aspect of the customers' needs and wants while under the care of the airline needs to be considered, and a decision made about the priority which will be given to each item. Such priority will, of course, vary from airline to airline. These differences are often the basis of the competitive stance an airline will take in relation to its rivals. There will even be differences within each airline, depending upon the type and duration of the flight. For example, the services available on a normal scheduled flight will be different from those on a charter, or the food and beverages provided on a long-haul, international flight will be different from those available on a short-haul, domestic flight.

This chapter examines each of the key aspects of effective on-board service. It begins by looking at issues related to cabin design and services, before discussing service staffing levels and training. Alternative policies with regard to on-board service are reviewed and the procedures for serving different kinds of passenger are explained. Finally, the approaches adopted by airlines for eliciting customer feedback are described.

Cabin design and services

The interior design of the aircraft is important in helping to set an appropriate mood for passengers. The careful use of colour schemes will help to create a calm, relaxing environment. Seat design is particularly important. Seats are in effect high-technology items of equipment which are medically and functionally researched. They incorporate communication and entertainment facilities and safety items, as well as table arrangements for use during meal service. The seats provided in the different class sections on each aircraft can vary considerably. For example, first class may have seats which have a 100 per cent incline, almost converting into a bed, while business-class seats may have a 49 per cent incline, and economy-class seats much less. Obviously, those seats with greater incline require a greater amount of space. Space availability can be a big competitive factor, a difference of 5 cm between seats can be crucial. The type of seat and spacing will also affect the type and style of meal service which is possible. In first class there can be sufficient space available for crew to have access to each individual passenger so that a much more personal level of service can be achieved.

Toilets have to be provided in sufficient quantity, and located conveniently in each section of the aircraft. The ratio of toilet facilities to passengers varies according to the class of passenger. Typically, the ratio in first class of toilets to seats is 1:10, in business class 1:18, and for economy passengers 1:40. Facilities for baby changing need to be provided in at least one of the toilets in each section, along with the special amenities which accompany this service.

All airlines are essentially governed by the same safety regulations and procedures on international flights, and by those in force in each country on domestic flights. Such regulations usually require that safety information is provided to all passengers by means of announcements, demonstrations, video, and printed materials.

Aircraft are also designed to provide both audio and video entertainment. This usually requires the passenger to use earphones so that a personal selection of entertainment can be made without disturbing or conflicting with other passengers. Video display may be on screens located on interior bulkheads or pulled down from the ceiling, while other aircraft are now equipped with individual video screens located in the back of seats.

Duty-free and other sales are also part of the overall 'entertainment package'. These need to be adjusted according to the type or nationality of passengers and what they are in the habit of buying. For example, Japanese passengers spend a lot of money on relatively high-priced items and so appropriate stocks need to be carried. An airline might take US$ 20–30 m. in sales per year which can make a significant contribution to profits as well as act as an incentive for the cabin crew. Sales need very careful planning. Catalogue sales may also be used.

Cosmetics and toiletries are normally available, either as a personal pack (first and business class), or in the toilet areas. A whole range of other basic necessities is often available from the cabin crew. Many of these may be included in a 'stewardess kit'. Such items might include tampons, disposable razors, first-aid supplies (all crew must have first-aid training), baby foods, children's games and entertainment (e.g. colouring books) according to age groups and safety, cards and other games (often chess) for adults, baby baskets and postcards, writing paper, and envelopes (possibly even postage service).

Staffing levels and training

Physical design will determine some of the constraints on the degree of personal service which is possible. However, personal service can be enhanced by the number of crew available, and the attention given to the training of the crew. The amount of personal attention which can be given to passengers is quite simply a function of the amount of staff available on the flight in each section. The proportion of crew to passengers will be much higher in first class than in economy. This allows not only greater attention to detail in actual services of food and beverages, but in general availability of crew to continuously check on passenger needs and to be proactive rather than reactive in the provision of services.

Staffing levels

By law each aircraft must have a minimum number of cabin crew according to the type of aircraft so that each exit door is covered by a crew member. More crew are needed to effect the provision of additional services for passengers. Additional services may involve the style and frequency of food and beverage services, as well as simply having sufficient staff so that they have time available in their schedule to talk to and spend time with passengers.

In deciding on the eventual staff level there is some comparison with competitors and agreement with crew (via the crew union), but first the airline needs to be clear on what it wants to do on board, and then to aim to provide the appropriate number of crew to properly fulfil the task required to achieve the decided level of service. For instance, the minimum number of cabin crew needed to staff a typical narrow-bodied plane is three staff, and for a wide-bodied aircraft, such as an A340, it is ten. However, some airlines have as many as six cabin crew on their 737s and 14 crew on A340s on some routes.

While every airline will have its own particular way to structure or organise its cabin crew and have its own titles for each position, Fig. 14.1 aims to show a the typical cabin crew arrangement for a 747-200 aircraft.

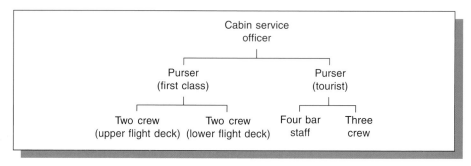

Figure 14.1
Cabin crew organisation for a 747-200 aircraft

Cabin crew training

Training of the crew is a very important aspect in ensuring that the required standards of service are achieved. It is also a very difficult thing to organise, as once new crew have completed their induction training they are effectively an 'absentee workforce'—they are not all together at one place or one time and so training has to be carefully planned with a view to crew availability and the normal needs of the airline.

A typical retraining programme is linked to upgrading or promotion of crew, as well as refreshing their existing skills and knowledge. Each airline will have its own training arrangement for the crew which will vary in detail to some extent. However, all airlines will have a similar pattern and content of training, which will always feature a high degree of safety training. The following sections reflect a typical pattern of training. The notes also provide an indication of the different seniority levels of the crew and the different duties and responsibilities which devolve to each level.

Induction training will involve approximately 1 month's full-time training. It will cover an introduction to the airline, general duties and responsibilities, first aid, and will place most emphasis on the safety aspects. All crew must be CAA certified. In addition new crew will be trained in specific duties relative to meal service, food and beverage knowledge, behaviour/cultural aspects, language training, interpersonal skills and personal appearance. About 30–40 per cent of the induction training will be involved with food and beverage related services. New crew are then allowed to fly, but are effectively on probation for about 3 months. During this time they are under close supervision. At the end of the period they are either recalled to receive further training in areas where they are found to be weak, or confirmed to work as crew members.

Cabin crew usually start on narrow body aircraft and serve domestic and short haul destinations in the beginning. For some a mix of short-haul and long-haul is also possible. Three types of licence are typical:

- 2–3 narrow-body aircraft/short-haul only
- 1 narrow-body, 1 wide-body/a mix of short-haul and long-haul
- 2 wide-body/long-haul only

Changes from one group to another are possible through applications and depending on seniority when free positions are announced by the airline. Tight union contracts play an important role, giving priority to seniority of cabin staff. Obviously planning of crews to work on various routes is much easier if more crew can be considered for any route whatever the type of aircraft in use on that route. However, this process of having cabin crew with multi-aircraft qualifications needs approval from the CAA to ensure that the highest standards of safety are maintained.

It is unlikely that a new crew member will work in first class during the first five years, especially since larger business class compartments have been introduced. Working in first class involves additional training, which may encompass a 3–4 day course and is a general upgrading of all skills. However, particular attention is given to the additional food and beverage and interpersonal skills needed to work in this part of the aircraft.

Crew will then normally work in the first-class cabin for about 3 years. This time frame depends upon the needs of the company in terms of the number of crew needed to work in first class, as well as the overall staffing situation at any time. For example, crew members may be on maternity leave, there may be resignations, and so on.

Many airlines now require their cabin staff to work on all positions in order to further complicate crew rotation planning. However, larger airlines may assign different ranks to their cabin staff within the individual classes, visibly demonstrated by stripes or other attachments to the uniforms. Galley purser training entails very specific food and beverage training and will normally take 2 weeks or more. This training will involve, for example, technical aspects of meal reheating and packing and organising all the items and equipment in the galley. It also deals with detailed food service skills such as slicing a roast and the service of caviar. However, with the introduction of the *a la carte* service even cabin staff on duty for 20 years will receive specialised training to ensure that service concepts are fully understood and put into practice on board. A crew member might then work as a galley purser for 3 or 4 years.

Additional training continues as crew become more senior, focusing on abilities in supervision, leadership, interpersonal skills with passengers, cultural abilities, and so on. The flight purser position is the equivalent of a section leader and will last for perhaps 2 years.

The senior purser is the next position in career development involving the supervision of a larger section, for example in charge of first class. Where business class is split between two levels of a 747, there will be a senior purser on each level. Training is focused again on supervisory and management skills. A crew member may spend 7 or 8 years working as a senior purser.

The chief purser is the highest level to which cabin crew can aspire on board. While the captain is ultimately responsible for everything which happens on board, the chief purser takes charge of all passenger-related activities. He or she is the flight service manager. Training involves all aspects of management and the many legal responsibilities which have to be fulfilled, such as immigration control, sealing of bars, and completing various documentation. This is an extremely responsible position, not made easier by the fact that the chief purser has to operate with different aircraft on different routes with different teams of people as the crew. Obviously, there is a great need for standardisation of procedures and information so that in such changing circumstances the service provided for passengers is assured.

Flight service policy

It is clear from the previous discussion that there are many more aspects to consider than simply food and beverage services during a flight. However, food and beverage services are probably the most important aspect from the perspective of most passengers, and technically one of the most difficult for airlines to achieve, and therefore an area which involves a great deal of planning and staff training. The previous chapters have covered aspects of markets and customers as well as the planning and operational details involved in the provision of the necessary food and beverage requirements for each flight.

Once on board the food and beverage products and their service become the responsibility of the cabin crew. In effect, they become just a part, although as already stated a very important part, of the total flight service programme.

The type and quantity of food and beverage services to be provided on any flight are subject to a detailed planning process which involves consideration of all the events which will be scheduled throughout the whole of the flight. These considerations will of course be made within the overall policy guidelines of each airline.

The policy may differentiate between the services offered on different sectors. For example, one sector may be particularly profitable because of a high ratio of full-price seats, and so services are tailored to give these passengers many extras in terms of food and beverage quality as well as other services provided. Most policies are not blanket ones but make allowances for different needs on different routes. This is of course reflected in a consideration of the passenger mix in national/cultural terms. Whenever possible, services are kept within normal parameters. Staff are highly trained in several service types, and each of these services is supported by extensive documentation for the cabin crew to follow. Any change to the normal service would involve the production of new guidelines, tasks lists and cards, and other support material and documentation. In addition, retraining of all the crews would be required and this would be a major task even for a relatively small airline like Cathay Pacific with about 5000 cabin crew employed. It would be a mammoth task for a larger airline, like Air France.

Flight service procedures

Each airline has its own set of standards and procedures in line with their general policy with respect to the level of service to be achieved. Each flight, whether domestic or international, short- or long-haul, and depending upon the time of day of departure, will have a predetermined and fairly precise service routine for each class of passengers on board. In view of the wide-ranging policy alternatives described above, it is not possible to describe in general terms how service is provided on board. However, the sequence of events a passenger experiences on a typical overnight flight from the USA to Europe consists of boarding the aircraft, taking a seat, departure and safety announcements, use of products available in the seat pocket (for instance magazine, headset), service of beverages, service of meal, provision of video entertainment, the opportunity to sleep, service of beverage and breakfast, landing announcements, and disembarkation.

Short-haul flights within Europe are similar to this, although only one meal will be served and there is usually no entertainment. In the USA internal flights, even of 4–5 hours, may not include any meal provision.

Special boarding and disembarkation arrangements are provided for first-class and business-class passengers. These passengers are always allowed to disembark before other passengers. The food and beverage service provided for them at the start of the flight (welcome drinks, snacks, etc.) can be considerable. Where the airline has a special airport lounge for such passengers, then the food and beverage service takes place in the more spacious comfort of the lounge, and boarding takes place as late as possible. Additional services, such as drinks, will still be offered on board. If lounge facilities are not available in the airport, then first- and business-class passengers are allowed to board before other passengers which allows the crew more time to offer these welcoming services on the aircraft itself.

A key factor in determining the type of meal service is the aircraft type. The two basic types of aircraft vary internally. Narrow-bodied aircraft, such as the Boeing 737, have a single aisle with passenger seats on either side and galleys at the front and rear, adjacent to the doors. Wide-bodied aircraft, such as the Tristar and Boeing 747, have twin aisles and three lots of seats, with as many as seven separate galley areas located near access doors. As explained in Chapter 13, each of these galleys can be configured in different ways, according to the policy of the airline. The interior layout of a Boeing 747 was illustrated in Fig. 13.2.

On narrow-body aircraft, trays containing all meal items are normally taken to the passengers by hand from the galleys, requiring the cabin crew to make repeated journeys back to the galley. On larger aircraft trolleys are used. A typical 747 economy-class trolley would hold as many as 42 trays. The crews move the trolleys along the aisles delivering trays to passengers as required. Careful planning and thorough staff training mean that it is possible for 400 passengers on a 747 to be served with cocktails, a three/four-course main meal with wine or other beverage, and a hot drink in about 90 minutes.

The following sections provide information about typical food and beverage service activities in relation to a main meal being provided on a long-haul flight on a wide-body aircraft in three class sections. Figures 5.6 and 5.7 illustrate the variation in menus—not only do the number and type of dishes on the menus reflect the different categories of passengers, but the menu itself, in terms of print style, layout, and weight and feel of paper, also reflects each class.

First-class meal service

The service of meals to first-class passengers is slightly more sophisticated than for business class. This is made possible by the smaller quantity of passengers and the greater amount of space available. For instance, a roast joint may be available carved at the passenger's seat. An hors d'oeuvre selection may be available for individual choice, or caviar may be served. Some airlines may even provide a buffet service for these passengers. In many respects the standard of service is quite traditional or classical in its approach, a great deal of individual attention is given to each passenger. This level of service requires cabin crew to have specialised training.

Business-class meal service

Drinks will have been served to these passengers before take-off, but then orders are taken for cocktails which will be served before the meal starts. Menus and wine lists are distributed, followed by order taking for the main meal entrée. After cocktail service the passenger table is commonly set with a tablecloth, and then the meal tray is distributed containing the appetiser and necessary cutlery, crockery, glassware, and accompaniments. Wine is offered and served. Appetiser plates are collected when finished and entrées served. Wine is offered again. After the collection of entrée plates, cheese and fruit are served. Hot beverages, normally tea or coffee, are then served, along with liqueurs and pralines. A second service of hot drinks is offered and served as requested. Finally, trays and table-cloths are collected and towels are distributed.

Economy-class meal service

Because of the greater number of passengers, it is not possible to offer the same level of service as experienced by first- and business-class passengers. Trays are stored in and distributed from trolleys which are moved along the aisles. At the start of service, trolleys will need to be moved to the appropriate locations so that service can start simultaneously from the back row of the section moving forward and from the first row of the section back.

On some aircraft two cabin crew will work from a single trolley, and commonly there would be four trolleys in use. The attendant pulling the trolley will hand out trays and the one pushing will offer beverages. The cabin crew need to coordinate and assist each other so that no passenger is kept waiting for either the tray or drinks. Sometimes a half-size trolley is used by a single crew member. This method allows service to start at eight places rather than four and helps to reduce the waiting time for the last passenger served.

Section leaders in the economy section are often given the responsibility for controlling the pace of the meal service and ensuring consistency of service on each aisle and at both ends of the section. There may also be a need to replenish some items on the trolley (hot entrées, bread rolls, specific beverages) depending upon the actual demand.

Flight service customer feedback

Standardised report forms are usually available for flight pursers and galley pursers to complete after a flight. This report may be related to food and beverage issues, and information will be at quite a detailed, or micro, level. For example, it might be reported that the beef was overcooked or that there were insufficient butter portions provided. It might also include information about equipment problems which need attention. The chief purser may also file a report. This is more of a macro-report looking at general events on the flight, some of which may be related to food and beverage products or services. For example, it might comment on the choice of main dishes made by the passengers, indicating that there was insufficient quantity of a particular choice.

These reports will go to a central department within the airline, perhaps the flight services or the cabin crew section. Copies of the report are then distributed to any other relevant section or department, for example, catering, engineering, safety training, lost and found. This allows follow-up to occur to ensure that any problems encountered are reported and checked with a view to controlling standards. There are plans by many airlines to introduce computerised management systems on board which will link via satellite with all ground stations. Thus the chief purser will be able to communicate problems or requirements directly with the relevant ground station to provide an even better and more efficient service.

There are various ways that feedback is received from passengers themselves. These might be letters, verbal messages, completion of survey cards, or detailed questionnaires. All such information is put into a data base in a central customer relations unit and such data are then available to any relevant department, such as catering, where the decision is made to take any action or not on the comments received.

Within the marketing department there is continuous market research which will cover approximately 1 per cent of all passengers. This provides valuable information on the flight profile achieved by the airline and passenger perceptions of services provided. The marketing department will also use focus groups as a feedback mechanism. However, both of these marketing devices are used more commonly in determining policy for the future and taking advance opinion from passengers about possible changes to routes or services. For example, the removal of first-class service from Cathay Pacific's South East Asia regional routes would have been subject to such market scrutiny.

Information flow from the flying passenger

So far we have been concerned with the flow of information between the major players involved in the provision of flight goods and services. As suggested at the beginning of this chapter, the most important 'customers' in the airline business are the fare-paying passengers and it is the flow of information from them that both starts and completes the information loop.

The passenger initially comes into contact with the airline either directly or through an intermediary such as a travel agent. It is at this stage that the airline receives its first information concerning the customer and is provided with data on which planning can commence. It is here that the passenger can also express any particular catering requirements he/she might have, perhaps by requesting one of the special menus the airline provides, for example, vegetarian or low-calorie meals. For the first-class passenger, special menu requests would also be considered and noted. Thereafter, apart perhaps from the collection of flight tickets, or a flight query, this will be the only contact with the airline until the flight takes place. The first occasion which the passenger encounters any of the flight catering provision will be once the aircraft has taken off. At this stage, the fare-paying passenger is very much in the hands of the airline and it is here that he/she will judge and form an impression of the airline catering provided. Although in many cases it is too late to effect any changes, it is important for both the caterer and the airline either to be provided with or seek feedback on the success, appropriateness and relevance of the current arrangements in order for changes to be made, either instantly because something has gone wrong, or so that future changes and modification can be planned for.

Feedback from the flying passenger can come from a number of sources. The group of people considered by some caterers to provide the most important feedback to the flight providers are the cabin crew who, in some cases, can contribute to the design of the product (Hartridge, 1991). Although the catering arrangements do not generally form part of the flight report, under exceptional circumstances it might be necessary for unusual incidents to be reported. Generally, the initial feedback on issues affecting the cabin service will come from the cabin crew who report on aspects of the flight that are considered unsatisfactory and require further attention. Occasionally, the incident might be such that a report needs to be faxed or telexed back to the originating station (flight discrepancy report). This is normally submitted in a standard format for clarity and might arise where something has been forgotten or omitted from the uplift and the situation needs to be rectified immediately for other flights. Where the situation is less urgent, the cabin crew will complete a more formal feedback report which is handed in on completion of the flight. This feedback normally applies to the more generic type of comment and in many airlines it is the responsibility of individual flight crew to complete the appropriate form.

When a passenger has a specific comment or complaint, the individual crew member receiving or dealing with the incident is in most cases required to log and record the details and nature of that complaint on a relevant form. This form is again returned at the end of the flight and the complaint would be investigated with appropriate action taken. Where a passenger considers the nature of comment to be sufficiently important or serious enough, or feels that the cabin crew might not be giving it the attention that it deserves, most airlines provide a mechanism whereby the passenger can write directly to the senior management of the airline. Many airlines provide prepaid, addressed envelopes in which passengers are invited to write and express views on matters they consider to be of importance.

This type of feedback is ongoing, and routinely provides much of the information required by airlines to keep them up to date on how they are performing and where improvements could be made. It also provides the opportunity to assess the quality and performance of the flight provider. Airlines obviously set targets in number of 'compliments' and 'complaints' they receive. The targets for BA, for example, based on analysis and comment cards received from passengers (Hartridge, 1991), were:

- compliments—35 per cent of passengers rating service as excellent
- complaints—less than one complaint per 10,000 meals

These targets should be set against the fact that BA 'produces' over 40 million meals per year. Aer Lingus had similar guidelines and, realising that not all passengers can be satisfied, aim for at least 85 per cent (O'Meara, 1993). Dobbs International Services noted that between 1988 and 1992 customer complaints dropped from one in every 62 flights to one in every 179 flights; an average improvement of 280 per cent (Lorenzini, 1992).

Other feedback can be obtained from continuous and ongoing market research. This would include consumer panels held with various groups of travellers; small but specific surveys designed to assess or measure particular aspects; general market intelligence gathering exercises such as staff attending meetings, conferences and other occasions designed to share and develop ideas; and travel on competitors' airlines to assess changes, standards, and any recent or new developments. However, from time to time, information is required to assess the need and impact of proposed action and on which major decisions might need to be taken. Under these circumstances it is necessary for the airline to conduct a much more comprehensive survey which might involve a major passenger survey. This type of survey is obviously very expensive to undertake and is therefore conducted much less frequently. They are often combined with other surveys in which the food service is a very small component. In a survey conducted by Lufthansa in 1994 on their business class, customers were asked to rate selected attributes as 'very important', 'important', and 'unimportant'. Of the 18 questions, two referred specifically to the provision of meals: 'I have a choice of flight meals' and 'I am served a hot meal on board'.

It would seem therefore that few airlines conduct comprehensive surveys specifically relating to food and rely very much on other types of feedback to ensure that the flight provision is adapted and best suited to their flying passengers' requirements.

Case study 14.1

Virgin upper class

The material for this case study was taken from Virgin Atlantic, 2003 [online] and Virgin Atlantic, 1999.

In November 1999 Virgin upper class cabin products and services underwent a £37 million relaunch. The launch encompassed the introduction of a new meal service, in-flight beauty products, over 100 new products and a new cabin design. The inspiration for the new upper class service came from the 'golden age of flying' when travelling was glamorous, romantic and exciting and Virgin built these ideals around the theme of 'the Modern Romance of Flight'.

Virgin has aimed to provide a total travel experience for its upper-class passengers, which begins when passengers leave for the airport. Virgin offer a selection of complimentary ways to get to the airport including a chauffeur-driven limousine or 'limobike' service for passengers from Central London or the Home Counties. At check in passengers have access to an exclusive upper-class check-in area. Alternatively, if the chauffeur-driven limousine or 'limobike' have been used, the chauffeur can check passengers in at a 'Drive Thru Check In'. This enables passengers to go directly to one of Virgin's Clubhouses. Each Clubhouse has its own unique characteristics and includes a full range of business facilities and less conventional services such as golf driving ranges, Wurlitzer juke-boxes, and skiing machines.

Regarding on-board service, research had indicated that business passengers did not like the restrictive routine they experienced on aircraft. As a consequence, Virgin wanted to create a simple, personalised experience for each traveller and this was reflected in the new upper-class service policy and procedures.

On all long-haul flights the new 'Freedom' meal service was adopted where passengers can order any item from the extensive Freedom menu at any time (very much in contrast to the fixed service provided in economy). The quality of the food and products are high with items such as caviar and fine vintage wines offered. In addition, all items are served on fine china, specialised cutlery, and glassware in a silver service style. Furthermore, Virgin blended the idea of beverage provision and flight entertainment through the inclusion of a bigger bar area for upper-class passengers.

In keeping with this new service concept, service procedures are much more flexible in the new upper-class cabin with customers able to eat what they want and when they want it. Moreover, every item is individually prepared to order by the crew. This unique preparation also allows plates to be piled high with food. This meant that the crew had to be specially trained for the new service. This training has allowed them to provide a more personal and intimate level of service.

Concerning the total travel experience once on board, the new seat design is fully adjustable, ranging from an upright position to a fully flat bed and in addition passengers are provided with a number of products to aid sleep. These include sleep suits for the passengers to change into, full-sized pillows, duvets, and fleece blankets. Entertainment facilities were also revamped with a cutting edge personal audio-visual entertainment system in every seat and a new designated treatment area was incorporated into the cabin so that beauty therapists can treat passengers in privacy.

Current-issues and future developments

The events of 11 September 2001 have had a significant effect on the airline industry. In the short-term passenger numbers declined, so airlines cut some unprofitable routes and reduced fares on others. Airlines also had to introduce new security measures and make efforts to rebuild confidence. This sudden downturn in revenues required companies to reduce their costs simply to stay in business and as *Airline Business* reported "spending on in-flight product and service is often the first to go when times get tough" (Pilling, 2003).

Given the complexity of introducing **new onboard service policies** and standards, those airlines that were in the process of doing so have tended to continue with their plans, despite the changed economic environment. For instance, during 2002, SAS Scandinavian Airlines, Gulf Air and Swiss all carried on with their planned refurbishment, product development, or rebranding exercises. Likewise, American Airlines continued with their $50 million project to increase the overhead bin space on their fleet of Boeing 757 and MD-80 aircraft.

However, major scheduled airlines have made changes to their on-board service, especially with regards to short-haul routes. This is due in large part to competition from the budget carriers. For instance, Air Canada launched a low-fares operation called Tango in late 2001, SAS introduced the Scandinavian Direct concept, and Air New Zealand launched its single-class express service on domestic flights in November 2002. Other airlines have looked at alternative ways in which to reduce costs, whilst trying to maintain service levels. Examples quoted in the trade press include:

- British Airways saved £5 million a year by using smaller meal trays on UK routes under 60 minutes. This means more trays can be loaded on board each aircraft, thereby enabling back catering
- American Airlines saved $2 million a year by not offering magazines
- American Airlines plans to save $6 million a year by offering free flight entertainment to passengers who buy a headset on-board or bring their own. It used to charge $5 per passenger, but this revenue was highly marginal as the cost of distributing and repairing headsets was too high

A key issue is whether or not scheduled airlines will adopt the practice of low-cost carriers of retailing (i.e. selling) meal, snack and drink products on board. During 2002, the only growth business for flight caterers, at least in Europe, was provision to carriers such as Virgin Express, easyjet and bmibaby (Pilling, 2003). Research suggests that on scheduled airlines ". . . European passengers expect a [free] meal service on board" (Abbott cited in Pilling 2003).

The role of cabin crew and their **training** is always evolving. As we saw in Chapter 1, originally female crew were selected because they were trained nurses (in the 1930s). Following concerns about security and air rage, the level of training with regards to dealing with conflict situations has increased. For a number of years El Al has had armed guards, so-called sky marshalls, in its passenger cabins, usually in cognito. This practice may be adopted by other airlines and may be compulsory if countries legislate for this. Cabin crew may also need be given more sales training if on-board meal and drink service becomes optional, carried out on a retail basis (see Chapter 3).

The emergence of **SARS** and its rapid distribution throughout the globe due to air transport has led to the introduction of a number of measures related to on-board services and at flight catering production units. On-board aircraft these include: increasing fresh air circulation, providing masks for passengers and crew on certain routes and isolating passengers that display SARS symptoms and alerting destination airports, and the provision of catering gloves for the crew to use while serving food and beverages (Momberger and Momberger, 2003). On the ground measures encompass the disposal of towels and leftover food, the sterilisation of catering utensils after use and the increased disaffection of aircraft including seats, meal tables, surfaces of lavatories, etc. on departure and arrival (Momberger and Momberger, 2003).

Conclusion

On-board service provides those 'moments of truth' from which customer satisfaction derives. It is the culmination of an extremely complex production and logistics process involving hundreds of unseen back-of-house employees. To ensure that the customer experience achieves the standard specified, cabin crew are highly trained in both technical aspects of on-board service and the interpersonal skills needed to deliver good service. The crew are also trained in safety procedures in the event they have to deal with an emergency situation. The job of cabin crew is often regarded by the average person as extremely glamorous, since it involves travelling around the world to exciting locations. The reality is not at all like that. Delivering on-board service is a very demanding job carried out in demanding circumstances.

On-board service is an area that is very susceptible to changes in the economic climate, as it is one of the few variable cost elements of the total travel experience. In recent years there has been a great deal of turbulence in this environment that has seen airlines adopt a variety of approaches to their on-board provision. In some cases, product and service have been simply reduced, or cut out all together; in others they have been modified to save money without too adversely affecting the passenger experience; and on long-haul some airlines have actually invested even more in their on-board service. It seems likely that this will continue to be a troubled, even contentious, aspect of flight catering. Thus in November 2002, Seeman in the editorial of the *IFCA Review* commented on this situation and suggested that airlines might think about "disbanding their total catering operation" by allowing caterers to provide take-on retail products to short-haul passengers and outsourcing long-haul operations. Seeman was clearly not pleased that "on a 2 hour flight in Business Class at lunchtime I received a bowl of lettuce with 4 small shrimps on top and on the way back again at lunchtime a bowl of lettuce with 3 very small and thin slices of cheddar cheese" (Seeman, 2002)!

Key terms

Cabin crew	Customer feedback	Flight service policy
Flight service procedure	On-board service	Seat design
Staffing levels	Training	

Discussion questions

1. What factors influence the level of on-board service given to passengers?
2. Discuss the importance of cabin crew training to the quality of on-board service.
3. Identify the advantages and disadvantages of the different ways in which customer feedback is elicited.
4. Discuss the importance of customer feedback to flight caterers.

References

Buzz. (2003) *Welcome to Café Buzz*, [online], Available from: http://www.café-buzz.com, [Accessed 22/01/03].

Hartridge A. (1991) *Quality in Flight Catering*, MSc dissertation, Oxford: Brookes University, UK, 55.

Lorenzini B. (1992) "Are You Committed to Quality?" *Restaurants & Institutions* 102: 71–75.

Momberger, K. and Momberger, M. (2003) "Handling SARS," *Momberger Airport Information*, 10 May, 6.

O'Meara A. (1993) "Aer Lingus—A Winning Team," *Hotel & Catering Review*, 23 Apr., 16–19.

Pilling, M. (2003) "Smarter Service," *Airline Business* vol. 19, no. 1, Jan. 36–39.

Seeman, W. (2002) "Food-Food Glorious Food," *IFCA/IFSA Review*. vol. 5, no. 4, Nov. 3.

Virgin Atlantic. (1999) *Flying High—Virgin Atlantic's New Upper Class Takes to the Air*, Virgin Atlantic Press Release.

Virgin Atlantic. (2003) *Upper Class*, [online], Available from: http://www.virgin-atlantic.com/flying_with_us_upper_class.view.do, [Accessed 21/01/03].

CHAPTER • • • • 15

Off-loading and recycling

- Understand ware-washing procedures
- Identify different disposal methods
- Understand the meanings of recycling
- Examine waste management
- Discuss environmental management policies in flight catering

Introduction

This chapter discusses what happens to the waste, crockery equipment and surplus food that is off-loaded from the aircraft at the end of each flight. Its remit begins from the moment the unloaded trolleys arrive at the unloading bay, and ends at the point where trays and trolleys are reassembled, ready for use. It includes crockery, cutlery, trays and trolleys, as well as bars and duty-free, service ware for tea and coffee, complimentary gift packs, and cabin staff equipment. A very significant problem of scale is involved, for example, a large airport with say 75 flights per day will produce about 25,000 tray sets for processing; anything up to 40,000 single items per aircraft (including linen/napkins, headrest covers, blankets, newspapers, headsets etc.), may need to be sorted, cleaned, polished, refurbished, or discarded. Flight meal production and service on this scale also produce around 10 tonnes of mixed waste, some of which may carry foreign pests or diseases and therefore requires specialist treatment.

In this context 'recycling' may have two meanings. In the first instance, recycling in the flight-catering industry refers to cleaning rotable equipment ready for re-use. Until relatively recently, all waste items were simply disposed of. However, in the last ten years environmental awareness has led to the idea than even so-called waste materials, such as paper, metal, and even food waste, should also be recycled. The trend towards waste recycling is more advanced in some countries than others, and may involve sorting waste into as many as eight different categories, all of which require separate storage and disposal facilities. Hence, in this chapter we will begin by looking at how rotable equipment is unloaded and handled in flight-production units ("re-using"), before going on to look at waste handling and environmental recycling.

Unloading procedures

Figure 15.1 outlines the ground services which support the flight-catering process. The level of dependence upon labour varies from country to country. It is much higher in the developing world. In Western countries, off-loading, recycling, and storage are frequently integrated into the whole servicing process by means of sophisticated automation. The process is comparatively standardised and repetitive and is therefore easy to describe in 'hard' systems terms (Johns and Edwards, 1994, and Kirk, 1994). System inputs are dirty ware and equipment, water and servicing chemicals. Outputs are clean ware and equipment, waste (sorted or unsorted), and dirty water. Sorting, ware washing and replenishment are readily envisaged as a series of parallel processes (Fig. 15.1), each consisting of stepwise process stages. This chapter considers each of these process stages in detail, identifying the implications in terms of equipment, labour, time, and space.

Virtually all of the rotables, waste and other materials return to the depots in the same trolleys from which they were served. The trolley system enables cabin staff to dispose rapidly of waste and used equipment. Crew equipment, complimentaries, bar, and duty-free goods are all housed in standard-sized trolleys, and there are additional trolleys to accommodate any loose waste collected from passengers. Some airlines, notably SAS, require cabin service

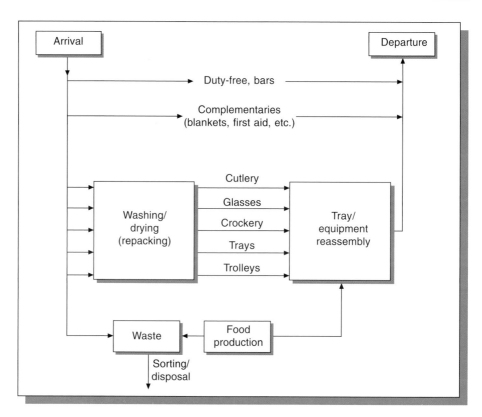

Figure 15.1
Schematic flow diagram of off-loading and recycling

staff to sort this waste during the flight by collecting it into compartmentalised trolleys. ATI Aero Design produce galley compaction units, with a hydraulic ram which can compress solid waste into special removable bins.

Trolleys are wheeled manually from the loading trucks and stored in a reception area. In a large plant, transporting and storing them is a major problem, because they must be moved over an enormous area. For example, one production unit at Heathrow South deals with British Airways long-haul flight requirements from a 4.7 ha site. Not all trolleys undergo the same treatment. Those used for duty-free goods are merely replenished, bar trolleys may need to be wiped, while all food trolleys are fully washed and sterilised. Trolleys awaiting different treatments may be stored (buffered) in different holding areas. Bar and duty-free holding areas must be secure.

With some help from robotics, the cleaning still requires some labour input removing trays from trolleys and then ensuring the right allocation of different type of dishes into the wash-up system. In some units, trolleys are raised hydraulically to a comfortable working level—one machine designed by a Swedish company—the Cart Pillar Lift—is able to swivel the meal trolley, allowing staff to clear trays from both sides of the trolley without having to move about. Currently, CIAS (the second caterer at Singapore's Changi Airport) have installed this trolley lift. They found it improved the washing process and enhanced productivity in their warewash department (Momberger and Momberger, 2002).

Trolleys are moved by hand in small plants, but this is not adequate for large operations. The invention of the 'power and free' transport system meant that the movement, storage and processing of trolleys could be scheduled and driven by computers. The 'power and free' system consists of double overhead rails, one above the other. Trolleys are loaded into special carrying baskets, which suspend from the lower 'free' rail. The automated system has electrical drivers, which move along the upper rail (the 'power' rail) and can be made to engage the trolley carriers on the lower rail and drive them along. In this way, trolleys can be carried to any destination, processed and buffered. For example they may pass through the washer, and then be buffered, awaiting loading; or they may go straight to the secure area for bar goods to be replenished. 'Power and free' systems are generally designed into a catering facility. AEG have this equipment in a production unit at Heathrow West, and United Airlines' Denver operation has a similar automated system.

Used trays are unloaded from trolleys within hours of landing, and transferred by hand onto conveyor belts associated with the ware washing system, which has special wash tunnels for trolleys, as well as for crockery, trays, and other equipment. Upon emerging from the washers, trays and ware are stacked in special baskets and taken to storage locations on trolleys, or via the automated transport system.

Washing ware and equipment

Non-disposable flight crockery and cutlery are known as 'rotables'. Crockery may be of melamine-formaldehyde copolymer (which is less prone to breakage), but increasingly it is ceramic, which has a more favourable image. Ware washing includes washing rotables, trays, and trolleys.

The large number of separate items which make up each aircraft's load means that it is always necessary to have an automated, or at least part-automated, ware-washing system. All washers work on a similar principle, exemplified by a typical small-scale operation. Trays are loaded by hand onto a conveyor. Items of ware are then removed by hand on to special trays, or onto mobile dish racks. These then pass through a tunnel washer on a conveyor. The tunnel washer sprays the ware successively with a hot detergent solution (c. 65°C) and then with heated rinse water (c. 85°C). Finally the ware is dried in a stream of hot air. Such a system is comparatively slow and labour-intensive. It is more usual to find at least three separate tunnel washers: one for glasses, one for crockery, and one for cutlery. It is still necessary to remove the glass and crockery manually from the trays, but cutlery can often be removed magnetically. Such large operations typically use a river or vacuum system to remove waste, which is tipped out on to the trays when the ware is picked off. Washing cycles in the different tunnels may also be altered to suit particular types of ware. For example, cutlery may be burnished and glassware treated with extra rinse-aid. Water for washer tunnels is deionised in bulk using reverse osmosis, i.e. it is pumped under pressure through a series of micro-diameter tubules, so that limescale and other minerals are left behind.

Meiko, a major supplier of tunnel washers to the flight-catering industry, have devised a further ware-washing refinement: a flight casserole washer. Many airlines offer their passengers food reheated in sauces. Frequently, a single spray-wash is inadequate for casserole dishes, but the specialised Meiko washer uses jets of high-pressure heated water to remove stubborn food materials. In order to do this, the washer has an upper conveyor rack, which comes down over the lower one, trapping the dishes and preventing breaking during the high-pressure treatment. Flight catering services usually have additional, separate washers to process trays. After the ware has been removed, the trays pass either under a vacuum hood, or through a torrent of 'river system' water to remove their loads of waste. They then undergo a complete wash–rinse cycle, similar to that used for ware. The trays are automatically stacked into the washer-tunnel conveyor; however, non-standard tray sizes present a significant problem, by becoming lost, or jamming in the tunnel. Specialised washers may also be required for bulk ware, for example tea and coffee pots, and for the trolleys themselves. In older plants, the latter may be loaded by hand onto a conveyor, but in automated systems the 'power and free' rails are designed to allow the trolleys to pass through the washer in their baskets.

Figure 15.2 shows a typical large-scale washing operation. Besides a two-track machine, capable of handling crockery and cutlery on separate conveyors, there are separate tunnels to deal with trays, casserole dishes, glasses, and trolleys. Waste is removed from the trays by a river system, after the different categories of ware have been taken off by hand. More recently, installed equipment would probably include vacuum waste removal. Washer installations are usually designed for specific operating sites and may differ substantially from country to country. For example, in India and the Far East there may be more reliance on manual labour to sort ware. Switzerland and Germany, where strict waste recycling policies prevail, tend to rely more on manual labour for removing and sorting waste, since this cannot as yet be accomplished by automated processes.

Refurbishment

Alcoholic drinks trolleys go to different secure areas, depending on whether they hold duty-free or duty-paid drinks. Drawers are removed and replenished and the trolleys are labelled ready for the next flight. Soiled trolleys may be set aside for steam cleaning, after which they are stored in a clean buffer zone, ready for re-use. Complimentary goods may be discarded or refurbished. Refurbishment includes repackaging cutlery, laundering blankets and sleeping suits, cleaning and refurbishing loan items such as stereo headsets, as well as checking and replenishing complimentary gift packs. Airlines have varying policies on equipment such as stereo headphones. For example, one airline may issue free complimentary headsets in their passenger pack, while another prefers to loan their customers better quality sets. These items have to be unloaded and sent to a contractor to be sterilised and repackaged after every run. Depending on the passenger class, gift packs include combs, toiletries, socks, and other items. All are enclosed in tamper-evident packages, and in some cases, unused goods can be returned to suppliers for checking and repackaging. In developing countries such services are not available, but (particularly in Africa) such items may be distributed to the local population. Aircrew equipment also includes blankets for passengers, games and toys for

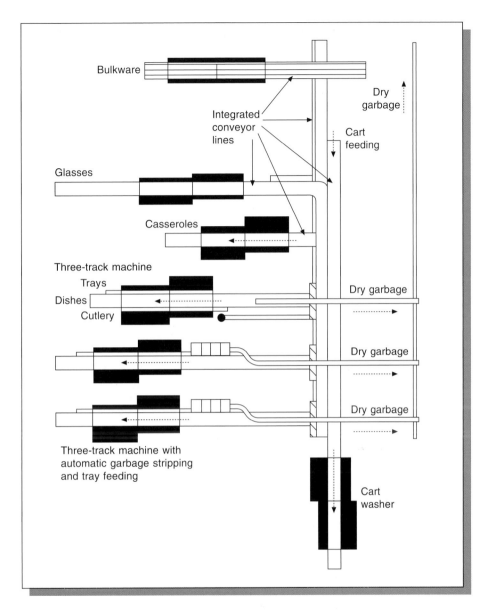

Figure 15.2
Plan of wash-up machinery
SOURCE: Meiko

children, and first-aid boxes. All equipment trolleys must be opened, checked, and replenished between flights. Damaged items and spent packaging join the main waste disposal routes, via bins or belts or, after shredding, through the vacuum system.

Sources of waste

Waste originates from several different sources, for example, uneaten passenger meals. The numbers of total meals and menu choices are calculated on the basis of previous experience for economy and club-class passengers, but higher numbers of all choices are carried for first-class customers. Thus, a proportion of first-class meals are generally likely to remain uneaten. In addition, passengers frequently refuse their meals, or accept them only to leave the food on their plates. Besides food waste, there are smaller but significant amounts of waste paper, aluminium foil, glass, and various types of plastics (from individually packed products).

Food-production facilities are another important source of waste. Production waste levels tend to be much higher in developing countries such as India, where the quality of raw materials is neither as high nor as standardised as in the West. However, no quantitative data are as yet available for such operations. Flight meal production operations also produce a considerable amount of packaging waste.

Organic waste from production facilities and passenger waste from many short-haul destinations are not likely to contain virulent pests or diseases. They do not have to be subjected to the same stringent treatments as waste from long-haul flights, which is usually quarantined and incinerated.

Another typical problem is that of intermediate storage or 'buffering'. The nature of air traffic means that used trolleys do not arrive in a steady flow, but come in batch consignments which vary in size according to the type of aircraft and the duration of the flight. Long-haul flights carry significantly more equipment and produce considerably more waste, and although airports work around the clock, more flights usually arrive during daylight hours. As a result, used trolleys from each aircraft may need to be stored for some time in 'buffer' areas, close to the unloading bays, until they can be processed. These include areas for general food equipment awaiting sorting and washing, and special secure areas for bars and duty-free trolleys. There may also be separate buffer areas for trolleys containing complimentary gift packs and other miscellaneous cabin equipment such as games for children, blankets, and first-aid boxes.

'Dead-heading' contributes to the logistical problems of recycling. An aircraft must carry a complete complement of tray sets whether it is full or empty. A part-empty plane carries enough meals for its passenger load, the remainder of its tray sets are sent empty as 'dead-heads'. On arrival, they must be checked, and often they are sorted and washed with the used sets. Simply to reuse them would be more cost-effective, but this incurs its own problems of logistics, buffering, and hygiene maintenance.

An important aspect of recycling in the flight-catering sector is the storage of ware. Each airline has its own styles of recyclable (rotable) equipment. These generally differ between travel classes, not only in style and quality, but also in number. First-class ware is usually distinctively marked and includes settings for different types of trays. Usually there is special first-class silverware for tea and coffee service as well as vases for flowers and other special equipment. Most airlines have separate sets of equipment for business, club and economy classes. All of these items must be stored in hygienic, dry and secure conditions, for all types of plane and for all the different airlines served by the airport facility.

The quantity of flight-catering waste

So far we have simply looked at the different types of waste, without identifying the scale of waste produced. Data is not easy to find, although more is becoming available as caterers start to consider recycling and record quantities in order to evaluate the relative economies of disposal versus recycling. One major problem is that waste produced in the-flight production unit from unwrapping supplies, preparing meals, and assembling trays is not always separated from waste removed from aircraft.

Table 15.1 illustrates some statistics from Switzerland in the early 1990s. This identifies the amount of waste generated by serving over 6.5 million flight meals, and separates waste into eight categories. Clearly, the two largest categories by weight at this time were paper and card (over 50 per cent of the total waste) and glass (over 30 per cent of the total). Between 1992 and 1993 glass usage fell, but aluminium increased. This data is useful in identifying the main types of waste, but does not identify if this waste was derived solely from unloading aircraft. More recent data from LSG Sky Chefs in 2001 identified the total amount of waste produced to be 40,771 tonnes from 73.3 million meals. Of this, 19,622 tonnes was described as "on board wastes and wastes

Category	Jan–Oct 1992			Jan–Oct 1993			Variance 1992/93	
	tonnes	kg per meal	kg per flight	tonnes	kg per meal	kg per flight	kg per meal	kg per flight
Paper and card	1,344.0	0.205	25.74	1,274.0	0.172	23.90	(0.034)	(1.84)
Aluminium (foil and cans)	10.7	0.002	0.20	35.7	0.005	0.67	0.003	0.47
Used frying oil	8.2	0.001	0.16	5.7	0.001	0.11	(0.000)	(0.05)
Glass	621.5	0.095	11.90	561.0	0.076	10.52	(0.019)	(1.38)
Polyethylene terephathalate (PET)	31.2	0.005	0.60	30.5	0.004	0.57	(0.001)	(0.02)
Stale bread	29.5	0.005	0.56	24.1	0.003	0.45	(0.001)	(0.11)
Styrofoam	2.0	0.000	0.04	2.5	0.000	0.05	(0.000)	0.01
Polyethylenes	0.224	0.000	0.00	1.7	0.000	0.03	(0.000)	0.03
Total	2048.0	0.313	39.21	1936.0	0.261	36.31	(0.520)	(2.90)
							Difference	
							No.	%
Meals produced	6,550,958			7,424,812			873,854	13.34
Flights handled	52,223			53,308			1,085	2.08

Table 15.1

Waste disposal statistics
Source: Gate Gourmet AG, Zurich

for disposal", so that 51.9 per cent was actually recycled (see also case study 15.1).

The data above suggests that the weight of non-food waste produced per passenger has remained at between 0.26 to 0.30 kg throughout this period. A study by Gate Gourmet in the UK specifically looked at waste per passenger by stripping inbound waste off tray sets, separating it, and weighing it. Results are shown below in Fig. 15.3 for the investigation conducted at their LHR unit providing mainly short-haul meals.

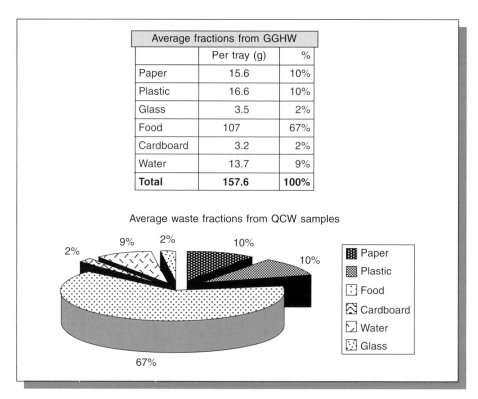

Average fractions from GGHW		
	Per tray (g)	%
Paper	15.6	10%
Plastic	16.6	10%
Glass	3.5	2%
Food	107	67%
Cardboard	3.2	2%
Water	13.7	9%
Total	**157.6**	**100%**

Average waste fractions from QCW samples

Figure 15.3
Waste statistics per passenger
SOURCE: Gate Gourmet, UK

This identifies that waste per passenger is lower, at around 0.16 kg per passenger. But two-thirds of this waste is food. The recyclable wastes identified in Table 5.1 make up only about 0.05 kg in total in this UK study.

The information presented above illustrates how difficult it is to collect data about flight waste. However, some general estimates are clear:

- The total amount of waste produced in a flight kitchen is large—roughly 0.5 tonnes per million meals
- Tray waste represents around one third of the waste produced in kitchens —roughly 0.2 tonnes per million meals
- Two thirds of tray waste is food
- Paper and card, glass and aluminium are the main types of non-food waste
- Over half of the total waste may now be recyclable

Waste-handling systems

Waste removed from trays may be carried to the waste-holding area by a number of different techniques, including bins, belt conveyors, screw conveyors, river or vacuum systems. These are described below.

Bins

Large-volume, wheeled bins are a convenient, low-capital option for moving general waste. Various systems are available from a number of manufacturers. Compactors located on the site can be used to make volumes manageable, and the bins interface with skips or hydraulic lift trucks. They are easy to handle and can cope with the output of a small to medium operation, but they are comparatively labour-intensive. Bins are often used in operations which have a waste-recycling policy. Sorting produces a number of comparatively low-volume waste categories, for which automated systems are not cost-effective except perhaps in the largest production units.

Trough conveyor

This term refers to a moving, easy-to-clean belt 800–1000 mm wide, running on lines of concave rollers, so that a dip, or trough, forms along its length. The central depression helps the waste to ride in the middle of the conveyor, increasing the carrying capacity and reducing spillage. Trough conveyors are a proven method of carrying waste. They can be cleaned easily and continuously by means of belt baths and scrapers. Trough conveyors are cost-effective for unsorted waste, and in large operations their use can be justified with comparatively small quantities of sorted materials. The length of each belt is limited by the load it carries and the gradient at which it operates, and this can limit this method's use.

Auger screw or ribbon screw conveyor

An auger or ribbon screw rotates inside a tube, drawing material up past it like a corkscrew. The viable length of such screws is even more limited than that of conveyors, but unlike belts they can lift materials up very steep gradients if required. Screw mechanisms are good for carrying liquids and soft, pliable materials, but they are not ideal for airline-catering waste. This is because bottles and cans, as well as escaped cutlery and crockery items, wear the stainless steel screws or cause them to flex and abrade the inside of the conveyor tube. This may also put damaging pressure on the screw bearings. Auger screw systems are satisfactory as long as the waste is well sorted by hand to remove hard materials, and major overhauls due to excessive wear are built into the maintenance programme.

River waste system

Waste rivers were incorporated into many of the large plants built in the 1970s and 1980s. A large volume of water circulates in a 'river' between the tray-cleaning operation and the waste-handling area. Crockery and cutlery are removed by hand from the trays, which are then cleared of waste food, paper, bottles, etc. by the torrent of circulating water.

At the waste extraction area the water passes through a rotating screen drum similar to those used at sewage works, which filters out all solid waste items and deposits them in a skip. River waste systems are effective and require comparatively little operating energy. A major disadvantage is the weight of the wet waste, which may be up to five times that of the dry material. This added water greatly increases the cost of incineration, because of the latent heat which must be supplied to drive it off before the waste will burn. Waste rivers are recirculated because it is not cost-effective to use clean water. They gradually dissolve more and more nutrients from the food waste and bacteria proliferate, eventually becoming a serious source of cross-contamination. Unless skips are watertight they will leak contaminated liquid onto floors and roadways.

Vacuum waste system

The most recent development in waste transport consists of a system of wide-bore vacuum lines, located in all parts of the operation. An outline diagram of a typical system is shown in Fig. 15.4. Tray waste is cleared by passing the hand-sorted trays under a vacuum hood, which removes all waste food as well as bottles, paper, etc. and carries them away for disposal. The on-line vacuum can also be used to dispose of kitchen waste from the food production area, and even for general vacuum cleaning of the whole unit, thus increasing its cost-effectiveness and convenience. Cans and cardboard are generally shredded before disposal. At the waste-handling area, the air is sucked into a cyclone, which removes solid materials by centrifugal force. They can then be sorted into waste categories, compacted and disposed of. Waste transported in this way is dry and comparatively inexpensive to transport and incinerate. Vacuum systems are capable of carrying waste throughout large plants and they can carry waste both horizontally and vertically, as required. Current systems may have several vacuum pipes which are used for different categories of waste, and microchip technology is used to control the flow of the different materials. However, vacuum waste disposal is currently in its infancy. More sophisticated means of separating waste for recycling, using less pipework but more efficient cyclones and separators will undoubtedly be developed.

Waste disposal

Solid waste and liquid effluent ultimately require treatment to disperse them back into the environment in a harmless form. Airlines are becoming increasingly sensitive of the need to minimise the environmental impact of their activities, but the waste produced by flight meal production and on-board airline service should be seen in the context of the total pollution loading. Spent fuel emission and noise pollution are more noticeable, and perhaps more serious problems. The general waste-disposal methods traditionally available to flight caterers are incineration, landfill and water treatment.

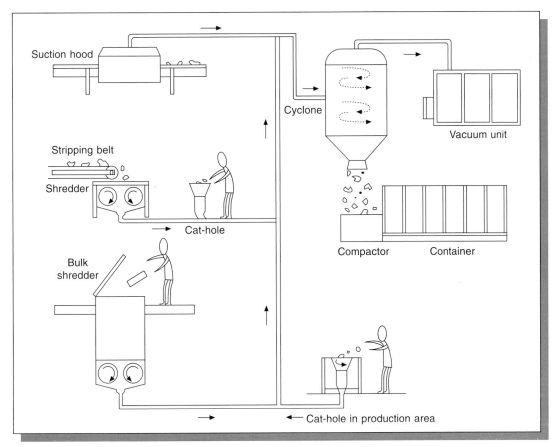

Figure 15.4
Typical large-scale vacuum waste-handling system

Incineration

The origin of much long-haul food waste makes incineration a necessity. Agricultural produce from distant countries is subject to quarantine restrictions, because it may infect local stock and produce pests and diseases. The only safe disposal method is incineration, which destroys living organisms, and converts the waste into carbon dioxide, water, and other harmless substances.

Incineration is expensive, because of the high water content of much of the organic waste. River disposal systems increase the water content, and hence the cost. Dry waste produces some heat during incineration, but heat is absorbed by water. To drive off each tonne of water requires at least 700 kWh of energy, and additional energy is required to maintain the high temperatures in order to convert the organic substances completely into harmless gases.

Gate Gourmet (UK) have identified three further factors against incineration:

- Public perception is not in favour of incineration. It is believed to be dirty, contributes to acid rain, releases PCBs and greenhouse gases, and affects the respiratory system

- Utilising waste to fuel energy facilities might reduce the impetus to seek alternatives for the waste stream such as reduction, reuse, and recycling
- BAA (British Airports Authority), a major stakeholder in the UK in-flight industry is opposed to the principle of incineration

If incineration is chosen as the disposal process for waste, then caterers must decide whether to contract to a municipal or community incinerator, or to build an on-site facility. The arguments for and against a municipal or on-site waste incinerator have been evaluated by Gate Gourmet (UK) as in Table 15.2.

Municipal waste incinerator		On-site waste incinerator	
For	**Against**	**For**	**Against**
No requirement for capital investment	Gate costs for the waste can fluctuate and will remain an ongoing cost to the operation	Energy surplus will convert waste disposal into a profit centre rather than a cost centre	Capital investment between £2–2.5 million per plant Ten-year-capital project needed: restriction of other environmental improvements
No requirement for planning permission	Transport of waste on public road	No transport of waste on public road, therefore meeting legislative requirements Guaranteed legislative compliance	Planning permission required
Management of the facility in the hands of a third party	Transporting of the waste to the site will still be required	Mitigation of road transport emission from daily movement of waste adding to GG green credentials	Plant-operation management skills not available within the current team Specialist or retraining required
Disposal of fly ash not required by GG	Energy recovery from the waste will not be directly available to GG	All energy recovered (after energy of activation) available for internal use (hot water or steam generation)	Disposal of fly ash: either to landfill or for road repair (material analysis of the fly ash required prior to final disposal)
To keep the facility in operation, minimum or maximum waste weights are required	No direct benefits for the units	Larger operating units can incinerate waste from smaller units extending the benefits to all sites	To maintain operational viability, minimum volumes of waste are required

Table 15.2

Comparison of Municipal versus On-Site waste Incinerator
Source: Gate Gourmet, UK)

However, operating an on-site incinerator is not without problems. The British Airways *Social and Environmental Report 2001* reported that "due to increased costs of incineration and pressure from local environmental groups on the (catering) site, the options for disposing of catering waste were reviewed." BA subsequently switched to using a registered landfill site.

Landfill

Landfill is an important means of disposal at many sites. Sorting of waste is not required, and the method can be used to reclaim quarry sites. For example, in the Thames basin, landfill is the preferred method for reclaiming exhausted road-gravel workings. In theory deeply buried waste is equivalent to quarantine and organisms will be destroyed during the decaying process. Landfill is relatively inexpensive, based on the cost of transport, site security, and subsequent landscaping.

However, there are a number of disadvantages. Friends of the Earth opposes landfill for 80 per cent of municipal solid waste that can be recycled or composted for the following reasons (FOE Briefing, 2002):

- It wastes valuable resources
- It exacerbates climate change because when materials are buried, more fossil fuel energy is used to replace the products through mining, manufacturing, and transportation around the world
- It produces methane, a potent greenhouse gas which contributes to climate change
- It creates water pollution through leaching
- It can lead to the contamination of land
- It gives rise to various nuisances including increased traffic, noise, odours, smoke, dust, litter and pests

Furthermore, in the UK the government has agreed targets of a reduction to 35 per cent of 1995 totals of biodegradable municipal waste going to landfill by the year 2014 with interim targets of 75 per cent of the total and 50 per cent of the total within 5 and 8 years respectively (DEFRA, Limiting Landfill, 1999). Cost for landfilling will rise significantly as the dual pressures from site reductions and increased landfill taxation, making landfill no longer the cheap disposal option.

Water treatment

Flight kitchens produce a considerable amount of wastewater from vegetable preparation, food residues, and cleaning operations. Dishwashers and waste river systems produce additional effluent. The water is often greater in volume and in organic content than public sewage facilities can handle, and most airports have their own water treatment plants. Effluent is typically passed through an anaerobic digester, where it is fermented by bacteria in the absence of air. This kills harmful micro-organisms and reduces the solids to a harmless, mild-odoured mulch which can be used as manure. The remaining liquid is usually then treated aerobically, by bubbling air passing through it so that a different population of bacteria grows, removing the last traces of nutrients. The water is then returned to the nearest river, although some European plants are currently exploring the idea of reusing it for washing or cleaning.

Recycling waste

Although much waste is currently disposed of, present efforts to recycle waste are likely to intensify. Companies can ill afford the publicity consequences of ignoring environmental issues, and the cost of waste disposal is climbing steadily, making recycling an increasingly economical proposition. Airline waste is usually generated in a highly mixed form, and needs to be sorted before any recycling is possible. Countries with a large, cheap unskilled labour force, such as India and parts of the Far East, tend to lack recycling facilities, so that although they can afford to sort the waste they are unable to use it profitably. However, they may distribute unopened individually packaged goods to the local populace. For instance, the Ambassador Sky Chef facilities at Mumbai and Delhi dispose of such items by donating them to charities, such as Mother Teresa's mission. Each charity is allocated one day of the week to come to the unit and sort items from the waste and no limitations are placed on what they may take. In some African countries, complimentary toiletries are also dispensed to the populace. Some airlines require cabin crews to sort waste on board, during flights. Specially adapted trolleys with compartmentalised compaction facilities are now available to assist this kind of development.

The categories of waste which may be recycled are steadily increasing. Most countries have facilities for glass, aluminium, steel and paper or card, but the quality of such services varies. For instance, recycled glass in the UK must not include aluminium bottle-tops, which react with silicates in the glass during remelting, causing impurities. In Switzerland, bottle tops are accepted by waste glass recycling operations. Switzerland and Germany currently lead the world in terms of waste recycling facilities. In 1993 waste at Zurich was sorted into eight different categories. Each of these requires a different specialist treatment, so that the flight service company has to set up disposal contracts with up to eight different specialists. The number of categories and the quantity of waste in each one tend to fluctuate from year to year. For instance, wood from packaging crates appeared in the 1991 audit, but was not recorded in 1992. Suppliers may change, and in addition the nature of packaging changes as flight caterers tend to purchase more pre-processed, pre-packaged foods.

The move towards waste recycling is driven by two forces. Growing public awareness of environmental issues implies that in eco-conscious countries customers are becoming sensitised to waste in all its forms: food, packaging, paper, and so on. Airlines are an easy target for environmental criticism, because they pollute in high-profile ways, such as urban noise, use of fossil fuels, global warming, and stratospheric pollution. Also, services such as flight catering increasingly make a feature of pampering customers with complimentary food and other goods. Many of these goods are individually packaged, frequently in heavy, quality-redolent materials such as glass. Thus, there is a cognitive dissonance between what conscientious customers feel they should receive and what they actually receive, in terms of potential environmental impact. Airlines, like other businesses, are subject to further pressures in the form of environmental standards such as BS 7750 and international awards such as those from the European Foundation for Quality Management (EQFM) in Brussels, which includes environmental and 'good neighbour' aspects with its other assessments of quality. Airlines are likely to lose important competitive advantage if they ignore environmental issues. Therefore, some companies are already seeking alternatives to flight service. SAS's gate buffet service on short-haul flights and BA's first-class overnight sleeper service are examples. The growing devolvement of catering services into independent companies marks airlines' desire not only to concentrate upon their core business, but also to shed peripheral pollution problems.

Besides influencing potential revenue, waste disposal affects costs. The cost of waste incineration is increasing sharply everywhere, due to a number of factors. As more people fly, waste levels increase sharply escalating the total demand for incineration. In addition airlines may try to out-do one another on service, increasing the amount of waste per meal. However, other developments such as the emergence and success of no-frills airlines and less service on short-haul flights may negate these factors. Nevertheless, fuel costs are also rising and at the same time clean air controls are becoming more stringent. Incineration technology thus has to improve in order to cope with the increasing volume and also to provide better conversion to non-pollutant gases. This usually requires higher temperatures and hence higher fuel input. The cost of incineration (which is always likely to be needed for quarantine waste) is expected to continue to rise. There is therefore an increasing interest in recycling as a means of cutting costs. Another likely growth area is the generation of heat and power from organic waste, by drying and pelleting it for use in specially adapted power stations. Recycling carries costs since it requires labour for sorting, and there may be a charge for recycling some categories of waste. Some airlines also transport sorted waste back from overseas destinations for recycling in the home country. Recycling will probably attract still higher premiums as the demand grows, but it is likely to establish itself as an alternative to other more general disposal techniques.

Compost organic waste[1]

"The process of composting is one of biological decomposition which degrades prutrescible organic material to leave a humus rich residue which is a valuable soil conditioner for both agricultural and horticultural applications" (Colebrand Waste Management, 2002). With the high proportion of organic material available in the flight waste, composting, both traditionally or by means of worm farming, would seem an immediate alternative to landfilling the waste. However, at present composting technology does not include sufficient heat treatment to guarantee the sterility of the waste as demanded by the 'processed' requirements of the Disease of Animals (Waste Food) Order 1973. Exceeding a temperature of 65°C will kill of the natural microbes (Trautmann et al., 2002) and worms if worm composting was chosen. Even *in-vitro* composting would not achieve

[1]This section and the next were written by Adrian Lee of Gate Gourmet as part of a report on alternative waste disposal alternatives and reproduced here with his permission.

the required temperature to satisfy the regulations, as explained below by John Wakefield, Director of Vital Earth Systems (specialist *in-vitro* composting company):

"The process itself is quite simple. Through the blending of waste streams we can achieve a carbon/nitrogen ratio of 30:1 and a moisture content compatible for the process. Our experience allows us to mix many different waste streams and still achieve a precise mix optimised to the In Vessel system. Mixing is carried out by a purpose built auger with integral scales and loaded into the digester by means of a conveyer. The process allows the temperature to rise to 55°C with the fans slowly increasing the airflow. This temperature is held for 2 days to ensure a uniform profile throughout the vessel. At this point the airflow is decreased to allow the temperature to rise to 65–70°C and is held at this temperature for 12 hours. This ensures the elimination of pathogens and weed seeds. Following this the temperature is reduced to 45°C for the remainder of the cycle. The achieved temperature profile is displayed and recorded in real time and data logged for future analysis. Great care is taken to comply with instructions from DEFRA on the composting of catering wastes. After 7 days the compost is removed from the digester and put through a secondary operation following screening. The compost is fed to worms in controlled conditions and the resultant worm cast is then passed to our sister company 'Vital Earth Vitaliser' for resale. This process takes a further 7 days after which the cycle is complete. Quality is ensured by regular independent analysis of the cast'.

All the organic products could be autoclaved prior to composting, thus ensuring the sterility, but would require the deliberate re-introduction of bacteria to the waste to aid the composting. Water and energy is also required and adds to the cost of composting.

Anaerobic digestion or fermentation (bio-gas)

"Anaerobic digestion is a biological process in which organic material is broken down by the action of micro-organisms (Fig. 15.5). Unlike composting, the process takes place in the absence of air. The residue remaining after digestion can be used as a soil conditioner and the process generates a gas which can be used as a fuel for domestic or industrial use" (Colebrand Waste Management, 2002). The fermentation of organic waste has been practised since the end of the 19th century. In the last decade, the tendency to segregate and compost organic household waste has increased but the disadvantages of composting has also become apparent. Therefore, people have started to think about fermenting organic kitchen waste as well. Today, two main fermentation processes can be distinguished, i.e. dry or wet fermentation. Wet fermentation is used for sewage sludge and due to the high water content, it is a less efficient process than dry fermentation, where a mixture from tree and grass cuttings and kitchen waste has proved itself.

The organic matter is deposited into a fermenting reactor, which provides the needed anaerobic conditions for fermentation. Methane-forming bacteria

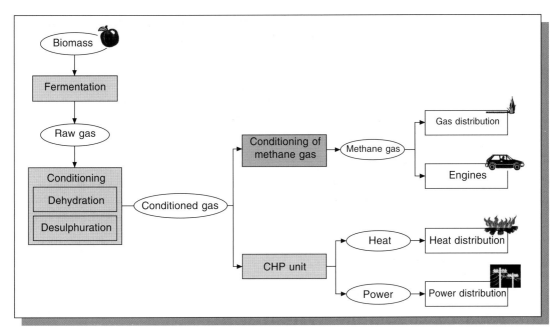

Figure 15.5
Flow diagram of a fermentation plant

decompose the organic matter best at anaerobic and humid conditions and at temperatures between 20 and 55°C. The residual time for organic waste in the fermentation tank is about 12 to 15 days (Energie Schweiz, 2001). After that time, about 0.9 m^3 fermentation gas per kg dry mass or 0.55 m^3 CH$_4$ per kg dry mass are produced. After the conditioning, which means de-sulphuring and dehydrating the raw fermentation gas, the gas can be fed into either the Combined Heat or Power (CHP) Unit or directly into generators. Pure and compressed CH$_4$ could also be directly fed into the natural gas distribution system. The residual organic waste is used as a soil conditioner and could possibly generate income.

During a fermentation process at temperatures above 60°C, pathogens should be sufficiently eliminated to meet food hygiene standards (Unternährer 1995). However, this temperature does not meet the required sterilisation temperatures required by legislation required in some countries (see below). Secondly, this higher thermophile process means a lower CH$_4$ proportion in the fermentation gas and as a consequence, less generated power per m^3 fermentation gas (Schulz and Eder, 2001). Both these issues could be surmounted with the inclusion within the bio-gas fermentation system an autoclave prior to the fermentation chamber to ensure the required sterility. With the autoclave *in situ*, the lower fermentation temperatures could be used.

Concerning current legislation, Article 4 of the recent EU Regulation 1774/ 2002 states that Category 1 waste of animal by-products (which includes catering waste from means of transport operating internationally) shall be:

(a) directly disposed of as waste by incineration in an incineration plant approved in accordance with Article 12: . . .

(d) in the case of catering waste referred to in paragraph 1(e), disposed of as waste by burial in a landfill approved under Directive 1999/31/EC;

However, Article 6 states that Category 3 waste which includes catering waste other than that from means of transport operating internationally (i.e. those emanating from flight production units) shall be:

(a) directly disposed of as waste by incineration in an incineration plant approved in accordance with Article 12: . . .

(f) transformed in a biogas plant or in a composting plant approved in accordance with Article 15;

Thus, at present, such alternative means of waste disposal can be utilised for waste generated in flight production units but not for the waste generated on board aircraft. However, paragraph 4 of Regulation 1774/2002 states:

"The Commission has given a commitment that by the end of the year 2004 a Directive on biowaste, including catering waste, will be prepared with the aim of establishing rules on safe use, recovery and recycling and disposal of this waste and of controlling contamination"

Therefore, alternative disposal techniques, such as composting, may be a permissible option for on-board waste in the not too distant future.

Case study 15.1

UK law and flight-catering waste[2]

The legal framework for disposal of waste material from international flights in the UK is outlined primarily in the Animal Health Act, 1981. Precisely, the Act states in paragraph 10 that:

"(1) The Ministers may by orders make such provision as they think fit for the purpose of preventing the introduction or spreading of disease into or within Great Britain through the importation of—

(a) animals and carcases;

(b) carcases of poultry and eggs; and

(c) other things, whether animate or inanimate, by or by means of which it appears to them that any disease might be carried or transmitted. . .

(2) Without prejudice to the generality or the powers conferred by this section and by section 1 above, for the purpose specified in subsection (1) above an order under this section—

(a) may prohibit or regulate the importation of any of the things specified in paragraphs (a) to (c) of subsection (1);

(b) may make provision not only with respect to imports (including vessels, boats, aircraft and vehicles of that descriptions), but

[2]This case is provided by Adrian Lee of Gate Gourmet UK

also with respect to persons, animals, and other things which have been or may have been in contact with imports; . . ."

(Animal Health Act 1981)

An order was issued (under the older legislation of the Disease of Animals Act 1950 and the Disease of Animals Act, 1975) and as yet has not been revoked. Under this Order, The Importation of Animal Products and Poultry Products Order 1980, specific duties regarding food from aircraft is specified.

"4. (1) Subject to paragraph (5) below, the landing in Great Britain of any animal product or poultry product from a place outside Great Britain is hereby prohibited except under the authority of a licence in writing issued by the appropriate Minister and in accordance with the conditions of that licence."

(The Importation of Animal Products and Poultry Products Order, 1980)

Therefore, if a product is landed, i.e. in the case of products from flight catering,

5. (1) Where any animal product or poultry product is landed in Great Britain in contravention of this order or of a licence . . . the person in charge of the animal product or poultry product require him, at the owners expense . . .
. . . (b) to destroy or otherwise dispose of the animal product or poultry product. . .

(The Importation of Animal Products and Poultry Products Order, 1980)

The legislation is further strengthened and made very much more precise regarding food waste from aircraft from an even older Order dating from 1973 (made under the previous legislation the Disease of Animals Act, 1950) and again not revoked. In this legislation precise prohibitions upon allowing food to be fed to animals is contained.

"4. Notwithstanding any provisions contained in article 3 of this order, no person shall in any circumstances feed or cause or permit to be fed to any animal or to any poultry or other birds any waste food removed from any ship, aircraft, hovercraft or road or other vehicle (being waste food which was or which originated from stores for the consumption of passengers, crew, animals, poultry or other birds carried on such ship, aircraft, hovercraft, road or other vehicle and imported into Great Britain) or any other waste food which has been in contact with imported waste food of the aforesaid description."

(The Disease of Animals (Waste Food) Order, 1973)

From the legislation it would seem that any food product or any material that came in contact with it (in flight catering this is considered to be all the material on a meal tray plus other materials such as newspapers that were placed in contact with the meal tray during the flight) must be destroyed or processed through an appropriate disposal system.

In terms of processing of the flight catering waste, again the law is very specific about the minimum amount of processing the waste can receive. Again, the Disease of Animals (Waste Food) Order 1973 defines this processing:

> "'processed' in relation to waste food means treated so that all of the waste food being treated was maintained for at least 60 minutes at a temperature of not less than 100°C (212°F). . ."
>
> (The Disease of Animals (Waste Food) Order, 1973)

Case study 15.2

SAS

SAS claim to take the environment into consideration in every decision they make (Lindegaard, 2001 in SAS, 2001). In 1997 alone they initiated 84 environmentally related projects (Anon, 1999). These projects, in combination with other initiatives "have a goal in part of reducing in-flight waste through work with it's major suppliers" (Anon, 1999).

The SAS environmental policy for in-flight operations places great demands on suppliers and this works in three main ways:

- All purchases are evaluated from an environmental standpoint
- Every major supplier is scrutinised with regards to its environmental policy and plan of action
- Environmental requirements are specified in existing and new supplier agreements (IFCA, 2001b [online])

These can be seen in practice with the Beijing Catering Co. developing an environmental policy and introducing environmental projects—including the recycling of cardboard boxes and aluminium waste—in order to meet the stringent environmental requirements of SAS (IFCA, 2001b [online]). SAS have also worked closely with their newspaper suppliers. Halvdanson (Director of Production at the Swedish daily *Expressen*) stated, "SAS contacted us early on and said that they wanted their suppliers to begin using more environmentally safe products" (Halvdanson in IFCA, 2001a [online]). Consequently, the paper has become the first major Swedish daily to receive permission to use the Nordic Council of Minister's official environmental seal of approval, the Swan (IFCA, 2001a [online]). This seal demands meeting a high number of environmental criteria that relate to the entire manufacturing process.

Regarding waste, SAS have introduced a number of initiatives to reduce the amount of waste stemming from on-board services. The biggest impact pertains to the introduction of a gate buffet program at three stations in Sweden, Karlstad, Kristianstad and Kiruna in 1996 (IFCA, 2001c [online]). Food service has been shifted to the ground with passengers able to compose their own meal or provided with a meal box at the gate. 'The advantages are the opportunity to offer a wider selection of food and beverages with greater freedom of choice for the passengers and reduced waste in the form of leftover goods (SAS in Anon, 1999). Trials at the three Swedish stations reported a reduction of waste of 40 per cent (IFCA, 2001c [online] and Anon, 1999).

Smaller projects have included the following:

- An agreement with six wine vendors to remove the sleeves on the neck of wine bottles, thus removing the plastic, aluminium and pewter alloys found in the sleeves (IFCA, 2001f [online] and Anon, 1999)
- The use of a pre-sorting trolleys on Norwegian flights in 1997, with an increase of aluminium collection of between 72 and 87 per cent. The service was then extended to Swedish routes where the collection of aluminium had fallen 10 per cent over the same period (Anon, 1999)
- Collaboration with Nestle in a project to develop a new type of environmentally safe coffee packaging that minimises the use of aluminium, plastics, paper, and boxes. The resulting packaging contain 12 per cent less aluminium and 34 per cent less PE plastic (IFCA, 2001d [online])
- In 1997, SAS recycled 150 tonnes of newspapers by asking passengers to carry off the newspapers they had read and place them in a special container by the exit (IFCA, 2001e [online]. This scheme was introduced on all domestic routes in Sweden and Norway in 1997

Case study 15.3

Oberoi Flight Kitchen, New Delhi

This flight kitchen was opened in 1980 and is located approximately three kilometres from Indira Gandhi International Airport. With a capacity of 5,000 meals a day it presently averages 4000 meals a day. Oberoi has long-standing contracts with a range of European, Middle-Eastern and Far-Eastern airlines like British Airways , KLM Royal Dutch Airlines, Thai Airways, etc. In addition, its latest contract is with the high profile domestic airline, Jet Airways. The unit employs 330 staff and is an ISO 9002 certified unit for Haccp by BSI, UK.

A feature of this operation is its very clear environmental management system. This includes:

- Published environmental policy (available on notice boards around the site)
- Clear responsibilities for activities and environmental issues
- Environmental committee meets regularly and points discussed are minuted
- Consumption of key energy resources such as light diesel oil (LDO), electricity units and fuel (cooking gas) are monitored on a daily basis by the Chief Engineer. The monitoring is done with the use of individual meters installed in each area which reflects the consumption each day and is recorded for comparison
- Each individual machine has been tagged with the consumption of electric units it consumes per running hour and the cost per running hour to increase awareness of the staff and the end user
- Staff are briefed on key issues/consumption patterns and encouraged to suggest ways of conserving energy
- Poster campaign on relevant environmental issues
- Company suggestion scheme covers environmental ideas

A number of recent initiatives have been taken to reduce the unit's environmental impact. These include:

- *Noise*—buildings and outlets associated with the back-up diesel generators have been acoustically treated to prevent noise nuisance
- *Atmospheric emissions*—height of the main chimney stack has been increased to meet new emissions regulations
- *Effluent discharges*—A new effluent treatment plant on site to treat water and allow recycling of the water for gardens and vehicle washing; the effluent is regulated and monitored regularly to ensure compliance

Key issues in waste and environmental management

There are a number of issues that are influencing airline and caterer's policies and actions in this area.

The **law** affecting the disposal and recycling of waste varies widely from one country to another. In most cases, there is no specific law in relation to flight waste, but only more general legislation. In some cases this may be legislation about waste, but often it may be contained in legislation concerned with other issues such as human or animal health. For example, the aforementioned EU Regulation 1774/2002 refers specifically to catering waste from transport operating internationally and distinguishes this from other catering waste. Case study 15.1 illustrates this by identifying the legislation in the UK that principally affects flight catering waste handling.

Apart from environmental issues, the main **quality concern** in the recycling process is the hygiene of rotable equipment. This is assured by frequently testing the wash water and the items emerging from washer tunnels. Two techniques may be used. Swabbing or contact agar plates may be used to obtain total viable counts (TVC) from surfaces and equipment, but a more recent development is the use of direct ATP monitoring. Adenosine triphosphate (ATP) is the energy 'currency' used by the cells of all living things, and is therefore a universal constituent of living and dead material, such as bacteria or food residues. ATP is the energy source which is used to generate the flash in a firefly's tail. This reaction, which involves a light-emitting substance called luciferin and a specific enzyme called luciferase, is the basis of ATP monitoring. A tiny flash is produced if luciferin and luciferase come into contact with any organic material containing ATP, and this flash can be detected using a sensitive light detector called a photomultiplier. Luciferin-lucife-rase-photomultiplier systems are sold by several distributors world-wide. British Airways in the UK use a system marketed by BioTrace International, which can detect bacterial populations instantly with the same accuracy as traditional methods, and can also detect food residues due to inefficient washing.

Other important considerations are the quality of the recycling/disposal process and of the waste material outputs. Process quality can be monitored by logging breakages. A steady increase in process quality and care has in fact been brought about by the increasing use of fragile items such as crockery and glassware, which are much more susceptible to rough handling and require sophisticated conveyor and washing technology. The quality of waste disposal outputs is usually the responsibility of the airport site-services contractor, rather than the flight caterer. Good management demands that regular checks be made on effluent from water treatments and on incinerator gases. Landfill site security must also be maintained.

In Western countries there is a trend towards completely **automating** the handling of waste and rotables, particularly in large operations. 'Power and free' transport and vacuum waste systems of the type discussed earlier in this chapter provide enormous economies of scale, and this contributes considerably to the overall cost-efficiency of the flight-catering process. As waste management costs rise, this may ultimately be enough to drive small companies out of business, particularly when large-scale, capital-intensive systems can automatically sort waste for recycling. Other productivity issues revolve around inventory management. Each airline has several types of crockery, cutlery and equipment, depending on the passenger class. Three-and-a-half sets are available for each aircraft, and both the number of craft and the number of different types of crockery are increasing. Current practices of dead-heading and inventory management are costly in terms of labour, equipment, and storage space, but represent large potential savings in process efficiency.

The effect of market forces in the early 1990s had been to sharpen the emphasis upon flight catering quality. Among other things, this meant increased use of rotables and therefore an increase in recycling requirements. This trend has been reversed since 2001. Following 9/11 metal cutlery has been replaced by plastic equipment for security reasons, and rotables have been replaced by disposables as scheduled airlines have cut costs. Increasingly, environmental considerations also affect the choice. For instance, "when SAS designs the tableware to be used on board, various environmental factors are considered. **Disposable** tableware made of paper and plastic weigh less than tableware made of porcelain, glass and utensils made of steel, but result in larger amounts of waste. Water and energy are required to wash non-disposable tableware, but are more pleasant to eat from. SAS has designed non-disposable tableware that weighs "as little as possible" (SAS, 2001).

The technology of recycling and waste management is also developing rapidly, and transport and waste management will probably be automated in most Western plants in the short to medium term. A key issue will be the sorting of waste, and as disposal costs increase this may include the use of organic waste (e.g. long-haul plate waste) for generating heat and power in installations.

It is clear that many airlines and caterers now acknowledge that **sustainability** is an issue. Most have policies in this area and management at a senior level with a commitment towards improving performance in this area. Jones et al. (2003) argue that the five main drivers for change towards sustainable development in an organisation are:

- the need for compliance with legislative and fiscal requirements
- opportunities for financial savings
- consumer attitudes and pressure
- public opinion
- enlightened senior management

A basic principle of sustainability is to *reduce*, reuse, and recycle. This chapter has tended to concentrate on reuse (rotables) and recycling waste, but has tended to ignore the notion of reduction. In fact, this option is the most environmentally friendly and cost efficient approach to this issue. In the past, airlines (and caterers) have tended to err on the side of caution by loading onto aircraft more than might be needed 'just in case'. This is not the case now.

Reducing what is put on board the aircraft not only reduces loading and off-loading costs and waste levels, but also the weight carried on board, which in return reduces the amount of fuel used and the pollution generated by the aircraft. British Airways' *Social and Environmental Report 2001* identified a number of recent initiatives of this kind, as follows:

- the number of china items used in First Class has been reduced by 20
- the number of magazines and childrens toys has been reduced
- the amount of ice carried on board was reduced
- the on-board catering and passenger number were more closely matched.

The report goes on to say, "This year we have significantly refined our catering product on domestic and short haul services and this should be reflected in a reduced volume of packaging consumed next year".

Conclusion

Flight catering produces an enormous amount of reusable crockery and cutlery as well as waste from uneaten food, and the packaging from many different types of individually portioned goods. The handling of these materials has been discussed in this chapter. Waste is also produced by food production processes in airport service operations. The huge volume of recycling, refurbishing, and waste disposal requires efficient stripping, transport, and washing procedures. In addition there must be separate storage areas for different categories of trolley. Transport of trolleys may be manual or automated. Some operations use an electronically controlled 'power and free' system to schedule the movement and storage of trolleys. Continuous movement of waste can be achieved in several ways, the most recent technique being online vacuum. Ware is cleaned by tunnel washers, which can be arranged in a number of ways depending on the throughput volume and the number of different categories of ware. Various aspects of waste management have been discussed in this chapter, including effluent treatment, disposal of solid waste by incineration, landfill, and recycling. The latter option is becoming increasingly desirable as disposal costs escalate and in the face of growing public interest in environmental issues. Quality issues of recycling include the testing of washed items for bacteria and food residues. The quality of the recycling process is increasingly important, particularly in terms of environmental impact, which affects company image and public relations. Automation of the recycling/waste disposal process will bring increasing economies of scale, as capital investment increases productivity and reduces the need for labour. This may result in the demise of small operations in favour of large centralised complexes. The demand for operational control may lead to the take-over by Western operations, of units in developing countries. In addition, changing attitudes to flight food service may lead to greater use of pre-flight meals and of alternative on-board services (for instance, electronics). The handling of rotables and waste is an important part of the flight catering process and its successful management may be vital to the cost structure of the business.

Key terms

Bins	Conveyor belts	Disposal	Incineration
Landfill	Legislation	Quality control	Recycling
Refurbishment	Waste	River waste system	
Sustainable		Vacuum waste system	
development		Water treatment	
Ware washing			

Discussion questions

1. Discuss the factors that are leading to flight caterers seeking alternative approaches to waste.
2. Identify the challenges to waste management in flight catering.
3. Discuss the pros and cons of disposal v. rotables in flight catering.
4. Identify the ways in which flight caterers can utilise reduction in their approach to waste management.

References

Anon. (1999) "SAS Report Shows more than 80 New Cabin Service Environmental Projects," *Pax International.* Mar./Apr., 42–44.

British Airways. (2001) *From the Ground Up: Social and Environmental Report 2001*, British Airways: London.

Colebrand Waste Management. (2002), *Incineration*, [online], Available from: http://www.colebrand.com/wastinc, [Accessed 03/05/02].

Colebrand Waste Management. (2002), *Anaerobic Digestion*, [online], Available from: http://www.colebrand.com/wasted [Accessed 03/05/02].

DEFRA. (1999) *Limiting Landfill: A consultation paper on limiting landfill to meet the EC landfill directive's targets for the landfill of biodegradable municipal waste*, [online], Available from: http://www.defra.gov.uk/environment/waste/strategy/landfill/1.htm.

EC. (2002) *Regulation (EC) No. 1774/2002 of the European Parliament and of the Council of 3 October 2002—Laying down health rules concerning animal by-products not intended for human consumption.*

Energie Schweiz. (2001) *Kompogasanlage Volketswil, gewerblich-industrielle Lösung*, [online], Available from: http://www.biomasseenergie.ch/inhaltdt.htm.

Friends of the Earth Briefings. (2002) *Waste Management Methods*, [online], Available from: http://www.foe.co.uk/pubsinfo/briefings.

IFCA. (2001a) 'A 'Greener' Newspaper,' [online], Available from: http://ifcanet.com/environment/useful-case-examples/useful-case-examples.html, [Accessed 23/04/01].

IFCA. (2001b) "Environmental Policy in Beijing," [online], Available from: http://ifcanet.com/environment/useful-case-examples/useful-case-examples.html, [Accessed 23/04/01].

IFCA. (2001c) "Food on the Ground," [online], Available from: http://ifcanet.com/environment/useful-case-examples/useful-case-examples.html, [Accessed 23/04/01].

IFCA. (2001d) "New Generation of Packaging," [online], Available from: http://

ifcanet.com/environment/useful-case-examples/useful-case-examples.html, [Accessed 23/04/01].

IFCA. (2001e) "Recycling Newspapers," [online], Available from: http://ifcanet.com/environment/useful-case-examples/useful-case-examples.html, [Accessed 23/04/01].

IFCA. (2001f) "Sleeveless Wine Bottles," [online], Available from: http://ifcanet.com/environment/useful-case-examples/useful-case-examples.html, [Accessed 23/04/01].

Johns N. and Edwards J.S. (1994), *Operations Management: a resource-based approach for the hospitality industry,* Cassell: London, 1–3.

Kirk D. (1994) "Hard and Soft Systems: a common paradigm for operational management, "*International Journal of Hospitality,* Regional Forum: New visions of hospitality operational management, Danbury Park Conference Centre, Colchester, UK, 23–28.

Momberger, M. and Momberger, K. (2002) "Aviation Catering News," *Momberger Airport Information,* 25 Apr.

SAS. (2001) *Fly with a clear environmental conscience!,* SAS: Stockholm.

Schulz, H. and Eder, B. (2001) *Biogas-Praxis, Grundlagen, Plnung, Anlagenbau, Beispiele,* Okobuch: Staufen bei Freiburg.

BROOKLANDS COLLEGE LIBRARY
WEYBRIDGE, SURREY KT13 8TT

Innovation in flight catering

Learning objectives

- Explain what is meant by innovation
- Compare and contrast new product and new service development
- Understand how suppliers, caterers and airlines go about innovation
- Identify the factors affecting in-flight innovation
- Understand the role of the Mercury Awards in promoting industry innovation

Introduction

This chapter reviews the nature of innovation in the flight catering industry. Innovation is explained and new product/service development is explored, before going on to describe the processes followed by airlines, flight caterers, and suppliers when they develop new products and services. It also examines how ideas are disseminated and discussed between these three parties. What emerges is a complex picture. Airlines adopt a process for innovation based largely around new service development, whereas caterers and suppliers adopt a new product development approach. In addition, suppliers in particular have to work largely in the dark as to what the airlines may be planning, as the lead time for developing new products can be longer than the time horizons of the airlines.

New products and services

New products and services have always been an important element of competitive strategy in the airline industry. In continental North America, strong competition and deregulation have resulted in a process of almost continual innovation. This has also become more significant for European and Asian carriers, particularly in the 1990s and early 2000s. After half a century of continuous growth, passenger volumes fell significantly in 1990, and over half of the 50 largest international airlines recorded losses. The immediate cause of these difficulties was the Gulf War. By the mid- and late 1990s the worst effects of this had passed, only for the tragic events of 9/11 to send the industry into yet another downturn. In 2003, at the time of writing, the industry continues to face a number of long-term challenges including the consequences of terrorism and the effects on worldwide travel, as well as significant changes in the dynamics of the flight-catering industry. All this has made it imperative for the all firms connected with the industry to develop a bolder, more innovative approach to flight catering and service, in an attempt to cut costs while maintaining quality. Many instances of such innovation have already been cited in previous chapters. For instance, tray lay-up may be revolutionised by the introduction of robotics (Chapter 7); inventory management can be computerised by the adoption of bar coding (Chapter 6); and aircraft loading can be assisted by adding sensors to high-lift trucks (Chapter 10). Another example of a major innovation includes airlines that have developed a quality cold-food concept for short-haul flights in their attempt to balance customer needs with cost reductions. SAS and Northwest Airlines have introduced a no-frills concept for short flights, consisting of pre-departure gate buffets, restricting on-board service to tea and coffee, with estimated cost reductions as high as 35 per cent. It seems certain that an innovative approach to flight catering will continue to be a prerequisite for survival in an increasingly competitive industry. Udo Luerssen (who currently holds a leading position at Aramark) has said that each airline must 'possess the creativity and courage to offer differential —something that stands you apart from your competitors".

Research into flight catering innovation confirms that most innovations are modifications to existing products or services as opposed to completely new, 'original' innovations. As in other industries, the level of innovation is greatest in larger companies and somewhat limited for smaller ones. With regards to flight catering in particular, it is the airlines that are the most systematic in their innovating processes due to their size. They are the companies most likely to have specialist research and development (R&D) departments. On the other hand, smaller companies owned or managed by highly creative entrepreneurs may also be highly innovative, although they may be less formal in their approach to the innovation process. The airlines are closest to the end user (the flying passenger) and as a consequence are more likely to innovate in 'service' (process). Suppliers and caterers tend to focus on 'product' and systems innovation. The chapter concludes that the continued need to cut costs while improving quality, combined with the constant need to differentiate, will require an ever-increasing level of inventiveness by the industry as a whole. Current trends suggest that caterers and suppliers will follow the lead of the airlines and recognise the need for a more systematic approach to innovation and enter more partnerships and joint ventures to introduce new ideas into the industry.

The nature of innovation

Definition

Much has been written about innovation and it is regarded as an essential element in sustaining strategic competitive advantage. Management gurus such as Tom Peters and Rosabeth Moss-Kanter firmly believe that constant innovation is of fundamental importance to a company's survival. Definitions are numerous, but the following are widely accepted:

- Innovation is the commercialisation of invention
- Innovation refers to the process of bringing any new, problem-solving idea into use
- The process of taking an invention forward into its first marketable form

The flight catering industry tends to focus on the problem-solving element of innovation. One major supplier to the industry believes that it is all about 'recognising problem solutions'. Many innovative ideas introduced into the industry have been very simple and solved problems that sometimes even the airlines did not realise existed. A good example of this is the development by a supplier of tray-size wine bottles that are flat on one side. The previous bottles were shaped like all wine bottles are, so when placed on their side to fit on a tray in a trolley, they rolled around.

The International Flight Catering Association (IFCA) annually sponsors the Mercury Awards, which provides a benchmark against which suppliers, caterers, and airlines world-wide are judged as to their innovativeness. The definition of innovation issued by IFCA, as the criteria to be met by the companies, is:

"The recent introduction or use of a product or service which produces an improved service to the passenger. It will demonstrate change, freshness, newness and will be modern and contemporary. Real progress in the context of the entrant will be achieved. The entry does not need to be unique."

Characteristics

There are a number of ways in which innovation can be categorised. In essence, there are three types—product, process, and systems. Each of these three types can range from being highly tangible to highly intangible. *Product innovations* are changes made to whatever it is that the customer purchases. For tangible products this means literally some kind of artefact; but intangible products are in effect services. With regards to the airline experience, it is a bundle of both tangible elements—the aircraft type, seat type, meal, etc.—and intangible elements—service level, speed of service, on-time delivery, etc. *Process innovation* refers to the way in which the product is made or delivered. For tangible products this kind of innovation may involve the introduction of a new technology that makes the artefact to a more consistent quality and/or at a lower cost. For services, process innovation may also involve a new technology but also redesigning the process flow to improve quality or reduce costs. Finally, *systems innovation* involves modifying the context in which processes are carried out. A high profile systems innovation is the adoption of a total quality management (TQM) strategy.

Although a firm may make changes to products, processes or the organisation that are for that firm 'innovative', it is not necessarily the case that they are original. Many firms apply ideas developed within one division of the company, or adapt ideas from other firms, or directly copy competitor practice. There has been a considerable amount of research carried out into new product development, the majority of which is based on manufacturing industries. The Booz, Allen & Hamilton (1982) studies made a distinction between products that are 'new to the company' and those which are 'new to the world'. They found that 90 per cent of 'new' products fell into the former category. What respondent companies considered as 'innovations' were in fact usually rather modest product improvements, cost reductions, product-line extensions, repositioning or repackaging of products, or the introduction of a new product line. They were often important and potentially profitable, but hardly radical innovations. Only 10 per cent of new products fell into the 'new to the world' category. These were major new products, new methods of delivering older products, new markets, or new ways of doing business. While this minority of innovations are what the general public think of as new products, most companies are much less ambitious in their definitions. Another study by Wan and Jones (1993), related to the UK fast food industry, suggests that nearly all innovation was as a result of copying other firms, rather than based on any formal, internal R&D from which original innovations were implemented.

The level of originality of innovation that a company develops may reflect their size, particularly in financial terms, since 'new to the world' innovations generally take years to develop. Even a consumer product that requires little R&D work would be expected to take approximately 18 months from the start of the developmental work to introduction. It is perhaps not surprising that so little innovation is original, especially in service firms. There are considerable costs attached to R&D work and the introduction of any new product or service is ultimately a risk. Service innovation has a potentially higher level of risk than product innovation. Services are largely intangible, produced and consumed simultaneously, heterogeneous and perishable. Services are not easily patentable, and although innovators may benefit from the launch of new services, companies who adopt them early enough may receive a disproportionate amount of benefit without having had any of the R&D costs. The late adopters (or majority) and the laggards usually do not have much to gain but may be forced to adopt in order to survive.

Innovation in manufacturing and service firms

There are well-established models of how manufacturing firms go about new product development. More recently, innovation in service firms has also been considered. Scheuing and Johnson (1989) proposed a model for new service development based on work in financial institutions. The approach to new product development is compared with that to new service development in Table 16.1. The sequence of activities in the proposed model goes beyond existing models on new product development to describe the interplay between the design and the testing functions during the development of a new service. At the start of the new service development process, management must chart the course of this effort and give it clear direction.

New product development*	New service development[†]
Strategy development	Objectives and strategy
Idea generation	Idea generation
Screening and evaluation	Idea screening
	Concept development
	Concept testing
Business analysis	Business analysis
Development	Service design and testing
Training	Process and system design and testing
	Marketing programme design and testing
	Personnel training
	Service testing
Commercialisation	Test marketing
	Launch
	Post-launch review

Table 16.1

Comparison of new product and new service development
SOURCES: *Booz, Allen & Hamilton (1982), [†]Secheuing and Johnson (1989)

The first part of both models focuses on how new ideas are generated and developed (steps 1 to 3 for new service development). Scheuing and Johnson (1989) recommended that the process must begin with a precise formulation of the objectives and strategy concerning the effort, "a well designed new service strategy drives and directs the entire service innovation effort and embues it with effectiveness and efficiency". Idea generation should draw on external sources for inspiration, e.g. suppliers and competitors, or internal consultation and brainstorming can add to the idea pool. It appears to be increasingly the case that airlines in particular are working much more closely with suppliers in order to innovate. Feasibility and profitability are often key considerations at the idea screening point, but this primarily judgemental activity should be handled carefully so as not to reject unusual ideas out of hand.

The idea formulation stage is followed by the design stage. For new product development this involves three stages, whereas for new service development greater consultation with employees, human resources, and marketing results in an eight-stage process. In the concept development stage, the surviving ideas are expanded into fully fledged concepts. Such development should normally be in conjunction with the company's own customer contact personnel, since it is these front-line staff who are an invaluable source of knowledge regarding customer needs and wants. A typical concept statement would include a description of the problem, the reasons why the new service is to be offered, an outline of its features and benefits and the rationale for its continued development and/or purchase. The next stage in the development process, the concept test, is a research technique designed to evaluate whether a prospective user understands the idea of the proposed service, reacts favourably to it and feels it offers benefits that answer unmet needs. Business analysis should represent a comprehensive investigation into the business implications of each concept. This should include a complete market assessment and the drafting of a budget for the development and introduction of each proposed new service. The project authorisation step occurs when top management commits corporate resources to the implementation of a new service idea. Next is the conversion of the new service concept into an operational entity. This requires service design and testing, an activity that should involve both the input of prospective users and the active cooperation of the operations personnel who will ultimately be delivering it. This stage should also cover the design and delivery of the process and system, since the delivery mechanism is very much part of the service itself. The introductory marketing programme should be formulated and tested in conjunction with prospective users. To complete the design phase of the process all employees should be familiarised with the nature and operational details of the new service (personnel testing).

The evaluation of a new product is largely carried out through market trials. For services trialing is slightly more involved (steps 12 to 15). Service testing should be used to determine potential customers' acceptance of the new service, while a pilot run ensures its smooth functioning. Test marketing examines the saleability of the new service and a field test should be carried out with a limited sample of customers, e.g. a specific route for an airline. With the delivery system and marketing in place and thoroughly tested, the company should next initiate the full-scale launch, introducing it to its entire market area. The final step, the post-launch review, should be aimed at determining whether the new service objectives were achieved or whether adjustments are needed.

Innovation in flight catering

It is these models of new product and new service development that form the basis for discussing how the flight catering industry carries out innovation. Two major studies of flight catering innovation have been carried out. Peirce

(1994) conducted a survey of 300 firms in the industry with a 40 per cent response rate. The respondents accurately reflected the three main constituent sectors of the industry—food manufacturers/suppliers, flight caterers, and airlines. Jones and Bertorello (2001) conducted face-to-face interviews with respondents from 38 different firms within the flight catering sector, from a range of countries including the UK, Germany, USA, Singapore, and Australia. The companies range from small entrepreneurial businesses up to global companies such as Mars, Qantas, and British Airways. The results of both studies are consistent with the findings of other similar surveys in other industries.

In the Peirce (1994) study, all the companies were asked if they had specific long-term objectives or strategies that involved developing new products or services. The majority of companies claimed to have specific company objectives that mention innovating new products and/or services. However, when asked whether their company had developed a new product or service in the past 12 months, very few were able to identify a specific example of such innovation. Only a small number of companies, around 10 per cent, have a specific department responsible for R&D. Of those firms that have such departments, these tend to be either food manufacturing companies or large airlines. The department most likely to generate new ideas was the sales and marketing department of firms. In the majority of firms, however, ideas were generated in an ad hoc way, either from listening and talking to customers, or the brainwave of an individual. This was especially true of all of the smaller firms surveyed. When asked what the most powerful idea sources are for companies, suppliers maintained it was customer feedback. Both airlines and caterers recognised this as important, but in combination with problem solving, i.e. advantageous modifications to existing products. A somewhat surprising 25 per cent of companies did not actively encourage staff to put forward innovative ideas— but of those that did, 30 per cent claimed that the general company culture promoted the idea of staff contributions through meetings.

With regards to the detailed design of the innovation, most companies chose to carry out concept testing through discussions with customer-contact personnel. New ideas were only formally screened/evaluated in terms of feasibility and profitability by 61 per cent of companies. In the case of most small companies, there was little or no formal business analysis. The number of small companies in the industry also helps to explain why 90 per cent of companies responding stated that one person/or department in the company authorized all innovative projects. The majority said this was usually the managing director or the 'committee leader'. The ad hoc way in which new ideas are generated is also reflected in how funding is agreed for projects. Research for new services/ products is also funded on an ad hoc basis by just over half of the firms surveyed. All three sectors found it difficult to identify the number of people specifically involved with innovation development, claiming that it depended on the product or service under development.

All firms agreed that operations personnel need to be involved in testing innovations. But there were some differences between sectors about the need to support innovations with marketing support and personnel training. Suppliers claimed that the products/services they developed required marketing programmes, whereas caterers and airlines were less likely to develop a marketing programme in support of the innovation. On the other hand, the opposite trend appeared when the different sectors were asked if their innovations required the training of personnel—91 per cent of airlines claimed they did, 87 per cent of caterers with only 68 per cent of suppliers.

Once developed, nearly all companies claimed to carry out 'pilot runs' to test new products/services. At the testing/development stage, the caterers and suppliers tended to rely on internal experience and/or satisfy legal requirements. Only the airlines carried out physical trials as part of the development process.

The sectors tend to evaluate new services/products once on the market in slightly different ways. The majority of airlines use market surveys, whereas caterers and suppliers both rely more on after-sales for feedback. All companies claimed to monitor customer satisfaction on a constant basis.

With regards to the type of innovation being carried out, all three sectors tend to think about innovation as product innovation. Food manufacturers and suppliers tend to think in terms of changing a food or drink item in such a way as to make it better meet the needs of the flight caterer and/or airline. The small- to medium-size suppliers do not have the financial or human resources needed to support large-scale process or organisational innovation. On the other hand, the larger suppliers may well be engaging in this kind of innovation, but across the whole of their organisation; therefore not identifying it as an innovation related solely to the flight catering segment of their activity. Flight catering firms also tend to think in terms of modifying the product, although there is some evidence to show that process innovation has been occurring in some cases. It is also likely that organisational innovation has been occurring, although the caterers do not think of it as such. This is because many such firms are instituting new approaches to quality management, especially BS 5750 in the UK or ISO 9000 in other parts of Europe. The airlines also tend to think in terms of the product/service bundle. From the survey results, each sector of the industry thought it was the most innovative with regard to the flight catering industry. For instance, one caterer responded:

> "Innovation through the caterer has its limitations due to the strict service and menu concepts of the airlines. The airlines should utilise the know-how of the caterers more. The experience of a large caterer with many clients gives a much broader basis for knowledge transfer than an individual airline can realise focused on its own requirements."

Likewise a supplier stated, "because of the narrower base, suppliers seem to be more focused on innovation".

Finally, with regards to the level of originality of innovation, there was little evidence of a major R&D activity producing highly original products, processes, or organisational forms. Many of the individual innovations cited in the research and reviewed from the IFCA annual Mercury Awards demonstrate that firms tend to adapt or adopt ideas from other firms, either within the industry or from other related industries. In the next section we shall look at some specific examples of flight innovation in the 1990s.

The Jones and Bertorello (2001) study of flight catering innovation adopted an interview approach which allows for a more detailed picture of innovation to emerge. The 38 firms varied in size from six employees up to several thousand employees. Twenty four per cent had fewer than 50 employees, 24 per cent were medium sized enterprises (50 to 1000 employees), and 52 per cent had more than 1000 employees. There was a fairly equal split between airlines (38 per cent), caterers (32 per cent) and suppliers (30 per cent). The majority of respondents (80 per cent) were male and two-thirds were employed in the operations or marketing function. Typical job titles of respondents were Managing Director, Flight Service Director, and Account Manager. The type of innovation was also almost equally split between food product (36 per cent), non-food product (32 per cent) and service (32 per cent). Examples of the innovations presented for an award were an oxygenated spring water, a multi-function plug for disposable earphones, a hot beverage trolley producing boiling water without electricity, and a new style first-class cabin.

Sixty per cent of the respondents were aware of their company having a mission statement, but many of these were vague as to precisely what it was. Of those that had such a statement only a quarter believe this to make explicit reference to innovation. However, most respondents were clear that their firm did have *objectives and a strategy* in relation to innovation, even if it was not in the mission. As one said, "There is no explicit reference to innovation . . . [but] to be the undisputed world leader in the travel market [means] a high degree of innovation must take place . . . ." Another said, "[Our mission statement says] providing superior solutions to the food service operator . . . [which] has something to do with being innovative I think."

With regards to *organisational structure*, respondents were asked if their firms had an R&D department. Only 20 per cent had such a department, of which the majority were large firms. In some cases the R&D department was technically based either with respect to engineering or food production, in other cases it was market research based reporting to the Sales or Marketing Director of the company. It was very clear that nearly all the companies, except for the very smallest, saw innovation as a team effort. This was always the case amongst the airlines in the sample. In terms of those with specific responsibility, the Managing Director of the firm played an important role for six out of the eleven caterers, whereas a key role was played by the flight service or catering department amongst the airlines. Chefs contributed to innovation in only five cases and ergonomic designers to only two.

Since all respondents were from firms that had innovated, all had experienced the *idea generation stage*. The most common form of this was though internal consultation and brainstorming, often stimulated by customer feedback. One caterer reported, "We have a weekly forum where everybody gets together to talk." In five instances, the innovation resulted from the "inspiration of a single individual." One equipment manufacturer stated, "I got the idea from a flight attendant." In most cases such inspiration was in small firms. Some respondents mentioned that trade shows or travelling led to the idea. One representative from an airline said, "We go to trade shows [or] see some nice things in a restaurant and think maybe we can adopt this to our business." Only one cited a supplier as providing the original idea.

Just over half (54 per cent) of the respondents identified some form of *idea screening*. The most common approaches to such consultation were with other people within the relevant division or department of the firm and/or with customers. In some cases, the factors taken into account were technical feasibility, practicality, time span and cost. For example, an executive from an airline said, "Each idea is evaluated for its effectiveness—cost, practicality, what regulatory approvals are needed. They go through a series of steps." However, the nature of the innovation may affect this screening process even within the same firm. Another airline executive identified that "It depends on the scale of and scope of the ideas. When you talk about a complete new service it's different from a product item . . . . For a large impact idea we go back to the customer and use our frequent flyers as a consumer panel. When it's a smaller idea . . . we try it out, introduce it for half a year and see if it's OK."

As the example above illustrates, *concept development and testing* may be carried out on an ad hoc basis. Two-thirds of the respondents reported that prior to development, their innovation was externally reviewed in some way. In nearly every case, such review was conducted by customers. An American airline manager stated, "We work closely with a consumer advocacy group. They are invited at all stages to give their views." In a very small number of cases, the concept was considered by suppliers and by technical experts. But some firms are reluctant to broaden consultation too widely—"if ideas were to leak out, our competitors would find out about them. A good idea can be easily copied" (airline representative) and "it was kept pretty quiet. I didn't talk to anyone until it was patented" (equipment manufacturer).

Most firms, 70 per cent, included some form of *business analysis* in their innovation process. This was usually in the form of a financial appraisal that identified some degree of payback on investment. Sixty per cent had to have project authorisation for the innovation to proceed. In small enterprises, this was often not necessary as the person carrying out the innovation was also the owner of the company. In larger firms, approval was often at board level (for major innovations) or at senior executive level, such as Vice President Foodservice Division or Marketing Director. Once approval has been given for the project to go ahead, the innovation process can vary quite widely both in terms of length of time and complexity. One airline's innovation "took a couple of months", while another's "took a long time—about two years from idea to implementation". This reflects very much the wide range of different innovations that were included in the sample.

In most cases (62 per cent), firms recognised that *training of personnel* was required. This applied especially to service and process innovations, but even product innovations may have required shop floor employees to be retrained. In very few cases (15 per cent) was a marketing programme developed in conjunction with the innovation. This is probably because so much of what was done was on a business-to-business basis rather than directly aimed at consumers. The low importance of marketing effort in relation to the innovation, also meant there was very little *test marketing*. However a very high proportion of firms (82 per cent) engaged in *product testing* the innovation. One airline "did some flight tests with the prototype"; another reported that "there was a trial period". For some products the testing was not done with flight caterers or airlines. One drinks manufacturer said that "testing took place in a London hospital"; a wine shipper "gave samples to customers in supermarkets"; and a food manufacturer has "a panel of twelve people who taste it on a score chart".

Firms adopted a wide variety of approaches to the *launch* of the new product, service or process. Some launched it with a press release, others ran an advertisement, yet others exhibited at trade shows. The IFCA trade show was specifically mentioned by 18 per cent of the respondents. However, in some cases the launch was very low key. One charter airline said, "There was nothing big." *Post launch review* for most firms seems to take place immediately, although it is not at all clear how systematic such review is. In effect, most review is not specific to the innovation but wrapped up in routine customer feedback. As one airline said, "it comes though from customer comments"; another stated, "we get feedback from the people on the ground, cabin staff and customers too."

The findings of the Jones and Bertorello (1989) study suggest there is a wide variety of practice with regards to innovation, supporting Jones' (1996) view that innovation is contingent. Few firms had explicit statements about innovation in their mission nor dedicated R&D departments. Those that did tended to be larger firms from across all types of firm—food suppliers, equipment suppliers, caterers, and airlines. However most firms used a variety of means of generating new ideas, in particular using customer feedback, staff feedback, brainstorming and other meetings to come up with new ideas. Individual 'inspiration' was relatively rare, and almost always in the smaller firms.

Idea screening is almost exclusively restricted to discussion in house or with customers, often through focus groups. Concept development and testing is typically carried out on an ad hoc basis, and also with customers. There is a real concern that ideas may be copied by competitors if they are discussed too openly. The most formal stage of the whole process, and common to most medium and large firms, is in relation to conducting some form of business appraisal of the innovation, along with having the project authorised formally by senior executives of the company.

Most innovation involves some training of personnel, but very little related to marketing. The latter is probably due to the nature of flight innovation, which is very much on a business-to-business basis. Nearly all innovative products, services or processes were trailed or tested before fully operationalised. In some cases such testing was out of the flight industry.

The new products, service, and processes examined in this study were launched in a wide variety of ways, with a review of their success being incorporated into routine customer feedback. There was very little specific review of the innovation process itself.

An analysis of the innovation process by type of firm—airline, caterer, or supplier—reveals no distinctive pattern. This is because although suppliers tended to be involved in product innovation, and airlines tended to report on service innovation, there was a fair amount of overlap between them. However, a pattern of innovation does emerge when the process is analysed by type—food, non-food product, or service. This is illustrated in Table 16.2.

It emerges that food products appear to go through an extremely abbreviated innovation process, without even the launch phase being included in the majority of cases. This is likely due to the fact that many food products have already been developed for other markets; what was innovative about them was their use in flight catering for the first time. The non-food innovation process is very close to the typical model of innovation described in the innovation literature.

Food	Non-food	Service
	Structure	
	Idea screening	Idea screening
Concept development	Concept development	
Business analysis	Business analysis	Business analysis
	Project authorisation	Project authorisation
	Personnel training	Personnel training
Product trialing	Product trialing	Service testing
	Launch	Launch
Customer feedback	Customer feedback	Customer feedback

Table 16.2
Stages in the Innovation Process by Type of Innovation

However, there is no evidence from this study that the service process is any more complex than that of products, contrary to what is proposed in the literature. The only three activities which are common to all types of innovation are business analysis, trialing/testing, and using customer feedback to evaluate the success of the innovation.

Case study 16.1

IFCA Mercury Awards

One way to examine the type and level of originality of innovation in flight catering is to examine the industry's own showcase for innovation, IFCA's Mercury Awards. This annual competition invited suppliers, caterers and airlines in 2001 to submit entries in five categories.

Category 1   Inflight service: an inflight service containing a food or beverage element
Category 2   Inflight meal product: a food or non-alcoholic beverage component
Category 3   Inflight service: non-food product or component of inflight service
Category 4   Equipment for inflight service and airline catering
Category 5   Systems or process

In 2002, the majority of entries were consistent with the Booz, Allen & Hamilton studies, not 'new to the world', but modifications of existing products. For example, drawing on the Mercury Awards it is possible to give some specific examples of the type of innovation the industry is engaged in. One good example of a tangible, product innovation was Pro-tek's disposable gloves. These polyethylene gloves create a micro atmosphere environment that kills harmful bacteria, such as e-coli, salmonella, and staphylococcus. They are also recyclable.

An example of an intangible product innovation or service innovation is the 2002 winner of the Mercury Award for skills development—Air CPU of Spain. Their citation reads, "Airline companies used to approach our Company with fixed ideas of meals they required for their passengers. However, there were comments that we could offer more innovation. We decided to take advantage of our own in-house skills and creativity to launch an internal competition to obtain new ideas for Breakfasts and Hot Meals, at the same time giving the opportunity to our own staff to reveal their creativity and culinary skills. This competition was open to any member of staff throughout Spain wishing to participate."

As the research has identified, process innovation is less common than product innovation in the industry, partly because of the high capital cost of introducing new process technology or systems. The winners of Mercury Awards in 2002 reflect this diversity.

Trends in the innovation process

Having considered the output of the innovation process, this section reviews the ways in which innovation is being developed and fostered within the flight catering industry. Two major developments are impacting on innovation. One is the extent that either forward or backward integration is taking place, and the second is the growth of joint ventures and other forms of partnership between firms.

As Chapter 2 explained, there are basically three links in the flight catering supply chain: manufacturer/supplier—caterer—airline. In the past, airlines have backwardly integrated to operate their own catering kitchens. This is no longer the trend. In the 1990s it was much more likely for airlines to contract out the catering function. So, for instance, a number of airlines set up separate companies to operate production units, such as Lufthansa's LSG Sky Chef and Swissair's Gate Gourmet business. At the same time food manufacturers and/or suppliers are forwardly integrating into the catering operations. So some suppliers also engage in tray lay-up and preparation. Such **integration** means that it is much more likely for suppliers to have to think about the service implications of new products than they may have to have done in the past. The second trend towards partnerships and joint ventures reflects the fact that innovation may often require capital investment and necessitate sufficient economies of scale to keep unit costs down to an acceptable level. For small-scale suppliers and caterers, effective linkages with either manufacturers and caterers is one way in which to generate the funds needed to support a new idea, as well as to ensure they sell at sufficient volume to keep costs down. For instance, one supplier developed the muffin as a product for use in airline meals by adapting the product significantly to the typical portion size. This involved collaboration with both the manufacturer of the muffin mix to assist with the production process development and with a catering company to assist with the promotion of the product to the airlines. In 1991 no airline in the world served muffins; by 1994 the innovative supplier was producing 15 000 per day.

In addition to formal links and partnerships, firms in the industry are also using more conventional ways to develop and promote new ideas. The **trade show** is a classic example of this. World-wide, there are two major trade shows each year. For instance, the IFCA trade show typically has over 150 companies exhibiting their products (as illustrated in Fig. 16.1). In addition, some companies have developed their own exclusive 'trade show' to which they invite their

Figure 16.1
IFCA Trade Show 2003

customers and potential customers. For instance, Pourshins PLC, a flight supplier based at London Heathrow, held for a number of years a 'menu development workshop' for a three-day period in which specially invited guests participated.

The interaction generated by trade shows and workshops is obviously a major **source of new ideas** and stimulates creative thinking. Other sources of information are the trade press, association newsletters and subscription services, such as Momberger Airport Information Service. The IFCA Mercury Awards also serve as a stimulus and have great prestige within the industry. In addition, firms themselves are increasingly developing ways in which creativity and innovation can be fostered. The research referred to above indicated that many firms do not have formal R&D departments. Instead they tend to rely on the creative entrepreneur, or hiring innovative personnel, or generating a culture in which new ideas are encouraged. It is not unusual for all three of these to exist within the same firm. Some operators in the industry include innovation explicitly in their mission statement or statement of company objectives. Others have introduced means by which innovation is encouraged. For instance, ALPHA Flight Services have introduced an award scheme into their company—the Golden Fleuron—based very much on IFCA's Mercury Awards scheme.

Conclusion

Referring to the models for new product and new service development, it can be concluded that it is the suppliers/caterers who engage in new product development and the airlines who follow the latter most closely. Due to their size and considerable financial resources, this sector of the industry is the most systematised when developing new products/services, although suppliers are catching up. It is the airlines who ultimately deliver the final service or product to the customer, and it is them who experience the unique characteristics of a service industry to the fullest. In contrast, the suppliers and caterers experience less of the service industry characteristics and behave more like manufacturing industries, with airlines as customers for their products. Consequently, the suppliers and caterers were recognised as following a process with less steps than the airlines.

The research confirms previous studies in the respect that the majority of innovations for all three sectors are those which are 'new to the company', i.e. adaptations building on existing knowledge. The examples cited show, however, that it is the airlines who produce 'original innovations' more often in response to the continuous demands of the customers, and the caterers and suppliers modify more products and services in response to market pressures. The airline industry is a particularly fragmented and competitive service industry; one in which companies constantly seek to differentiate themselves from the competition. Through the unique characteristics of a service industry, however, the 'innovativeness' of others is easily imitated, for example, North West's decision to copy Lufthansa's meal restriction on short-haul flights. Customer feedback is the most powerful idea source for all three sectors, as would be expected for service firms.

It can be said, however, that the emphasis is on quantity not quality. The majority of innovations are small modifications to existing products or services. As successful as these may be, it is usually original innovation that sustains competitive advantage. With an increasing trend towards the contracting out of flight catering, the emphasis on cost cutting while improving and maintaining quality, calls for increased inventiveness, with the responsibility for innovation shifting away from the airlines and being increasingly expected of the caterers and suppliers. As such, companies in these sectors with no specific R&D department are beginning to set up inter-departmental committees or working groups to meet and brainstorm new ideas on new service/product development, as well as engage in joint ventures and partnerships.

The research reported in this chapter identified the supply and catering sectors, and particularly the smaller companies in those sectors, as those least systematic when developing new products and services. This puts them at a considerable disadvantage in that they are the furthest from the customers and therefore distanced from the best market research. If such companies are to continue in their present role, it would be to the mutual advantage of themselves and the airlines they serve to work together on new service/product innovation. The service companies in the industry appear to have the right emphasis on new service/product development, but many lack the systematic procedures. The entrepreneurial spirit and creativity exist but it could be harnessed and channelled in a more structured way to ensure maximum profitability.

Key terms

Business analysis	Competition	Concept development
Concept testing	Differentiation	Idea generation
Idea screening	Innovation	Launch

Product innovation   Process innovation   Post-launch review
Research and development   System innovation

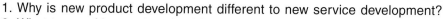

Discussion questions

1. Why is new product development different to new service development?
2. What types of innovation do airlines engage in?
3. What stages in the innovation process are most likely to be adopted by firms engaged in flight innovation?
4. What factors influence the innovation process?

References

Booz, Allen and Hamilton Consultants. (1982) *New Product Management for the 1980s*, Booz, Allen and Hamilton Consultants: New York.

Jones, P. and Bertorello, V. (2001) *The Process of Innovation in Flight Catering*, CHME National Research Conference.

Jones, P. (1996) "Managing Hospitality Innovation," *Cornell HRA Quarterly*, vol. 37, no. 5, 86–95.

Peirce, A.M., (1994) *Innovation in Flight Catering*, Unpublished dissertation: University of Brighton.

Scheuing, E.E. and Johnson, E.M. (1989) "A Proposed Model for New Service Development," *The Journal of Services Marketing*, vol. 3, no. 2, 25–34.

Wan, L. and Jones, P. (1993) "Innovation in the UK Foodservice Industry," *International Journal of Contemporary Hospitality Management*, vol. 5, no. 2, 32–38.

Index

BROOKLANDS COLLEGE LIBRARY
WEYBRIDGE, SURREY KT13 8TT